HANDBOOK OF RESEARCH METHODS FOR MARKETING MANAGEMENT

HANDBOOKS OF RESEARCH METHODS IN MANAGEMENT

Series Editor: Mark N.K. Saunders, *University of Birmingham, UK*

This major series provides the starting point for postgraduate research students in business and management and associated social science disciplines. Each *Handbook* offers a definitive overview of a range of research methods appropriate for a particular subject area within business and management and allied subjects. The series aims to continue to produce prestigious high-quality works of lasting significance, providing insights into methodological issues alongside qualitative, quantitative and mixed methods. Each *Handbook* comprises original contributions by leading and up-and-coming researchers, selected by an editor who is an acknowledged international leader in their field. International in scope, these *Handbooks* provide an invaluable guide to those embarking on a research degree and to researchers moving into a new subject area.

Titles in the series include:

Handbook of Research Methods on Intuition
Edited by Marta Sinclair

Handbook of Research Methods on Human Resource Development
Edited by Mark N.K. Saunders and Paul Tosey

Handbook of Research Methods on Trust
Second Edition
Edited by Fergus Lyon, Guido Möllering and Mark N.K. Saunders

Handbook of Qualitative Research Methods on HRM
Innovative Techniques
Edited by Keith Townsend, Rebecca Loudoun and David Lewin

Handbook of Methods in Leadership Research
Edited by Birgit Schyns, Rosalie Hall and Pedro Neves

Handbook of Research Methods for Tourism and Hospitality Management
Edited by Robin Nunkoo

Handbook of Research Methods on the Quality of Working Lives
Edited by Daniel Wheatley

Handbook of Qualitative Research Methods for Family Business
Edited by Alfredo De Massis and Nadine Kammerlander

Handbook of Research Methods on Creativity
Edited by Viktor Dörfler and Marc Stierand

Handbook of Research Methods in Careers
Edited by Wendy Murphy and Jennifer Tosti-Kharas

Handbook of Research Methods for Marketing Management
Edited by Robin Nunkoo, Viraiyan Teeroovengadum and Christian M. Ringle

Handbook of Research Methods for Marketing Management

Edited by

Robin Nunkoo

Associate Professor of Management, University of Mauritius, Mauritius

Viraiyan Teeroovengadum

Senior Lecturer, University of Mauritius, Mauritius

Christian M. Ringle

Professor of Management, Hamburg University of Technology, Germany

HANDBOOKS OF RESEARCH METHODS IN MANAGEMENT

Edward Elgar
PUBLISHING

Cheltenham, UK • Northampton, MA, USA

Published by
Edward Elgar Publishing Limited
The Lypiatts
15 Lansdown Road
Cheltenham
Glos GL50 2JA
UK

Edward Elgar Publishing, Inc.
William Pratt House
9 Dewey Court
Northampton
Massachusetts 01060
USA

Paperback edition 2023

A catalogue record for this book
is available from the British Library

Library of Congress Control Number: 2021945174

This book is available electronically in the **Elgar**online
Business subject collection
http://dx.doi.org/10.4337/9781788976954

ISBN 978 1 78897 694 7 (cased)
ISBN 978 1 78897 695 4 (eBook)
ISBN 978 1 0353 1549 9 (paperback)

Printed and bound by CPI Group (UK) Ltd, Croydon, CR0 4YY

Contents

v

Contributors

Edina Ajanovic, Faculty of Tourism, Akdeniz University, Turkey

Shabanaz Baboo, Curtin Mauritius, Charles Telfair Campus, Moka, Mauritius

Nika Balomenou, School of Management, Swansea University, UK

Nilay Bıçakcıoğlu-Peynirci, Department of International Business and Trade, Dokuz Eylul University, Turkey

Mehraz Boolaky, University of Lincoln, UK

Birgit Bosio, MCI Management Center Innsbruck, Austria

Beykan Çizel, Faculty of Tourism, Akdeniz University, Turkey

Germà Coenders, Department of Economics, University of Girona, Spain

Jan Dul, Department of Technology and Operations Management, Rotterdam School of Management (RSM), Erasmus University Rotterdam, Netherlands

Sumeyra Duman, Department of Business Administration, Dokuz Eylul University, Turkey

Berta Ferrer-Rosell, Department of Business Management, University of Lleida, Spain

Brian Garrod, School of Management, Swansea University, UK

Mridula Gungaphul, Department of Management, University of Mauritius

Arghavan Hadinejad, Business Unit, University of South Australia, Australia

Sven Hauff, Helmut Schmidt University, Hamburg, Germany

Rachel Hay, College of Business Law and Governance, James Cook University, Australia

Mine Inanc, Dokuz Eylul University, Turkey

İlayda İpek, Department of Business Administration, Dokuz Eylul University, Turkey

Metin Kozak, Dokuz Eylul University, Turkey

Anna Kralj, Department of Tourism, Sport and Hotel Management, Griffith University, Australia

Roopanand Mahadew, Department of Law, University of Mauritius

Eva Martin-Fuentes, Department of Business Management, University of Lleida, Spain

D. Anthony Miles, Miles Development Industries Corporation

Brent Moyle, Department of Tourism, Sport and Hotel Management, Griffith University, Australia

Robin Nunkoo, Department of Management, University of Mauritius, Reduit

Katharina Rainer, More than Metrics, Austria

Christian M. Ringle, Hamburg University of Technology (TUHH), Germany

Soujata Rughoobur-Seetah, Curtin Mauritius, Moka, Mauritius

Noel Scott, Sustainability Research Centre, University of the Sunshine Coast, Australia

Ashley Seebaluck, Fortree

Marc Stickdorn, More than Metrics, Austria

Noorjahan Banon Teeluckdharry, Department of Management, University of Mauritius, Reduit

Viraiyan Teeroovengadum, Department of Management, University of Mauritius, Reduit

Zsófia Tóth, Nottingham University Business School, University of Nottingham, UK

Marie Valerie Uppiah, Department of Law, University of Mauritius

Marina Vives-Mestres, Department of Computer Science, Applied Mathematics and Statistics, University of Girona, Spain

John Williams, Otago Business School, University of Otago, New Zealand

Introduction: advances in marketing research methods
Robin Nunkoo, Viraiyan Teeroovengadum and Christian M. Ringle

INTRODUCTION

As a discipline, marketing has matured after evolving for decades (Korai & Souiden, 2019; Leonidou et al., 2010; Witkowski, 2010). Marketing research has achieved high methodological sophistication and theoretical awareness, whereas it previously lacked both. It has currently reached a stage of active scholarship in theory development and empirical testing. The proliferation of academic journals is one of the dominant features of this evolution, as these journals have taken a leading position in respect of the various knowledge dissemination channels. These journals serve the following important functions: first, academic journals play a central role in knowledge production and, by dispersing knowledge, are key to its advancement in all disciplines. Second, they indicate the existence of a scientific domain, niche discipline, or school of thought (Nie et al., 2009). Third, marketing journals are the main reservoir of knowledge for researchers, students, and practitioners alike. Fourth, these journals are, in their own right, the focus of investigations, which Figueroa-Domecq et al. (2015, p. 88) describe as "the scholarship on the scholarship" of marketing research.

Consequently, it is no surprise that the various studies investigating the marketing discipline's intellectual structure fervently debate published research's philosophical underpinnings, as well as the resulting theoretical and methodological approaches. In terms of these studies' contributions to the field, Hanson and Grimmer (2007) reviewed articles published in three leading marketing journals between 1993 and 2002. They found that quantitative research dominated, with only very few scholars approaching their topics by means of qualitative approaches. Leonidou et al. (2010) assessed leading mainstream marketing journals' contribution to the international marketing discipline. These scholars found that the investigated studies' research designs became increasingly formalized and causal, as well as statistical and cross-sectional, suggesting quantitative approaches' dominance. Davis and colleagues carried out an extensive content analysis

1

of articles published over a 20-year period (1990–2009) in the following five leading marketing journals: *Journal of the Academy of Marketing Science, Journal of Consumer Research, Journal of Marketing, Journal of Marketing Research*, and *Marketing Science*. The researchers noted a "disturbing downward trend in methods diversity resulting from increasing reliance on two methods, experiments and modeling" (Davis et al., 2013, p. 1245). Research assessing the state of mixed-method research in marketing also concluded that studies prioritize quantitative rather than qualitative data (Harrison & Reilly, 2011). These researchers were concerned that, while marketing researchers recognize the benefits of mixing qualitative and quantitative approaches, the discipline does not demonstrate adequate knowledge of mixed-methods research's good practices and procedures. It is not surprising, therefore, that several researchers have criticized positivistic paradigms' over-dominance in marketing research, with some wondering whether the "marketing discipline [is] in trouble" (Korai & Souiden, 2019), whether "marketing research suffers from methods myopia" (Davis et al., 2013, p. 1245), and whether "current research approaches in marketing [are] leading us astray" (Gummesson, 2001, p. 27).

Such epistemological and methodological debates have informed this *Handbook of Research Methods for Marketing Management*, with the aforementioned researchers presenting the methodological issues in marketing research clearly. In addition, these researchers present specific methods and share their experiences of what works, what does not, and what the challenges and innovations are. Our handbook generates wider methodological debates by offering in one volume a wealth of research methods that marketing researchers have experienced. It comprises 18 chapters written by researchers from diverse educational and research backgrounds and geographical locations. The book is divided into four sections: quantitative research approaches; qualitative research approaches; mixed-method approaches; and other research issues. Each part of this handbook and its various chapters have their own internal logic; together the chapters serve as a "one-stop shop" for marketing scholars and practitioners interested in research. Given the differences between quantitative, qualitative, and mixed-method research approaches, and their unequal use, we next provide a detailed explanation of how the authors of this handbook have used and applied them.

PART I   QUANTITATIVE RESEARCH METHODS

Marketing practitioners rely enormously on marketing phenomena's quantification for decision making (Terblanche & Boshoff, 2008).

However, while constructs such as sales performance, profitability, and financial performance can be measured objectively, others relating to consumer attitudes and behaviors, such as satisfaction and loyalty, are unobservable—and often referred to as latent variables (Borsboom et al., 2003). The latter cannot be measured objectively, yet their role in marketing decisions is conspicuous. Gupta and Zeithaml (2005) maintain that consumers' perceptual, attitudinal, and behavioral aspects are key to corporate success, and their measurement a prerequisite for enhanced marketing decision making. It is therefore not surprising that latent variables underlie much marketing research, and that their measurement has attracted scholars' attention. Appropriate measurement indicators that adequately represent such variables are fundamental for understanding consumer behaviors (Ambler, 2003). Consequently, the standard question that should be asked from a marketing manager's perspective is: Are the scales we use in marketing research truly valid and reliable?

In this volume's opening chapter, Noorjahan Banon Teeluckdharry, Viraiyan Teeroovengadum, and Ashley Seebaluck, using established theoretical and methodological guidelines, examine the paradigm for scale development. In addition, the authors examine scale evaluation, in which each phase includes several steps that the researcher must follow to ensure a valid and reliable measure of the latent variable. Further, the authors discuss the scale development process's reliability and validity issues by providing various illustrations to facilitate the readers' understanding.

The notion of causality is often used in marketing to infer relationships between variables. Causality has two distinct components, i.e., sufficiency and necessity (Abbott, 1974; Goertz, 2003). For example, in a relationship proposing that the variable X influences the variable Y, most researchers assume that X causes Y in terms of sufficiency. The second component of causality implies that X is necessary for Y; in other words, that there is no Y without X—although such hypotheses are rarely formulated and tested in marketing research. Consequently, researchers often confuse necessity with sufficiency, although the two terms are very dissimilar. However, necessity and sufficiency have rarely been discussed in the marketing literature. Jan Dul, Sven Hauff, and Zsófia Tóth address this literature gap in Chapter 2 by familiarizing the reader with necessary condition analysis (NCA). This technique, they argue, is a new and promising approach for identifying necessary conditions in empirical data. The authors provide the basic logic and steps required to conduct NCA. They then discuss opportunities to use it in marketing research, explaining the necessity logic before discussing the principles of NCA. The authors illustrate the application and the main functions of NCA software, using data from the Hogan Personality Inventory (Hogan & Hogan, 2007) in order to discuss

NCA as an effective method to apply in marketing research. Also, NCA may represent an interesting extension of other methods, such as partial least squares structural equation modeling (Richter et al., 2020).

Compositional data are those that only contain relative information and are a unique case in terms of marketing research. That is, these data "represent parts of some whole; therefore, they convey only relative information" (Pawlowsky-Glahn & Egozcue, 2006, p. 1). Such data are always positive and usually constrained to a constant sum. Values in compositional data are not free to range from $-\sim$ to $+$ oo (as unconstrained variables are), which conditions the relationships between variables (Pawlowsky-Glahn & Egozcue, 2006). While compositional data are widely used in natural sciences, they are also relevant for the marketing discipline. Various marketing research questions are either related to the distribution of a whole (e.g., distribution, share, allocation, etc.) or to the relative importance (e.g., dominance, concentration, profile, etc.). However, compositional data cannot be analyzed by using conventional statistical techniques. In Chapter 3, Berta Ferrer-Rosell, Eva Martin-Fuentes, Marina Vives-Mestres, and Germà Coenders discuss the application of compositional data analysis in marketing research by using data from an e-word-of-mouth platform. The authors introduce compositional data's peculiarities and draw on their own experiences to discuss compositional data analysis's various steps.

The scientific-positivistic imperative, based on a deductive form of logic involving hypothesis testing, has traditionally informed marketing research (Gummesson, 2001). The analysis of quantitative marketing data has been enhanced due to advanced statistical software made possible by increasing computational power. In Chapter 4, John Williams argues that this trend, combined with researchers' access to big data, has led to a de-emphasis of traditional frequentist statistics, specifically null-hypothesis significance testing (NHST), in favor of resampling-based methods, such as bootstrapping, cross-validation, and Empirical Bayesian methods. In this chapter, the author discusses modern data analysis as a paradigm for robustness in marketing research. He argues that the recent advances in data analysis due to increased computational power have led to many of the implicit assumptions underlying traditional statistical techniques being questioned. The author identifies current norms' deficiencies and suggests a way to improve marketing research quality. He notes that some issues with the current norms include the replication crisis, problems with NHST, shrinkage, linearity, and additivity. He therefore proposes an alternative machine learning paradigm as a way to improve data analysis in marketing research.

Meta-analysis is an important technique for codifying knowledge in various fields. The term is defined as "the statistical analysis of a large collection of results from individual studies for the purpose of integrating the findings. It connotes a rigorous alternative to the casual, narrative discussions of research studies which typify our attempt to make sense of the rapidly expanding research literature" (Glass, 1976, p. 3). A meta-analysis allows researchers to describe, identify, and analyze the variations in the results that previous studies of a specific relationship obtained (Gursoy et al., 2019; Nunkoo et al., 2020). Meta-analyses help identify and clarify theoretical and methodological contributions, and offer insights into avenues for future research that could advance a discipline. In Chapter 5, İlayda İpek and Nilay Bıçakcıoğlu-Peynirci contribute to our current understanding of meta-analysis by introducing this technique and explaining the key steps in its application. The authors subsequently apply this technique to study the relationship between export market orientation and export performance.

Much marketing research relies on emerging survey data, which are subsequently used to test causal relationships and make inferences. However, surveys have several inherent limitations that pose challenges for marketing research. One of the main limitations is total survey error (Eckman & de Leeuw, 2017), which is defined as "the accumulation of all errors that may arise in the design, collection, processing, and analysis of survey data. In this context, a survey error is defined as the deviation of a survey response from its underlying true value" (Biemer, 2010, p. 817). Survey errors could therefore pose challenges regarding research findings' reliability and validity. An experimental design approach is a superior method for testing theories and examining causal relationships, which are known to increase research findings' internal validity and, eventually, their robustness (Bradley & Sparks, 2012; Khan, 2011; Namasivayam, 2004). In Chapter 6, Sumeyra Duman discusses experimental design research in marketing. The author defines and explains the meaning of causality, the conditions required for causality, and the conditions required for experimental design research. Thereafter, she discusses the internal and external validity issues that experimental research requires. The author subsequently uses relevant examples from the literature to present experimental designs' classification. She continues with a discussion of the ethical aspects of experimental research in marketing, drawing on her own experiences to discuss the advantages and challenges of experimental designs.

In their research and investigations, marketing researchers deal with complex and multidimensional issues. They are interested in analyzing the associations between various dependent and independent variables. Univariate and bivariate statistical techniques are limited when they are simultaneously applied to examine the relationships between different constructs, but yet leave some interactions unexplained (Crowley

& Fan, 1997). This omission requires researchers and scholars to use multivariate statistical analysis to solve complex research problems. Consequently, the use of multivariate statistical techniques in the social science literature has grown, enabling researchers to answer complex research questions and test multivariate models (Nunkoo & Ramkissoon, 2012; Nunkoo et al., 2013a; Weston & Gore, 2006). Partial least squares structural equation modeling (PLS-SEM; Hair et al., 2021; Sarstedt et al., 2017) has specifically emerged as a popular multivariate statistical technique in marketing research (Hair et al., 2012, 2017; Henseler et al., 2009). In Chapter 7, Soujata Rughoobur-Seetah, Robin Nunkoo, and Viraiyan Teeroovengadum discuss the use of PLS-SEM applications in marketing. These authors present PLS-SEM's various benefits, such as the method's ability to deal with small sample sizes, formative constructs, and complex structural models that include first- and second-order factors. The authors also explain PLS-SEM's contributions to theory advancement in detail.

PART II   QUALITATIVE RESEARCH METHODS

There is little doubt that positivism is the dominant paradigm in marketing research, as there are far fewer studies on interpretive approaches. Nevertheless, in the preceding discussion, we argue that studies using subjective approaches are on the rise. Our handbook and discussion do not aim to discredit either of the two methods or favor one approach over the other. Instead, we argue that both methods are legitimate and, in their own way, contribute to advancing marketing research. However, the paucity of qualitative data research provides an obvious research area in terms of using more interpretive approaches in marketing studies (Valtakoski, 2020). Although replication is an essential task in science, quantitative methods are often criticized for refining and testing what is already known, rather than developing new concepts and generating new theories. Quantitative methods also prevent researchers from using insight and intuition, especially when studying consumers' feelings, which require diverse forms of evidence and information. Several marketing phenomena, such as consumers' attitudes and behaviors, are formed in historical and social contexts that give meaning to marketing as a social process, and require the use of subjective research approaches.

In the following, we focus on case study research, which has made invaluable contributions to our understanding of marketing phenomena by allowing researchers to investigate real-life phenomena in their socioeconomic and political contexts. Contrary to quantitative research, the contextual conditions are not delineated and/or controlled, but become part of the investigation (Ridder, 2017). Despite case study research's methodological and theoretical progress, researchers sometimes understand it poorly and use it inappropriately (Harrison et al., 2017; Ridder, 2017; Yin, 2012). In Chapter 8, Edina Ajanovic and Beykan Çizel present a guide for the successful use of case studies in marketing management research. These authors start by defining case study research and discussing its use and its philosophical underpinnings. Thereafter, they explain how to define a case and select an appropriate design and theory, before explaining the various steps required when writing a case study. The authors provide useful guidelines to help novice case study researchers avoid methodological pitfalls.

Visual research methods have attracted the attention of many social science researchers (Hicks, 2018; Mannay, 2010; Pauwels & Mannay, 2019; Rose, 2014). Visuals such as photographs and virtual images have been used as research evidence, as stimuli to generate further data, and as a way of eliciting research participants' affects and reflections for decades (Dockett et al., 2017; Knowles & Sweetman, 2004; Rose, 2016). The proliferation of research approaches through the use of visual materials is, we believe, due to visual images' importance in contemporary social and cultural practices (Rose, 2014). Visual research methods allow researchers to get "one step closer to the field" (Rohani et al., 2014, p. 300). In Chapter 9, Brian Garrod and Nika Balomenou explore the use of visual research methods in marketing. These authors argue that visual materials—such as artworks, photographs, and film—have often been considered inferior to the more familiar figures, words, and texts associated with the established social research methods canon. In this context, the authors review the use of visual methods across the social sciences, focusing particularly on the use of volunteer-employed photography (VEP). In the opening paragraphs of the chapter, the authors explain visual research methods by first delving into their history. This is followed by a discussion of their reliability, validity, intent, and timing issues. Thereafter, the authors explain a visual research method, using VEP in the context of a case study.

Although the positivistic paradigm has traditionally dominated marketing research, post-positivist approaches are becoming an alternative research approach (Alvesson & Sköldberg, 2000; Svensson, 2007). Marketing researchers are increasingly using phenomenology to study consumer experiences. Phenomenology distinguishes itself from other scientific forms of inquiry through its emphasis on subjective experiences (Cohen, 1979; Li, 2000; Goolaup et al., 2018). Scholars regard phenomenology as the study of essence: the essence of perception or the essence of consciousness. The literature, dating back as far as the 1980s, has emphasized phenomenology's benefits for marketing research (Askegaard & Linnet, 2011;

Houston et al., 2019; Thompson et al., 1989; Wilson, 2012). In Chapter 10, Mine Inanc and Metin Kozak join the debate on phenomenology by discussing its prospects and challenges in respect of marketing research. With qualitative methods being increasingly emphasized as an alternative method for understanding the cause of consumer behavior in its natural settings, the authors discuss the benefits and challenges of phenomenology, as well as its applications in marketing research. They subsequently outline the procedures that a phenomenological study should follow.

Technological advancements have provided several opportunities for scholars to improve the ways they conduct research and collect data. For example, increased smartphone usage has led to the emergence of a new research method known as mobile ethnography. Unlike traditional ethnographic research, which involves face-to-face data collection, mobile ethnography employs technology-based devices, such as smartphones (Muskat et al., 2018; Rebernik et al., 2020; Stickdorn et al., 2014). In Chapter 11, Birgit Bosio, Katharina Rainer, and Marc Stickdorn present mobile ethnography as an emerging research approach that integrates customers as active researchers with mobile devices. In this chapter, the authors discuss the benefits of using mobile ethnography for marketing research. They argue that mobile ethnography enables researchers to get closer to customers through a better understanding of the problems and challenges they face when using their product or service. The chapter outlines a typical research process, and discusses this emerging method's potentials and challenges.

PART III   MIXED-METHOD APPROACHES

Quantitative and qualitative approaches have their specific advantages as well as drawbacks, which are all well documented. Their drawbacks are not a problem per se; but the ways researchers have positioned these approaches are. For example, Gummesson (2001) argues that positivist researchers claim that quantitative approaches "are better, even the only science; and their far too successful warfare to implant that claim in the academic system and acquire disproportionate 'market share' [is] close to monopoly" (p. 28). This positioning has unfortunately led to a divide between qualitative and quantitative researchers, who view themselves as competing with one another (Onwuegbuzie & Leech, 2005). This divide has led to self-proclaimed purists; that is, researchers restricting themselves to either qualitative or quantitative approaches. However, mono-method study designs are critiqued as being the biggest threat to social science research (Onwuegbuzie & Leech, 2005).

A robust research design is one that adopts a mixed-method approach (Nunkoo et al., 2013b). Mixed-methods research is where a researcher "combines elements of qualitative and quantitative research approaches (e.g., use of qualitative and quantitative viewpoints, data collection, analysis, inference techniques) for the broad purposes of breadth and depth of understanding and corroboration" (Johnson et al., 2007, p. 123). The literature provides a range of well-rehearsed arguments about the advantages of mixing methods, which include validating data or analysis and providing a fuller picture of the phenomenon (Bryman, 2004; Davies, 2003; Harrison & Reilly, 2011; Kowalczuk, 2018; McGoldrick & Liu, 2017; Onwuegbuzie & Leech, 2005). Consumers' social experiences and lived realities—which are multidimensional by nature rather than comprising a unique, "absolute" truth—influence consumer behaviors. Studying these experiences and realities as a single dimension could be inadequate and limit our understanding of marketing phenomena. Methodology and methods are needed that open researchers' perspectives to the multidimensional nature of social experiences and lived realities. Mixing methods offers the potential to explore new dimensions in marketing research that allow researchers and scholars to think differently and "outside the box." Integrating tools of qualitative and quantitative approaches enables fact verification and the investigation of complex and multidimensional reality. This can be achieved if mixed-method approaches are viewed multidimensionally instead of simply in qualitative–quantitative terms (Onwuegbuzie & Leech, 2005).

In Chapter 12, Rachel Hay adopts a mixed-methods approach in the context of agricultural marketing research. Her approach involves face-to-face interviews, followed by an online survey to determine the extent to which rural women use technology and to establish their views of the role they play in managing emerging livestock management tools. A media campaign supported the methodology, which aimed to build the participants' trust in the researchers. The chapter outlines the methodological steps involving the sampling strategy, data collection, validity, reliability, and data analysis. The author applies an emic approach to her research of participants with unique personalities, such as farmers. The author's contribution lies in her application of a mixed-methods approach to research by involving participants who are difficult to reach.

Emotions influence consumer behaviors; therefore their role in marketing cannot be disputed, and is well discussed in the literature (Addis et al., 2018; Babin et al., 1998; Bagozzi et al., 1999; Gaur et al., 2014; Hosany et al., 2020; Huang, 2001). Emotions in the marketing literature are "mental states of readiness that arise from appraisals of events or one's own thoughts" (Bagozzi et al., 1999, p. 184). The measurement of emotions has been thoroughly debated. In Chapter 13, Arghavan Hadinejad, Noel Scott, Anna Kralj, and Brent Moyle apply multi-methods to measure emotion in tourism marketing. These authors argue that, while most studies on tourism use self-reported measures to capture individuals' emotions, this approach cannot capture moment-to-moment emotions, and is therefore unsuitable for a continuous measurement of emotions in real time. Self-report surveys have been criticized for allowing retrospective reflection, which might not reflect participants' actual emotions. In response to such criticism, the contributors apply a multi-method approach involving FaceReader™, skin conductance, self-report surveys, and post hoc interviews to capture individuals' emotional responses (emotional arousal and valence in particular) to a promotional video of a destination in Switzerland.

While a scale development process can be based solely on a quantitative approach, a mixed-methods approach to generate scale items has more recently also gained popularity in the literature (Harrison, 2013). Researchers have advocated a mixed-method approach to developing reliable instruments, including the generation and validation of measurement items since the early 2000 (Collins et al., 2006). Researchers such as Creswell and Plano Clark (2011) recommend a sequential mixed-methods approach to scale development that includes: a qualitative phase to define the constructs; an instrument development phase that includes item generation and revision; and a quantitative phase to test the instrument and confirm the measurement items. In Chapter 14, Shabanaz Baboo adopts a mixed-method approach to develop a social media attachment scale. Her approach involves in-depth interviews with social media users, from which she generated the scale items and refined these on the basis of an expert panel's feedback. Following this process, she applies an exploratory factor analysis to ensure the scales' unidimensionality, and a confirmatory factor analysis to confirm the scale items by using data collected from two different surveys. She demonstrates the benefits of using a mixed-method approach to develop valid and reliable scale items.

PART IV   OTHER ISSUES IN MARKETING RESEARCH

The final part of this handbook deals with other issues that are relevant for marketing researchers. In Chapter 15, D. Anthony Miles illustrates and discusses forensic marketing—a new investigative research model based on marketing dynamics. The discussion includes the following forensic science model and evidence framework: industry position and competitors evidence; law and policy evidence; pricing and product line evidence; brand offering evidence; and distribution channels evidence. The author also presents the forensic marketing competencies and abilities that investigators require. His discussions contribute to the ongoing, but limited, debate on the usefulness of forensic marketing (Anderson et al., 2008; Bussière, 2005; Volkov & Laing, 2015).

In Chapter 16, Marie Valerie Uppiah and Roopanand Mahadew explore the application of legal theories and legal research methods to marketing research, and provide an overview of the different legal theories and legal research methods that can be used throughout a marketing research process. They argue that such a multidisciplinary approach adds value to the outcome of research by providing a multifaceted way of analyzing and interpreting data. They delve into legal theories, paying specific attention to natural law theory. In Chapter 17, these contributors further the debate by assessing the legal implications and parameters of marketing research. They discuss the legal implications of data collection and privacy, the use and dissemination of information, misleading and illegal advertisement, and pricing strategies, using appropriate sections of the law to support their arguments.

Research ethics have for long attracted the attention of researchers (Borgerson & Schroeder, 2002; Crawford, 1970; Gajjar, 2013; Wester, 2011). In the final chapter, Mridula Gungaphul and Mehraz Boolaky discuss ethical considerations in marketing research. After situating the role of ethics in marketing research, the authors discuss its historical evolution. They examine the importance of upholding ethical standards throughout the marketing research process, taking marketing researchers, clients, respondents, and the public into consideration. The authors also highlight some of the innovative marketing research techniques and ethical issues related to these techniques. They provide researchers and students writing dissertations with practical recommendations and guidelines on ethical issues in marketing research.

REFERENCES

Abbott, B. (1974). Some problems in giving an adequate model-theoretic account of cause. In C. Fillmore, G. Lakoff, & R. Lakoff (Eds.), *Berkeley Studies in Syntax and Semantics* (Vol. I., pp. 1–14). Berkeley: University of California.

Addis, M., Miniero, G., & Soscia, I. (2018). Facing contradictory emotions in event marketing: Leveraging on surprise. *Journal of Consumer Marketing, 35*(2), 183–193.

Alvesson, M., & Sköldberg, K. (2000). *Reflexive Methodology: New Vistas for Qualitative Research*. London: Sage.

Ambler, T. (2003). *Marketing and the Bottom Line: The Marketing Metrics to Pump Up Cash Flow* (2nd ed.). Harlow: FT Prentice Hall.

Anderson, S. J., Volker, J. X., & Philips, M. D. (2008). The forensic marketing case study methods. *SAM Advanced Management Journal, 73*(1), 4.

Askegaard, S., & Linnet, J. T. (2011). Towards an epistemology of consumer culture theory: Phenomenology and the context of context. *Marketing Theory, 11*(4), 381–404.

Babin, B. J., Darden, W. R., & Babin, L. A. (1998). Negative emotions in marketing research: Affect or artifact? *Journal of Business Research, 42*(3), 271–285.

Bagozzi, R. P., Gopinath, M., & Nyer, P. U. (1999). The role of emotions in marketing. *Journal of the Academy of Marketing Science, 27*(2), 184–206.

Biemer, P. (2010). Total survey error: Design, implementation, and evaluation. *Public Opinion Quarterly, 74*(5), 817–848.

Borgerson, J. L., & Schroeder, J. E. (2002). Ethical issues of global marketing: Avoiding bad faith in visual representation. *European Journal of Marketing, 36*(5), 570–594.

Borsboom, D., Mellenbergh, G. J., & Van Heerden, J. (2003). The theoretical status of latent variables. *Psychological Review, 110*(2), 203–219.

Bradley, G. L., & Sparks, B. A. (2012). Antecedents and consequences of consumer value: A longitudinal study of timeshare owners. *Journal of Travel Research, 23*(2), 191–204.

Bryman, A. (2004). *Social Research Methods* (2nd ed.). Oxford: Oxford University Press.

Bussière, D. (2005). Forensic marketing: The use of the historical method in a capstone marketing course. *Journal of Marketing Education, 27*(1), 61–67.

Cohen, E. (1979). A phenomenology of tourist experiences. *Sociology, 13*(2), 179–201.

Collins, K. M., Onwuegbuzie, A. J., & Jiao, Q. G. (2006). Prevalence of mixed-methods sampling designs in social science research. *Evaluation & Research in Education, 19*(2), 83–101.

Crawford, C. M. (1970). Attitudes of marketing executives toward ethics in marketing research. *Journal of Marketing, 34*(2), 46–52.

Creswell, J. W., & Plano Clark, V. L. P. (2007). *Designing and Conducting Mixed Methods Research*. Thousand Oaks, CA: Sage.

Crowley, S. L., & Fan, X. (1997). Structural equation modeling: Basic concepts and applications in personality assessment research. *Journal of Personality Assessment, 68*(3), 508–531.

Davies, B. (2003). The role of quantitative and qualitative research in industrial studies of tourism. *International Journal of Tourism Research, 5*(2), 97–111.

Davis, D. F., Golicic, S. L., Boerstler, C. N., Choi, S., & Oh, H. (2013). Does marketing research suffer from methods myopia? *Journal of Business Research, 66*(9), 1245–1250.

Dockett, S., Einarsdottir, J., & Perry, B. (2017). Photo elicitation: Reflecting on multiple sites of meaning. *International Journal of Early Years Education, 25*(3), 225–240.

Eckman, S., & de Leeuw, E. (2017). Editorial: Special issue on total survey error (TSE). *Journal of Official Statistics, 33*(2), 301.

Figueroa-Domecq, C., Pritchard, A., Segovia-Pérez, M., Morgan, N., & Villacé-Molinero, T. (2015). Tourism gender research: A critical accounting. *Annals of Tourism Research, 52*, 87–103.

Gajjar, D. (2013). Ethical consideration in research. *Education, 2*(7), 8–15.

Gaur, S. S., Herjanto, H., & Makkar, M. (2014). Review of emotions research in marketing, 2002–2013. *Journal of Retailing and Consumer Services, 21*(6), 917–923.

Glass, G. V. (1976). Primary, secondary, and meta-analysis of research. *Educational Researcher, 5*(10), 3–8.

Goertz, G. (2003). The substantive importance of necessary condition hypotheses. In G. Goertz & H. Starr (Eds.), *Necessary Conditions: Theory, Methodology, and Applications* (pp. 65–94). New York: Rowman & Littlefield.

Goolaup, S., Solér, C., & Nunkoo, R. (2018). Developing a theory of surprise from travelers' extraordinary food experiences. *Journal of Travel Research, 57*(2), 218–231.

Gummesson, E. (2001). Are current research approaches in marketing leading us astray? *Marketing Theory, 1*(1), 27–48.

Gupta, S., & Zeithaml, V. (2005). Customer metrics: The past, the present, and the future in academia and practice. Marketing Science Institute Special Report No. 05-200.

Gursoy, D., Ouyang, Z., Nunkoo, R., & Wei, W. (2019). Residents' impact perceptions of and attitudes towards tourism development: A meta-analysis. *Journal of Hospitality Marketing & Management*, *28*(3), 306–333.

Hair, J. F., Hult, G. T. M., Ringle, C. M., and Sarstedt, M. (2021). *A Primer on Partial Least Squares Structural Equation Modeling (PLS-SEM)*. Thousand Oaks, CA: Sage.

Hair, J. F., Hult, G. T. M., Ringle, C. M., Sarstedt, M., & Thiele, K. O. (2017), Mirror, mirror on the wall: A comparative evaluation of composite-based structural equation modeling methods. *Journal of the Academy of Marketing Science*, *45*(5), 616–632.

Hair, J. F., Sarstedt, M., Ringle, C. M., & Mena, J. A. (2012). An assessment of the use of partial least squares structural equation modeling in marketing research. *Journal of the Academy of Marketing Science*, *40*(3), 414–433.

Hanson, D., & Grimmer, M. (2007). The mix of qualitative and quantitative research in major marketing journals, 1993–2002. *European Journal of Marketing*, *41*(1–2), 58–70.

Harrison, H., Birks, M., Franklin, R., & Mills, J. (2017). Case study research: Foundations and methodological orientations. *Forum Qualitative Sozialforschung/Forum: Qualitative Social Research*, *18*(1), Art. 19.

Harrison, R. L. III (2013). Using mixed methods designs in the *Journal of Business Research*, 1990–2010. *Journal of Business Research*, *66*(11), 2153–2162.

Harrison, R. L., & Reilly, T. M. (2011). Mixed methods designs in marketing research. *Qualitative Market Research: An International Journal*, *14*(1), 7–26.

Henseler, J., Ringle, C. M., & Sinkovics, R. R. (2009). The use of partial least squares path modeling in international marketing. In R. R. Sinkovics & P. N. Ghauri (Eds.), *New Challenges to International Marketing* (pp. 277–320). Bingley: Emerald.

Hicks, A. (2018). Developing the methodological toolbox for information literacy research: Grounded theory and visual research methods. *Library & Information Science Research*, *40*(3–4), 194–200.

Hogan, R., & Hogan, J. (2007). *Hogan Personality Inventory Manual* (3rd ed.). Tulsa, OK: Hogan Assessment.

Hosany, S., Martin, D., & Woodside, A. G. (2020). Emotions in tourism: Theoretical designs, measurements, analytics, and interpretations. *Journal of Travel Research*, doi. org/10.1177/0047287520937079.

Houston, M. B., Blocker, C. P., & Flint, D. J. (2019). Business buyers are people too: Phenomenology and symbolic interaction in buyer relationships. In C. A. Ingene, J. R. Brown & R. P. Dant (Eds.), *Handbook of Research on Distribution Channels* (pp. 337–354). Cheltenham, UK and Northampton, MA, USA: Edward Elgar Publishing.

Huang, M. H. (2001). The theory of emotions in marketing. *Journal of Business and Psychology*, *16*(2), 239–247.

Johnson, R. B., Onwuegbuzie, A. J., & Turner, L. A. (2007). Toward a definition of mixed methods research. *Journal of Mixed Methods Research*, *1*(2), 112–133.

Khan, J. (2011). Validation in marketing experiments revisited. *Journal of Business Research*, *64*(7), 687–692.

Knowles, C., & Sweetman, J. (2004). Introduction. In C. Knowles and J. Sweetman (Eds.), *Picturing the Social Landscape: Visual Methods and the Sociological Imagination* (pp. 1–17). London: Routledge.

Korai, B., & Souiden, N. (2019). The marketing discipline in trouble? Academic voices vying for supremacy. *Management Decision*, *57*(9), 2555–2569.

Kowalczuk, P. (2018). Consumer acceptance of smart speakers: A mixed methods approach. *Journal of Research in Interactive Marketing*, *12*(4), 418–431.

Leonidou, L. C., Barnes, B. R., Spyropoulou, S., & Katsikeas, C. S. (2010). Assessing the contribution of leading mainstream marketing journals to the international marketing discipline. *International Marketing Review*, *27*(5), 491–518.

Li, Y. (2000). Geographical consciousness and tourism experience. *Annals of Tourism Research*, *27*(4), 863–883.

Mannay, D. (2010). Making the familiar strange: Can visual research methods render the familiar setting more perceptible? *Qualitative Research*, *10*(1), 91–111.

McGoldrick, P. J., & Liu, C. (2017). Application of mixed methods by consumer marketing practitioners: Lessons for the academy? Abstract. In M. Stieler (Ed.), *Creating Marketing Magic and Innovative Future Marketing Trends: Proceedings of the 2016 Academy of Marketing Science (AMS) Annual Conference* (pp. 1463–1464). Cham: Springer.

Muskat, B., Muskat, M., & Zehrer, A. (2018). Qualitative interpretive mobile ethnography. *Anatolia, 29*(1), 98–107.

Namasivayam, K. (2004). Repeated measures experimentation in hospitality research: A brief overview. *Journal of Hospitality & Tourism Research, 28*(1), 121–129.

Nie, K., Ma, T., & Nakamori, Y. (2009). An approach to aid understanding emerging research fields: The case of knowledge management. *Systems Research and Behavioral Science, 26*(6), 629–643.

Nunkoo, R., & Ramkissoon, H. (2012). Structural equation modelling and regression analysis in tourism research. *Current Issues in Tourism, 15*(8), 777–802.

Nunkoo, R., Ramkissoon, H., & Gursoy, D. (2013a). Use of structural equation modeling in tourism research: Past, present, and future. *Journal of Travel Research, 52*(6), 759–771.

Nunkoo, R., Seetanah, B., Jaffur, Z. R. K., Moraghen, P. G. W., & Sannassee, R. V. (2020). Tourism and economic growth: A meta-regression analysis. *Journal of Travel Research, 59*(3), 404–423.

Nunkoo, R., Smith, S. L., & Ramkissoon, H. (2013b). Residents' attitudes to tourism: A longitudinal study of 140 articles from 1984 to 2010. *Journal of Sustainable Tourism, 21*(1), 5–25.

Onwuegbuzie, A. J., & Leech, N. L. (2005). On becoming a pragmatic researcher: The importance of combining quantitative and qualitative research methodologies. *International Journal of Social Research Methodology, 8*(5), 375–387.

Pauwels, L., & Mannay, D. (Eds.). (2019). *The SAGE Handbook of Visual Research Methods*. Los Angeles: Sage.

Pawlowsky-Glahn, V., & Egozcue, J. J. (2006). Compositional data and their analysis: An introduction. In A. Buccianti, G. Mateu-Figueras & V. Pawlowsky-Glahn (Eds.), *Compositional Data Analysis in the Geosciences: From Theory to Practice* (pp. 1–10). London: Geological Society.

Rebernik, N., Favero, P., & Bahillo, A. (2020). Using digital tools and ethnography for rethinking disability inclusive city design: Exploring material and immaterial dialogues. *Disability & Society*, 1–26.

Richter, N. F., Schubring, S., Hauff, S., Ringle, C. M., & Sarstedt, M. (2020). When predictors of outcomes are necessary: Guidelines for the combined use of PLS-SEM and NCA. *Industrial Management & Data Systems, 120*(12), 2243–2267.

Ridder, H. G. (2017). The theory contribution of case study research designs. *Business Research, 10*(2), 281–305.

Rohani, L. S., Aung, M., & Rohani, K. (2014). One step closer to the field: Visual methods in marketing and consumer research. *Qualitative Market Research: An International Journal 17*(4), 300–318.

Rose, G. (2014). On the relation between 'visual research methods' and contemporary visual culture. *Sociological Review, 62*(1), 24–46.

Rose, G. (2016). *Visual Methodologies: An Introduction to the Researching with Visual Materials* (4th ed.). Los Angeles: Sage.

Sarstedt, M., Ringle, C. M., & Hair, J. F. (2017). Partial least squares structural equation modeling. In C. Homburg, M. Klarmann & A. Vomberg (Eds.), *Handbook of Market Research* (pp. 1–40). Cham: Springer.

Stickdorn, M., Frischhut, B., & Schmid, J. S. (2014). Mobile ethnography: A pioneering research approach for customer-centered destination management. *Tourism Analysis, 19*(4), 491–503.

Svensson, P. (2007). Producing marketing: Towards a social-phenomenology of marketing work. *Marketing Theory, 7*(3), 271–290.

Terblanche, N. S., & Boshoff, C. (2008). Improved scale development in marketing: An empirical illustration. *International Journal of Market Research, 50*(1), 105–119.

Thompson, C. J., Locander, W. B., & Pollio, H. R. (1989). Putting consumer experience back into consumer research: The philosophy and method of existential-phenomenology. *Journal of Consumer Research, 16*(2), 133–146.

Valtakoski, A. (2020). The evolution and impact of qualitative research in *Journal of Services Marketing*. *Journal of Services Marketing, 34*(1), 8–23.

Volkov, M., & Laing, G. (2015). Forensic marketing and consumer behaviour: Admissibility of evidence. *e-Journal of Social and Behavioural Research in Business, 6*(1), 11–20.

Wester, K. L. (2011). Publishing ethical research: A step-by-step overview. *Journal of Counseling & Development, 89*(3), 301–307.

Weston, R., & Gore, P.A., Jr. (2006). A brief guide to structural equation modeling. *The Counselling Psychologist, 34*, 719–751.

Wilson, T. (2012). What can phenomenology offer the consumer? *Qualitative Market Research: An International Journal, 15*(3), 230–241.

Witkowski, T. H. (2010). The marketing discipline comes of age, 1934–1936. *Journal of Historical Research in Marketing, 2*(4), 370–396.

Yin, R. K. (2012). Case study methods. In H. Cooper, P. M. Camic, D. L. Long, A. T. Panter, D. Rindskopf & K. J. Sher (Eds.), *APA Handbook of Research Methods in Psychology, 2. Research Designs: Quantitative, Qualitative, Neuropsychological, and Biological* (pp. 141–155). Washington, DC: American Psychological Association.

PART I

QUANTITATIVE
RESEARCH METHODS

1. Scale development in marketing research

Noorjahan Banon Teeluckdharry, Viraiyan Teeroovengadum and Ashley Seebaluck

Marketing is mostly what can be termed as an empiricism-driven discipline, whereby survey methods are often used for data collection and regression or structural equation modelling for data analysis (Kock et al., 2016). However, like in most social sciences, the phenomenon on its own cannot be directly observed and has to be assessed by proxy variables (Diamantopoulos et al., 2008). As such, a structured and comprehensive process of developing measurement models is of utmost importance since poorly conceived processes are likely to lead to highly inaccurate results.

Scale development practices mainly follow established theoretical and methodological guidelines (e.g., Churchill, 1979; DeVellis, 2016), but the emergence of new methods and software offers opportunities to develop and employ new approaches. This chapter provides an overview of the best practices for developing and validating scales. The aim is to provide a primer for scale development in a way that facilitates the development of new, valid and reliable scales, and to help improve existing ones. DeVellis (2016) is by far one of the most cited references when it comes to scale development, and here we have incorporated the guidelines suggested therein, among others. However, we found the flowchart in Boateng et al. (2018) to be more structured and comprehensive as well as more straightforward. The latter have identified three phases that span into nine steps. Therefore, building on their work (Figure 1.1), Phase 1 is about the item and domain development, whereby items are generated and their validity is assessed by the various stakeholders. Phase 2 showcases the steps in the scale construction and includes steps such as pre-testing questions, sampling and survey administration, item reduction and factor extraction. In Phase 3 we consider the test of dimensionality, reliability and validity.

Phase 1: ITEM DEVELOPMENT	Step 1: Identification of domain and item generation
	Step 2: Content validity
	Step 3: Pre-testing of questions
Phase 2: SCALE DEVELOPMENT	Step 4: Sampling and survey administration
	Step 5: Item reduction
	Step 6: Extraction of factors
Phase 3: SCALE EVALUATION	Step 7: Tests of dimensionality
	Step 8: Tests of reliability
	Step 9: Tests of validity

Source: Adapted from Boateng et al. (2018).

Figure 1.1   Framework elaborating steps for scale development

PHASE 1: ITEM DEVELOPMENT

Step 1: Identification of the Domain(s) and Item Generation

Domain identification

Having a well-defined domain serves several purposes; but, most importantly, it provides us with the knowledge to specify the boundaries of the phenomenon under study, and to smooth out the process of item generation and content validation (Boateng et al., 2018). The identification of any domain calls for a thorough overview of existing literature. Having a well-formulated definition of the phenomenon to be measured helps avoid unintentional drifting and crossing over into other domains, especially when similar items are present that may tap into quite different constructs. Prior to providing the preliminary conceptual definition, apt focus should be given to reviewing appropriate related theories. In cases where the dimensions of the domain exist a priori, each dimension should be clearly defined. When there is a lack of any substantive theory that can be utilized as a guide to develop the scale, researchers should try to provide a tentative theoretical model while stipulating how the new construct relates to existing phenomena and their operationalization (DeVellis 2016).

When taking on a new scale development, it is important to specify the purpose for which the construct is being developed and whether there are existing measurement scales. If this is the case, justification is to be provided as to why the development of a new scale is being undertaken, and emphasis should be laid on the differences between existing scales and the new proposed one.

Furthermore, it is helpful to clarify the level of scale specificity, i.e., the extent to which the scale aims to measure a phenomenon – whether as a general global measure of a particular phenomenon or as a detailed and specific one. A good example is satisfaction with respect to a particular outcome, as opposed to overall satisfaction. Usually, the relative broadness or narrowness of the scale is context-specific, and will depend on the aim of the research.

Item generation

Item generation can also be referred to as question development. There are basically two ways to view this step: we can either apply a deductive approach, working from the domain to identify items from existing literature and existing scales; or we can use an inductive approach to generate items from the responses recorded during exploratory studies involving methodologies such as focus groups and interviews. However, it is best to combine both approaches into a hybrid one. This is because existing theory is not only a source of accumulated knowledge about the items; it also provides the theoretical underpinning for better pragmatic decisions related to the constructs. On the other hand, the use of a qualitative approach helps transmute occasionally abstract market perspectives into simple manifested forms of the phenomenon.

When it comes to what should be included in the pool of items, selection is rather subjective. For example, DeVellis (2016) advocated caution since items of a homogeneous nature would reflect the latent variable and, as such, they should be sensitive to the true score of the latent variable. They should not venture beyond the boundaries of the defining construct, yet they should exhaust all possibilities within those boundaries to accurately capture the essence of the construct. On the other hand, some authors, like Boateng et al. (2018), favour a more liberal approach and suggest incorporating all the items identified even though at first glance they do not appear to be a perfect fit to the domain, as successive evaluations at later stages will remove all undesirable items that lack clarity, show questionable relevance or display undesirable similarity to other items.

The number of items to be included will usually depend on the scale being developed – whether it is multidimensional as opposed to monodimensional. Since internal consistency reliability is dependent on the strength of correlations among items, and by extension with the latent variable, the greater the number of items, the better will be internal consistency. However care is advocated to ensure that non-related items are not included since they are likely to induce error variance within the scale, leading to the latter's invalidation. Some authors suggest the initial item pool should be five times as big as the final pool so as to offer enough margin for the optimal grouping of items (Schinka et al., 2012); but the general rule of thumb is that the initial pool of items should be at least double the desired scale (Kline, 1993; Schinka et al., 2012).

As for the forms of the items, the wording and the types of responses being induced should be considered. Items should be straightforward and worded in simple language; they should follow the conventions of normal conversation and be as unambiguous as possible. Lengthy items should be avoided as they are likely to induce complexity and decrease clarity. Unnecessary wordiness should be avoided. However, the meaning of an item should never be sacrificed for the sake of brevity. Furthermore, the reading difficulty level of items should be well thought out. It is best to eliminate potential confusion associated with the use of multiple negatives within a sentence – for example: *It is not unlikely for me not to have a certain bias concerning a particular brand.*

Another important consideration is the avoidance of ambiguous items that convey two or more ideas simultaneously, such that an endorsement of the item might refer to either or both ideas. Items similar to a package deal that renders it impossible to endorse one part without agreeing to the other part should therefore be avoided. Sometimes it may be that the whole sentence describing an item is ambiguous and possibly open to numerous interpretations. This can get very perplexing for some respondents and can also create varying levels of bias within the responses given, and hence should be avoided.

The use of both positively and negatively worded items is rather common in scales. The proponents of such an approach suggest that its application is to reduce various forms of response bias, such as the tendency to select positive responses regardless of the content of the items or to select all high or all low ratings – either due to lack of engagement or confusion on behalf of the respondents. However, opponents are just as numerous. It has been demonstrated in several studies to induce another bias such as the negative items loading on one or more separate factors, that is, the inaccurate perception of factors being related to positively and/ or negatively worded items. Henceforth such an approach should be used with caution, if not avoided. As reflected upon by DeVellis (2016), the disadvantages of using both positive and negative wording within a scale outweigh the benefits.

There is an additional aspect to consider when pooling items for the scale: the redundancy of items. It is recommended to have different ways of expressing a similar idea. This allows the most suitable version to be selected in the subsequent stages, thus yielding more reliable item sets. Furthermore, by using multiple and seemingly redundant items, the core common ground will summate across the items while cancelling out irrelevant idiosyncrasies (DeVellis, 2016). Risk of under-representation and narrow focus is also mitigated. However, when several construct-irrelevant statements display similarities in wording, this can cause respondents to react similarly to these items, and thus produces an inflated estimate of reliability when this isn't truly the case.

Lastly, in terms of wording, there should be due ethical consideration such that proposed items are not offensive or discriminatory towards any individual or social entity.

When it comes to questions with dichotomous response categories (e.g., true/false), no ambiguity should be present. When Likert scales are used the responses should be represented in an ordinal, meaningful manner which is clear to the respondents so that they are interpreted in the same way by each participant. Also, scales with 2–3 points tend to display lower reliability than Likert-type response scales with 5–7 points. When the items are reflecting the relative degrees of a single response quality – for example, *not satisfied to very satisfied* – it is advisable to use a five-point Likert scale. On the other hand, when the items reflect the relative degrees of two qualities, such as *completely disagree* to *completely agree*, a 7-point scale is a better option (Boateng et al., 2018).

Step 2: Content Validity

Content validity was first defined as: "the extent to which a subject's responses to the items of a test may be considered to be a representative sample of his/her responses to a real or hypothetical universe of situations which together constitute the area of concern to the person interpreting the test" (Lennon, 1956, p. 295). Despite the numerous subsequent definitions, it is generally agreed that content validity refers to the extent to which the sampled items adequately reflect the domain and operational definition of the construct. In scale development, this step is known as theoretical analysis, whereby the initial pool of items is checked to see: whether they genuinely reflect the desired construct; whether the scale is measuring what it presumes to measure; and whether related items which are beyond the conceptual boundaries of the construct are being unintentionally added. Content validity is also about capturing the relevant experience of the target population.

According to Guion (1977) there are five conditions of content validity:

1.   There is consensus on the behavioural content.
2.   There is unambiguity in the construct definition.
3.   Content is construct-relevant.
4.   Experts agree that domains have been adequately sampled.
5.   Response content must be reliably observed and re-evaluated.

Content validity is a precondition to other forms of validity and, as such, must first be checked. Its purpose is to minimize the potential error associated with instrument operationalization in the initial stages and to increase the probability of obtaining supportive construct validity in the later stages (Shrotryia & Dhanda, 2019). Content validity assessment relies on the use of panel experts to evaluate the scale. When done correctly in a systemic and comprehensive manner invaluable information can be gathered (Rubio et al., 2003). Addressing content validity begins with the development of the instrument itself. It involves a two-stage process of instrument development and judgement. We agree with Carr et al. (1985) that the two stages (development and judgement/quantification) are crucial for any developed instrument. Furthermore, a third step of revising and reconstruction/reformation is also needed.

In most cases the opinions sought for content validation are those of expert judges (knowledgeable people in the content area or in the development of scales) or the target population, the lay experts, who are the potential users. Optimally the panel of experts should consist of both content experts and lay experts, although the opinions of expert judges are given more emphasis, especially in cases where resources are limited and only of the group being chosen (Boateng et al., 2018). The number of expert judges used for a study depends on the scale developer. Some studies, such as Shrotryia and Dhanda (2019), recommend a minimum of 3 judges, whereas others (for instance Haynes et al., 1995) recommend around 5 to 7 expert judges; but it is generally agreed that using more than 10 expert judges decreases the chance of consensual agreement (Polit & Beck, 2006).

The experts are likely to confirm or invalidate the definition proposed as well as provide recommendations with respect to grammar; the correct use of words and the position of key words are obtained from the panel of experts (Safikhani et al., 2013). The threats that typically arise during scale development are construct-irrelevant content – that is, the presence of unnecessary elements beyond the core intended concept of the construct – and content under-representation. To cater for construct-irrelevant content, the scale developers should apply both existing theory and the judgements of content experts to validate excluding or including a certain element while considering the research objective. The same goes for under-representation of certain elements, the presence of which can jeopardize the internal consistency of the construct and interfere with the relationships and correlations between the items under certain factors or domains (Almanasreh et al., 2019).

Content validity procedures usually entail the experts rating how relevant each item is using techniques such as content validity ratio (CVR), content validity index (CVI) or Cohen's kappa coefficient (κ) for measuring inter-rater or expert agreement (Almanasreh et al., 2019). Figure 1.2 depicts a typical flowchart of the steps involved in content validity.

Content validity ratio is computed according to the Lawshe test. It provides confidence in selecting the most important and correct content in an instrument. Basically, CVR is a numeric value which varies from 1 to −1, and is determined from expert ratings indicating the instrument's degree of validity. The experts are requested to rate the necessity of each

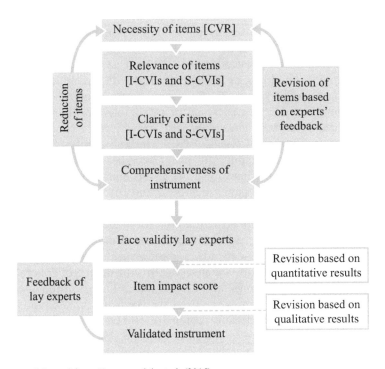

Source: Adapted from Zamanzadeh et al. (2015).

Figure 1.2   Flowchart illustrating typical steps in content validity

item for operating a construct using scores of 1–3, with a three-degree range of "not necessary", "useful but not essential" and "essential" respectively. The formula for calculating CVR is (Ne – N / 2) / (N / 2), where Ne is the number of panellists indicating "essential" and N is the total number of panellists. One rule of thumb suggests that a CVR of at least 0.78 on a scale is necessary to deem an item or scale as valid (Frey, 2018).

To cater for agreement among experts not due to chance, critical CVR (CVR critical) values have been proposed by Lowell Schipper (Lawshe, 1975). CVR critical is the minimum value of CVR such that the level of agreement exceeds that of chance for a given item, for a given alpha (Type I error probability, one tailed test P = 0.05) (Lawshe, 1975). Methods for calculating the critical values of CVR can be found in Ayre and Scally (2014). CVR critical values can be utilized to identify the number of panel experts required to agree on an item as essential and the items which should be retained or discarded from the final instrument.

Alternatively, the Delphi technique (or method) may be used for content validity. This is a distinct type of survey method for soliciting and obtaining group consensus on an important subject (Lindeman, 1975; Notter, 1983), and is described as the technique "for structuring group communication process so that the process is effective in allowing a group of individuals, as a whole, to deal with a complex problem" (Linstone & Turoff, 1975, p. 3). This method is particularly convenient when content is either controversial or intangible, or when one of the expert judges potentially lacks sufficient knowledge or expertise of the subject matter (Tersine & Riggs, 1976). The key points of the Delphi technique are: (1) anonymity of panel members; (2) anonymity of responses; (3) numerous iterations; (4) group consensus; (5) controlled feedback of responses to panel members; and (6) statistical analysis of data (Lindeman, 1975; Notter, 1983). Its goal is to reach a consensus of opinions through a series of structured questionnaires sent to the experts which build upon their responses to previous rounds of questionnaires. The number of rounds is dependent upon several factors, namely: the level of consensus desired by the investigator; the degree of concreteness of items; unexpected findings; and the number of items on the question-naire (Perroca, 2011). However, there are typically three rounds. The expert panel should preferably comprise stakeholders with relevant experience and facilitators in the field (Scheele, 1975). The size of the panel varies with the research objective; for instance, in Brockhoff's study of Delphi performance (1975), groups with 11 participants were more accurate in their predictions than larger groups, whereas for fact-finding questions groups with seven participants performed better. On the other hand, error decreases with larger Delphi panels (Linstone & Turoff, 1975).

Content validity index (CVI)

The CVI is the method used for quantifying the content validity of an instrument, based on expert ratings for each item in terms of its relevance to the underlying construct, generally applying on Likert scales ranging from 1 (not relevant) to 4 (extremely relevant). CVI can be computed at each item level (I-CVI) or for overall scale (S-CVI).

For each item, the I-CVI can be calculated by counting the number of experts who rated the item as 3 or 4 and dividing that number by the total number of experts – that is, the proportion of agreement about the content validity of an item. For example, if 8 out of 10 content experts rated an item as relevant (3 or 4), the CVI would be 8/10 = 0.80. Zamanzadeh et al. (2015) suggest the following: if I-CVI > 0.79, the item is relevant; between 0.70 and 0.79, the item needs revision; and if the value is below 0.70 the item is eliminated.

Literature reports two methods for computing the overall content validity index. The first is universal agreement (UA-CVI), which is defined as the proportion of items on an instrument that achieved a rating of 3 or 4 (valid) by all the content experts. Not only is this approach rather conservative, but the increase in the number of experts made its achievability rather difficult. The second approach is Average CVI (Ave-CVI), which is defined as the average proportion of items rated as 3 or 4 (valid) across the various experts. There are basically three methods to calculate the Ave-CVI, though all will yield the same results:

1. Calculate the average CVI across the items by adding together the I-CVIs and dividing them by the number of items.
2. Count the total number of ratings multiplied by the number of items rated relevant by all experts combined, and divide by the total number of ratings.
3. Average the proportion of items rated relevant across experts.

Davis (1992) suggested a standard criterion of 0.8 as the lower limit of acceptability of a CVI of an instrument. Polit and Beck (2006) have criticized aspects of the CVI and recommended using Lynn's criteria for calculating the I-CVI (I-CVI = 1 with 3 or 5 experts and a minimum I-CVI of 0.78 for 6–10 experts), and an Ave-CVI of 0.90 or higher to have an excellent content validity of an instrument. It should be noted that Polit et al. (2007) slightly modified the above criteria and recommended perfect agreement only when there are three or four experts.

Table 1.1 *Sample ratings of 10 items using a 4-point rating relevance scale (3,4 relevant), (1,2 not relevant)*

Item	Expert 1	Expert 2	Expert 3	Expert 4	Expert 5	Expert 6	Expert 7	No of agreement	Item-CVI*
1	3	4	4	3	3	4	4	7	1
2	3	2	4	3	3	3	4	6	0.72
3	2	2	4	4	3	3	1	4	0.58
4	4	3	2	4	3	3	4	6	0.86
5	4	3	3	3	1	2	4	5	0.72
6	3	4	1	3	3	3	3	6	0.86
7	3	4	4	1	3	3	2	5	0.72
8	3	4	4	3	3	4	4	7	1
9	3	4	3	4	4	3	3	7	1
10	1	3	4	3	3	4	3	6	0.86
								AVE-CVI**	0.84
								UA-CVI***	0.3
No of agreements	8	8	8	9	9	9	8	59	
Proportion of agreements with respect to total items	0.8	0.8	0.8	0.9	0.9	0.9	0.8	5.9	

Mean expert agreement proportion** 0.85

Notes: *Item-CVI = [number of items having 3 or 4 rating] / [number of experts] = content validity index of an item.
** Ave-CVI = [summation of all item-CVI] / [no. of items] = content validity of scale.
*** UA-CVI = [number of items that achieved rating 3 or 4 by all experts] / [total number of items] = content validity of scale.
**** Mean expert agreement proportion = [agreements with respect to total items by each expert] / [number of experts].

Source: Adapted from Almanasreh et al. (2019).

It is important to know that while CVI is easy to compute and interpret, and provides content validity of each item and the instrument as a whole, it is the call of the scale developer which item(s) to include or exclude, as shown in Table 1.1 (Almanasreh et al., 2019).

Evaluation by lay experts (face validity)
Face validity can be defined as the "degree that respondents or end users or lay persons judge that the items of an assessment instrument are appropriate to the targeted construct and assessment objectives" (Haynes et al., 1995, p. 243n4). If a measure looks, on the face of it, as though it measures a particular attribute, then the existence of face validity can be assumed (McGartland Rubio & Kimberly, 2005). While face validity and content validity may sound similar, they are not. Content validity is established through structured and rigorous procedures; in comparison, face validity is rather subjective and established through cognitive interviews to establish whether the construct is a good measure of the domain. Since the target population are the lay experts for face validity, they can be asked to confirm the researchers' ideas of "what looks as if" it might be correct, and to make adjustments to the scale as necessary so that the scale is truly crafted for the targeted audience and is context appropriate.

PHASE 2: SCALE DEVELOPMENT

Step 3: Pre-Testing of Questions

The primary purpose of pre-testing is to ensure that items are meaningful to the target population prior to administering the survey so as to minimize misinterpretation and subsequent measurement error. It also eliminates poorly worded items, reduces the cognitive burden on the surveyed population, eases out the rephrasing of statements for higher scale efficiency, and is an overall additional way for the target population to input further insights into the scale being developed (Boateng et al., 2018).

Qualitative methods chiefly identify items having certain wording concerns, such as being hyphenated, leading or confusing (Leech, 2002). While some of these tests are able to pinpoint those items with face validity concerns, they do not provide a direct numerical indicator. Hence, they may be able to remove items with large face validity concerns, but they cannot be used to solely retain the items with the greatest face validity. Howard (2018) provides a guideline of procedures to adopt depending on the main concerns at hand (Figure 1.3).

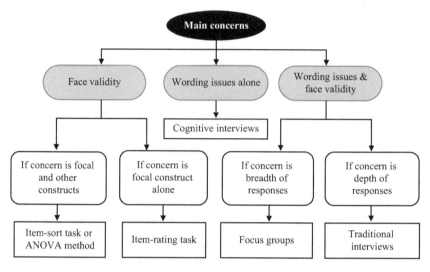

Source: Adapted from Howard (2018).

Figure 1.3   Flowchart of which procedure to use with regard to face validity and wording issues

Cognitive interviews

Cognitive interviewing incorporates a wide range of techniques for eliciting data about interpretation of the scale and how responses are formulated. Techniques may include verbal probing and thinking aloud (Collins, 2003). Verbal probing is about encouraging respondents to verbalize their interpretation of items and to paraphrase and/or comment on the wording of items in an effort to identify ambiguous or poorly worded questions as well as to comment on the perceived accuracy of their response. The think aloud technique is utilized when the scale developer wants to elicit data on participants' thought processes as they respond to each item, thus providing insights into the kinds of information participants retrieve from memory as they determine their response to an item. By eliciting thought processes associated with responses, investigators gain useful insights into participants' decision-making processes. Cognitive interviews ensure that the questions are producing the intended data, that they are clear to the respondents, that they are easy and simple to interpret, and that the options are appropriate and adequate. It is advocated that the outcomes of the interviews should be reported together with the solutions used to remedy the situation. Though there are some difficulties in determining whether the participants are interpreting items correctly or are completely off the mark, or to what extent a particular participant is struggling to answer a question, it is up to the developers to know where to draw the line, especially since there is no hard and fast rules to coding participant responses (Howard, 2018). Likewise, researchers may choose whether to apply non-essential coding methods, such as behaviour coding or response latency, whereby items with longer latencies are believed to perform poorly.

Item-rating tasks

This is among the most common quantitative pre-test methods. In this method, participants are asked to evaluate the extent to which the item represents the principal construct, using scales such as "clearly representative", "somewhat representative" and "not representative", or "very good", "good", "fair" and "poor." While there is no recommended sample size for item-rating tasks, typical sample sizes range from 10 to 30 (Goetz et al., 2013; Heene et al., 2014). There are three approaches that can be used for item-retention decisions:

1. Each item rating is allocated a number (e.g., very good 4, good 3, fair 2, poor 1), and the highest scoring items are retained.
2. Items that receive a certain percentage of highest or second highest responses (i.e., very good, good) are retained.
3. Items that receive any of the lowest responses (e.g., poor) are discarded.

Item-sort task

At the beginning of any item-sort task, the participants are presented with the items list and a list of constructs to which they have to match those items. Those with frequent assignments to the posited construct are retained. The typical number of participants for this step is 20–30, although Howard and Melloy (2016) demonstrated that sample sizes as small as five can be used. The researchers can choose a cut-off that would result in the desired number of items to be retained or can use the cut-off values provided by Howard and Melloy. Using this latter approach, which is based on traditional statistical significance testing, the results of item-sort tasks have sound statistical justification and have been shown to replicate exploratory factor analysis (EFA) results.

Step 4: Survey Administration and Sample Size

Survey administration

The aim at this stage is to allow for collection of data with the minimum of measurement errors from an adequate sample. We shall explore what constitutes an adequate sample size shortly, but first let us consider some possible ways that data can be collected. These range from typical paper and pen/pencil interviewing (PAPI) to computer-assisted personal interviewing (CAPI), with each approach having its pros and cons.

For instance, in the case of CAPI, the use of technology can reduce errors associated with data entry, permit data collection from a larger sample at lower cost, enhance response rates, reduce enumerator errors, and allow for instant feedback along with providing space to get more confidential sensitive information (Goldstein et al., 2012; Fanning & McAuley, 2014; Dray et al., 2016). The fact that CAPI allows for the inclusion of photos and videos makes the survey even more engaging for the respondents, and at the same time allows researchers to convey their questions to the target audience with greater clarity. In audio computer self-assisted interviewing (A-CASI), questions may be recorded and read out loud to participants with low literacy levels. Furthermore, self-interviewing using CAPI allows participants to respond to the questions without the interviewer's involvement, which may give the responder a sense of comfort and privacy to answer sensitive questions with greater honesty and transparency. This is particularly true when participants are anonymized, allowing for less social desirability (Gosling et al., 2004) and fewer ethical problems (Nosek et al., 2002). While there may be a few start-up costs with the use of CAPI – such as the purchase of the software, along with more time and resources needing to be spent on configuring the questionnaire in the software and programming the consistency checks – there is a growing body of evidence supporting the idea that CAPI is a cheaper and faster form of data collection than PAPI. For example, Leisher (2014, p. 264) found that "the cost per completed interview for the tablet-based survey was 74% less than the paper-based survey average." Also, the electronic data capture approach eliminates the need for post-interview data entry, and thus allows for immediate data retrieval. Hence the main benefits of the CAPI method can be summarized as the prevention of error in the data collected through its in-built automated routing, consistency checks and use of images for uniformity of data interpretation. This in turn leads to cost savings for the organizations involved and reduces the time between fieldwork and publication of final results.

As for the traditional PAPI method, the advantages lie in averting crisis in case data is lost: software crashes, devices can be lost or stolen; and it may be more suitable in areas with irregular electricity supplies and internet connections. Still, as the sample size increases, so the risk of human error increases as interviewing becomes more labour- and time-intensive (Fanning & McAuley, 2014; Greenlaw & Brown-Welty, 2009). Based on the merits of CAPI over PAPI, we recommend that researchers use CAPI in data collection for surveys when feasible.

Establishing sample size

The sample size to be used for scale development is often contentious, and the adequate size varies from study to study. However, the rule of thumb dictates at least ten participants for each scale item (Nunnally, 1978), though Hair et al. (2019b) recently suggested that a ratio of five respondents per item scale may be adequate. They also suggested that, in addition to the rule of thumb for calculating the minimum size of the sample population, the final sample size should be at least 20 per cent larger than the calculated one so as to cater for missing responses or any other issues related to data collection. Others have suggested sample sizes that are independent of the number of survey items. For example, Comrey (1988) recommended a range of 200–300 as appropriate for factor analysis, while Guadagnoli and Velicer (1988) suggested a minimum of 300–450 since replication might be needed for a sample below 300. Moreover, item reduction techniques such as bootstrapping may require larger data sets; but, generally, with larger samples sizes measurement errors are lower, factor loadings are more stable and the results can be better generalized to be applicable to the targeted population (Osborne & Costello, 2004). Furthermore, statistical issues play a central role when calculating the required sample size, which is often based on the confidence level (95 per cent), margin of error (3–5 per cent) and expected variability. Since the methodological rigour of the study and the generalizability of the results are heavily dependent on a sample size which is representative of the targeted population, there should be proper planning and execution for sampling design (Teeroovengadum & Nunkoo, 2018).

Determining the type of data to use

Normally scale development would require data from a single point in time; but to fully test the reliability of a scale, as will be demonstrated in subsequent steps, an independent data set is required. Data from longitudinal studies may be used for initial scale development (e.g., initial data), to conduct confirmatory factor analysis (follow-up data) and to assess test–retest reliability (using baseline and follow-up data). However, the use of longitudinal data may lead to common error variance because the same participants are involved (Boateng et al., 2018). Hence, ideally the scale development should be developed on sample A, whether it is longitudinal or cross-sectional data collection, and then use an independent sample B for confirmatory factor analysis (CFA). For example, Hill et al. (2019) conducted two studies to develop a scale to measure the components for meaning in life. In Study 1, they conducted an exploratory factor analysis of the items and assessed the test–retest reliability of the new measure, called the Meaning in Life Measure (MILM). In Study 2, they tested the replicability of the factor structure of the MILM with a new sample using CFA and tested the MILM's validity and reliability.

Step 5: Factor Reduction

The purpose of item reduction is to ensure that only parsimonious, functional and internally consistent items are ultimately included (Thurstone, 1947). It is about identifying items that are the least related to the domain under study for deletion or modification. Functional items can be described as those that are correlated with each other, discriminate between individual cases, underscore a single or multidimensional domain and contribute significantly to the construct (Boateng et al., 2018).

The measurement theories that underpin scale development are the Classical Test Theory (CTT) and the Item Response Theory (IRT) (Fan, 1998; DeVellis, 2016). Each theory can be used on its own or in conjunction with another (Glockner-Rist & Hoijtink, 2003). The basic idea underlying CTT is that an observed score is simply the result of the respondent's true score plus error, which is differentiated into different categories. By contrast, IRT differentiates errors with respect to characteristics of individual items. Therefore, with IRT methods the researcher is able to examine the item information and standard error functions for the item pool and determine the effect of adding or deleting a given item (Harvey & Hammer, 1999). One of the objectives of IRT is to establish certain characteristics of items that are independent of the respondent assessing the items, and the emphasis is placed on items as opposed to the scale as a whole. For guidelines on how to perform IRT, these sources are recommended: Alaya (2009) and Baker and Kim (2017).

Depending on which test theory is driving the scale, several techniques are used to reduce the item pool, including:

- item difficulty and item discrimination indices (primarily for binary responses); and
- inter-item and item–total correlations (categorical items).

Item difficulty index
The item difficulty index pertains to both CTT and IRT, and assesses the relative difficulties of test items. It is important to note that these difficulties are defined in terms of the likelihood of correct response, not in terms of perceived difficulty or amount of effort required. Knowing the item difficulty is useful when building a scale to match the levels of a target population. For example, an instrument aimed at measuring wellbeing within an

organization should not be constituted solely of items that resonate only with those who have clinical depression. When used under the CTT framework, the item difficulty index refers to the proportion of participants who answer an item correctly: the higher the score, the greater the proportion of the sample who understood and answered the question correctly. Low scores would suggest a need to modify items or delete them from the pool of items. When it comes to the IRT framework, the item difficulty index refers to the probability of a particular test taker correctly answering any given item. This enables identification of levels of individual performance on specific questions, as well as allowing for the selection of questions specific to a segment of the targeted population (Hambleton & Jones, 1993). Depending on the type of scale being developed, the researcher must determine whether they need items with low, medium, or high difficulty. For instance, researchers interested in general-purpose scales will focus on items with medium difficulty (0.4–0.6) (Raykov, 2011).

Item discrimination index
The item discrimination index, also called the item-effectiveness test, is a measure of how well an item is able to distinguish between participants who are familiar with the context being studied and those who are not. It basically measures the difference in performance between groups. On an attitude scale, it would discriminate between those with positive attitudes and those with negative attitudes.

In CTT, the item discrimination index can be computed through correlational analysis between the performance on an item and an overall criterion using either the point biserial correlation coefficient or the phi coefficient (Sim & Rasiah, 2006). This index considers the relationship between an examinee's performance on the given item, whether it is correct or incorrect, and the examinee's score on the overall test. Under the IRT framework, item discrimination is a slope parameter that determines how sharply the probability of a correct response changes as the trait being investigated increases (DeMars, 2010).

For an item that is highly discriminating, in general the examinees who responded to the item correctly also did well on the test, while in general the examinees who responded to the item incorrectly also tended to do poorly on the overall test. While the range of the discrimination index is within −1.0 to 1.0, an item with discrimination below 0.0 would suggest a problem. Likewise, an item discriminating negatively may indicate that the item is measuring something other than what the rest of the test is measuring. Moreover, when interpreting the value of a discrimination it is important to be aware that there is a relationship between an item's difficulty index and its discrimination index. If an item has a very high (or very low) item difficulty index, the potential value of the discrimination index will be much less than if the item has a mid-range p-value.

Inter-item and item–total correlations

Inter-item correlations consider the degree to which the scores on one item are related to the scores on all other items in a scale. They provide an assessment of item redundancy by examining the extent to which items on a scale are assessing the same content (Cohen & Swerdlik, 2005; Raykov, 2011). When the inter-item correlations are too low, this indicates that the items may not be representative of the same domain. When the value is too high, this may suggest that the bandwidth of the construct captured is too narrow or that each of the items is not contributing something unique to the construct. According to Piedmont (2014), the average inter-item correlation for a set of items should be between 0.20 and 0.40. The reason stipulated is that, while being reasonably homogenous, the items do contain sufficiently unique variance, and thus are not isomorphic. On the other hand, Clark and Watson (2016) endorsed a mean inter-item correlation range of 0.15 to 0.20 for scales that measure broad characteristics and 0.40 to 0.50 for those tapping narrower ones.

Item–total correlations examine the relationship between each item and the total score of scale items. There are two types of item-scale correlation – corrected and uncorrected. For example, if there are ten items, in the corrected version the item being assessed is correlated with all the remaining nine other items excluding itself, while in the uncorrected correlation the item under consideration is correlated with all ten items. Since the uncorrected version is likely to inflate the correlation coefficient, the use of the corrected version is advisable (DeVellis, 2016). The higher the correlation coefficient, the more clearly an item belongs to the scale. As a rule of thumb, if it is less than 0.3 then the item is dropped from the scale. However various cut-off points are adopted. For example, Cristobal et al. (2007) recommend 0.30; Loiacono et al. (2002) and Ladhari (2010) suggest 0.40; and Francis and White (2002) and Kim and Stoel (2004) 0.50. Calculating an item-to-scale coefficient for each of the initial items and dropping the inappropriate ones should result in a unidimensional scale.

Examine the quality of data

For the findings to be accurate and reliable, missing data, absence of outliers, linearity and extreme multicollinearity should be given due importance by researchers (Beavers et al., 2013). When it comes to missing data, patterns should be inspected. Usually, it is advisable to consider deleting cases when the majority of responses (50 per cent or more) contain missing data (De Vaus, 2002). There are several ways to deal with missing data, including ad hoc procedures such as listwise deletion and pairwise deletion (Marsh, 1998; Roth, 1994), but these do not have any theoretical justification. We also have theory-based maximum likelihood (ML) approaches and similar response pattern imputation. While going into detail about these specific approaches is beyond the scope of this chapter, there are numerous manuals about data-cleaning best practices (e.g., Hair et al., 2019a; Meyers et al., 2016) that may be referred to on how to deal with missing data, outliers, or other potential issues.

DeVellis (2016) also suggests examining the item performance in terms of reversing scoring if needed, item variance and item means. High difference within the item variances may indicate different sources of error among the items. Furthermore, a mean close to the mid-range of possible scores is also desirable since items with means too near to an extreme of the response range will have low variances, and those that vary over a narrow range will correlate poorly with other items.

Step 6: Extraction of Factors

Factor analysis examines whether, based on the patterns in the responses collected in a survey, we can summarize the variables into fewer, more general factors. A simple example is provided in Table 1.2, whereby the variables are grouped under different factors.

According to De Vaus (2002) there are four main steps in forming scales using factor analysis, namely: selecting the variables to be analysed; extracting an initial set of factors, extracting a final set of factors by "rotation"; and constructing scales based on the results at step 3 and using these in further analysis.

Selecting the variables prior to factor analysis
One of the issues of factor analysis is that, regardless of the variables used, a set of "underlying" factors will be produced, whether they make sense or not. When selecting variables to be factor analysed, it is important to be able to assume that correlations between the variables will not be causes of other variables in the analysis. It is also necessary to ensure that the

Table 1.2   Example of variables grouped under different factors

Factor 1: Location	Factor 2: Value for money	Factor 3: Efficiency
X_1: Convenient location X_2: Near home	X_3: Low prices X_4: Attractive promotions	X_5: Ease of parking X_6: Great customer service X_7: Ease of locating items

variables to be analysed have at least reasonable correlations with some other variables. Hence the factorability of the data is verified through inspection of the correlation matrix, Bartlett's test of sphericity and the Kaiser-Meyer-Olkin (KMO) measure. The correlation matrix should include numbers at levels of 0.30 or higher; Bartlett's chi-square should be significant at a probability of 0.05 or less; and a KMO value of 0.60 or higher is recommended before proceeding with factor analysis (Pett et al., 2006; Tabachnick et al., 2007, pp. 481–498).

Initial set of factors

Extraction of factors is usually done using exploratory factor analysis (EFA), whereby latent factors that represent the shared variance in responses among the multiple items are extracted. Prior to extracting factors there are two decisions to consider: the method of extraction and the number of factors to be extracted. Based on a number of statistical theories, there are many factor-extraction methods, but the two most common are principal component(s) analysis (PCA) and common factor analysis (FA). The purpose of PCA is to reduce the number of items while retaining as much of the original item variance as possible, while that of FA is to understand the latent factors or constructs that account for the shared variance among items – and thus is more appropriate for scale development (Worthington & Whittaker, 2006). Furthermore, error variance included in PCA tends to inflate the size of components, causing researchers to retain too many components (Goldberg & Velicer, 2006). On the other hand, common factor analysis results are more generalizable for confirmatory factor analysis (Haig, 2005; Worthington & Whittaker, 2006), as illustrated in Box 1.1.

BOX 1.1

An example of the use of FA versus PCA in a simulated data set might illustrate the differences between these two approaches. Imagine that a researcher at a public university is interested in measuring campus climate for diversity. The researcher created 12 items to measure three different aspects of campus climate (each using four items): (a) general comfort or safety; (b) openness to diversity; and (c) perceptions of the learning environment. In a sample of 500 respondents, correlations among the 12 variables indicated that one item from each subset did not correlate with any other items on the scale (e.g., no higher than r = 0.12 for any bivariate pair containing these items). In FA, the three uncorrelated items appropriately drop out of the solution because of low factor loadings (loadings < 0.23), resulting in a three-factor solution (each factor retaining three items). In PCA, the three uncorrelated items load together on a fourth factor (loadings > 0.45). This example demonstrates that, under certain conditions, PCA may overestimate factor loadings and result in erroneous decisions about the number of factors or items to retain.

Source: Worthington & Whittaker (2006).

In scale development, the methods to determine the number of factors to retain include a scree plot (Cattell, 1966), the variance explained by the factor model, and the pattern of factor loadings. The eigenvalue is a measure indicating the amount of variance in the entire set of items accounted for by a given factor. Kaiser (1958) believed that eigenvalues of less than 1.0 reflect potentially unstable factors, while the scree test is considered more accurate than the eigenvalue rule (Pett et al., 2006; Preacher & MacCallum, 2003; Reise et al., 2007), whereby the number of factors to be retained is determined by when a line elbows off from a somewhat subjectively straight dotted line. The amount of the total variance in the original set of variables that is explained by the factors is an indication of good factor analysis. Since to increase the total variance explained we have to increase the number of factors, it becomes important to retain stable factors with an eigenvalue of 1 or higher used (De Vaus, 2002). The number of factors to be retained can also be computed using methods such as parallel analysis (Horn, 1965), minimum average partial procedure (Velicer, 1976) or the Hull method (Lorenzo-Seva et al., 2011).

The rotation method

Rotation is necessary in order to more clearly identify the scale's factors (or dimensions) since the unrotated results from a factor analysis are not easy to interpret. The term "rotation" is used because, historically and conceptually, the axes are being rotated so that the clusters of items fall as closely as possible to them. There are two broad categories of rotation, namely oblique and orthogonal, which refer to the angle maintained between the X and Y axes. Therefore, orthogonal rotations produce factors that are uncorrelated (i.e., maintain a 90-degree angle between axes), while oblique methods allow the factors to correlate (i.e., allow the X and Y axes to assume an angle other than 90 degrees). However, in social sciences like marketing, it is very common for factors to correlate with one another (DeVellis, 2016). Hence, if factors are substantially correlated, an oblique rotation provides a better and more accurate solution. Oblique rotation options include Direct Oblimin and Promax. Though both allow factors to correlate, Promax begins with an orthogonal solution and then transforms it to an oblique solution (Hendrickson & White, 1964), and it has been argued to be more robust (Thompson, 2004). If factors do not correlate, it is advisable to assess whether two separate constructs are being measured rather than one.

Retention or deletion of items

It is suggested that items for retention should be evaluated based on theory, communalities, item loadings, no significant cross-loadings, minimum of three salient loadings, factor reliability levels and parsimony (Carpenter, 2018).

One example of how theory can affect the item to retain is to consider "price". Often when service quality scale is being conceptualized customers are likely to mention price and value as dimensions of the service quality, though the consensus in existing marketing literature is that price is often considered as a separate construct such as perceived value (Dabholkar et al., 1996; Brady & Cronin, 2001; Martínez & Martínez, 2010). Henceforth items to be retained should be backed by theory.

While there is a fixed level for what degree of communality qualifies a variable as having sufficient common variation to retain in a factor solution, there are various suggestions for the communalities cut-off. For example, Osborne et al. (2008) suggest that communality above 0.4 is acceptable. Items loading highly on more than one factor should be removed (Hair et al., 2010). As for factor item, there are various suggested cut-off points, which normally range from 0.3 to 0.4 or above (Worthington & Whittaker, 2006; Hair et al., 2010).

When it comes to the number of items per subscale, many methodologists would recommend being over-inclusive with the number (Kline, 1993), but usually a minimum of three is recommended in order to capture the true centre of each dimension (Carpenter, 2018). Two-item scales are plausible only if items are highly correlated (i.e., $r < 0.70$) (Worthington & Whittaker, 2006).

PHASE 3: SCALE EVALUATION

Step 7: Tests of Dimensionality

The term "test dimensionality" does not only refer to the particular set of items comprising a test; it is also the function of the interaction between the set of items and the group of examinees responding to those items (Gessaroli & de Champlain, 2005). Earlier definitions related to testing homogeneity and reliability, while the current definition extends to incorporate some form of local independence. According to Brown (2015), the test of dimensionality is one in which extracted factor structure is tested at a different time point in a longitudinal study or in a new sample using CFA, bifactor modelling or measurement invariance.

Confirmatory factor analysis
Confirmatory factor analysis is a multivariate statistical procedure that is used to test how well the measured variables represent the number of constructs. CFA borrows similar concepts from exploratory factor analysis (EFA). However, instead of letting the data tell us the factor structure, we specify an a priori hypothesized model to which systematic fit assessment procedures are applied and the relationship between latent constructs are estimated. Wieland et al. (2018) suggest that item removal should be considered when the Goodness of Fit (GFI) index indicates insufficient model fit based on the standardized residuals, estimated improvements in the $\times$ 2 value with corresponding degrees of freedom, the magnitude of modification indices, the normed fit index, the value of the comparative GFI index and the overall interpretability. The techniques for testing dimensionality include the chi-square test of exact fit, Root Mean Square Error of Approximation (RMSEA ≤ 0.06), the Tucker–Lewis Index (TLI ≥ 0.95), Comparative Fit Index (CFI ≥ 0.95), Standardized Root Mean Square Residual (SRMR ≤ 0.08) and Weighted Root Mean Square Residual (WRMR ≤ 1.0) (Morin et al., 2016; Yu, 2002).

CFA is a well-established method in the literature for confirmatory studies (Hair et al., 2019b) and has often been utilized in the past for scale reliability, identification of items whose removal may enhance content validity, and testing of convergent and divergent reliability (Hair et al., 2020). However, confirmatory composite analysis (CCA) has recently been proposed as a scale validation process and as a replacement for traditional scale development procedures. CCA as an alternative means to confirm linear composite constructs in measurement models is just emerging (Hair et al., 2019b, 2020; Henseler et al., 2014). While both CCA and CFA aim at confirming the measurement models, CCA is different from CFA based on its statistical objective, which is to maximize the variance extracted from dependable variables, and facilitating the prediction of these exogenous variables (Hair et al., 2020).

In addition to its ability similarly to CFA to carry out the checks mentioned above in terms of scale reliability, composite reliability, content validity, and convergent and discriminant validity, there is an emerging literature suggesting the superiority of CCA over CFA. Its advantages are given in terms of the following: the number of items retained being on the higher end with CCA leading to improved construct validity with more items available to serve as proxies (Hair et al., 2020); determinant construct scores are available (Rigdon et al., 2019); and the potential of CCA to assess both reflective and formative measurement models (Hair et al., 2020; Motamarri et al., 2020). More details on how to perform a CCA can be found in Hair et al. (2020).

Bifactor modelling

Bifactor modelling, also referred to as nested factor modelling, is a form of item response theory used in testing dimensionality of a scale (Reise et al., 2007). In a bifactor model, items are influenced by what can be referred to as a global factor, and also display evidence of sets of items tapping into coherent, homogeneous subcomponents referred to as local factors. It is important to note that bifactor models are not the same as hierarchical models as displayed in Figure 1.4, since they imply different causalities.

By carrying out the factor analysis we can identify whether there is inherent multidimensionality and clusters within items essentially previously identified as unidimensional. The bifactor model partitions the total covariance among the items into a global factor component underlying all items and local factor components explaining the residual covariance not explained by the global factor (Morin et al., 2016).

To assess whether to retain a construct as unidimensional or multidimensional, the factor loadings from the general global factor are

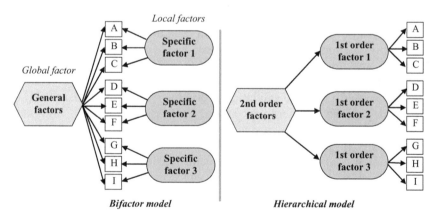

Source: Authors.

Figure 1.4   Example of bifactor model versus hierarchical model

then compared to those from the group local factors. Understanding of residual properties of specific factor score estimates is important for their interpretation. Whether the specific factor scores or weighted combinations of the general and specific factors should be reported will depend on how the scores will be used (DeMars, 2013). Where the factor loadings on the general factor are significantly larger than the group factors, a unidimensional scale is implied (Reise et al., 2007). While these analyses can be rather complex, and require specific software packages, DeMars (2013) and Morin et al. (2016) provide some guidelines on how to interpret the bifactor modelling scores.

Measurement of invariance
Chan (2011) states that "we cannot assume the same construct is being assessed across groups by the same measure" without tests of measurement invariance (p. 108). Multigroup confirmatory factory analysis is often used to test measurement invariance across participants from various groups (Milfont & Fischer, 2010). It permits the examination of whether the same measure is interpreted in conceptually similar ways across different groups (Bialosiewicz et al., 2013). There are three typical phases of measurement invariance testing, namely configural invariance, metric invariance and scalar invariance. Though there are stricter tests of measurement invariance, researchers agree that these three sequential steps are sufficient for establishing measurement invariance (Bialosiewicz et al., 2013; Milfont & Fischer, 2010). For example, if we use age to check invariance, for configural invariance we will need to examine whether the overall factor structure fits well for all age groups in the sample. Metric invariance will examine whether factor loadings are similar across groups, and scalar invariance will examine whether the item intercepts are equivalent across groups.

Step 8: Tests of Reliability

Reliability is the degree to which the measure of a construct is consistent or dependable when a measurement is repeated under identical conditions. The tests developed to assess reliability of a scale includes Cronbach's alpha (Vandenberg & Lance, 2000), test–retest reliability (coefficient of stability) (DeVellis, 2016), McDonald's Omega (McDonald, 1999), Raykov's rho (Raykov, 2011), split-half estimates, the Spearman-Brown formula, alternate form method (coefficient of equivalence) and inter-observer reliability (DeVellis, 2016). However Cronbach's alpha and test–retest reliability are the mostly utilized to assess reliability of scales (Raykov, 2011).

Cronbach's alpha considers the degree to which a set of items in the scale co-vary, relative to their sum score (DeVellis, 2016). Gardner (1995) noted that alpha is maximized when every item in a scale shares common variance with at least some other items in the scale. Coefficients of internal consistency increase as the number of items goes up, to a certain point. For instance, a five-item test might correlate 0.45 with true scores, and a 12-item test might correlate 0.85 with true scores. Hence there should be a trade-off between the reliability and the brevity of the scale.

An alpha coefficient of 0.70 has often been regarded as an acceptable threshold for reliability (Nunnally, 1978). DeVellis (2016) suggests that, below 0.65, the reliability level is undesirable; between 0.65 and 0.70 it is minimally acceptable; between 0.70 and 0.80 it is respectable; between 0.80 and 0.90 it is very good; and much above 0.90 one should consider short-ening the scale. Likewise, dropping items with poor inter-item correlation is likely to increase the internal consistency.

Test–retest reliability refers to the temporal stability of a test from one measurement session to another: that is, the test is administered to the same group of respondents at two different times whereby the correlation between scores on the identical tests operationally defines the test–retest reliability. Rosnow and Rosenthal (1991) identify a few limitations to test–retest: namely, shorter intervals between tests might cause the answers to be affected by memory; or, conversely, a longer interval might witness the maturation of the respondents which is reflected in their opinions. Pearson's correlation is often used to estimate the theoretical reliability coefficient between parallel tests, while some authors prefer the intra-class correlation coefficient (Weir, 2005).

Step 9: Tests of Validity

Scale validity is defined as the extent to which a measurement instrument is measuring the construct it was developed to evaluate (Raykov, 2011). It is important to understand that throughout scale development valida-tion is an ongoing process which starts right from Step 1 with proper identification of the items and construct under study to its generalizability in this last step.

There are numerous ways of examining validity, but the most common validity tests for scale development are content validity, criterion validity and construct validity. Content validity has already been discussed in Step 2.

Criterion validity
This type of validity has two subcategories, namely concurrent validity and predictive validity. In concurrent criterion validity there is usually a known standardized instrument, or even a known criterion that measures the same underlying concept of interest. It is defined as the extent to which

test scores have a stronger relationship with the criterion, which is also known as the gold standard.

Concurrent criterion validity is the extent to which test scores have a stronger relationship with the criterion (gold standard), which is in most cases a more valid and established measurement. The validity is appraised using Pearson product moment correlation or latent variable modelling (Boateng et al., 2018). Establishing concurrent validity is particularly beneficial when a new measure is created that claims to be better than the prior instrument. In marketing, criterion validity can be crucial – as seen in the infamous case when Coca-Cola decided to alter the flavour of their trademark drink. Surveys were carried out to assess whether or not people liked the new flavour, which they did; however the researchers did not consider using the original taste as a benchmark to question the target audience on which one they preferred. Consequently, the company incurred heavy losses.

Nunnally (1978, p. 87) provides a useful definition of predictive validity as: "when the purpose is to use an instrument to estimate some important form of behaviour that is external to the measuring instrument itself, the latter being referred to as criterion [predictive] validity". In predictive validity we assess the operationalization's ability to predict something it should theoretically be able to predict. For example, we can consider the predictive validity for measure of attitude towards the advertisement (predictor) and the brand attitude (criterion). As rightly stipulated by Becker et al. (2013), it is important to look beyond any given set of phenomena for additional connections and for new opportunities to challenge the existing knowledge; and this is where predictive validity is important. Worthington and Whittaker (2006) firmly recommend cross-validation of re-specified structural equation models to establish predictive validity. Predictive validity can be estimated by examining the association between the scale scores and the criterion in question.

Construct validity
Construct validity is the extent to which the identified items are tapping into the underlying theory or model of behaviour. Boateng et al. (2018) suggest four indicators of construct validity relevant to scale development: convergent validity, discriminant validity, differentiation by known groups and correlation analysis.

Convergent validity is determined by examining the average variance extracted, which indicates the amount of variance explained by a latent variable. An average variance extracted value of 0.50 or higher indicates that convergent validity has been achieved (Hair et al., 2010). Convergent validity states that tests having the same or similar constructs should be

highly correlated. Two methods are often applied to test convergent validity. One is to correlate the scores between two assessment tools or tool
sub-domains that are considered to measure the same construct. The other
method is the multitrait-multimethod matrix (MTMM) approach.

Discriminant validity, on the other hand, ensures that a construct
measure is empirically unique and represents phenomena in a way that
does not merely reflect some other construct (Hair et al., 2010; Raykov,
2011). It requires that a test does not correlate too highly with measures
from which it is supposed to differ (Campbell, 1960). Traditionally, in
marketing it is established using the Fornell and Larcker (1981) criterion
and cross-loadings (Chin, 1998), though recent research suggests that
the Fornell-Larcker criterion is not effective under certain circumstances
(Henseler et al., 2015). For example, it overestimates indicator loadings
(Hui & Wold, 1982; Lohmöller, 1989). Henseler et al. (2015) carried out
a simulation and their study revealed that the Fornell-Larcker criterion
and assessment of the cross-loadings are insufficiently sensitive to detect
discriminant validity problems. Henceforth the heterotrait-monotrait
ratio of correlations (HTMT) is proposed as a better approach to assess
discriminant validity.

Known-groups validation or differentiation between known groups
involves examining the distribution of a newly developed scale score and
showing that some scales can differentiate between different groups based
on their score (DeVellis, 2016). The validity of the measure is established
if the measure is able to discriminate between the groups through statistically significant findings.

Bivariate correlation can also be used to establish convergent and discriminant validity by providing evidence based on the relationship between
a test score and a conceptually related construct. Convergent validity is
identified by strong relationships, whereas discriminant validity was indicated by weak relationships (Swank & Mullen, 2017).

CONCLUSION

A rigorous scale development process is vital to increase the trustworthiness of research results. As rightly put by DeVellis (2016), the cost of using
a poorly conceptualized scale, even if it is the only one available, might be
greater than any benefits attained. Accurately defining and operational-
izing the phenomenon helps tackle resulting challenges of poor validity
and reliability or limited the scale's generalizability. The use of a systematic approach along with multiple methods increases the likelihood of
constructing a valid, reliable and applicable scale (Streiner et al., 2015).

We support Wieland et al.'s (2017) dualistic approach to scale purification: that the scales should take into account not only statistical criteria usually related to statistical heuristics or tests but also judgemental criteria that focus both on theoretical and empirical meanings. While statistical criteria are essential to evaluate the quality of scales, judgemental criteria are what give theoretical meaning to the construct (Borsboom et al., 2004). Henceforth, throughout scale development, judgemental criteria should also be applied, especially when considering scale purification. Another important side of scale development is ensuring that the scale is parsimonious. It is about minimizing the amount of data required while ensuring that all relevant aspects of the construct are captured (Wieland et al., 2017). This calls for a balance between the statistical and judgemental criteria.

We acknowledge that there are a number of issues not addressed here, such as interpretation of the tests or the different software to use, and therefore we recommend reading on each suggested test to assess its suitability to the measures being developed. Likewise, the necessity of the nine steps that we have outlined in this chapter is very likely to vary from study to study, and it is at the researcher's discretion which method is most suited for their studies. While some of the steps may have been labelled differently, on a global level the essence of scale development remains the same.

REFERENCES

Alaya, R.J. (2009). *The theory and practice of item response theory*. New York: Guilford.

Almanasreh, E., Moles, R., & Chen, T.F. (2019). Evaluation of methods used for estimating content validity. *Research in Social and Administrative Pharmacy*, *15*(2), 214–221.

Ayre, C., & Scally, A.J. (2014). Critical values for Lawshe's content validity ratio: Revisiting the original methods of calculation. *Measurement and Evaluation in Counseling and Development*, *47*, 79–86.

Baker, F.B., & Kim, S.H. (2017). *The basics of item response theory using R*. Cham: Springer.

Beavers, A.S., Lounsbury, J.W., Richards, J.K., & Huck, S.W. (2013). Practical considerations for using exploratory factor analysis in educational research. *Practical Assessment, Research, and Evaluation*, *18*(6), 1–13.

Becker, J.M., Rai, A., & Rigdon, E. (2013). Predictive validity and formative measurement in structural equation modeling: Embracing practical relevance. Proceedings of the 34th International Conference on Information Systems (ICIS), Milan.

Bialosiewicz, S., Murphy, K., & Berry, T. (2013). An introduction to measurement invariance testing: Resource packet for participants. Demonstration Session, American Evaluation Association, October, Washington, DC, 1–37.

Boateng, G.O., Neilands, T.B., Frongillo, E.A., Melgar-Quiñonez, H.R., & Young, S.L. (2018). Best practices for developing and validating scales for health, social, and behavioral research: A primer. *Frontiers in Public Health*, *6*, 149.

Borsboom, D., Mellenbergh, G.J., & Van Heerden, J. (2004). The concept of validity. *Psychological Review*, *111*(4), 1061–1071.

Brady, M.K., & Cronin Jr, J.J. (2001). Some new thoughts on conceptualizing perceived service quality: A hierarchical approach. *Journal of Marketing, 65*(3), 34–49.

Brockhoff, K. (1975). The performance of forecasting groups in computer dialogue and face-to-face discussion. In H.A. Linstone and M. Turoff (Eds.), *The Delphi method: Techniques and applications*. Reading, MA: Addison-Wesley.

Brown, T.A. (2015). *Confirmatory factor analysis for applied research*. New York: Guilford.

Campbell, D.T. (1960). Recommendations for APA test standards regarding construct, trait, or discriminant validity. *American Psychologist, 15*(8), 546–553.

Carpenter, S. (2018). Ten steps in scale development and reporting: A guide for researchers. *Communication Methods and Measures, 12*(1), 25–44.

Carr, J.H., Shepherd, R.B., Nordholm, L., & Lynne, D. (1985). Investigation of a new motor assessment scale for stroke patients. *Physical Therapy, 65*(2), 175–180.

Cattell, R.B. (1966). The scree test for the number of factors. *Multivariate Behavioral Research, 1*(2), 245–276.

Chan, D. (2011). Advances in analytical strategies. In S. Zedeck (Ed.), *APA handbook of industrial and organizational psychology* (Vol. 1, pp. 85–113). Washington, DC: American Psychological Association.

Chin, W.W. (1998). The partial least squares approach to structural equation modeling. *Modern Methods for Business Research, 295*(2), 295–336.

Churchill, G.A. Jr (1979). A paradigm for developing better measures of marketing constructs. *Journal of Marketing Research, 16*(1), 64–73.

Clark, L.A., & Watson, D. (2016). Constructing validity: Basic issues in objective scale development. In A.E. Kazdin (Ed.), *Methodological issues and strategies in clinical research* (pp. 187–203). Washington, DC: American Psychological Association.

Cohen, R.J., & Swerdlik, M.E. (2005). *Psychological testing and assessment: An introduction to tests and measurement* (6th ed.). Boston: McGraw-Hill.

Collins, D. (2003). Pretesting survey instruments: An overview of cognitive methods. *Quality of Life Research, 12*(3), 229–238.

Comrey, A.L. (1988). Factor-analytic methods of scale development in personality and clinical psychology. *Journal of Consulting and Clinical Psychology, 56*(5), 754–761.

Cristobal, E., Flavian, C., & Guinaliu, M. (2007). Perceived e-service quality (PeSQ): Measurement validation and effects on consumer satisfaction and web site loyalty. *Managing Service Quality: An International Journal, 17*(3), 317–340.

Dabholkar, P.A., Thorpe, D.I., & Rentz, J.O. (1996). A measure of service quality for retail stores: Scale development and validation. *Journal of the Academy of Marketing Science, 24*(1), 3–16.

Davis, L.L. (1992). Instrument review: Getting the most from a panel of experts. *Applied Nursing Research, 5*(4), 194–197.

De Vaus, D.A. (2002). *Surveys in social research*. Crows Nest, NSW: Allen and Unwin.

DeMars, C. (2010). *Item response theory*. Oxford: Oxford University Press.

DeMars, C.E. (2013). A tutorial on interpreting bifactor model scores. *International Journal of Testing, 13*(4), 354–378.

DeVellis, R.F. (2016). *Scale development: Theory and applications* (4th ed.). Los Angeles: Sage.

Diamantopoulos, A., Riefler, P., & Roth, K.P. (2008). Advancing formative measurement models. *Journal of Business Research, 61*(12), 1203–1218.

Dray, S., Dunsch, F., & Holmlund, M. (2016). Electronic versus paper-based data collection: Reviewing the debate. World Bank Development Impact blog. https://blogs.worldbank.org/impactevaluations/electronic-versus-paper-based-data-collection-reviewing-debate (Accessed 15 June 2020).

Fan, X. (1998). Item response theory and classical test theory: An empirical comparison of their item/person statistics. *Educational and Psychological Measurement, 58*(3), 357–381.

Fanning, J., & McAuley, E. (2014). A comparison of tablet computer and paper-based questionnaires in healthy aging research. *JMIR Research Protocols, 3*(3), 38.

Fornell, C., & Larcker, D.F. (1981). Evaluating structural equation models with unobservable variables and measurement error. *Journal of Marketing Research, 18*(1), 39–50.

Francis, J.E., & White, L. (2002). PIRQUAL: A scale for measuring customer expectations and perceptions of quality in internet retailing. In K. Evans & L. Scheer (Eds.), *2002 AMA Winter Educators' Conference* (pp. 263–270). Austin, TX: American Marketing Association.

Frey, B.B., ed. (2018). *The SAGE encyclopedia of educational research, measurement, and evaluation.* Los Angeles: Sage.

Gardner, W. (1995). On the reliability of sequential data: Measurement, meaning, and correction. In J.M. Gottman (Ed.), *The analysis of change* (pp. 339–359). Mahwah, NJ: Erlbaum.

Gessaroli, M.E., & de Champlain, A.F. (2005). Test dimensionality: Assessment of. In B.S. Everitt & D.C. Howell (Eds.), *Encyclopedia of statistics in behavioral science.* Hoboken, NJ: Wiley.

Glockner-Rist, A., & Hoijtink, H. (2003). The best of both worlds: Factor analysis of dichotomous data using item response theory and structural equation modeling. *Structural Equation Modeling, 10*(4), 544–565.

Goetz, C., Coste, J., Lemetayer, F., Rat, A.C., Montel, S., Recchia, S., Debouverie, M., Pouchot, J., Spitz, E., & Guillemin, F. (2013). Item reduction based on rigorous methodological guidelines is necessary to maintain validity when shortening composite measurement scales. *Journal of Clinical Epidemiology, 66*(7), 710–718.

Goldberg, L.R., & Velicer, W.F. (2006). Principles of exploratory factor analysis. In S. Strack (Ed.), *Differentiating normal and abnormal personality* (pp. 209–237). New York: Springer.

Goldstein, M., Benerjee, R., & Kilic, T. (2012). Paper v plastic part 1: The survey revolution is in progress. World Bank Development Impact blog. https://blogs.worldbank.org/impactevaluations/paper-v-plastic-part-i-the-survey-revolution-is-in-progress (Accessed 15 June 2020).

Gosling, S.D., Vazire, S., Srivastava, S., & John, O.P. (2004). Should we trust web-based studies? A comparative analysis of six preconceptions about internet questionnaires. *American Psychologist, 59*(2), 93–104.

Greenlaw, C., & Brown-Welty, S. (2009). A comparison of web-based and paper-based survey methods: Testing assumptions of survey mode and response cost. *Evaluation Review, 33*(5), 464–480.

Guadagnoli, E., & Velicer, W.F. (1988). Relation of sample size to the stability of component patterns. *Psychological Bulletin, 103*(2), 265–275.

Guion, R.M. (1977). Content validity: The source of my discontent. *Applied Psychological Measurement, 1*(1), 1–10.

Haig, B.D. (2005). Exploratory factor analysis, theory generation, and scientific method. *Multivariate Behavioral Research, 40*(3), 303–329.

Hair, J.F., Black, W.C., Babin, B.J., & Anderson, R.E. (2010). *Multivariate data analysis* (7th ed.). Upper Saddle River, NJ: Prentice Hall.

Hair, J.F., Black, W.C., Babin, B.J., & Anderson, R.E. (2019a). *Multivariate data analysis* (8th ed.). Andover: Cengage Learning.

Hair, J.F., Gabriel, M.L.D.S., da Silva, D., & Braga Jr., S. (2019b). Development and validation of attitudes measurement scales: Fundamental and practical aspects. *RAUSP Management Journal, 54*(4), 490–507.

Hair, J.F., Howard, M.C., & Nitzl, C. (2020). Assessing measurement model quality in PLS-SEM using confirmatory composite analysis. *Journal of Business Research, 109*, 101–110.

Hambleton, R.K., & Jones, R.W. (1993). Comparison of classical test theory and item response theory and their applications to test development. *Educational Measurement: Issues and Practice, 12*(3), 38–47.

Harvey, R.J., & Hammer, A.L. (1999). Item response theory. *The Counseling Psychologist, 27*(3), 353–383.

Haynes, S.N., Richard, D., & Kubany, E.S. (1995). Content validity in psychological assessment: A functional approach to concepts and methods. *Psychological Assessment, 7*(3), 238–247.

Heene, M., Bollmann, S., & Bühner, M. (2014). Much ado about nothing, or much to do about something? Effects of scale shortening on criterion validity and mean differences. *Journal of Individual Differences, 35*(4), 245–249.

Hendrickson, A.E., & White, P.O. (1964). Promax: A quick method for rotation to oblique simple structure. *British Journal of Statistical Psychology, 17*(1), 65–70.

Henseler, J., Dijkstra, T.K., Sarstedt, M., Ringle, C.M., Diamantopoulos, A., Straub, D.W., . . . & Calantone, R.J. (2014). Common beliefs and reality about PLS: Comments on Rönkkö and Evermann (2013). *Organizational Research Methods, 17*(2), 182–209.

Henseler, J., Ringle, C.M., & Sarstedt, M. (2015). A new criterion for assessing discriminant validity in variance-based structural equation modeling. *Journal of the Academy of Marketing Science, 43*(1), 115–135.

Hill, C.E., Kline, K.V., Miller, M., Marks, E., Pinto-Coelho, K., & Zetzer, H. (2019). Development of the meaning in life measure. *Counselling Psychology Quarterly, 32*(2), 205–226.

Horn, J.L. (1965). A rationale and test for the number of factors in factor analysis. *Psychometrika, 30*(2), 179–185.

Howard, M.C. (2018). Scale pretesting. *Practical Assessment, Research, and Evaluation, 23*(1), Art. 5.

Howard, M.C., & Melloy, R.C. (2016). Evaluating item-sort task methods: The presentation of a new statistical significance formula and methodological best practices. *Journal of Business and Psychology, 31*(1), 173–186.

Hui, B.S., & Wold, H. (1982). Consistency and consistency at large of partial least squares estimates. In K.G. Joreskog & H.O.A. Wold (Eds.), *Systems under indirect observation, part II* (pp. 119–130). Amsterdam: North-Holland.

Kaiser, H.F. (1958). The varimax criterion for analytic rotation in factor analysis. *Psychometrika, 23*, 187–200.

Kim, S., & Stoel, L. (2004). Apparel retailers: Website quality dimensions and satisfaction. *Journal of Retailing and Consumer Services, 11*(2), 109–117.

Kline, P. (1993). *A handbook of psychological testing* (2nd ed.). London: Routledge.

Kock, F., Josiassen, A., & Assaf, A.G. (2016). Advancing destination image: The destination content model. *Annals of Tourism Research, 61*, 28–44.

Ladhari, R. (2010). Developing e-service quality scales: A literature review. *Journal of Retailing and Consumer Services, 17*(6), 464–477.

Lawshe, C.H. (1975). A quantitative approach to content validity. *Personnel Psychology, 28*(4), 563–575.

Leech, B.L. (2002). Asking questions: Techniques for semistructured interviews. *PS: Political Science and Politics, 35*(4), 665–668.

Leisher, C. (2014). A comparison of tablet-based and paper-based survey data collection in conservation projects. *Social Sciences, 3*, 264–271.

Lennon, R.T. (1956). Assumptions underlying the use of content validity. *Educational and Psychological Measurement, 16*(3), 294–304.

Lindeman, C.A. (1975). Delphi survey of priorities in clinical nursing research. *Nursing Research, 24*(6), 434–441.

Linstone, H.A., & Turoff, M., eds. (1975). *The Delphi method: Techniques and applications.* Reading, MA: Addison-Wesley.

Lohmöller, J.-B. (1989). Basic principles of model building: Specification, estimation, evaluation. In H.O.A. Wold (Ed.), *Theoretical empiricism: A general rationale for scientific model-building* (pp. 1–26). New York: Paragon House.

Loiacono, E.T., Watson, R.T., & Goodhue, D.L. (2002). WebQual: A measure of website quality. *Marketing Theory and Applications, 13*(3), 432–438.

Lorenzo-Seva, U., Timmerman, M.E., & Kiers, H.A. (2011). The Hull method for selecting the number of common factors. *Multivariate Behavioral Research, 46*(2), 340–364.

Marsh, H.W. (1998). Pairwise deletion for missing data in structural equation models: Nonpositive definite matrices, parameter estimates, goodness of fit, and adjusted sample sizes. *Structural Equation Modeling: A Multidisciplinary Journal, 5*(1), 22–36.

Martínez, J.A., & Martínez, L. (2010). Some insights on conceptualizing and measuring service quality. *Journal of Retailing and Consumer Services, 17*(1), 29–42.

McDonald, R.P. (1999). *Test theory: A unified treatment.* Mahwah, NJ: Erlbaum.

McGartland Rubio, D., & Kimberly, K.L. (2005). Content validity. In K. Kempf-Leonard (Ed.), *Encyclopedia of Social Measurement.* Pittsburgh: Elsevier.

Meyers, L.S., Gamst, G., & Guarino, A.J. (2016). *Applied multivariate research: Design and interpretation* (3rd ed.). Thousand Oaks, CA: Sage.

Milfont, T.L., & Fischer, R. (2010). Testing measurement invariance across groups: Applications in cross-cultural research. *International Journal of Psychological Research, 3*(1), 111–130.

Morin, A.J., Arens, A.K., & Marsh, H.W. (2016). A bifactor exploratory structural equation modeling framework for the identification of distinct sources of construct-relevant psychometric multidimensionality. *Structural Equation Modeling: A Multidisciplinary Journal, 23*(1), 116–139.

Motamarri, S., Akter, S., & Yanamandram, V. (2020). Frontline employee empowerment: Scale development and validation using confirmatory composite analysis. *International Journal of Information Management, 54,* 102177.

Nosek, B.A., Banaji, M.R., & Greenwald, A.G. (2002). E-research: Ethics, security, design, and control in psychological research on the internet. *Journal of Social Issues, 58*(1), 161–176.

Notter, L.E. (1983). *Essentials of nursing research* (3rd ed.). New York: Springer.

Nunnally, J.C. (1978). *Psychometric theory* (2nd ed.). New York: McGraw-Hill.

Osborne, J.W., & Costello, A.B. (2004). Sample size and subject to item ratio in principal components analysis. *Practical Assessment, Research, and Evaluation, 9*(1), Art. 11.

Osborne, J.W., Costello, A.B., & Kellow, T.J. (2008). Best practices in exploratory factor analysis. In J.W. Osborne (Ed.), *Best practices in quantitative methods* (pp. 86–99). Los Angeles: Sage.

Perroca, M.G. (2011). Development and content validity of the new version of a patient classification instrument. *Revista latino-americana de enfermagem, 19*(1), 58–66.

Pett, M., Lackey, N., & Sullivan, J. (2006). *Making sense of factor analysis in health care research: A practical guide.* London: Sage.

Piedmont, R.L. (2014). Inter-item correlations. In A.C. Michalos (Ed.), *Encyclopedia of quality of life and well-being research* (pp. 3303–3304). Dordrecht: Springer.

Polit, D.F., & Beck, C.T. (2006). The content validity index: Are you sure you know what's being reported? Critique and recommendations. *Research in Nursing & Health, 29*(5), 489–497.

Polit, D.F., Beck, C.T., & Owen, S.V. (2007). Is the CVI an acceptable indicator of content validity? Appraisal and recommendations. *Research in Nursing & Health, 30*(4), 459–467.

Preacher, K.J., & MacCallum, R.C. (2003). Repairing Tom Swift's electric factor analysis machine. *Understanding Statistics: Statistical Issues in Psychology, Education, and the Social Sciences, 2*(1), 13–43.

Raykov, T. (2011). Evaluation of convergent and discriminant validity with multitrait–multimethod correlations. *British Journal of Mathematical and Statistical Psychology, 64*(1), 38–52.

Reise, S.P., Morizot, J., & Hays, R.D. (2007). The role of the bifactor model in resolving dimensionality issues in health outcomes measures. *Quality of Life Research, 16*(1), 19–31.

Rigdon, E.E., Becker, J.M., & Sarstedt, M. (2019). Parceling cannot reduce factor indeterminacy in factor analysis: A research note. *Psychometrika, 84*(3), 772–780.

Rosnow, R.L., & Rosenthal, R. (1991). If you're looking at the cell means, you're not looking at only the interaction (unless all main effects are zero). *Psychological Bulletin, 110*(3), 574–576.

Roth, P.L. (1994). Missing data: A conceptual review for applied psychologists. *Personnel Psychology, 47*(3), 537–560.

Rubio, D.M., Berg-Weger, M., Tebb, S.S., Lee, E.S., & Rauch, S. (2003). Objectifying content validity: Conducting a content validity study in social work research. *Social Work Research*, *27*(2), 94–104.

Safikhani, S., Sundaram, M., Bao, Y., Mulani, P., & Revicki, D.A. (2013). Qualitative assessment of the content validity of the Dermatology Life Quality Index in patients with moderate to severe psoriasis. *Journal of Dermatological Treatment*, *24*(1), 50–59.

Scheele, D. (1975). Reality construction as a product of Delphi interaction. In H.A. Linstone & M. Turoff (Eds.), *The Delphi method: Techniques and applications* (p. 37). Reading, MA: Addison-Wesley.

Schinka, J.A., Velicer, W.F., & Weiner, I.R. (2012). *Handbook of psychology, vol. 2: Research methods in psychology*. Hoboken, NJ: Wiley.

Shrotryia, V.K., & Dhanda, U. (2019). Content validity of assessment instrument for employee engagement. *SAGE Open*, *9*(1).

Sim, S.M., & Rasiah, R.I. (2006). Relationship between item difficulty and discrimination indices in true/false-type multiple choice questions of a para-clinical multidisciplinary paper. *Annals of the Academy of Medicine Singapore*, *35*(2), 67–71.

Streiner, D.L., Norman, G.R., & Cairney, J. (2015). *Health measurement scales: A practical guide to their development and use*. New York: Oxford University Press.

Swank, J.M., & Mullen, P.R. (2017). Evaluating evidence for conceptually related constructs using bivariate correlations. *Measurement and Evaluation in Counselling and Development*, *50*(4), 270–274.

Tabachnick, B.G., Fidell, L.S., & Ullman, J.B. (2007). *Using multivariate statistics* (5th ed.). Boston, MA: Pearson.

Teeroovengadum, V., & Nunkoo, R. (2018). Sampling design in tourism and hospitality research. In R. Nunkoo (Ed.), *Handbook of research methods for tourism and hospitality management* (pp. 477–488). Cheltenham, UK and Northampton, MA, USA: Edward Elgar Publishing.

Tersine, R.J., & Riggs, W.E. (1976). The Delphi technique: A long-range planning tool. *Business Horizons*, *19*(2), 51–56.

Thompson, B. (2004). *Exploratory and confirmatory factor analysis*. Washington, DC: American Psychological Association.

Thurstone, L.L. (1947). *Multiple-factor analysis: A development and expansion of the vectors of mind*. Chicago: University of Chicago Press.

Vandenberg, R.J., & Lance, C.E. (2000). A review and synthesis of the measurement invariance literature: Suggestions, practices, and recommendations for organizational research. *Organizational Research Methods*, *3*(1), 4–70.

Velicer, W.F. (1976). The relation between factor score estimates, image scores, and principal component scores. *Educational and Psychological Measurement*, *36*(1), 149–159.

Weir, J.P. (2005). Quantifying test–retest reliability using the intraclass correlation coefficient and the SEM. *Journal of Strength & Conditioning Research*, *19*(1), 231–240.

Wieland, A., Durach, C.F., Kembro, J., & Treiblmaier, H. (2017). Statistical and judgmental criteria for scale purification. *Supply Chain Management: An International Journal*, *22*(4), 321–328.

Wieland, A., Kock, F., & Josiassen, A. (2018). Scale purification: State-of-the-art review and guidelines. *International Journal of Contemporary Hospitality Management*, *30*(11), 3346–3362.

Worthington, R.L., & Whittaker, T.A. (2006). Scale development research: A content analysis and recommendations for best practices. *The Counseling Psychologist*, *34*(6), 806–838.

Yu, C.Y. (2002). Evaluating cutoff criteria of model fit indices for latent variable models with binary and continuous outcomes (Unpublished doctoral dissertation). University of California Los Angeles.

Zamanzadeh, V., Ghahramanian, A., Rassouli, M., Abbaszadeh, A., Alavi-Majd, H., & Nikanfar, A.R., (2015). Design and implementation content validity study: Development of an instrument for measuring patient-centered communication. *Journal of Caring Sciences*, *4*(2), 165–178.

2. Necessary condition analysis in marketing research

Jan Dul, Sven Hauff and Zsófia Tóth

SUMMARY

This chapter introduces necessary condition analysis (NCA), which represents a new and promising approach for identifying necessary conditions in empirical data. The reader will become familiar with the basic logic and steps needed to conduct an NCA. We will also discuss the opportunities of using NCA in marketing research.

INTRODUCTION

Necessary condition analysis (NCA) (Dul, 2016; Dul et al., 2020) is a new approach and analysis technique for identifying necessary conditions. Necessary conditions represent constraints, bottlenecks, or critical factors that must be present for a desired outcome. They cannot be compensated by other factors, and will lead to guaranteed failure if absent. For example, the assumption that reciprocity is necessary for cooperative outcomes (Jap & Ganesan, 2000) implies that cooperative outcomes cannot be achieved without reciprocity. Similarly, if researchers state that research and development are necessary for innovativeness (Rubera & Kirca, 2012), they assume that there will be no innovativeness if there are no research and development activities.

The logic of NCA differs from additive logic implied in conventional methods (e.g. correlation, regression, or structural equation modelling) where contributing factors add up to produce an outcome and can compensate for each other. In contrast to these methods, NCA does not try to predict the presence of an outcome when the condition is present, but the absence of an outcome when the condition is absent instead. Therefore, NCA provides a different view on theory, methodology and practical relevance. With this different view, NCA can enrich marketing research by exploring (levels of) conditions without which (levels of) desired outcomes of marketing strategies, planning, advertising and so on cannot occur.

In this chapter, we introduce NCA and discuss its applications in marketing management. First, we will look at the underlying logic of necessary conditions. Building on that, we describe the basics of NCA (for a more thorough introduction see Dul, 2020) and show how it can be applied to identify necessary conditions of relevant marketing phenomena. Finally, we will discuss the advantages of using NCA in marketing research.

NECESSITY LOGIC

Necessity statements are very common in all research disciplines. Researchers use different words to express that a condition X is a necessary cause for an outcome Y. Common expressions are, for example, *"X is needed for Y"*, *"X is critical for Y"*, *"X must be there for Y to succeed"*, *"X is a precondition for Y"* or *"Y requires X"*. All these expressions refer to a necessity logic implying that an outcome Y can only be achieved if a specific condition X is present. This is different from sufficiency logic. Sufficiency logic implies that a change in X is sufficient for a change in Y, whereby X is not automatically necessary for Y since Y may also be achieved if X is not present.

Figure 2.1 exemplifies the difference between necessity and sufficiency logic by illustrating three types of cause. On the left we see possible combinations of values of X and Y when X is a sufficient but not necessary cause for Y. When X is present (value 1) Y is also present: X produces Y. However, when X is absent (value 0) Y can be absent or present. For example, when a relationship between customers is not very strong (high tie-strength is absent), word-of-mouth (WOM) marketing between them may still be present or absent (Groeger & Buttle, 2014). In the middle of Figure 2.1 we see possible combinations of values of X and Y when X is a necessary but not sufficient cause for Y. In this situation Y is absent when X is absent (value 0). Thus the absence of X produces the absence of Y. However, when X is present (value 1) Y can be absent or present.[1] For example, customer participation is necessary for collaborative marketing relationships (Lacey, 2009). If customer participation is absent, collaborative marketing relationships cannot be built. On the right in Figure 2.1 we see the possible combination of values of X and Y when X is a necessary and sufficient cause for Y. When X is present (value 1) Y is also present, and when X is absent Y is also absent. The presence of X produces the presence of Y, and the absence of Y produces the absence of Y. For example, an individual or company paying a fee to access a market research database will result in their being able to access the database, and not paying the fee produces the inability to access it.

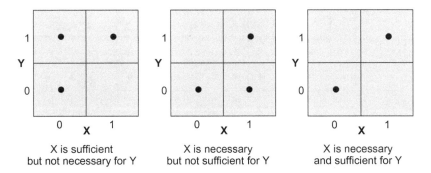

Figure 2.1   Types of causes

Notably, causal statements do not need to be universally true; they usually refer to a specific context. For example, building *guanxi* (networks, relationships) is necessary for the success of small- and medium-sized enterprises (SMEs) in China (Hu & Stanton, 2011) but not necessary in some other international business contexts.

So far, we have discussed necessary conditions in terms of "X is necessary for Y". However, the idea of necessity is not limited to the dichotomous case but can also refer to discrete or continuous variables. With discrete and continuous variables, necessary conditions can be formulated by degree, i.e. in terms of "A certain level of X is necessary for certain level of Y." Figure 2.2 provides several examples of discrete necessary conditions. In contrast to the dichotomous case, discrete variables allow more precise statements on necessity. For example, the first example in Figure 2.2 shows a case in which a medium level of X (X = 1) is necessary for a superior level of Y (Y = 2). In contrast, the second example shows a case in which a high level of X (X = 2) is necessary for a superior level of Y (Y = 2).

The examples in Figure 2.2 show a discrete situation with three levels. This can be extended to more levels (four, five, etc.) up to the continuous situation where the condition and the outcome can have an infinite number of levels (Figure 2.3). In this situation level X = Xc or level Y = Yc is necessary, where c is a point on the "ceiling line" that separates the dark area with observations from the light area without observations.[2]

In sum, necessary conditions can be formulated in different ways. This can be in terms of "X is necessary for Y" in the dichotomous case or in terms of "A certain level of X is necessary for a certain level of Y" for discrete or continuous variables. This gives countless options for marketing research. In the next section, we introduce necessary condition analysis as a methodology for analysing necessary conditions empirically.

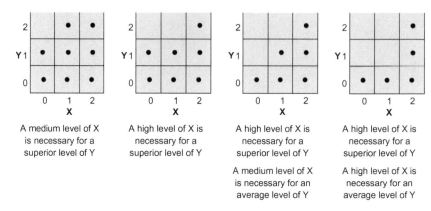

Figure 2.2   Discrete necessary conditions

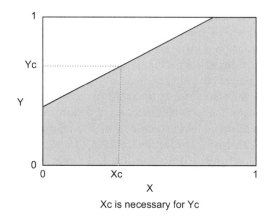

Xc is necessary for Yc

Figure 2.3   Basic continuous necessary condition

BASICS OF NCA

Necessary condition analysis (NCA) (Dul, 2016; Dul et al., 2020) is a novel approach and data analysis method that is based on the logic that certain conditions are necessary (but not sufficient) to achieve a specific outcome. By applying necessity logic, NCA differs fundamentally from conventional methods like correlation, regression, or structural equation modelling. In contrast to these methods, NCA does not try to predict the presence of an outcome; instead, it tries to predict the absence of an outcome.

In order to identify necessary conditions, NCA looks for an empty space in the upper left-hand corner of a scatter plot.[3] Therefore, instead of drawing a regression line "through the middle" of the data in a scatter plot, NCA draws a ceiling line "on top" of the data. Several techniques can be used to draw ceiling lines. Two currently recommended techniques are Ceiling Envelopment – Free Disposal Hull (CE-FDH) and Ceiling Regression – Free Disposal Hull (CR-FDH). The *ceiling envelope* (CE) technique puts a piecewise linear envelope along the upper-left observations. CE-FDH assumes that the ceiling is non-decreasing, resulting in a non-decreasing step function. *Ceiling regression* (CR) smooths the piecewise linear function obtained by the CE techniques by using OLS regression through the upper-left corners of the piecewise linear functions. Thus, CR-FDH draws a line through CE-FDH corners. The percentage of cases that are on or below the ceiling line defines the *accuracy* of a ceiling line (c-accuracy). The c-accuracy of CE-FDH is by definition 100 per cent. The c-accuracy of the CR-FDH line is below 100 per cent. CE-FDH is recommended for dichotomous and discrete (with few levels) necessary conditions, or when the ceiling pattern is irregular. CR-FDH is recommended for discrete (with many levels) and continuous necessary conditions, or when the ceiling is assumed to be linear.

Figure 2.4 illustrates the CE-FDH and the CR-FDH ceiling lines in an example where Sociability is assumed to be a necessary condition for the Sales ability of a salesperson (for more details on this example see below).

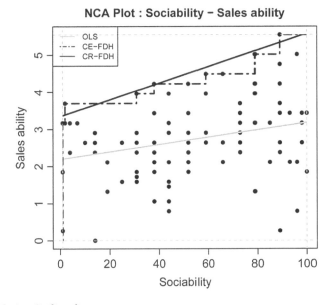

Figure 2.4   Ceiling lines

Table 2.1   Bottleneck table

Y Sales ability (%)	X Sociability (%)
0	NN
10	NN
20	NN
30	NN
40	NN
50	NN
60	NN
70	23
80	48
90	73
100	98

The figure also shows the OLS regression line. While the OLS line addresses the average trend within the data, the ceiling line separates the zones with and without observations. Therewith, the ceiling line indicates which maximum Y (Sales ability) can be achieved for a given value of X (Sociability) or, in other words, which value of X is necessary for which level of Y.

The ceiling line(s) can also be displayed in a tabular form, which is called a *bottleneck table*. The first column in a bottleneck table is the outcome; any subsequent columns are the conditions. Outcome and conditions can be expressed as a percentage of the range, actual values or as percentiles. Table 2.1 shows the bottleneck table for the previous example. The bottleneck indicates the necessary levels (minimum required levels) of the condition for a given value of outcome Y. For example, when an outcome level of only Y = 50 per cent is desired, the condition (Sociability) is not necessary to achieve that outcome (NN = Not Necessary). However, when the desired Y is 80 per cent, the condition must have a level of at least 23 per cent. For 100 per cent Sales ability, the bottleneck table predicts that Sociability must be also close to 100 per cent.

The size of the empty space above the ceiling line ("ceiling zone") relative to the size of the entire area that can have observations ("scope") defines the strength of the necessary condition. This can be expressed as $d = C/S$, with d being the *effect size*, C the ceiling zone, and S the scope. The scope is defined by the minimum and maximum values of X and Y. This can either be the empirically observed minimum and maximum values ("empirical scope") or the theoretically possible minimum and maximum values ("theoretical scope"). The theoretical scope and the corresponding empty space are larger than the empirical scope and the corresponding empty space, and the effect size calculated with the theoretical scope is usually larger than the effect size calculated with the empirical scope. Thus, the empirical scope should be preferred in order to avoid over-estimation.

The range of d can be from 0 to 1 ($0 \leq d \leq 1$). In order to establish whether the effect size is practical and meaningful, Dul (2016) suggested the following thresholds:

$0 < d < 0.1$	"small effect"
$0.1 \leq d < 0.3$	"medium effect"
$0.3 \leq d < 0.5$	"large effect"
$d \geq 0.5$	"very large effect"

Since the observed effect size may be the result of random chance, NCA also allows us to evaluate the statistical significance of the effect (Dul et al., 2020). NCA uses an approximate permutation test that estimates the probability p that the data is the result of random chance when X is unrelated to Y. If this probability is very small (e.g. $p < 0.05$) it can be concluded that the observed sample is not the result of a random process of unrelated variables (the null hypothesis is rejected). Subsequently, the researcher may conclude that the hypothesis of interest (the alternative hypothesis) is supported.

Notably, NCA is fundamentally a bivariate analysis: only two variables are analysed at a time (one X and one Y). When more variables are potential necessary conditions (multiple NCA), the analysis is done for these conditions separately. This is possible because a necessary condition operates in isolation from the rest of the causal structure: The necessity of X_1 on Y does not depend on the necessity of X_2 on Y. A multivariate analysis that includes *all* variables plus "control factors" (e.g. as in multiple regression) is thus not needed.

When performing an NCA, researchers should perform an *outlier* analysis since NCA is very sensitive to some outliers. Indeed, the cases around the ceiling line are particularly important for two reasons. First, these cases determine the ceiling line. These cases may have sampling error or measurement error, or may be outliers (very high value of Y compared to other cases with similar X values). When there is only one case in the "empty space" due to measurement error or sample error (e.g. the case does not belong to the population of interest), a wrong conclusion can be made. Thus NCA researchers must pay particular attention to avoid measurement error and sample error. Second, cases around the ceiling line are "best cases" in the situation that X is a scarce resource and Y is a desired output. These cases are apparently able to have relatively high desired outcome with relatively low resources. The question of how to deal with few "outliers" that are not caused by measurement or sample error is not an easy one. In a *deterministic view* on necessity, every single case can falsify a necessity theory. Thus, if there is one single case in the upper-left corner, the necessity hypotheses should be rejected. However, researchers could also opt for a more *probabilistic view* on necessity in that a few cases above the ceiling line are acceptable. Therewith, necessity statements are more flexible in terms like "practically", "virtually", or "almost always" necessary.

NCA can be performed with a free software package for R. The NCA software's main functions are to draw scatter plots with ceiling lines, calculate NCA parameters (e.g. ceiling zone, scope, effect size) and bottleneck tables, and perform the significance test. The next section will illustrate the software's application and main functions (for a quick guide on how to apply NCA with R, see also Dul, 2019).

APPLICATION AND MAIN FUNCTIONS OF THE NCA SOFTWARE

Data and Model

In order to illustrate the application and the main functions of the NCA software, we use data from the Hogan Personality Inventory (HPI; Hogan & Hogan, 2007). This data contains information on personality traits and the sales ability of 108 sales representatives of a large US food manufacturer: 81.7 per cent of the respondents are male, and the average age is 36.7 years (SD = 10.7 years).

The dependent variable in our example is *Sales ability*, measured as the degree to which a person has effective demonstration, promotion and sales of products and services. This was measured through supervisor rating of employee performance bases on a seven-item scale (alpha = 0.83). The independent variables are four personality traits of the HPI, namely:

Ambition (the degree to which a person seems leader-like, status-seeking, and achievement-oriented);
Sociability (the degree to which a person needs and/or enjoys social interaction);
Interpersonal sensitivity (the degree to which a person has social sensitivity, tact, and perceptiveness); and
Learning approach (the degree to which a person enjoys academic activities and values education as an end in itself).

Our guiding assumption is that these four traits are necessary conditions for the sales ability of sales representatives (Figure 2.5).

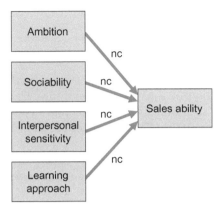

Figure 2.5   Personality traits as necessary conditions of sales ability

How to Conduct an NCA

In order to perform an NCA you first need to install and load the NCA R package in R. You can use the following commands:

```
install.packages("NCA")
library(NCA)
```

The first command downloads the NCA R package, which needs to be done to use NCA for the first time. To update to the latest NCA version you can use the `update.packages()` function. After the NCA package is installed, the `library()` function runs the software. This needs to be done in every new R session.

In the next step you need to import the data you want to analyse. To do this you can use the `read.csv()` function (or another data import function, depending on the format you are using – SPSS, Stata, Excel, etc.).

Once the data is loaded you can run a basic NCA with the `nca()` function. Thereby, you need to specify your data, and the independent and dependent variable. In our example, this looks as follows:

```
nca(Hogan, "Ambition", "Sales ability")
```

Our data set is called *Hogan*, the independent variable is *Ambition* and the dependent variable is *Sales ability*. By default, the `nca()` function provides the CE-FDH and the CR-FDH effect sizes as well as a scatter plot with the OLS, CE-FDH and CR-FDH lines. For our example, the following output is provided:

```
Effect size(s):
ce_fdh cr_fdh
 0.204  0.179
```

The scatter plot (Figure 2.6) shows an empty space in the upper-left corner which is an indication of a necessary condition. This is also supported through the effect size. Since independent and dependent variables are continuous, we focus on the CR-FDH effect size, which is $d = 0.18$ and can be characterized as "medium effect".

You can also integrate multiple necessary conditions in the nca() function to analyse different necessary conditions (multiple NCA) together:

```
nca(Hogan, c("Ambition", "Sociability", "Interpersonal
    sensitivity", "Learning approach"), "Sales ability")
```

This provides the following outputs:

```
Effect size(s):
                            ce_fdh cr_fdh
Ambition                    0.204  0.179
Sociability                 0.221  0.193
Interpersonal sensitivity   0.113  0.108
Learning approach           0.129  0.139
```

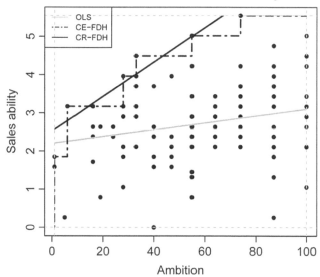

Figure 2.6   R plot for ambition and sales ability

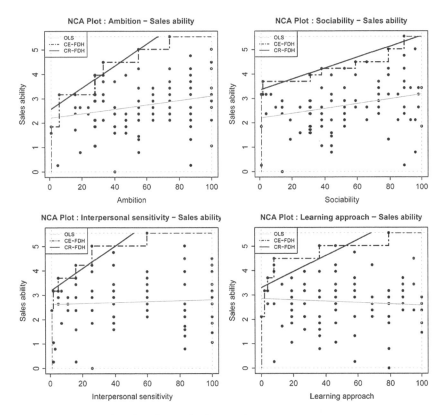

Figure 2.7   R plots for the multiple NCA

All four scatter plots (Figure 2.7) show an empty space in the upper-left corner, and the CR-FDH effect sizes are all above 0.1. Thus, according to the thresholds for a practical meaningful effect (Dul, 2016), Ambition (d = 0.18), Sociability (d = 0.19), Interpersonal sensitivity (d = 0.11), and Learning approach (d = 0.14) represent a medium necessary condition.

For a more detailed output you can use the `nca_analysis()` function followed by the `nca_output()` instruction. Thereby, the analysis can be given a specific name, like "model". The command structure is as follows:

```
model <- nca_analysis (Hogan, c("Ambition", "Sociability",
   "Interpersonal sensitivity", "Learning approach"),
   "Sales ability")
nca_output(model)
```

This provides you with a summary of key NCA parameters for all inte-grated necessary conditions. For the relationship between Ambition and Sales ability, this looks as follows:

```
------------------------------------------------------------
NCA Parameters: Ambition — Sales ability
------------------------------------------------------------

Number of observations 108
Scope                          549.224
Xmin                             1.000
Xmax                           100.000
Ymin                             0.000
Ymax                             5.548

                      ce_fdh   cr_fdh
Ceiling zone         112.011   98.246
Effect size            0.204    0.179
# above                    0        4
c-accuracy              100%    96.3%
Fit                     100%    87.7%

Slope                           0.045
Intercept                       2.530
Abs. ineff.          279.235 352.732
Rel. ineff.           50.842  64.224
Condition ineff.      26.263  33.230
Outcome ineff.        33.333  46.418
------------------------------------------------------------
```

The `nca_output` instruction can be modified in order to also provide a bottleneck table for all necessary conditions:

```
nca_output(model, bottlenecks=TRUE)
```

This respective output looks like this:

```
------------------------------------------------------------
Bottleneck CR-FDH (cutoff = 0)
Y Sales ability                   (percentage.range)
1 Ambition                        (percentage.range)
2 Sociability                     (percentage.range)
3 Interpersonal sensitivity       (percentage.range)
4 Learning approach               (percentage.range)
------------------------------------------------------------
Y          1     2     3     4
0          NN    NN    NN    NN
10         NN    NN    NN    NN
20         NN    NN    NN    NN
30         NN    NN    NN    NN
40         NN    NN    NN    NN
50         4.5   NN    NN    NN
60         16.9  NN    2.7   0.8
70         29.4  23.2  14.8  17.7
80         41.8  48.3  27.0  34.6
90         54.3  73.3  39.1  51.5
100        66.8  98.4  51.2  68.4
------------------------------------------------------------
```

Furthermore, the `nca_analysis()` function can be used to test the statistical significance of the effects. Therefore, you need to integrate the "test.rep" argument into the `nca_analysis()` function, and specify a large number of random samples (e.g. 10 000) which are created to obtain a distribution of effect sizes when the null hypothesis is true (X and Y are not related). This distribution is used for comparison with the observed effect size and for calculating the p value. If the p value is small enough (e.g. $p < 0.05$), it is unlikely that the observers' effect size is caused by random chance (for more details see Dul et al., 2020). The command structure looks as follows:

```
model<-nca_analysis(Hogan, c("Ambition", "Sociability",
    "Interpersonal sensitivity", "Learning approach"),
    "Sales ability", test.rep=10000)
model
```

The respective output is:

```
-----------------------------------------------------------------
Effect size(s):
                            ce_fdh p      cr_fdh p
Ambition                    0.204  0.040  0.179  0.044
Sociability                 0.221  0.003  0.193  0.004
Interpersonal sensitivity   0.113  0.315  0.108  0.380
Learning approach           0.129  0.190  0.139  0.165
-----------------------------------------------------------------
```

Thus, we find that the effects of Ambition and Sociability are statistically significant, while the effects of Interpersonal sensitivity and Learning approach are not statistically significant.

NCA vs. Regression Analysis

The results of the NCA have shown that Ambition and Sociability are meaningful and statistically significant necessary conditions for Sales ability. How do these results compare to traditional regression-based analysis? Table 2.2 shows the results of both OLS regression analysis and NCA. For each method we provide the results of a full model (i.e. a model where all independent variables were considered) and a reduced model (a model where Sociability is not considered as an independent variable).

The OLS results from the full model show that Sociability is the only personality trait that has a significant relationship with Sales ability. Based on these results researchers might conclude that Sociability is the only personality trait that is relevant for the selection of salespeople. This stands, however, in contrast to the NCA results – where Ambition and Sociability are both statistically significant necessary conditions for Sales ability. Both

Table 2.2 *OLS vs. NCA results*

	OLS full model		NCA full model		OLS reduced model		NCA reduced model	
	B	p value	D	p value	B	p value	d	p value
(Constant)	2.115	0.000	–	–	2.363	0.000	–	–
Ambition	0.007	0.059	0.179	0.044	0.010	0.006	0.179	0.044
Sociability	0.009	0.012	0.193	0.004	–	–	–	–
Interpersonal sensitivity	0.000	0.883	0.108	0.380	0.000	0.952	0.108	0.380
Learning approach	-0.006	0.055	0.139	0.165	-0.005	0.135	0.139	0.165
Adjusted R squared	0.101	–	–	–	0.053	–	–	–

analyses refer to a different logic and provide different implications. The results of the OLS analysis point out that Sales ability can be increased (on average) if salespeople show a higher score on the Sociability index. In contrast, the results of the NCA imply that a high level of Sales ability cannot be achieved without a certain level of Ambition and Sociability.

The comparison between the full and the reduced model highlights another feature of NCA: while the results of the OLS regression become biased through the omitted variable, because Sociability correlates with the other independent variables and the dependent variable, the results of the NCA are stable. The reason is that each necessary condition is analysed separately; thus omitting a variable does not affect the results of the other variables.

APPLYING NCA IN MARKETING RESEARCH

First of all, NCA can be applied as a novel method in various marketing research frameworks and domains. It can add value with new insights as well as shed light on long-lasting dilemmas about what conditions are necessary for an outcome and which ones are only nice to have. Domains may include but are not restricted to the study of consumer markets, strategic marketing and marketing planning, marketing communications, personal selling and sales, and business-to-business (B2B) marketing.

Consumer markets is an exciting field to study necessary conditions as it can inform ongoing academic discussion on understanding the necessary but not sufficient conditions of purchase decisions. Research shows that being isolated in terms of a lack of seeking and giving advice about brand appears to be a necessary condition for pamper buying. This refers to the purchase of products and services that the customer would normally be able to achieve without the purchase, and are thus used for pleasure (Rauch et al., 2015). Evaluations of alternatives and motivational factors of customer needs, such as the need for recognition (Lambert & Desmond, 2013), also have the potential for the exploration of new necessary conditions. There are remarks, for example, about the necessary nature of transparency for effective market functioning (Simintiras et al., 2015) that could be further investigated.

Strategic marketing plays a key role in the creation of vision, mission and effective strategic marketing campaigns as part of a comprehensive system, aligned with the organization's corporate identity (Peloza & Shang, 2011). Among other NCA applications, this domain would benefit from studying the necessary conditions of ensuring a good fit between strategic marketing campaigns and corporate identity. Marketing planning

(Madhavaram & Hunt, 2008) is the next level towards implementing strategic marketing principles: this systematic process involves assessing marketing opportunities, setting up objectives and scheduling steps to achieve the planned objectives. Applying NCA in this context could result in a better understanding of what steps are necessary for achieving certain objectives, and where the bottlenecks are.

The *marketing mix* is a set of controllable tactical marketing tools that a firm combines to achieve the desired response from its target audience (Kotler & Armstrong, 2010) – which tools are necessary within the marketing mix to effectively reach customers. While the emphasis is on the combination of different tools, there might be certain tools without which a desired outcome (for example, purchase or reputational benefits) cannot occur.

Necessary conditions are widely discussed but not always empirically investigated (or at least not from a necessity perspective) in the *marketing communications* domain. For example, consumer learning is posited as a necessary but not sufficient condition of persuasion (Yeh et al., 2013). Also, lobbying appears to be a necessary but not sufficient condition for obtaining preferential treatment (Anderson et al., 2018), or maintaining communication is necessary for firms to articulate and transfer knowledge (Park et al., 2012). NCA could be applied for theory testing in these marketing communication contexts.

The same applies to research on *personal selling and sales*: some examples of the discussed sales issues are the need for perceived organizational justice for the effective functioning of a sales organization (Miao et al., 2017), and certain personal traits of salespeople being necessary for high performance (Rubel & Prasad, 2016). Further characteristics of salespeople that appear as potential necessary conditions of high performance include customer orientation (Homburg et al., 2011), opportunity recognition ability (Leff Bonney & Williams, 2009) and competitive intelligence (Mariadoss et al., 2014).

In *business-to-business marketing* trust is discussed as a necessary condition for continued inter-organizational interactions (Laaksonen et al., 2008), customer involvement for efficient solution provision (Haas et al., 2012) and familiarity for attraction to occur (Hüttinger et al., 2012). Furthermore, a healthy financial situation appears as a necessary but not sufficient condition of successful service provision in business-to-business contexts (Kowalkowski et al., 2017) and reciprocity as a criterion of maintaining effective supplier–buyer relationships (Blonska et al., 2013). International marketing embraces various contextual factors inherent to international markets, such as market size (Bausch & Krist, 2007), economic growth (Sun et al., 2012) of the country and political stability

(Rosado-Serrano et al., 2018) as potential necessary conditions for successful internationalization. Further potential necessary conditions are discussed in relation to different modes of market entry, such as finding the right timing (Makadok, 1998) and possessing locally specific skills (Anand & Delios, 2002).

The reviewed necessary conditions in marketing research can be grouped into three distinct categories: they are actor-specific (for example, specific salesperson personality traits as necessary conditions for high sales performance); they are relationship-specific (for example, reciprocity to maintain business relationships); or there are contextual factors (such as political stability for successful internationalization). Future research should identify and empirically investigate more necessary conditions in marketing research – several of which are already discussed in the literature but not yet tested. Illustrative cases of remarks on specific necessary conditions in marketing research are demonstrated in Table 2.3; the

Table 2.3   *Illustrative cases for remarks on specific necessary conditions in marketing research*

Source	Research Design and Sample	Necessary but Not Sufficient Statement
Agustin & Singh (2005)	1230 randomly selected consumers	"Satisfaction is a *necessary but not sufficient* component of loyalty" (p. 96)
Bhattacharya & Sen (2003)	Theoretical review	"[I]dentity attractiveness in the customer–company context is likely to be a *necessary but not sufficient condition* for identification" (p. 81)
Ellis & Pecotich (2001)	Theoretical review	"[E]xports cannot be initiated without the coexistence of three *necessary but not sufficient conditions:* (1) the capability to go abroad, (2) the motive to go abroad, and (3) the awareness of a particular market opportunity" (p. 119)
Gebhardt et al. (2006)	Theoretical review	"These cultural values, however, appear to be *necessary, but not sufficient*, for the presence of market-oriented behaviors" (p. 52)
Kennedy et al. (2003)	Observations, in-depth interviews, focus groups, documentation	"[I]f senior leadership is *necessary but not sufficient*, what are the key factors that differentiate successful from unsuccessful implementation?" (p. 71)

Table 2.3   Continued

Source	Research Design and Sample	Necessary but Not Sufficient Statement
Lilien (2004)	Theoretical review	"A problem focus and an insights-actions correspondence are *necessary but not sufficient* conditions for success" (p. 190)
Noble et al. (2002)	Case studies	"In this view, market orientation is described as a *necessary, but not sufficient*, factor in the creation of a learning organization" (p. 30)
Im & Workman (2004)	1080 project managers drawn from CorpTech Directory of Technology Companies field survey	"All innovation begins with creative ideas . . . creativity by individuals and teams is a starting point for innovation; the first is a *necessary but not sufficient condition* for the second" (p. 114)
Ulaga & Eggert (2006)	Theoretical review, with a qualitative study	"[C]ost competitiveness emerges as a *necessary but not sufficient* condition to gain key supplier status" (p. 131)

examples are far from extensive but should offer some starting points for future research investigations.

CONCLUSION

NCA has been welcomed in a steadily increasing number of research fields such as psychology (Karwowski et al., 2016), human resource management (Hauff et al., 2021), hospitality and tourism management (Lee & Jeong, 2021), education (Tynan et al., 2020) and international business (Aguinis et al., 2020). The method has also recently entered the marketing field when Shahjehan and Qureshi (2019) studied the necessary personality characteristics for impulse buying. In our perspective, NCA is very promising for marketing research. This assessment is based on two reasons. First, the method sharpens theoretical thinking and engenders new theoretical insights. In every research field we find assumptions on necessity (Goertz, 2003), and researchers use various expressions that refer (explicitly or implicitly) to necessity logic. However, necessity logic differs from sufficiency logic, and researchers should be aware of the differences. Second, the results of NCA are highly relevant for marketing practice. If a necessary condition is identified, the condition must be in place in virtually every single case to reach the outcome. If the condition is not in place, the outcome will not occur and it makes no sense to focus on other causes to influence the outcome.

NCA can be applied either alone or in combination with other methodologies (e.g. Richter et al., 2020). For example, when NCA is combined with regression analysis, insights about the necessary variable for the outcome (evaluated with NCA) can be combined with insights about the average contribution of the variable to the outcome (evaluated with regression analysis). Thereby, NCA provides different and additional insights.

ACKNOWLEDGEMENT

We are grateful to Karen Fuhrmeister of Hogan Assessments for providing the data for the illustrative examples.

NOTES

1. Necessary conditions can be formulated in different ways, depending on the presence or absence of X and Y. Thus different combinations of the presence or absence of X and Y allow different formulations of necessary causes. For example, researchers can assume that absence of X is necessary for the presence of Y, or that presence of X is necessary for the absence of Y. In this chapter we only focus on necessary conditions, in that the presence of X is necessary for the presence of Y, since this is the standard case in most situations.
2. Notably, the ceiling line can be linear or non-linear.
3. Again, necessary conditions can refer to the presence and/or absence of the condition and/or the outcome. This implies looking for empty spaces in different corners of a scatter plot. By default, the NCA software identifies empty spaces in the upper left-hand corner; thus we focus on this case here. However, if researchers want to analyse necessary conditions that do not follow the standard logic implied here, they just need to choose another corner, which is facilitated in the NCA software.

REFERENCES

Aguinis, H., Ramani, R. S., & Cascio, W. F. (2020). Methodological practices in international business research: An after-action review of challenges and solutions. *Journal of International Business Studies*, *51*, 1593–1608.

Agustin, C., & Singh, J. (2005). Curvilinear effects of consumer loyalty determinants in relational exchanges. *Journal of Marketing Research*, *42*, 96–108.

Anand, J., & Delios, A. (2002). Absolute and relative resources as determinants of international acquisitions. *Strategic Management Journal*, *23*, 119–134.

Anderson, J. E., Martin, S. L., & Lee, R. P. (2018). Lobbying as a potent political marketing tool for firm performance: A closer look. *Psychology & Marketing*, *35*, 511–521.

Bausch, A., & Krist, M. (2007). The effect of context-related moderators on the internationalization–performance relationship: Evidence from meta-analysis. *Management International Review*, *47*, 319–347.

Bhattacharya, C. B., & Sen, S. (2003). Consumer–company identification: A framework for understanding consumers' relationships with companies. *Journal of Marketing*, *67*, 76–88.

Blonska, A., Storey, C., Rozemeijer, F., Wetzels, M., & de Ruyter, K. (2013). Decomposing the effect of supplier development on relationship benefits: The role of relational capital. *Industrial Marketing Management*, *42*, 1295–1306.

Dul, J. (2016). Necessary condition analysis (NCA): Logic and methodology of "necessary but not sufficient" causality. *Organizational Research Methods*, *19*, 10–52.

Dul, J. (2019). Necessary condition analysis (NCA) with R (Version 3.0.2): A quick start guide. Retrieved from https://www.erim.eur.nl/fileadmin/user_upload/_generated_/download/Quick_Start_Guide_NCA_3.0.2_November_22__2019___.pdf.

Dul, J. (2020). *Conducting necessary condition analysis for business and management students.* London: Sage.

Dul, J., van der Laan, E., & Kuik, R. (2020). A statistical significance test for necessary condition analysis. *Organizational Research Methods*, *23*, 385–395.

Ellis, P., & Pecotich, A. (2001). Social factors influencing export initiation in small and medium-sized enterprises. *Journal of Marketing Research*, *38*, 119–130.

Gebhardt, G. F., Carpenter, G. S., & Sherry Jr., J. F. (2006). Creating a market orientation: A longitudinal, multifirm, grounded analysis of cultural transformation. *Journal of Marketing*, *70*, 37–55.

Goertz, G. (2003). The substantive importance of necessary condition hypotheses. In G. Goertz & H. Starr (Eds.), *Necessary conditions: Theory, methodology, and applications* (pp. 65–94). New York: Rowman & Littlefield.

Groeger, L., & Buttle, F. (2014). Word-of-mouth marketing: Towards an improved understanding of multi-generational campaign reach. *European Journal of Marketing*, *48*, 1186–1208.

Haas, A., Snehota, I., & Corsaro, D. (2012). Creating value in business relationships: The role of sales. *Industrial Marketing Management*, *41*, 94–105.

Hauff, S., Guerci, M., Dul, J., & Rhee, H. (2021). Exploring necessary conditions in HRM research: Fundamental issues and methodological implications. *Human Resource Management Journal*, *31*, 18–36.

Hogan, R., & Hogan, J. (2007). *Hogan Personality Inventory manual* (3rd ed.). Tulsa, OK: Hogan Assessment.

Homburg, C., Müller, M., & Klarmann, M. (2011). When should the customer really be king? On the optimum level of salesperson customer orientation in sales encounters. *Journal of Marketing*, *75*, 55–74.

Hu, J., & Stanton, J. (2011). A study of how mainland Chinese small and medium privately owned businesses engage in networking. *Industrial Marketing Management*, *40*, 534–539.

Hüttinger, L., Schiele, H., & Veldman, J. (2012). The drivers of customer attractiveness, supplier satisfaction and preferred customer status: A literature review. *Industrial Marketing Management*, *41*, 1194–1205.

Im, S., & Workman Jr., J. P. (2004). Market orientation, creativity, and new product performance in high-technology firms. *Journal of Marketing*, *68*, 114–132.

Jap, S. D., & Ganesan, S. (2000). Control mechanisms and the relationship life cycle: Implications for safeguarding specific investments and developing commitment. *Journal of Marketing Research*, *37*, 227–245.

Karwowski, M., Dul, J., Gralewski, J., Jauk, E., Jankowska, D. M., Gajda, A., . . . Benedek, M. (2016). Is creativity without intelligence possible? A necessary condition analysis. *Intelligence*, *57*, 105–117.

Kennedy, K. N., Goolsby, J. R., & Arnould, E. J. (2003). Implementing a customer orientation: Extension of theory and application. *Journal of Marketing*, *67*, 67–81.

Kotler, P., & Armstrong, G. (2010). *Principles of marketing*. New York: Pearson Education.

Kowalkowski, C., Gebauer, H., & Oliva, R. (2017). Service growth in product firms: Past, present, and future. *Industrial Marketing Management*, *60*, 82–88.

Laaksonen, T., Pajunen, K., & Kulmala, H. I. (2008). Co-evolution of trust and dependence in customer–supplier relationships. *Industrial Marketing Management*, *37*, 910–920.

Lacey, R. (2009). Limited influence of loyalty program membership on relational outcomes. *Journal of Consumer Marketing*, *26*, 392–402.

Lambert, A., & Desmond, J. (2013). Loyal now, but not forever! A study of narcissism and male consumer–brand relationships. *Psychology & Marketing*, *30*, 690–706.

Lee, W., & Jeong, C. (2021). Distinctive roles of tourist eudaimonic and hedonic experiences on satisfaction and place attachment: Combined use of SEM and necessary condition analysis. *Journal of Hospitality and Tourism Management*, *47*, 58–71.

Leff Bonney, F., & Williams, B. C. (2009). From products to solutions: The role of salesperson opportunity recognition. *European Journal of Marketing*, *43*, 1032–1052.

Lilien, G. L. (2004). Special section introduction by the ISMS Practice Prize competition chairman. *Marketing Science*, *23*, 180–191.

Madhavaram, S., & Hunt, S. D. (2008). The service-dominant logic and a hierarchy of operant resources: Developing masterful operant resources and implications for marketing strategy. *Journal of the Academy of Marketing Science*, *36*, 67–82.

Makadok, R. (1998). Can first-mover and early-mover advantages be sustained in an industry with low barriers to entry/imitation? *Strategic Management Journal*, *19*, 683–696.

Mariadoss, B. J., Milewicz, C., Lee, S., & Sahaym, A. (2014). Salesperson competitive intelligence and performance: The role of product knowledge and sales force automation usage. *Industrial Marketing Management*, *43*, 136–145.

Miao, C. F., Evans, K. R., & Li, P. (2017). Effects of top-performer rewards on fellow salespeople: A double-edged sword. *Journal of Personal Selling & Sales Management*, *37*, 280–297.

Noble, C. H., Sinha, R. K., & Kumar, A. (2002). Market orientation and alternative strategic orientations: A longitudinal assessment of performance implications. *Journal of Marketing*, *66*, 25–39.

Park, C., Vertinsky, I., & Lee, C. (2012). Korean international joint ventures: How the exchange climate affects tacit knowledge transfer from foreign parents. *International Marketing Review*, *29*, 151–174.

Peloza, J., & Shang, J. (2011). How can corporate social responsibility activities create value for stakeholders? A systematic review. *Journal of the Academy of Marketing Science*, *39*, 117–135.

Rauch, A., Deker, J. S., & Woodside, A. G. (2015). Consuming alone: Broadening Putnam's "Bowling Alone" thesis. *Psychology & Marketing*, *32*, 967–976.

Richter, N. F., Schubring, S., Hauff, S., Ringle, C. M., & Sarstedt, M. (2020). When predictors of outcomes are necessary: Guidelines for the combined use of PLS-SEM and NCA. *Industrial Management & Data Systems*, *120*, 2243–2267.

Rosado-Serrano, A., Paul, J., & Dikova, D. (2018). International franchising: A literature review and research agenda. *Journal of Business Research*, *85*, 238–257.

Rubel, O., & Prasad, A. (2016). Dynamic incentives in sales force compensation. *Marketing Science*, *35*, 676–689.

Rubera, G., & Kirca, A. H. (2012). Firm innovativeness and its performance outcomes: A meta-analytic review and theoretical integration. *Journal of Marketing*, *76*, 130–147.

Shahjehan, A., & Qureshi, J. A. (2019). Personality and impulsive buying behaviors: A necessary condition analysis. *Economic Research-Ekonomska Istraživanja*, *32*, 1060–1072.

Simintiras, A. C., Dwivedi, Y. K., Kaushik, G., & Rana, N. P. (2015). Should consumers request cost transparency? *European Journal of Marketing*, *49*, 1961–1979.

Sun, S. L., Peng, M. W., Ren, B., & Yan, D. (2012). A comparative ownership advantage framework for cross-border M&As: The rise of Chinese and Indian MNEs. *Journal of World Business*, *47*, 4–16.

Tynan, M. C., Credé, M., & Harms, P. D. (2020). Are individual characteristics and behaviors necessary-but-not-sufficient conditions for academic success? A demonstration of Dul's (2016) necessary condition analysis. *Learning and Individual Differences*, *77*, 101815.

Ulaga, W., & Eggert, A. (2006). Value-based differentiation in business relationships: Gaining and sustaining key supplier status. *Journal of Marketing*, *70*, 119–136.

Yeh, M. A., Jewell, R. D., & Hu, M. Y. (2013). Stereotype processing's effect on the impact of the myth/fact message format and the role of personal relevance. *Psychology & Marketing*, *30*, 36–45.

ANNOTATED FURTHER READING

Dul, J. (2016). Necessary condition analysis (NCA): Logic and methodology of "necessary but not sufficient" causality. *Organizational Research Methods*, *19*(1), 10–52.

This is the core paper that introduces NCA. It discusses necessity logic compared to conventional average effect additive logic. The paper shows that traditional regression-based methods cannot be used for testing necessary condition hypotheses. The paper distinguishes between dichotomous, discrete, and continuous necessary conditions, and provides a step-wise approach for testing necessary conditions with data.

Dul, J. (2020). *Conducting necessary condition analysis for business and management students.* London: Sage.

This book provides a hands-on primer for conducting NCA in qualitative and quantitative research. It provides background to NCA, its main components, data analysis with NCA and examples of NCA applications, and discusses the strengths and weaknesses of NCA.

Dul, J., van der Laan, E., & Kuik, R. (2020). A statistical significance test for necessary condition analysis. *Organizational Research Methods*, *23*, 385–395.

This paper provides a statistical significance test of NCA to establish whether or not the data are compatible with the null hypothesis that the (assumed) necessary condition is unrelated to Y. This test helps researchers prevent false positive conclusions: concluding that the condition is necessary when it actually is a random result of unrelated variables.

Karwowski, M., Dul, J., Gralewski, J., Jauk, E., Jankowska, D. M., Gajda, A., . . . Benedek, M. (2016). Is creativity without intelligence possible? A necessary condition analysis. *Intelligence*, *57*, 105–117.

This paper is one of the first applications of NCA that properly tests the long-existing theory in psychology that intelligence is necessary for creativity. This much-cited paper re-analyses nine existing data sets to conclude that high levels of intelligence are indeed necessary for high levels of creativity.

3. When size does not matter: compositional data analysis in marketing research

Berta Ferrer-Rosell, Eva Martin-Fuentes, Marina Vives-Mestres and Germà Coenders

SUMMARY

Many research questions in marketing concern distribution of a whole or relative importance of magnitudes. Compositional Data Analysis focuses on testing relative hypotheses, and solves problems when analysing relative importance data with classical statistical methods. This chapter introduces and illustrates the method with data from an electronic word-of-mouth (e-WOM) platform.

INTRODUCTION

Compositional Data Analysis (CoDa) is the standard statistical methodology when data contain relative information or parts of a whole, typically (but not necessarily) with a fixed sum. The seminal work by Aitchison (1986) laid the foundations of CoDa based on the fields of chemistry and geology. Researchers in these fields are interested in the proportion of each component, since absolute amount (size of the sample) is irrelevant (Buccianti et al., 2006).

Nowadays, almost all hard sciences employ CoDa, and it has started to be used and expanded in the fields of marketing, communication and consumer behaviour, which often face similar research questions (Blasco-Duatis et al., 2019; Coenders and Ferrer-Rosell, 2020; Ferrer-Rosell et al., 2015, 2016a, 2016b, 2019, 2020; Ferrer-Rosell and Coenders, 2018; Joueid and Coenders, 2018; Marine-Roig and Ferrer-Rosell, 2018; Morais et al., 2018; Vives-Mestres et al., 2016). All those applications show that what is ultimately compositional is the research question (not the data) focusing on relative rather than absolute values.

Typical compositional research questions in the marketing field are related either to the distribution of a whole (e.g. share or allocation) or to the relative importance (e.g. dominance, profile, prevalence). Morais et al.

(2018) study the determinants of market share in the automobile industry. Joueid and Coenders (2018) analyse the role of marketing innovation in the relative importance of products with various innovation grades in the firm's portfolio. Marine-Roig and Ferrer-Rosell (2018) quantify the gap between the relative presence of contents in the two sides of tourist destination images (projected vs perceived image). Ferrer-Rosell et al. (2016a) and Ferrer-Rosell and Coenders (2018) segment tourists according to how they allocate their trip budget. Blasco-Duatis et al. (2019) study the relative importance of contents in e-communication by means of Twitter. In what follows we show the rationale for using CoDa in the context of one particular research question regarding online customer reviews.

When considering the reviews posted on a customer opinion platform the dominant type of review matters more than the total number of reviews. The dominance is usually computed as the number of each type of review out of the total number of reviews. The analysis of fixed-sum (or constant-sum) data, such as percentages adding to 100, poses considerable statistical challenges, which often are not properly addressed. Most classical statistical methods applied to percentages do not take into account the proportionality or the restricted nature of the data, and may cause serious problems, for example, when interpreting results: one percentage can only increase if one or more percentages decrease.

This chapter is organized as follows. In the next section we briefly introduce compositional data analysis. Then two sections follow on research validity and caveats of the method and the history of its use. Next, personal experience of using CoDa on data from hotel reviews on TripAdvisor and Booking.com is used to illustrate the methodology. The last sections provide our discussion and further reading. The syntax of the analyses is included in the Appendix.

ABOUT COMPOSITIONAL DATA ANALYSIS

What Makes Compositions Special

Compared to absolute data, compositional data – such as the number of each review type out of total reviews – lie in a constrained space. Let $\mathbf{x}$ be a vector with D positive components: $\mathbf{x} = (x_1, x_2, \ldots, x_D)$, with $x_j > 0$ for all $j = 1, 2, \ldots, D$.

In this illustration D represents the number of review types (also called components or parts) and x_j the number of reviews per each review type for a given hotel. Since what matters is the percentage of each part, it is common practice to close $\mathbf{x}$ to a constant sum. In the case of percentages

(100) this yields the compositional vector **z**, which lies in a bounded space between 0 and 100, known as the simplex:

$$\mathbf{z} = C(\mathbf{x}) = \left(\frac{x_1}{S}, \frac{x_2}{S}, \ldots, \frac{x_D}{S} \right) \cdot 100 = (z_1, z_2, \ldots, z_D)$$

with $z_j > 0$ for all $j = 1, 2, \ldots, D$; $\sum_{j=1}^{D} x_j = S$; $\sum_{j=1}^{D} z_j = 100.$ (3.1)

The so-called compositional equivalence property ensures that the relative information carried out by the D components remains the same regardless of whether the closure is performed (or not), or whether the constant sum is 1 (proportions) or 100. Since z_j is constrained by positiveness and 100 sum, using classical statistical methods will lead to meaningless results to a greater or lesser extent. In other words, one part can only increase if one or more of the others decrease(s), so negative spurious correlations among parts emerge (Pearson, 1897). On the other hand, the Euclidean distance considers the pair of percentages 1 and 2 to be as mutually distant as 11 and 12, while in the first pair the relative difference is far greater than in the second, so that Euclidean distances among individual compositions are also meaningless. In addition, the common distributional assumptions of most classical models are also somehow violated on **z** (Aitchison, 1986; Pawlowsky-Glahn et al., 2015). That is, modelling with unbounded distributions (e.g. normal) may lead to prediction interval limits outside the [0,100] range.

Exploring a Composition

The closed geometric mean is the central tendency measure of a sample of n compositions, and is expressed as $C(g_1, g_2, \ldots, g_D)$, where g_j is the sample geometric mean of review type z_j for all n hotels.

The most common approach to analyse compositional data is to transform the original compositional vector of D parts into logarithms of ratios among parts (Aitchison, 1986; Egozcue et al., 2003). Log-ratios present a series of advantages: (1) they are unbounded; (2) they tend to meet the distributional assumptions of classical statistical models; (3) they carry all needed information about the relative importance of components; and (4) they are the basis for defining association and distance in a meaningful way. Log-ratios yield the same result when computed from **x** or **z** (Pawlowsky-Glahn et al., 2015). Log-ratios may, for instance, be computed among all possible pairs of parts:

$$\ln \frac{z_j}{z_k} = \ln \frac{x_j}{x_k}$$

(3.2)

with $j < k$; $k = 2, 3, \ldots, D$; $j = 1, 2, \ldots, k - 1$.

The so-called centred log-ratio transformation is computed between each part and the geometric mean of all parts:

$$\ln \left(\frac{z_j}{\sqrt[D]{z_1 z_2 \ldots z_D}} \right)$$

(3.3)

with $j = 1, 2, \ldots, D$.

Association in CoDa is computed as the proportionality between pairs of components (Lovell et al., 2015). The variance of a pairwise log-ratio is computed as:

$$Var \left(\ln \left(\frac{z_j}{z_k} \right) \right)$$

(3.4)

with $j < k$; $k = 2, 3, \ldots, D$; $j = 1, 2, \ldots, k - 1$.

Like correlations, variances (Equation 3.4) can be arranged in a symmetric matrix known as variation matrix where parts define D rows and D columns. The interpretation of variances of log-ratios is as follows: hotel review types z_j and z_k behaving perfectly proportionally have a zero variance, and vice versa; the further the variance is from zero, the lower the association between parts.

The CoDa Biplot

Compositional data require visualization tools to help researchers interpret large data sets with many components and individuals. Principal component analysis can be applied to compositional data when it is based on the covariance matrix and applied to the centred log-ratios (Equation 3.3). Results can then be plotted on a CoDa biplot, whose accuracy is the percentage of explained variance by the two first dimensions.

The CoDa biplot can be understood as the most accurate representation of the variation matrix in two dimensions. Rays emanating from a common origin represent parts, and points represent individual compositions. The interpretation is as follows (see Aitchison and Greenacre, 2002; Van den Boogaart and Tolosana-Delgado, 2013; Pawlowsky-Glahn et al., 2015 for further details):

1. Distances between the vertices of the rays of two parts are approximately proportional to the square root of the variance of their corresponding pairwise log-ratio. Review types that behave proportionally for all n (hotels in our example) appear close together.
2. The orthogonal projection of all individual compositions (hotels) in the direction defined by a ray shows an approximate ordering of the importance of that review type for all hotels.

Transformation in Balance Coordinates and Sequential Binary Partition

Since the D-centred log-ratios (Equation 3.3) are perfectly collinear and cannot be used as such in a statistical model, an alternative log-ratio transformation, named balance coordinates, was developed in Egozcue and Pawlowsky-Glahn (2005). In fact, a D-part composition subject to a fixed sum constraint is inherently D-1 dimensional. Standard statistical models can be applied on balance coordinates.

The appeal of balance coordinates is that they can be investigator-driven; that is, they can be built based on the investigator's research questions. Balance coordinates are formed from a sequential binary partition (SBP) of parts. To create the first balance coordinate, the complete composition is partitioned into two groups of parts: one for the numerator and the other for the denominator. In the following step, one of the two groups is further split into two new groups to create the second balance coordinate. In step k, when the y_k balance is created, a group containing $r_k + s_k$ parts is split into two: the r_k parts $(z_{n1}, \ldots, z_{nr})$ in the first group are placed in the numerator; and the s_k parts $(z_{d1}, \ldots, z_{ds})$ in the second group appear in the denominator. The balance coordinate obtained is a normalized log-ratio of the geometric means of each group of parts:

$$y_k = \sqrt{\frac{r_k s_k}{r_k + s_k}} \ln \frac{\sqrt[r_k]{(z_{n1} \cdots z_{nr})}}{\sqrt[s_k]{(z_{d1} \cdots z_{ds})}}, \text{with } k = 1, \ldots, D-1. \quad (3.5)$$

Positive balance coordinates show a higher relative weight of parts in the numerator, while negative values show the opposite.

SBPs, and hence balance coordinates, are flexible and can be tailored to the particular research question of interest. To this end, SBPs may be constructed according to conceptual similarity of parts, or in order to obtain balance coordinates that express theoretically meaningful comparisons of numerator and denominator parts. The resulting log-ratios can be included in a statistical model as variables.

RESEARCH VALIDITY AND CAVEATS

The most relevant limitation of CoDa is that, strictly speaking, it cannot deal with zero values because log-ratios cannot be computed. If x or z contain zeros, they must be replaced beforehand (Martín-Fernández et al., 2011) and treated depending on the assumed reason for the zeros' occurrence. This situation is analogous to a missing data imputation problem under the restriction that, given the original zero values, imputed values cannot be large. The most common reasons for having zero values are rounding or values below detection limits (continuous-valued compositions), and count compositions (integer compositions). The composition of occurrence of each review type per hotel clearly belongs to the second case.

Zero imputation started in a rather ad hoc manner (Martín-Fernández et al., 2011), but nowadays rigorous statistically grounded procedures have been developed: the modified expectation-maximization (EM) algorithm (Palarea-Albaladejo and Martín-Fernández, 2008) for the continuous case and the Geometric Bayesian Multiplicative (GBM) approach (Martín-Fernández et al., 2015b) for the count case. The references in this paragraph acknowledge the fact that zero imputation can introduce distortion when the proportion of zero values to be imputed in the data set is large. What constitutes a large proportion may depend on many circumstances, but in many cases sizeable distortion starts occurring at around 15 or 20 per cent.

HISTORY OF CODA'S USE

In his seminal work about CoDa, Aitchison (1982) included an example with geological data and another with economic data. Since then, the number of articles published using CoDa in both the hard and social sciences has increased notably. In 1990 we found 14 articles in hard science and one article in social science citing the first handbook on compositional analysis by John Aitchison in 1986 (search made on Web of Science, 1 June 2018). In 2010 these numbers had increased to 87 and 13 respectively; and from then on in the field of social sciences the number of articles published citing Aitchison (1986) never again fell below five per year. The applications in fields related to management and business administration are relatively recent, and currently include relative prices, finance, management education, organizational culture and accounting – besides, of course, marketing.

Accessible handbooks have also contributed to extending the use of CoDa (Van den Boogaart and Tolosana-Delgado, 2013; Filzmoser et al., 2018; Greenacre, 2018; Pawlowsky-Glahn et al., 2015), as has dedicated user-friendly software (R library compositions by Van den Boogaart and Tolosana-Delgado, 2013; R library zCompositions by Palarea-Albaladejo and Martín-Fernández, 2015; and a stand-alone program CoDaPack by Thió-Henestrosa and Martín-Fernández, 2005).

PERSONAL EXPERIENCE OF USING CODA IN MARKETING RESEARCH

Data

In April 2016, data was downloaded from TripAdvisor and Booking. com via an automatically controlled webscraper tool developed in Python, using a library device called Python's Scrapy that simulated user navigation.

Out of the top 100 Euromonitor cities of 2016 (Geerts, 2016), those with at least 150 hotels were selected for the analysis, resulting in the following city selection: Bangkok, Dubai, Hong Kong, Istanbul, London, New York, Paris, Rome, Singapore and Taipei. After city selection, hotels with at least 100 reviews were retained for analysis. The final data set contains 2605 hotels: Bangkok 253, Dubai 134, Hong Kong 125, Istanbul 127, London 418, New York 227, Paris 627, Rome 440, Singapore 174 and Taipei 80.

The variables collected from TripAdvisor were: hotel name, address, city, country, global score, hotel category, number of reviews and number of reviews by types or categories (excellent, very good, average, poor, terrible), and segment posting the review (families, business, solo, friends, couples).

TripAdvisor rating categories "excellent", "very good", "average", "poor" and "terrible" comprise a composition in which each category is a component with its specific number of reviews – that is, out of the total number of reviews, how many are categorized under each component. In this case, the total number of reviews does not matter; what actually matters is the percentage of reviews included in each hotel rating category. The other TripAdvisor composition to analyse is the travelling group (segment), that is, total reviews distributed to the following components: "families", "business", "solo", "friends" and "couples". Table 3.1 shows the centres of both compositions.[1]

From Booking.com the variables downloaded were hotel name, address, city and country; also included were hotel characteristics: number of rooms (mean 76 rooms); category from 1–2 to 5 stars (1–2: 298, 3: 930, 4: 962 and

Table 3.1   Geometric mean (centres) of components per review type and segment

Composition hotel rating

Excellent	Very good	Average	Poor	Terrible	Total
33.1	42.3	16.2	5.1	3.3	100

Composition group travelling

Families	Solo	Friends	Business	Couples	Total
20.2	8.9	13.8	15.0	42.1	100

5: 415 hotels); price category ordered from 1 to 5, with 1 meaning a cheap hotel and 5 an expensive hotel (1: 204, 2: 393, 3: 515, 4: 653 and 5: 840 hotels); and whether the hotel is part of a chain (yes: 748, no: 1857).

Hotels were merged automatically from two sources (TripAdvisor and Booking.com), the city being the base to merge hotels (note that there are hotels with the same name in different cities). The same hotel name in the same city was clearly the same hotel if the hotel name on one site is entirely contained in the name on the other site. If none of the previously mentioned points were fulfilled, then we applied the Ratcliff text similarity method (Ratcliff and Metzener, 1988): given two hotel names, the algorithm calculates the number of common characters; if hotels had a lower than 85 per cent similarity, then they were discarded.

On an opinion platform, the number of reviews (called volume) may be important because it allows businesses to be more visible and is a sign of popularity (Martin-Fuentes et al., 2020). However, the valence (e.g. positive, negative or neutral review) brings users with even more information of the product and service, and influences other consumers; positive reviews may encourage other consumers to book, and negative reviews may discourage them (Dellarocas, 2003). Moreover, the category of the review allows researchers to calculate the real score of a hotel on TripAdvisor.

Two different analyses have been carried out to show how to apply the most common CoDa tools: linear models and visualization. The first is a multivariate analysis of covariance (MANCOVA) in order to answer the following research question: are hotel characteristics affecting hotel review composition ("terrible", "poor", "average", "very good" and "excellent")? The second analysis uses the CoDa biplot, creating a visual representation of the two TripAdvisor compositions – type of review by hotel rating, and type of review by travelling segment – with the aim of observing associations between them. Analyses were carried out with R software, version 3.4.2.

Linear Model

Balance coordinates were computed after replacing the 0.69 per cent of count zeros in the hotel rating composition. Figure 3.1 shows a visual representation of the SBP as a tree diagram. Drawing from the "excellent" component, the composition is split into two groups – "excellent" versus the other four components. In the following step, the group with the other four components is again split into two groups resulting in the component "very good" versus the other three components. The last partition splits the component "poor" versus "terrible". The balance coordinates are:

$$y_1 = \sqrt{\frac{1 \cdot 4}{1 + 4}} \ln \frac{x_5}{\sqrt[4]{x_4 x_3 x_2 x_1}}$$

$$y_2 = \sqrt{\frac{1 \cdot 3}{1 + 3}} \ln \frac{x_4}{\sqrt[3]{x_3 x_2 x_1}}$$

$$y_3 = \sqrt{\frac{1 \cdot 2}{1 + 2}} \ln \frac{x_3}{\sqrt{x_2 x_1}}$$ (3.6)

$$y_4 = \sqrt{\frac{1 \cdot 1}{1 + 1}} \ln \frac{x_2}{x_1}$$

Balance coordinates are the dependent variables in the multivariate model; and, since we have continuous and categorical predictors, a MANCOVA is performed. Global model tests such as Pillai's trace are invariant to how the balance coordinates are constructed (Martín-Fernández et al.,

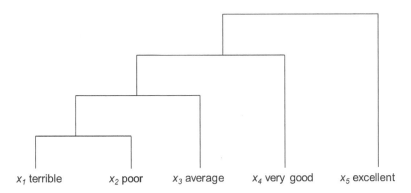

Figure 3.1   Representation of an SBP as a tree diagram

2015a). However, individual tests referring to each balance coordinates are not invariant and are interpreted according to the interpretability of each balance.

Table 3.2 shows the estimates and individual tests for each predictor. As regards the global model tests, all five predictors' Pillai's traces are significant (p-values< 0.001).

When interpreting the model, the compositional nature of data has to be taken into account by considering which component increases when others decrease. The positive effect on y_1 shows that hotels located in the

Table 3.2   Parameter estimates and individual tests for each predictor

Variable	Category	y_1	y_2	y_3	y_4
Intercept		−1.0653***	0.4857***	0.7554***	−0.0191
City	Singapore	−0.1198	−0.1361*	−0.0050	0.0132
	Bangkok	0	0	0	0
	Istanbul	0.0523	−0.0793	0.0171	−0.0964
	Hong Kong	0.0876	0.1633*	0.1378**	0.0105
	Rome	0.1820*	−0.1281*	−0.1293***	−0.0255
	London	0.3017***	−0.1523**	−0.1990***	−0.0407
	Paris	0.4620***	0.1412**	−0.0441	0.0307
	Taipei	0.5984***	0.6246***	0.4166***	0.0561
	Dubai	0.7680***	0.2530***	0.0248	−0.1154*
	New York	0.9939***	0.2184***	−0.1013*	−0.0528
Chain membership	No	0	0	0	0
	Yes	0.2833***	0.1442***	0.0617**	0.0612**
Price	1	0	0	0	0
	2	0.7906***	0.6777***	0.3497***	0.2281***
	3	1.2799***	1.0049***	0.4797***	0.2995***
	4	1.9116***	1.3888***	0.5974***	0.4122***
	5	2.5133***	1.6380***	0.6251***	0.3931***
Stars	1–2	0	0	0	0
	3	0.1089	0.0724	0.0139	0.0133
	4	0.0756	−0.1070	−0.1365***	−0.0079
	5	0.5660***	−0.2549***	−0.3015***	−0.0340
No. of rooms		−0.0009***	−0.0004***	0.0000	0.0000
F-test p-value		<0.001	<0.001	<0.001	<0.001
R-squared		0.4707	0.3164	0.1536	0.0544

Note: P-value: <0.001***; 0.001**; 0.01*.

cities with statistically significant estimates (Rome, London, Paris, Taipei, Dubai and New York) are associated with an increase in the frequency of the "excellent" rating at the expense of a decrease in the geometric mean of all other ratings with respect to Bangkok hotels. On the other hand, the negative effects of Rome, London and New York on y_3 show that hotels located in these three cities are associated with a decrease in the frequency of the "average" rating at the expense of an increase in the geometric mean of "poor" and "terrible" ratings.

Being part of a chain also affects y_1; that is, the positive effect shows that hotel members of a chain tend to have a higher frequency of "excellent" ratings at the expense of all other rating categories. Regarding price, all estimates are significant, meaning that price category is associated with ratings, as confirmed by Martin-Fuentes (2016). In fact, the higher the price category the higher the estimate; and thus, as the price category increases, it also increases the frequency of the "excellent" rating, at the expense of the geometric mean of the other ratings. Five-star hotels are likewise related to the excellent rating but three- and four-star hotels are undistinguishable from the lowest categories. The negative effect of number of rooms on y_1 shows that hotels with more rooms tend to have a higher geometric mean of all four ratings except for "excellent", at the expense of "excellent" ratings. Regarding y_4 and cities, only the effect of hotels located in Dubai is significant. This negative effect shows that being located in Dubai is associated with an increase in the frequency of "poor" ratings at the expense of a decrease in the frequency of "terrible" when comparing this city with Bangkok.

CoDa Biplot

Biplots can be extended to cases in which there is more than one composition (Filzmoser et al., 2018; Kynčlová et al., 2016). To this end the centred log-ratios (Equation 3.3) of both compositions are combined into a single data set, which is submitted to a principal component analysis based on the covariance matrix. Both hotel rating and travel group composition are represented in Figure 3.2. The percentage of explained variance by the two first dimensions is 72.9.

Distances between the vertices of the rays of two parts of the same composition are interpreted as an approximation of the standard deviation of their corresponding pairwise log-ratio. Parts that behave proportionally for all individuals appear close together. This is the case for "poor" and "terrible" reviews, or reviews written by families and couples. The cosine of the angle between two rays corresponding to different compositions is approximately equal to the correlation between their two centred

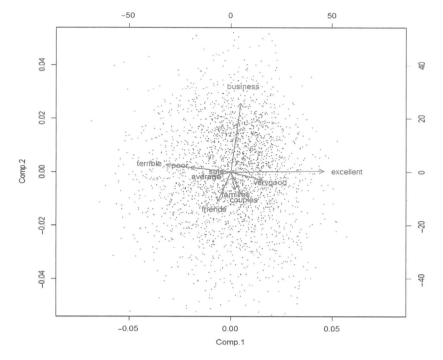

Figure 3.2   Biplot of hotel rating and travel group compositions

log-ratios. For instance, when the frequency of reviews written by solo travellers increases in relative terms the frequency of "average", "poor" and "terrible" reviews also increases in relative terms.

Hotels on the right-hand side of the biplot have a comparatively high proportion of "excellent" and "very good" reviews and a comparatively low proportion of "poor" and "terrible" reviews. Hotels on the top of the biplot have a comparatively high proportion of reviews written by business travellers and a comparatively low proportion of reviews written by families, couples and friends.

As in standard biplots, hotel points could be labelled according to the values of an external variable, or their scores on the first two dimensions could be used as data in subsequent statistical analyses.

DISCUSSION

This chapter constitutes the first overview of CoDa in the marketing management field. We have strived to keep to the point and write an easy-to-follow invitation to use the method, which can be complemented in the annotated further reading section.

A common statistical saying goes that one should not "fit square pegs into round holes": compositional questions have to be answered with compositional methods. Aitchison pointed out in 1997 that "compositional data analysis is simple" – and we agree with that. CoDa is the simple way out for researchers who want to be on the safe side when interpreting their results by taking into account the relative information of interest. An added appeal of the CoDa methods we have presented in this chapter is that, once the data have been transformed, researchers can use standard and well-understood statistical tools.

Given the fact that many research questions and measures in marketing are relative rather than absolute, it can be argued that CoDa methodology has not yet reached its full usage potential. To offer just a few suggestions, CoDa can be used on a general basis to analyse survey questionnaires with the common response format "Please divide 100 points among the following product attributes according to the importance they have to you", which is quite common in product development and market segmentation. Moreover, audience research is focused on the concept of share, which is compositional by nature. Likewise, consumer time use adds up to 24 hours a day and can only be studied in relative terms.

Analysing the relative importance of reviews by type is important in marketing because it has been demonstrated that the valence is correlated with the expectations created by customers about a product or a service and their intention to purchase (Mauri and Minazzi, 2013), and influences other consumers' decisions (Vermeulen and Seegers, 2009). Moreover, the relative importance of the reviews according to the traveller group that has posted them is a source of segmentation that allows for better positioning (Martin-Fuentes et al., 2018).

Ultimately CoDa can be traced back to the old distinction between "size" and "shape" in morphometrics and multivariate statistics. It goes without saying that CoDa focuses on shape, as if size would not matter. This is not always true; and more advanced CoDa methods, which are beyond the scope of this chapter, consider both shape and size.

NOTE

1. All tables and figures in this chapter were created by the authors based on their own empirical data obtained from TripAdvisor and Booking.com.

REFERENCES

Aitchison, J. (1982), "The statistical analysis of compositional data", *Journal of the Royal Statistical Society: Series B (Methodological)*, Vol. 44 No. 2, pp. 139–177.

Aitchison, J. (1986), *The Statistical Analysis of Compositional Data*, Chapman and Hall, London.

Aitchison, J. (1997), "The one-hour course in compositional data analysis or compositional data analysis is simple", in Pawlowsky-Glahn, V. (Ed.), *Proceedings of IAMG '97: The Third Annual Conference of the International Association for Mathematical Geology*, pp. 3–35, International Center for Numerical Methods in Engineering (CIMNE), Barcelona.

Aitchison, J. and Greenacre, M. (2002), "Biplots of compositional data", *Journal of the Royal Statistical Society: Series C (Applied Statistics)*, Vol. 51 No. 4, pp. 375–392.

Blasco-Duatis, M., Coenders, G., Sáez, M., Fernández García, N. and Cunha, I. (2019), "Mapping the agenda-setting theory, priming and the spiral of silence in Twitter accounts of political parties", *International Journal of Web Based Communities*, Vol. 15 No. 1, pp. 4–24.

Buccianti, A., Mateu-Figueras, G. and Pawlowsky-Glahn, V. (2006), *Compositional Data Analysis in the Geosciences: From Theory to Practice*, Geological Society of London, London.

Coenders, G. and Ferrer-Rosell, B. (2020), "Compositional data analysis in tourism: Review and future directions", *Tourism Analysis*, Vol. 25 No. 1, pp. 153–168.

Dellarocas, C. (2003), "The digitization of word of mouth: Promise and challenges of online feedback mechanisms", *Management Science*, Vol. 49 No. 10, pp. 1407–1424.

Egozcue, J.J. and Pawlowsky-Glahn, V. (2005), "Groups of parts and their balances in compositional data analysis", *Mathematical Geology*, Vol. 37 No. 7, pp. 795–828.

Egozcue, J.J., Pawlowsky-Glahn, V., Mateu-Figueras, G. and Barcelo-Vidal, C. (2003), "Isometric logratio transformations for compositional data analysis", *Mathematical Geology*, Vol. 35 No. 3, pp. 279–300.

Ferrer-Rosell, B. and Coenders, G. (2018), "Destinations and crisis: Profiling tourists' budget share from 2006 to 2012", *Journal of Destination Marketing and Management*, Vol. 7, pp. 26–35.

Ferrer-Rosell, B., Coenders, G. and Martínez-Garcia, E. (2015), "Determinants in tourist expenditure composition: The role of airline types", *Tourism Economics*, Vol. 21 No. 1, pp. 9–32.

Ferrer-Rosell, B., Coenders, G. and Martínez-Garcia, E. (2016a), "Segmentation by tourist expenditure composition: An approach with compositional data analysis and latent classes", *Tourism Analysis*, Vol. 21 No. 6, pp. 589–602.

Ferrer-Rosell, B., Coenders, G., Mateu-Figueras, G. and Pawlowsky-Glahn, V. (2016b), "Understanding low-cost airline users' expenditure patterns and volume", *Tourism Economics*, Vol. 22 No. 2, pp. 269–291.

Ferrer-Rosell, B., Martin-Fuentes, E. and Marine-Roig, E. (2019), "Do hotels talk on Facebook about themselves or about their destinations?", in Pesonen, J. and Neidhardt, J. (Eds.), *Information and Communication Technologies in Tourism 2019*, pp. 344–356, Springer, Cham.

Ferrer-Rosell, B., Martin-Fuentes, E. and Marine-Roig, E. (2020), "Diverse and emotional: Facebook content strategy by Spanish hotels", *Journal of Information Technology and Tourism*, Vol. 22 No. 1, pp. 53–74.

Filzmoser, P., Hron, K. and Templ, M. (2018), *Applied Compositional Data Analysis: With Worked Examples in R*, Springer, Cham.

Geerts, W. (2016), *Top 100 City Destinations Ranking*, available at: http://blog.euromonitor.com/2016/01/top-100-city-destinations-ranking-2016.html.

Greenacre, M. (2018), *Compositional Data Analysis in Practice*, Chapman and Hall/CRC, New York.

Joueid, A. and Coenders, G. (2018), "Marketing innovation and new product portfolios: A compositional approach", *Journal of Open Innovation: Technology, Market, and Complexity*, Vol. 4 No. 2, p. 19.

Kynčlová, P., Filzmoser, P. and Hron, K. (2016), "Compositional biplots including external non-compositional variables", *Statistics*, Vol. 50 No. 5, pp. 1132–1148.

Lovell, D., Pawlowsky-Glahn, V., Egozcue, J.J., Marguerat, S. and Bähler, J. (2015), "Proportionality: A valid alternative to correlation for relative data", *PLoS Computational Biology*, Vol. 11 No. 3, e1004075.

Marine-Roig, E. and Ferrer-Rosell, B. (2018), "Measuring the gap between projected and perceived destination images of Catalonia using compositional analysis", *Tourism Management*, Vol. 68, pp. 236–249.

Martín-Fernández, J.A., Daunis i Estadella, J. and Mateu i Figueras, G. (2015a), "On the interpretation of differences between groups for compositional data", *SORT: Statistics and Operations Research Transactions*, Vol. 39 No. 2, pp. 231–252.

Martín-Fernández, J.A., Hron, K., Templ, M., Filzmoser, P. and Palarea-Albaladejo, J. (2015b), "Bayesian-multiplicative treatment of count zeros in compositional data sets", *Statistical Modelling*, Vol. 15, pp. 134–158.

Martín-Fernández, J.A., Palarea-Albaladejo, J. and Olea, R.A. (2011), "Dealing with zeros", in Pawlowsky-Glahn, V. and Buccianti, A. (Eds.), *Compositional Data Analysis: Theory and Applications*, pp. 47–62, Wiley, New York.

Martin-Fuentes, E. (2016), "Are guests of the same opinion as the hotel star-rate classification system?", *Journal of Hospitality and Tourism Management*, Vol. 29, pp. 126–134.

Martin-Fuentes, E., Mateu, C. and Fernandez, C. (2018), "Does verifying users influence rankings? Analyzing Booking.com and TripAdvisor", *Tourism Analysis*, Vol. 23 No. 1, pp. 1–15.

Martin-Fuentes, E., Mateu, C. and Fernandez, C. (2020), "The more the merrier? Number of reviews versus score on TripAdvisor and Booking.com", *International Journal of Hospitality & Tourism Administration*, Vol. 21 No. 1, pp. 1–14.

Mauri, A.G. and Minazzi, R. (2013), "Web reviews influence on expectations and purchasing intentions of hotel potential customers", *International Journal of Hospitality Management*, Vol. 34, pp. 99–107.

Morais, J., Thomas-Agnan, C. and Simioni, M. (2018), "Using compositional and Dirichlet models for market share regression", *Journal of Applied Statistics*, Vol. 45 No. 9, pp. 1670–1689.

Palarea-Albaladejo, J. and Martín-Fernández, J.A. (2008), "A modified EM alr-algorithm for replacing rounded zeros in compositional data sets", *Computers & Geosciences*, Vol. 34 No. 8, pp. 902–917.

Palarea-Albaladejo, J. and Martín-Fernández, J.A. (2015), "zCompositions: R package for multivariate imputation of left-censored data under a compositional approach", *Chemometrics and Intelligent Laboratory Systems*, Vol. 143, pp. 85–96.

Pawlowsky-Glahn, V., Egozcue, J.J. and Tolosana-Delgado, R. (2015), *Modeling and Analysis of Compositional Data*, Wiley, Chichester.

Pearson, K. (1897), "Mathematical contributions to the theory of evolution: On a form of spurious correlation which may arise when indices are used in the measurement of organs", *Proceedings of the Royal Society of London*, Vol. 60 No. 359–367, pp. 489–498.

Ratcliff, J.W. and Metzener, D.E. (1988), "Pattern-matching: The gestalt approach", *Dr Dobbs Journal*, Vol. 13 No. 7, p. 46.

Thió-Henestrosa, S. and Martín-Fernández, J.A. (2005), "Dealing with compositional data: The freeware CoDaPack", *Mathematical Geology*, Vol. 37 No. 7, pp. 773–793.

Van den Boogaart, K.G. and Tolosana-Delgado, R. (2013), *Analyzing Compositional Data with R*, Springer, Berlin.

Vermeulen, I.E. and Seegers, D. (2009), "Tried and tested: The impact of online hotel reviews on consumer consideration", *Tourism Management*, Vol. 30 No. 1, pp. 123–127.

Vives-Mestres, M., Martín-Fernández, J.A. and Kenett, R.S. (2016), "Compositional data methods in customer survey analysis", *Quality and Reliability Engineering International*, Vol. 32 No. 6, pp. 2115–2125.

ANNOTATED FURTHER READING

Van den Boogaart and Tolosana-Delgado (2013) is the first guide to CoDa with R, using a library developed by the authors. The book contains many step-by-step examples from different fields, and covers most standard statistical methods.

Pawlowsky-Glahn et al. (2015) is a comprehensive guide to the CoDa methodology. It does not follow any software in particular, but rather focuses on principles, interpretation and threats to the validity of conclusions.

Filzmoser et al. (2018) is another guide to CoDa with R, using a library developed by the authors and including some novel features, among which we highlight missing data, high-dimensional compositions, robust methods and two-way compositions.

APPENDIX

```
library(compositions)
library(zCompositions)
#data frame "data" contains the rating category
#components in columns 2 to 6.
#travel group components are columns 7 to 11
#computing percentage of zero values
zPatterns(data[,2:6],label=0)
zPatterns(data[,7:11],label=0)
#imputation by GBM method
comp_rating<-acomp(cmultRepl(data[,2:6]))
comp_group<-acomp(cmultRepl(data[,7:11]))
#center
mean(comp_rating)
mean(comp_group)
#linear model
#Defining an SBP for balance coordinates
#(1: numerator, -1: denominator, 0 not present)
W<-matrix(c(
  1,-1,-1,-1,-1,
  0,1,-1,-1,-1,
  0,0,1,-1,-1,
  0,0,0,1,-1), nrow=5)
rownames(W)<-c("excellent","very good","average",
"poor","terrible")
colnames(W)<-c("y1","y2","y3","y4")
```

```
W

#balance computation

comp_ratingbalances<-ilr(comp_rating,gsi.
buildilrBase(W))

#estimation

model=lm(comp_ratingbalances~factor(city)+factor
(chain)

+factor(price)+factor(stars)+rooms, data=data)

summary(model)

anova(model)

#biplot

#merging centred log ratios of both compositions

comps2<-cbind(clr(comp_rating),clr(comp_group))

#principal component analysis

pcx=princomp(comps2)

#biplot data point labels

data$point=".''

biplot(pcx, xlabs=data$point)
```

4. Modern data analysis – a paradigm for robustness: lessons for marketing researchers from the machine learning literature

John Williams

1. INTRODUCTION

This chapter is written for the practising marketing researcher who deals with quantitative data and is interested in producing valid and reliable results, as opposed to merely publishable results. In other words, for researchers who want to participate in the advancement of scientific knowledge about marketing. Part of a scientific approach is using the best tools and workflows for the task at hand. Recent advances in data analysis due to increased computing power call into question many of the implicit assumptions about appropriate analysis methods, as evidenced by the current marketing literature; hence the purpose of the chapter is to outline the main deficiencies of current norms and to illustrate a way forward.

Considering the progress of knowledge accumulation in marketing, some papers that make claims to have detected a generalisable empirical regularity will contain errors, because to err is human. The system we have in place to guard against the most egregious errors, the double-blind peer review model, is well suited to detect and guard against the more obvious *methodological* errors or ill-founded knowledge claims. Peer review is unlikely to detect outright fraud; the best we can do as reviewers and editors is to check the manuscripts we receive against current discipline-specific norms of best practice. However those norms are outdated.

Hence the purpose of this chapter is to discuss and demonstrate current best practices with respect to one aspect of our knowledge-generating process: the analysis of quantitative data. Modern best practice in quantitative data analysis exploits the advances in statistical methods that have been made in recent years, largely based on increased computing power (see, for example, Efron & Hastie, 2016; Harrell, 2015; Hastie et al., 2009; James et al., 2013). Modern methods combined with modern data sets (which tend to be larger than in the recent past) emphasise the decreasing importance of classical null-hypothesis significance testing (NHST) in favour of learning from data via resampling methods, Bayesian statistics (primarily Empirical Bayes) and triangulating over, or combining, the results of many algorithms or models to obtain a more robust result.

In this chapter, elements of advances in modern data analysis practice are outlined insofar as they are relevant to a marketing researcher who is interested in analysing their data to examine the tenability of some theoretical model, most usefully expressed in terms of dependence relationships, e.g. a regression model, possibly involving latent variables, and possibly involving multiple dependent variables.

Statistical inference, or data analysis more generally, can be seen to have related but distinct goals of prediction vs. explanation. This chapter is written for researchers who are not interested in mere prediction (which is often sufficient for commercial marketing purposes); i.e. they want to assess the weight of evidence regarding their theories. Hence the "black box" models of machine learning, e.g. artificial neural networks, are not considered.

2.   ELEMENTS OF MODERN DATA ANALYSIS

Modern data analysis can be characterised as a paradigm that takes advantage of current computing power and the statistical models and algorithms they enable. It encompasses the following broad and inter-related principles:

1.   A de-emphasis on, or elimination of, null-hypothesis significance testing
2.   Triangulation over data by bootstrapping and/or cross-validation
3.   Triangulation over methods by using multiple models, either to combine their results in some way or to find the best tool for the job.

These principles are covered in the following section.

2.1   Some Problems with Current Norms

In this section we examine several issues with the vast majority of current practice as evidenced by recent publications in top-ranked marketing journals. Most of these issues are relatively well known in the methodological literature, although methods of addressing them are less well known.

2.1.1   The replication crisis
Meyer (2015) calls attention to the "replication crisis" that originated in social psychology and has since made its presence felt in many other

disciplines, not least marketing. This term refers to things that a discipline "knows" but that, on closer inspection, are based on a single paper or set of connected papers by the same author(s). When independent researchers attempt to replicate the results on which this knowledge is based, they often obtain conflicting results. This situation calls many of the foundational tenets of the discipline into question.

The replication crisis is not the result of any specific single cause, if one leaves aside the "publish or perish" model of academic careers, which leads to corner-cutting (high quality vs. "will this get past the reviewers?") and a bias against replication. Independent replication is a foundation of scientific knowledge, but in most social "sciences", novel research is far easier to publish than replication and extension studies.

The issues outlined in the sections below may seem like statistical pedantry until one ponders the reasons for the replication crisis in social psychology. To be sure, some of the reasons behind this "crisis" may be more due to matters of experimental design and measurement validity (i.e. data gathering) as opposed to data analysis. However most methodological experts agree that mindless association of statistical significance with scientific relevance or "real-world" impact (usually called "clinical significance" in the medical literature) has played no small part in the widespread acceptance of psychological principles or "knowledge" that may have very little credible evidential basis.

In addition to conflation of statistical with substantive significance, much of the false "knowledge" we may have accumulated due to reliance on NHST is almost certainly due to inflated rates of Type I error, well above the nominal level (e.g. 5 per cent) that we *think* we have controlled for when conducting our analyses. It is worth repeating that α-inflation is almost certainly not the *sole* cause of lack of replicability; but the point is that other, non-statistical, sources of error due to data-gathering and measurement issues are *hard*, and expensive to control for (in researcher time as well as money), even when the issues are well known (e.g. social desirability bias, self-selection bias, common-method bias, and so on).

In contrast, the problems due to statistical issues are *easy* to deal with, if they are known. In data gathering, knowledge plus non-trivial time and effort are needed; in statistical analysis, only knowledge is necessary. Once one has learned better procedures and obtained the appropriate software to implement them, doing analysis the "right" way takes roughly the same effort as doing it the "wrong" way.

2.1.2 The trouble with NHST

An editorial published in *The American Statistician* (Wasserstein & Lazar, 2016) starts with the following:

Q: Why do so many colleges and grad schools teach $p = 0.05$?
A: Because that's still what the scientific community and journal editors use.
Q: Why do so many people still use $p = 0.05$?
A: Because that's what they were taught in college or grad school.

(Presumably, "people" above means "the scientific community and journal editors", and either $p < 0.05$ or $\alpha = 0.05$ is more accurate.) In short, there is really no good reason to use the "golden rule" of statistics; it is merely a social convention, a historical accident that may have been relevant when statistics was in its infancy, but is regarded by many methodological scholars as being past its use-by date in the 21st century, for reasons discussed below.

The problems of NHST have been well known for decades (Cohen, 1988, 1990, 1994; Harlow et al., 1997; Meehl, 1978; Rozeboom, 1960; Tukey, 1969), so a detailed exposition will not be given here. What might be less well known is that even the inventor of the NHST paradigm, Sir Ronald Aylmer Fisher, was aware of these problems and was trying to develop an alternative (at a time when Bayesianism was equated with subjective probability, so that was not an acceptable alternative for Fisher) up until his death in 1962 (Efron, 1998, sec. 8).

Although problems have been known for decades, the Marketing community (and social sciences in general) has been slow to address these problems. Every so often, someone from within our discipline will call attention to these issues and the fact that they have been discussed before (see Williams, 2014, for example); but such efforts typically have little or no discernible effect. The most obvious reason for lack of progress seems to be little more than the institutional inertia effect alluded to in the introductory epithet above; however there are signs that in some sub-disciplines pressure may finally be building to a sufficient degree that change may be coming soon. Some recent events include publication of several articles that address issues raised by the "replication crisis" in social psychology, a discipline that Marketing borrows from in no small measure – for example:

- NHST "banned" by editors of *Basic and Applied Social Psychology* (Trafimow & Marks, 2015; also reported in *Nature*).
- *Why most findings are false* (Ioannidis, 2005), in which a case for a much lower "gold standard" criterion is made.
- *American Statistical Association*'s statement on *p*-values (Wasserstein & Lazar, 2016), which, in a nutshell, says that the vast majority of users of NHST are doing it all wrong.
- Two articles in *Nature Human Behaviour*, one of which proposed redefining "statistically significant" from $p < 0.05$ to $p < 0.005$

(Benjamin et al., 2018), the other proposing (yet again) abandoning the notion altogether (Amrhein & Greenland, 2018).

Briefly, the problems include:

- Practical issues:
  - Large sample sizes make trivial effects "significant" (i.e. over-powered research designs).
  - The vast majority of scientific papers contain dozens or even hundreds of cases of NHST, but almost no papers explicitly control for α-inflation.
  - The "golden rule" is a common criterion that applies to all judgements but ignores risks and costs associated with Type I vs. Type II error (e.g. making a Type II error can be seen to be an opportunity cost in new product development research, or the cost of a Type I error is effectively zero in an academic publication, but may be millions of dollars in a commercial setting).
- Logical and philosophical issues:
  - The null hypothesis is never false, so why pretend it is?
  - Why should we pretend we know nothing about the likely range of values of the parameters we're trying to estimate (e.g. the population mean) when we may have reliable and valid prior information available? (i.e. use Bayesian statistics).
  - Why should we treat the sample statistic or population parameter as fixed and the data as random?

In summary, classical NHST was developed to address relatively small samples – often as a result of carefully planned experiments – of measures of continuous variables (e.g. plant height, amount of fertiliser applied), and to be mathematically tractable, e.g. the OLS solution $\beta = (X'X)^{-1}X'Y$. These conditions, particularly the last, are no longer the norm in the social sciences or the business world. More importantly, classical NHST relates to probable error in *one* statistical test, considered in isolation.

Although these problems are well known, papers that reject null hypotheses for small effect sizes in over-powered designs still get published. One example is one of the "Top Articles" from the *Journal of Marketing Research* (arguably the paragon and exemplar of rigour in marketing research) website (accessed 23 November 2016). This described an analysis of the "sales funnel" model (Hoban & Bucklin, 2014), where a test of the difference between two proportions (2 per cent vs. 3 per cent) was rejected at $p < 0.05$ with $n > 100\ 000$ (and grossly unbalanced sub-samples: 106 690 vs. 1414). The study used the term "marginally significant" for rejection at $p < 0.1$ and stated "these results provide strong model-free evidence for the efficacy of online display advertising and differences in that efficacy along the purchase funnel" (Hoban & Bucklin, 2014, p. 380). Furthermore, the authors assessed the error rate independently for four separate pairwise comparisons without making any adjustment for α-inflation.

Even when one has firmly internalised both mantras – "correlation is not causation" and "statistical significance is not clinical significance" – there is still the problem of the best way to control for two forms of α-inflation.

2.1.2.1 Multiple testing   The first, and most familiar, form of α-inflation is how to control the *joint* probability of a set of statistical hypotheses. A very special formulation of this problem is taught in most undergraduate business school research methods courses: "post hoc tests" examined after a one-way ANOVA test has been found to be significant. In most statistical software there is a fairly large selection of such tests available, each of which has been developed under a set of more or less restrictive assumptions, e.g. homogeneity of variance and equal sample sizes. The most generally applicable procedure, due to Bonferroni, is the most conservative: if one has q tests, for the probability of Type I error with respect to the entire set of q hypotheses to be less than α we must reject the null hypothesis for each test at the level of α/q. This is conceptually simple, but many researchers feel that the procedure is too conservative; hence the development of alternative procedures.

However the problem of α-inflation is not restricted to post hoc inference in ANOVA, as seems to be a relatively common misconception. Error inflation is a simple consequence of probability theory, and hence applies to *any* set of hypothesis tests considered jointly, e.g. in a regression or SEM setting where we conclude that such-and-such variables were significant *and* the rest were not; so we are going to make inferences about the variables that were significant, and ignore the rest.

In a typical academic marketing paper there are often dozens of hypothesis tests; but in the "data-mining" field there may be thousands or even tens of thousands, and so the problem is simply too large to ignore. Hence alternatives to the Bonferroni procedure have been developed, as we shall see below.

2.1.2.2 Cherry picking   The other, and less well-known, form of α-inflation refers to the *process* by which a set of tests were judged to be significant. Suppose one has a theory, and a corresponding statistical model. One gathers data, then analyses it as a plausible statistical model by running a procedure with one's favourite statistical software, and then makes a decision about the theory. Does anyone actually do that? Most of us run many procedures, multiple times with small variations, often using NHST in an exploratory manner and adjusting our theoretical model based on those results. So although in our paper there may be 20 hypothesis tests, the process to get to that point may have involved hundreds of tests, where the decision about which test to run next *depends* on the outcome of a previous test. This is known as "cherry picking", and inflates the nominal α in addition to that inflation simply due to the number of tests involved. A familiar context for this phenomenon to occur is during stepwise regression, or developing a Structural Equation Model (SEM) iteratively, perhaps by thoughtlessly adding paths based on modification indices, to achieve fit indices above the acceptable criteria.

Again, in an academic paper this problem is pernicious but costless; but in a commercial data-mining process, where managerial effort and financial resources could be wasted on a pipe dream, the problem is much larger and the consequences more severe. This is known as the problem of *selective inference*.

2.1.2.3 False Discovery Rate and related procedures In response to these problems, theorists have developed a number of responses, each trying to balance Type I with Type II error. Initiated by Hochberg and Benjamini (1990) and Benjamini and Hochberg (1995), there are now quite a few methods available to not only balance Type I and Type II error but also to control the probability of various aspects of sets of hypotheses. Table 4.1 shows the (hopefully familiar) possible outcomes of NHST, and the quantities included represent the *count* of events: for example, in m hypothesis tests V is the count of Type I errors and V/m is the Type I error *rate*.

The **Family-wise error-rate** (FWER) is the probability of making *at least one* Type I error when making a joint probability statement regarding NHST, i.e. $\Pr(V > 0)$. These procedures were mostly developed within the context of multiple pairwise comparisons of means.

The **False Discovery Rate** (FDR), due to Benjamini and Hochberg (1995), sometimes called the BH procedure, is less conservative than

Table 4.1   Outcomes of NHST

Truth	Called not significant	Called significant	Total
H_0 true	U	V	m_0
H_0 false	T	S	m_1
Total	$m-R$	R	m

FWER, and is similar conceptually to Holm's procedure (Holm, 1979) in that in the set of m hypothesis tests the procedure begins by ordering the associated p-values from smallest to largest, and then rejecting the null hypothesis for the first k tests according to some stopping rule. It is the stopping rule that differentiates the procedures. For the Holm procedure, the rule is (Equation 4.1):

$$P_{(k)} > \frac{\alpha}{m+1-k} \tag{4.1}$$

where k is the kth test of $i = 1 \ldots m$ tests. In contrast, the FDR stopping rule is (Equation 4.2):

$$P_{(k)} \leq \frac{k}{m}\alpha \tag{4.2}$$

and aims to control the *proportion* of Type I errors, i.e. $\Pr(V/R > \alpha)$. This feature makes it less conservative than Bonferroni-based procedures, and explicitly allows for the realistic assumption that some (small) rate of Type I error is acceptable, in exactly the same way that the conventional "reject H_0 if $p < \alpha$" mantra taught to all undergraduate students of statistics accepts that a non-zero probability of Type I error is acceptable. The stopping rule above is for when the m tests are independent. When they are not independent, the BY procedure (Benjamini & Yekutieli, 2001) can be used (Equation 4.3):

$$P_{(k)} \leq \frac{k}{m \cdot c(m)}\alpha \tag{4.3}$$

In addition to these major procedures, others have been proposed: notably the *False Coverage Rate*, an analogous procedure to FDR for confidence intervals as opposed to NHST (Benjamini & Yekutieli, 2005), and an Empirical Bayes formulation of the same problem (Zhao & Gene Hwang, 2012).

A notable recent attempt to control the confidence intervals at the end of a selective inference procedure ("cherry picking") was proposed by Taylor and Tibshirani (2015), which was Rob Tibshirani's inaugural article after being elected to the National Academy of Sciences of the United States of America. Their procedures apply to processes where the picking of cherries is done in a well-defined way, by an algorithm. The cited work covers three such algorithms: stepwise regression; the lasso (Tibshirani, 1996, 2011, see Section 3.2.2.2); and principal components analysis – although work is under way to extend their method to other scenarios. For example, their stopping rule for forward regression is as follows, where p_i is the ith p-value (Equation 4.4):

$$\hat{k} = max\left\{k : -\frac{1}{k}\sum_{i=1}^{k}log\left(1 - p_i\right) \le \alpha\right\} \tag{4.4}$$

Essentially, it is "stop when the average *p*-value up to that point is below a target FDR". Their method also allows computing confidence intervals that account for selective inference.

2.1.3   Shrinkage

A phenomenon related to the cherry picking problem is the tendency for a model developed using one data set to have a lower fit on data subsequently gathered. If one only has a single data set, how can one estimate the degree to which one's final model is *over-fitted*; i.e. the fit will be higher than subsequent replications? The obvious answer is, of course, by resampling. Both bootstrapping and cross-validation can be used to estimate shrinkage/over-fitting. This procedure will be illustrated below.

2.1.4   Single methods of analysis

Every statistical method has its assumptions; however, examining whether these assumptions are met is rarely reported in most journal articles, and the implications of violating those assumptions are almost never discussed in any but the most superficial terms. In the past this was forgivable because the statistical theorists who invented the methods were silent on the issue. However, now that it's trivial to conduct large-scale simulation studies, empirical examination of the effects of assumption violation are possible.

In scenario modelling (for example, banks planning for financial shocks) it is canonical practice to conduct sensitivity analysis, i.e. to test how the mathematical model being used reacts to perturbations of inputs that reflect assumptions. With modern computing power it takes longer to plan a simulation study than to actually run it, in many cases. But reporting the results of simulation studies is unlikely to result in publication in top journals, so there is a disincentive to conduct such useful work.

What one can do in the absence of guidance from the literature regarding how robust or fragile one's single model is, is to run alternative, equally valid, models. Many researchers do this already, for example using parametric tests and their equivalent non-parametric alternatives, such as examining both Pearson and Spearman correlations for skewed 5-point rating scale variables or conducting both *t*-tests and Mann-Whitney *U* tests for comparing two groups. An example of a more recent practice is that many researchers are now using PLS-SEM instead of CB-SEM, in no small part due to the more restrictive and unrealistic assumptions of CB-SEM.

With modern computing power, a much wider range of alternatives can be examined, and the whole process automated, given appropriate software, as we shall see below.

2.1.5   Linearity and additivity

In the regression context, most classical methods assume linearity: i.e. the effect of an explanatory variable on an outcome is the same over the entire range of the explanatory variable, exemplified by the regression coefficient estimates from OLS regression. Moreover, effects of explanatory variables are assumed to be independent; the goal is to obtain a *ceteris paribus* interpretation.

However most marketing phenomena are unlikely to be reflected by these assumptions. For example, marketing mix modelling examines the effect of expenditure in different media on sales, e.g. pay-per-click digital advertising, TV advertising, sales-force remuneration, etc. It is extremely unlikely for these effects to be linear and additive.

With a small number of explanatory variables this is not a problem: non-linearities and interactions can be modelled by adding polynomial and multiplicative terms in OLS regression, for example. However with a large number of explanatory variables, the practical problem faced by the marketing analyst using traditional tools is that introducing terms to model non-linearity and interaction increases the number of parameters to estimate, which can (a) exceed the number of observations, making the model unidentified; and (b) make the model very difficult to interpret.

2.2   Alternative Paradigms from Machine Learning

The attempts to deal with the problems of quantitative data analysis scenarios that are described above have their origin in the machine learning field, notably related to genomics. Many of those innovations are well within the NHST fold; i.e. they try to adjust *p*-values and confidence limits according to frequentist or Fisherian thinking. But the machine learning field has also developed other responses to the problems of NHST that do not totally abandon NHST, but substantially downplay the centrality of asymptotic *p*-values to decision making.

The term "machine learning" has been used above, and many readers have no doubt come across the term before. In this section a few aspects of machine learning are considered, from the point of view of a researcher who deals with moderate sized data sets (say, a few hundred or fewer than 5000 cases, and few hundred variables or less) and has some theoretical model in mind that can be operationalised as a sub-model of the Generalised Mixed Linear Model (Laird & Ware, 1982; McCullagh &

Nelder, 1983, 1989; Pinheiro & Bates, 2000), e.g. one-way ANOVA or Structural Equation Modelling, whether covariance based (Jöreskog & Wold, 1982) or PLS (see Hair et al., 2013, for example).

Machine learning includes a wide array of methods, largely characterised by their applicability and relevance for problems of analysing "large" data sets and ongoing data *streams*, e.g. sales records over time or ongoing web metrics. A recent driver of innovation has been the analysis of "wide" or "high-dimensional" data sets, where the number of variables (q) is greater than the number of cases (n). This is the situation faced in the analysis of genomic data, where the analyst is faced with a sample of perhaps a few hundred patients, each of whom has measurements relating to thousands of genes. In most of these scenarios, in addition to the $q > n$ problem, there is also the expectation that, of the thousands of possible correlates of a given outcome, only a handful are expected to have a clinically significant (let alone statistically significant) relationship with the outcome. This is known as the "sparsity problem". We can see an immediate parallel for market researchers here: the medical binary outcome of "alive vs. dead" could translate to "buy vs. not", and the number of data point measures on each customer could be very large in commercial settings, and the number of potential leads (people who see an online ad, for example) is much larger than warm leads (people who click on that ad).

In these situations – where "big" can refer to cases, correlates or both – classical approaches based on NHST have proved less than useful, primarily because of the following issues:

1. Excessive statistical power (small effect sizes are "significant")
2. Alpha inflation (probability of Type I error greater than the nominal rate)
3. The untenable assumption of lack of prior knowledge (past data in a stream provide information about likely values of parameters)
4. Linear models
5. Additive models.

How, then, should data analysts decide which correlates or "explanatory" variables are worthy of further investigation, or management attention?

Classical methods are based on parametric statistical models, which were almost all developed using simplifying assumptions to achieve mathematical tractability. In contrast, more machine learning *algorithms* often do not have an explicit statistical model, and are sometimes characterised as "black box" methods, which will give prediction but not explanation (e.g. effect sizes and simple methods of describing effects, for instance beta coefficients that are interpretable in a *ceteris paribus* manner).

In addition to the classical methods described above ("classical" because they are based on NHST and frequentist inference, notwithstanding some Empirical Bayes variations), some fundamentally new *paradigms* of data analysis have emerged from the machine learning community, the most important of which (from the point of view described above) are outlined below.

2.2.1   Prediction versus explanation

As discussed above, a glaring feature of over-reliance (or reification) of NHST is the idiom of discussing statistically significant results with no substantive significance; e.g. the parameter estimate or overall model fit is trivial. This leads to consideration of overall model performance *first*, and consideration of impact of individual correlates second. An illustrative example is a logistic regression model of an outcome with roughly 50 per cent prevalence in the population. Imagine the "hit rate", i.e. the proportion of model predictions that are correct, is 55 per cent. In a commercial setting, an enterprise would spend a lot of money gathering data, both to develop the model and to put it into production. Why bother if you could get comparable accuracy by flipping a coin?

2.2.2   Triangulation over data: bootstrapping and cross-validation

2.2.2.1 Bootstrapping   Many readers will already be familiar with the fundamentals of the bootstrap, so the details will not be repeated here. Bootstrapping is an old idea (Efron, 1979, 1981); but it took a *very* long time before it was implemented in commercial software (notably SPSS), and even today it is not available at the click of a mouse everywhere that it could, or should, be used.

Most researchers familiar with the ideas of the bootstrap will probably think of it as an alternative to asymptotic *p*-values when the assumptions of some parametric procedure, e.g. maximum likelihood estimation of a SEM, are not met. Perhaps a smaller proportion will realise that the fundamental basis of inference from sample to population differs between asymptotic and bootstrap *p*-values. Even fewer will be aware that there are several variations on the bootstrap. And even fewer will be aware that bootstrapping is not just a way to obtain *p*-values or confidence intervals, but can be used to study other aspects of models, such as goodness of fit, as we shall see below.

2.2.2.2 Cross-validation   Cross-validation is an extension of a very old idea: split-half testing. Textbooks from the 1990s and earlier advocated splitting your data in half, developing your model based on one half and then testing it on the other half and comparing the estimates and goodness of fit. This is good advice; but some of us were wondering: Would the results be any different if we used different halves? – i.e. selecting the halves at random, perhaps more than once. Many researchers would regard this as unnecessarily tedious. Others would think that this approach was costly: to apply it one needed to gather twice as much data, assuming that data were gathered according to some minimum sample size to achieve the desired statistical power approach.

However, with cheap computing power the basic idea can be developed further. One could apply the split-half multiple times, then average or aggregate the results. And, if one does it enough times, one "borrows" power from replication, so the fraction of the data left out on each replication can be smaller. The modern application of this procedure is known as *cross-validation*, and the most common method is *k*-fold validation, where one leaves *n*/*k* of the data out as a test sample and the remaining cases for the "training" data. Most commonly $k = 10$, i.e. 10 per cent of the cases for testing and 90 per cent for training at each iteration.

2.2.3 Triangulation over methods

In addition to methods of assessing the relevance of correlates or explanatory variables, and assessing the quality of estimates from a given model, there is an increasing realisation that in many situations there is no single algorithm or method that could be regarded a priori as being "optimal", and hence triangulating over methods (as opposed to data in resampling approaches) is a useful way of assessing the trustworthiness of any conclusions derived from data analysis.

There are several different reasons for using multiple methods:

- Bake-offs: One can simply try a set of methods/models/algorithms and pick the one with the best performance to report as the final model.
- Method bias assessment: A more useful way to approach comparing several models is to assess the degree to which one's substantive conclusions depend on the patterns in the data, as opposed to the methods used to detect those patterns.
- Ensembles: Algorithmically combining the results of several comparable models – random forests being the canonical example.

Modern approaches to data analysis strongly suggest that, for anything but the most trivial theoretical models or research questions, best practice includes fitting several different statistical models and examining their congruence. For example, if we wish to examine influences on a binary outcome (for instance a customer buys, or not) there are several statistical models that are applicable, such as discriminant analysis or logistic regression. How can we, as researchers, assess the possibility that our results depend not only on our (random) sample but also on our chosen analysis method? One way to assess this is to triangulate over methods. However this principle, which is in common use in the machine learning discipline, has not yet made its way into the mainstream methodological toolbox of modern academic marketing researchers, despite the fact that machine learning is mainstream in many enterprises.

For example, Williams (2013) advocated an ensemble approach to clustering time-series data, rather than searching for the One Method to Rule Them All, as many researchers seem to advocate (especially those who have developed or recently learned about a new method).

2.3　Software

One of the reasons for the slow adoption of modern best practices may be the unavailability of the latest methods in the *software* that comprises the traditional toolbox of our discipline. Commercial software seems to suffer from conservative bias, whereby it takes years for new methods to become available. In contrast, using open-source statistical software allows the researcher access to the *current* best practice methods, rather than those of a decade or more previously.

Probably the best software available today, in terms of reflecting current best practice and the latest methods, is **R**; however Python, especially using the scikit-learn module, is catching up fast in terms of capability and usability. For the serious data analyst in marketing research there seems to be few other choices in terms of power, flexibility and expressiveness. And both are free and open-source software.

There's another reason to use **R** and Python, and that is to free marketers from Excel. Many business students learn to do data analysis with SPSS, sometimes with SAS or maybe Stata; but when they enter the workforce they find their enterprise has no budget for SPSS, and definitely not SAS, so all they can work with is Excel. If we trained students with **R** and/ or Python, they could carry their skills into the workplace.

As an example of the ability of **R** to reflect the absolute cutting-edge of data analysis methods, a very popular package, **caret** (Classification and **Regression Training**), lists over 100 functions for each of a number of regression and classification problems.

With 190 methods for classification problems and 136 methods for regression, one might think that it is unreasonable to try over 100 models on the same data; but modern computing power makes this quite straightforward. It is not as interactive and instantaneous as running a single OLS regression in SPSS; but for moderate problems, e.g. around 1000 cases and 50 or so covariates, setting a script running on one's computer (with, say, four or eight i5 or i7 cores and 8 or 16GB of RAM), and then going for a coffee while it runs and inspecting the results on one's return to the office is quite feasible. This is a small price to pay for the reassurance that one's results don't depend to a large degree on the arbitrary choice of methods to analyse one's data.

Another advantage of using a genuine programming language that was designed for statistical analysis and graphics is that it allows (relatively) easy collection of results from several different algorithms or models, which allows one to programmatically prepare summary tables and reports. If your boss, supervisor or colleague says to you "Great work! But could you add another ten methods, and run it on this month's data", then a couple of modifications to your scripts (rather than repeating the original work entirely) will accomplish this task. The importance of this ability, for someone who analyses data regularly, cannot be overstated.

A particular strength of **R** is that it incorporates very strong support for "reproducible research" – i.e. authoring a single source file that contains both text and code to run analyses, construct tables, produce graphics and so on. This has the advantage that if a mistake is discovered in the analysis or a colleague changes his or her mind about which subset of the data to include, such that one or more tables or figures are invalidated, then the entire report, article, blog post, chapter or entire book can be regenerated with minimal effort. It should be no surprise to the reader that this chapter was produced using just such a workflow, namely the **bookdown** package (Xie, 2016, 2018).

3.   AN EXAMPLE

In this section we'll examine an example of putting these principles into action, and where a modern approach corroborates the classical approach, giving confidence in the conclusions.

3.1   Data

We're going to use data from the BEATS (**B**uilt **E**nvironment and **A**ctive **T**ravel to **S**chool) project (Mandic et al., 2016), which was a multi-year, multi-disciplinary study into factors that affect transport to school among secondary students. The project sampled one class from every secondary school in Dunedin, New Zealand (a hilly provincial city of around 100 000 people), and investigated correlates of active transport to school (walking, cycling, scootering, etc.). Over 1000 responses to a questionnaire, as well as anthropometric measurements, were collected, resulting in a total of 63 covariates considered to possibly affect active travel to school (ATS). These included:

- personal factors
- attitudes to ATS
- social factors
- environmental factors.

The outcome was modelled using ATS as a binary variable; hence logistic regression was used, in part to fit with the norms of the medical science literature, where this aspect of the study was published (Mandic et al., 2015). But the logistic regression model (LRM) is not the only statistical model for binary outcomes, as we shall see. More importantly, the published model has extremely high goodness of fit (area under the ROC curve 97 per cent), which can sometimes indicate over-fitting or numerical problems with the fitting algorithm. Hence it is of interest to examine the method-dependence of any conclusions from this model.

The variables used for this demonstration are as follows: distance is measured in metres; the other items are either 7- or 4-point Likert scales.

- **Distance**: Distance from school to home (actual walking/driving distance, not straight line); modelled in the LRM using a regression cubic spline.
- **WSpsh**: My parents think I should walk to school.
- **WSf5ws**: Some of my best friends walk to school.
- **WSpunsafe**: My parents think it's unsafe to walk to school.
- **WCSone**: School is on the way of my parents' commute to work.
- **WSno**: I can't be bothered walking to school.
- **WSbstuff**: I've got to carry too much stuff to walk to school.
- **WSbplan**: Walking to school conflicts with my after-school activities.

Other variables appear in some of the output below, but they will not be discussed.

3.2   Methods

In this section some different ways of modelling these data are illustrated. The aim is not to show the "optimal" statistical model, but to illustrate that for most situations faced by quantitative marketing researchers there are several equally valid ways to analyse the data. Moreover, if the substantive interpretation of results differs across analytical methods, there is prima facie evidence that the results are a feature of the somewhat arbitrary choice of analysis methods, as opposed to genuine non-random patterns in the data – i.e. our view of the world as opposed to the way the world really is, putting aside measurement issues.

We'll see several "manual" methods, i.e. where the algorithm that implements the statistical model does not "learn" from the data; and then in Subsection 3.2.3 we'll see a few illustrative machine learning methods.

3.2.1 Logistic regression

A logistic regression model (LRM) was fitted manually, first by entering all the theoretically relevant variables, and then removing them one by one based on deviance reduction, and at each step inspecting the change in the remaining parameter estimates. This procedure was continued until only variables significant at the 1 per cent level remained. This level was chosen because the sample size was over 1000 and because of potential α-inflation due to cherry picking.

The final model fits well, as shown by the fit indices in Table 4.2. The odds ratios are shown in Table 4.3, and the influence of the explanatory variables is shown graphically in Figure 4.1. Shrinkage estimates are shown in Table 4.4. We can see little evidence of over-fitting; there's not much shrinkage in R^2, for example. I have chosen to include a couple of variables that are non-significant, to illustrate how these variables are treated using alternative methods.

According to Hosmer et al. (2013, p. 177), an AUC of 97 per cent is "Excellent"; hence we are justified in interpreting the feature coefficients. Coefficients of logistic regression models are sometimes interpreted in raw form, or as raw odds ratios (ORs), each of which is problematic. It's better to "standardise" the ORs for features on different scales by calculating the OR for a one quartile change in the feature (rather than

Table 4.2 Fit indices for LR model

Index	Value
AUC	0.972
D_{xy}	0.943
R^2	0.796
Brier score	0.060

Note: AUC is the area under the ROC curve; D_{xy} is Somers' *D*, i.e. the correlation between the predicted and actual outcome; and R^2 is the Nagelkerke R^2.

Table 4.3   Odds ratios for LR model

Correlate	Low	High	IQR	OR	Lower CI	Upper CI	p-value
Distance	1.61	7.53	5.92	0.02	0.01	0.04	0.00
WSpsh	2.00	6.00	4.00	11.36	5.86	22.02	0.00
WSf5ws	1.00	3.00	2.00	2.01	1.38	2.92	0.00
WSpunsafe	1.00	3.00	2.00	0.55	0.26	1.14	0.11
WCSone	2.00	4.00	2.00	0.34	0.21	0.55	0.00
WSno	2.00	3.00	1.00	0.57	0.43	0.74	0.00
WSbstuff	2.00	4.00	2.00	1.00	0.58	1.72	0.99
WSbplan	1.00	3.00	2.00	0.33	0.15	0.71	0.00

a unit change). The "Low" and "High" columns in Table 4.3 refer to the 25 per cent and 75 per cent (first and third) quartiles.

Effect plots reveal a surprising feature: as expected, the odds of using ATS decline sharply with distance; however at 10km the odds increase again. Note also that the confidence band widens, due to fewer observations of larger distances. The inflection and upward slope is a result of a very small number of students who claimed to live more than 30km from school but used ATS.

Whenever a model fits close to 100 per cent, suspicions should be raised about whether you have (a) trivial model, (b) a numerical accident or (c) a model arrived at by cherry picking – i.e. over-fitted, and hence likely to suffer from shrinkage. The latter can be partially addressed by resampling. Table 4.4 shows the results refitting the model to 1000 bootstrap resamples, and the resulting fits compared to the original fit, to give an estimate of shrinkage.

The results are pleasing, i.e. there is very little evidence of over-fitting. However this still leaves open the possibilities of numerical accidents and a trivial model. One might be tempted to say that because distance is such an obvious factor in ATS, it probably swamps or masks the other effects, and is responsible for the "Outstanding" fit. However re-estimating the model with Distance removed (not shown here) still has "Excellent" fit, and the substantive interpretation of the remaining covariates remains unchanged.

This still leaves the possibility that some numerical quirk or accident is responsible for the pleasing fit. This can be assessed by using equally plausible but algorithmically different statistical models, as illustrated below.

3.2.2   Other manual methods

There are *many* methods for modelling a binary outcome; so why do our textbooks only cover logistic regression and discriminant analysis? One

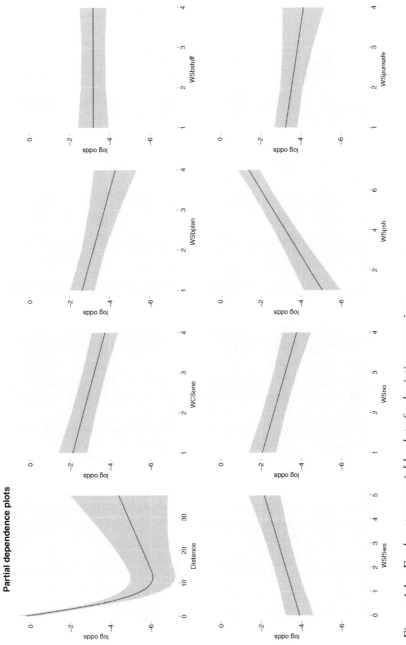

Figure 4.1   Explanatory variable plots for logistic regression

Table 4.4   Shrinkage evaluation

	Original index	Training	Test	Optimism	Corrected index
D$_{xy}$	0.943	0.946	0.941	0.004	0.939
R^2	0.796	0.801	0.791	0.010	0.786
Intercept	0.000	0.000	−0.002	0.002	−0.002
Slope	1.000	1.000	0.957	0.043	0.957
E$_{max}$	0.000	0.000	0.010	0.010	0.010
D	0.814	0.822	0.806	0.016	0.798
U	−0.002	−0.002	0.001	−0.002	0.001
Q	0.815	0.823	0.805	0.018	0.797
B	0.060	0.058	0.061	−0.003	0.063
g	5.126	5.335	5.083	0.253	4.873
gp	0.389	0.389	0.388	0.001	0.388

reason is that a single book that covers all, or even several, methods would be large and expensive. However there is no reason why the existence of alternative methods cannot be mentioned briefly and the canonical references cited, with an encouragement to the reader to learn more about them.

Of interest for this example is whether "cutting-edge" methods or algorithms can beat the LRM. In other words, are the LRM results an *artefact of the method*? Do all methods that *could* be used give similar results? For the reason mentioned above (limited space), we'll only look at a few of the more interesting methods, i.e. those that seem to be most popular among the machine learning community. For space reasons, only the output of these methods will be shown, and discussed very briefly.

The methods demonstrated below have been chosen to illustrate three general advances in dependence modelling that have yet to appear as part of the standard toolbox of marketing research: the Generalised Additive Model (GAM), i.e. meaningful modelling of non-linear response functions; the LASSO (an algorithm to combat shrinkage and alpha inflation); and a Bayesian Mixed Model GAM. Also included is FLAM: a recent and interesting hybrid approach between the realism of the GAM and easy and familiar interpretability of the GLM.

3.2.2.1 The Generalised Additive Model   The GAM (Hastie & Tibshirani, 1995) is fairly simple conceptually. Instead of the usual linear model (Equation 4.5),

$$\hat{y} = \beta_0 + \sum_{j=1}^{p} \beta_j \, x_{ij} + \in \qquad (4.5)$$

we have the following model (Equation 4.6):

$$\hat{y} = \beta_0 + \sum_{j=1}^{p} f_j(x_{ij}) + \epsilon \qquad (4.6)$$

where each $f(\cdot)$ can be any smooth function, which means that the relationship between each covariate and the outcome can be (highly) non-linear, giving tremendous modelling flexibility.

Output is illustrated in Figure 4.2, which shows evidence of non-linearity for the effect of distance and WSpsh: "My parents think I should walk to school." The effect of distance shows a rapid drop-off in the odds of using ATS, and three inflection points. This is due to outliers, and shows the usefulness of the GAM in detecting such features of the data.

The GAM corroborates the LRM, and suggests a previously undetected non-linearity in WSpsh ("My parents think I should walk to school"), indicating that perhaps the 7-point Likert scale should be collapsed into binary, split at 4.

3.2.2.2 LASSO The LASSO (Least Absolute Shrinkage and Selection Operator) is due to Rob Tibshirani (see Tibshirani, 1996, 2011). The basic idea is to force parameter estimates of the GLM toward zero, in contrast to relying on NHST to decide if they probably are zero. The LASSO is an algorithm to minimise Equation (4.7):

$$\sum (y_i - \beta_0 - \sum \beta_j x_{ij})^2 + \lambda \sum |\beta_j| \equiv RSS + \lambda \sum |\beta_j| \qquad (4.7)$$

where λ is a penalisation factor that encourages the βs to be exactly 0. When $\lambda = 0$ the estimates are just the OLS estimates. With λ sufficiently large, all the βs will be exactly 0. So the task is to select the optimal value of λ, which is done by cross-validation, as shown in Figure 4.3. Choosing the minimum value of λ gives the coefficients and corresponding odds ratios shown in Table 4.5.

For readers unfamiliar with the statistical modelling approach (in contrast with NHST), "deviance" is the difference between the fitted and predicted values, similar to R^2 in OLS regression, and is hence a criterion to be minimised in many fitting algorithms.

We can see that the LASSO has selected quite different variables from the other methods, and in particular Distance has been selected out by penalisation. This highlights the peril of relying on single models. As we shall see, there is a high degree of consistency among the other models illustrated in this chapter, in terms of both fit and important variables, so the LASSO results will not be considered further.

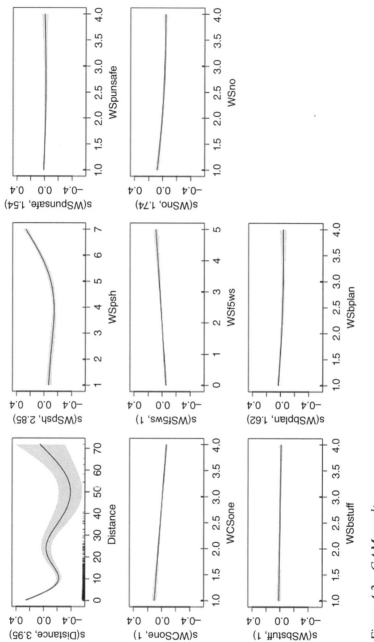

Figure 4.2 GAM results

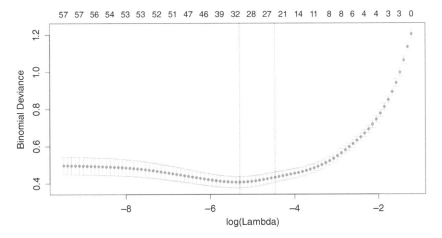

Figure 4.3   Choosing λ by cross-validation

Table 4.5   All non-zero LASSO estimates

Term	Beta	OR
GIS_Intersection_count	0.965	2.626
WCSone	0.553	1.738
WSbsched	0.421	1.523
WStime	0.377	1.458
WSno	0.373	1.453
WSbplan	0.357	1.429
WSpunsafe	0.350	1.420
WSbdist	0.258	1.295
WSbfri	0.196	1.216
GIS_LandMixUse	0.155	1.168
WCShills	0.129	1.138
WCStraffic	0.116	1.123
HMcars	0.092	1.096
WSbwant	0.084	1.088

3.2.2.3 FLAM   However an extension of LASSO, the Fused Lasso Additive Model (Petersen et al., 2016), is a recently developed model that may improve on the bare LASSO. The main idea behind FLAM is to force the influence of the correlates to be zero – that is, flat (i.e. LASSO); but it is also to detect change points. This is a hybrid between linear and smooth curve modelling, e.g. by including polynomial terms. Estimates are shown in Figure 4.4.

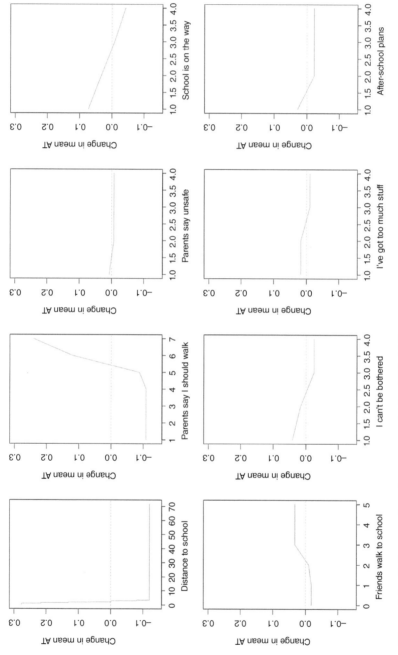

Figure 4.4   Influence of explanatory variables (FLAM)

We can see how FLAM is resistant to outliers, retains the sharp break point of WSpsh (but indicating a binary split point at 5) and indicates possible break points in some other explanatory variables.

3.2.2.4 SpikeSlabGAM   Due to Scheipl et al. (2012), this model is based on two core ideas:

1.   a Bayesian "Spike and Slab" model (Ishwaran & Rao, 2005)
2.   Generalised Additive Mixed Models (GAMMs) (Fahrmeir et al., 2004, 2010).

The **R** package provides an easy and flexible interface for exploring interaction and non-linearity; specification of covariates as binary, categorical, ordinal or continuous; and "automagic" variable, function and interaction selection. However it is relatively computer-intensive (because of MCMC estimation, e.g. up to a minute for this model).

Learning from the FLAM output that suggests WSpunsafe and WCSone are linear while the remaining variables may have non-linearities, the SpikeSlabGAM model was specified this way, and also interactions between WSpsh, WCSone and Distance were explored. Figure 4.5 shows an example of the easy-to-interpret graphical output that depicts interactions, and modelling rating scales as both linear and discrete variables.

This method corroborates other methods that allow flexibility of modelling the relationships between each correlate and the dependent variable, in that there is evidence of interactions (non-additivity) and non-linearity, both smooth and threshold points.

3.2.2.5 Summary of manual methods   Table 4.6 shows a comparison of the methods on the basis of AUC, including some methods not shown here for space reasons (such as forward and backward stepwise algorithms). The "full" model includes all 63 potential covariates. There is not much to choose between the models, implying that it is meaningful to compare their substantive interpretations.

The point of such a comparison is to assess how much better or worse one's favoured model is, compared to several equally plausible and possibly superior models. In this case the LRM is reasonable and is appropriate to communicate to a health/medical research audience, who are familiar with, and expect to see, odds ratios and risk factors.

3.2.3   Machine learning methods

All the above methods were "manual": that is, although some rely on cross-validation or bootstrapping to select tuning parameters, they do

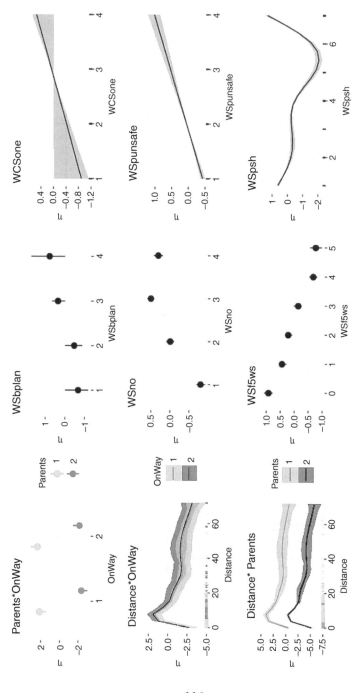

Figure 4.5 Influence of explanatory variables (SpikeSlabGAM)

Table 4.6   Comparison of manual methods by AUC criteria

LRM full	LRM backward	LRM forward	LRM final	HDGLM	SSGAM	FLAM
98	97	96	97	98	97	97

not modify the *entire* model based on resampling. Real "machine learning" methods are characterised by the latter, and applying them typically involves resampling over "training" and "test" data sets.

The **caret** package for **R** was used for the analyses in this section, as its purpose is to help streamline many of the steps in a machine learning approach to data analysis (i.e. using multiple statistical models, using algorithms to select their parameters to maximise some quality index, and using cross-validation).

Of interest here is whether "cutting-edge" methods and algorithms can beat the LRM. In other words: (a) are the LRM results an *artefact of the method*?; (b) is the fit of the LRM as near the maximum fit of competing models?; and (c) do competing and comparable models be used give similar results? Space restrictions prevent showing dozens of models, so only a few are presented as an illustration of the general principles of MDA in action. The models are:

- Decision trees (CART) and random forests (Therneau & Atkinson, 2018)
- Multivariate adaptive regression splines (MARS) (Milborrow, 2019)
- Gradient boosting (GB-GLMM) (Greenwell et al., 2019)
- Flexible discriminant analysis (Leisch et al., 2017).

The last three items in this list are variations on the general linear model, and will not be explained here; however, as some readers may be unfamiliar with tree methods, they will be illustrated briefly below.

3.2.3.1 Tree methods   Both Kuhn and Johnson (2013) and Harrell (2015) suggest using a CART/MARS approach (Breiman et al., 1984; Friedman, 1991) to initial modelling, to get a feel for the important factors and to identify possible interactions. Advantages of decision trees are:

- They easily handle differing levels of measurement of covariates
- They allow automatic identification of interactions
- They are more intuitively understandable for non-technical audiences.

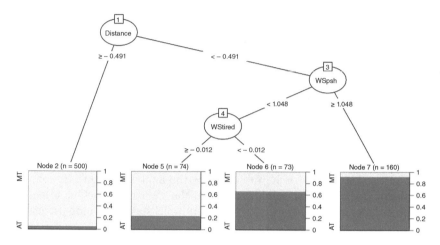

Figure 4.6   Simple decision tree example

But decision trees have the major disadvantage that they are often (highly) unstable in the face of data permutation/resampling. A simple example is shown in Figure 4.6, which indicates that distance is the most important variable, followed by time. The terminal bar plots indicate the probability of the outcome. In these examples, the variables have been scaled, and hence the split points are not directly interpretable; however the scaled distance −0.5 corresponds to approximately 2.3km, indicating that if the distance is less than that, students walk or cycle to school. But *if* the student lives further away, parental attitudes are the determining factor, *unless* the student complains that they're often too tired to walk or cycle. You can see how this is a more intuitively understandable and realistic interpretation, as opposed to the *ceteris paribus* interpretation of OLS regression coefficients, for example.

A more complex example is shown in Figure 4.7, which shows a different story because a different CART algorithm and different maximum tree depth were used.

This illustrates the fundamental problem with CART: fragility to seemingly minor analytical choices, and perturbations of the data. Because of this problem, an innovation in tree methods was required. What do you call a set of trees? A forest. Hence the name of Breiman's next innovation: estimate many trees and add an element of randomisation (Breiman, 2000, 2001). Random forests (RFs) are the go-to method in modern machine learning. Why? Simple: outstanding predictive accuracy over a wide range of problems. There is no NHST in the final output, but it is possible to construct "variable importance" metrics. These outputs do

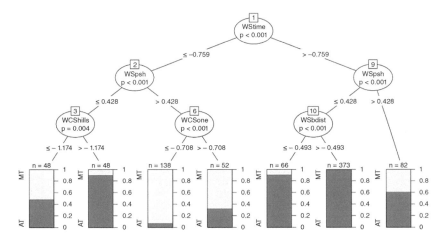

Figure 4.7   More complex decision tree example

not indicate the *direction* of influence, which must be investigated using other methods.

Figure 4.8 shows the output used to help tune a random forest – the number of trees to include, and Figure 4.9 shows the variable importance plot.

3.2.3.2 Summary of ML methods   Influential covariates (where the AUC of those methods ≈ AUC of the LRM shown in Tables 4.2 and 4.3) are shown in Table 4.7, with Goodness of Fit (GoF). Examining the variable importance metrics, we can see that although there are some differences between methods, there is also a large degree of consensus. Comparison of methods in execution time, fit in training and test data sets, and estimated shrinkage, is shown in Table 4.8. Box plots help summarise the differences in accuracy within and between methods (in terms of dispersion as well as typical values), as shown in Figure 4.10.

4.   SUMMARY

We've seen a few different ways of analysing the data at hand; now it's time to see what we've learned from this. One thing that you, the reader, cannot learn from reading this material is how easy the tables and figures were to produce. The *first* time you put these principles into practice using reproducible research methods, you will face a learning curve, and will have to write some custom code to suit your way of working and the style

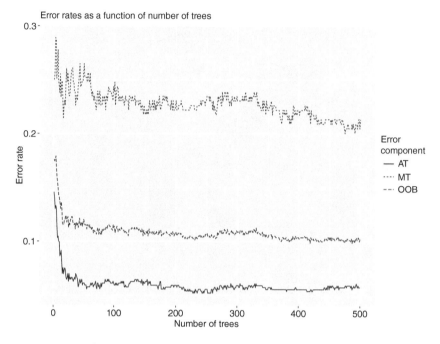

Figure 4.8   Choosing the number of trees

requirements of the publication. But the next time you have some data to analyse all the infrastructure will be in place, and you will be much more productive.

For these data and the initial model, alternative methods didn't *add* much, but rather gave *confidence* that the results are not an *artefact of the statistical model* (as opposed to the empirical world). Moreover, we have seen how easy it is to implement this approach, using **R**.

4.1   Discussion

MDA is not simply using modern *statistical models* or software for data analysis; rather, the principles covered above comprise a new *paradigm*, one characterised by scepticism of simplistic, unrealistic models/algorithms, and single models. Here are some principles that seem to be embraced to a varying degree of explicitness in modern data analysis:

- Controlling for Type I error using FDR, FCR or similar methods – i.e. something less conservative than a simple Bonferroni adjustment

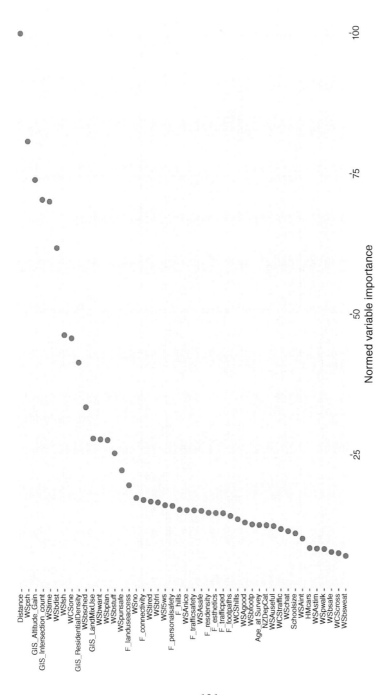

Figure 4.9 *Variable importance for random forest*

Table 4.7   The seven most important variables in each model

Model	AUC	1	2	3	4	5	6	7
LRM 0	98	WSpsh	Distanc	WCSone	WSno	WSf5ws	WSbcool	F_trffc
LRM F	97	D(F+HOF)	WS(F+OF)	WCSone	WSno	WSbschd	WCSrbor	WSf5ws
HDGLM	98	Dist	WSpsh	WCSone	WSf5ws	WSno	WSbsched	
bagEarth	96	WSpsh	Distanc	gender	Ag_t_Sr	WSbwthr	NZDepCt	HMcars
fda	97	Distanc	WSpsh	WCSone	WSbschd	WSchat	WSno	WSAusfl
gbm	100	Distanc	WSpsh	WSbdist	WSbschd	WStime	WCSone	GIS_A_G
multnom	98	GIS_A_G	Distanc	GIS_In_	WSpsh	WCSone	WSbplan	F_trffc
rf	100	Distanc	WSpsh	GIS_A_G	GIS_In_	WStime	WSbdist	WSfsh
ctree	94	Distanc	gender	Ag_t_Sr	WSbwthr	NZDepCt	HMcars	WSpsh

Table 4.8   Comparison of GoF and shrinkage across methods

Method	Run time	Acc. (train)	Acc. (test)	Acc. Shrink	AUC train	AUC test	AUC Shrink
bagEarth	4.93 mins	12.27	16.42	−4.15	95.5	93.1	2.4
ctree	14.02 secs	88.10	86.94	1.16	94.4	93.4	1.1
fda	12.91 secs	92.07	92.16	−0.09	97.2	97.7	−0.4
gbm	26.38 secs	98.14	88.43	9.71	99.8	95.2	4.6
multinom	12.53 secs	94.05	90.30	3.75	98.3	96.9	1.4
pls	4.03 secs	91.57	91.04	0.53	97.2	96.2	0.9
rf	53.19 secs	100.00	90.30	9.70	100.0	96.6	3.4
rpart	4.42 secs	90.46	85.07	5.39	92.1	85.2	6.9

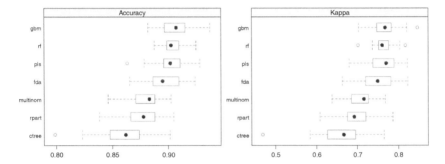

Figure 4.10   Comparison of GoF measures between methods

- Applying several statistical models to the same theoretical model to gain insight into refinements and threats to validity
- Cross-validation and/or bootstrapping for CIs and GoF indices
- Concern with, and employment of, methods to ameliorate shrinkage
- Focus on fit (aka "predictive" validity) as well as effect size and confidence intervals; de-emphasis of NHST
- Relaxing the linearity assumption
- Relaxing the additivity assumption
- Abandoning the assumption of zero prior knowledge, e.g. using an Empirical Bayes approach where appropriate
- Embracing *reproducible research*, i.e. producing all the necessary output for the final document with code.

How does one put MDA into practice? The good news is that the most capable software is open-source and free, and there are many high-quality, free online resources to help one learn, including university-level textbooks. If you want to follow this approach, Kuhn and Johnson (2013) cover many, *many* alternative methods. The lead author maintains the **caret** package (Kuhn, 2017). One or two good books are all that's necessary for introduction to these ideas (e.g. Kuhn & Johnson, 2013; Harrell, 2015). For more details the following are highly recommended and free to download, and in order of increasing technical detail:

- *An Introduction to statistical learning* (James et al., 2013)
- *Elements of statistical learning* (Hastie et al., 2009)
- *Computer age statistical inference* (Efron & Hastie, 2016).

4.2   Implications for Marketing Research

To put the foundations of marketing knowledge on a more firm and credible foundation, addressing the low-hanging fruit of threats to validity, i.e. using MDA, seems relatively straightforward. Although we can't expect all reviewers to be interested and competent in more "advanced" methods of statistical analysis, the twin problems relating to conflation of statistical and substantive significance, and α-inflation, are conceptually simple. Demanding effect sizes and multiple testing adjustment procedures are simple and easy to implement.

However a more important piece of the puzzle remains: replication. Although replication is gaining acceptance very slowly in some major journals, it is not the norm or even a major enterprise in marketing research. A large-scale replication project, along the lines of that under way in social psychology, would go a long way toward establishing a credible evidence base for marketing knowledge. For this to happen, the attitudes of journal editors and reviewers would have to change. Currently novelty is not only highly valued, it is a minimum barrier to entry in many journals. "This is already known" is one of the most feared sentences that authors encounter when reading reviews of their articles.

4.3   Conclusion

In this chapter I have outlined some principles implicit in the practices of machine learning, principles that the marketing discipline would benefit from adopting in the quest for scientific knowledge about the phenomena that interest us. I feel compelled to emphasise a final time: the ideas described here are *relatively* easy to implement. All that's required is a few hours or days of self-study (depending on one's prior knowledge) for the practising marketing researcher who's familiar with analysing data with code. And that self-improvement effort will pay off for years to come.

REFERENCES

Amrhein, V., & Greenland, S. (2018). Remove, rather than redefine, statistical significance. *Nature Human Behaviour, 2*(1), 4. http://doi.org/10.1038/s41562-017-0224-0.

Benjamin, D. J., Berger, J. O., Johannesson, M., Nosek, B. A., Wagenmakers, E.-J., Berk, R., ... Johnson, V. E. (2018). Redefine statistical significance. *Nature Human Behaviour, 2*(1), 6–10. http://doi.org/10.1038/s41562-017-0189-z.

Benjamini, Y., & Hochberg, Y. (1995). Controlling the false discovery rate: A practical and powerful approach to multiple testing. *Journal of the Royal Statistical Society, Series B, 57*(1), 289–300.

Benjamini, Y., & Yekutieli, D. (2001). The control of the false discovery rate in multiple testing under dependency. *Annals of Statistics, 29*(4), 1165–1188. http://doi.org/10.1214/aos/1013699998.

Benjamini, Y., & Yekutieli, D. (2005). False discovery rate: Adjusted multiple confidence intervals for selected parameters. *Journal of the American Statistical Association, 100*(469), 71–93. http://doi.org/10.1198/016214504000001907.

Breiman, L. (2000). Randomizing outputs to increase prediction accuracy. *Machine Learning, 40*, 229–242.

Breiman, L. (2001). Random forests. *Machine Learning, 45*, 5–32.

Breiman, L., Friedman, J. H., Olsen, R. A., & Stone, C. J. (1984). *Classification and regression trees*. New York: Chapman & Hall.

Cohen, J. (1988). *Statistical power analysis for the behavioral sciences* (2nd ed.). Hillsdale, NJ: Lawrence Erlbaum.

Cohen, J. (1990). Things I have learned (so far). *American Psychologist, 45*(12), 1304–1312.

Cohen, J. (1994). The Earth is round ($p < .05$). *American Psychologist, 49*(12), 997–1003.

Efron, B. (1979). Bootstrap methods: Another look at the jackknife. *Annals of Statistics, 7*(1), 1–26.

Efron, B. (1981). Nonparametric estimates of standard error: The jackknife, the bootstrap and other methods. *Biometrika, 68*(3), 589–599.

Efron, B. (1998). R. A. Fisher in the 21st century. *Statistical Science, 13*(2), 95–114. Retrieved from http://www.jstor.org.ezproxy.otago.ac.nz/stable/2676745.

Efron, B., & Hastie, T. (2016). *Computer age statistical inference: Algorithms, evidence, and data science*. New York: Cambridge University Press.

Fahrmeir, L., Kneib, T., & Konrath, S. (2010). Bayesian regularisation in structured additive regression models. *Statistics and Computing, 20*(2), 203–219.

Fahrmeir, L., Kneib, T., & Lang, S. (2004). Penalized structured additive regression for space-time data: A Bayesian perspective. *Statistica Sinica, 14*, 731–761.

Friedman, J. H. (1991). Multivariate adaptive regression splines (with discussion). *Annals of Statistics, 19*(1), 1–141.

Greenwell, B., Boehmke, B., Cunningham, J., & GBM Developers. (2019). *GBM: Generalized boosted regression models*. Retrieved from https://CRAN.R-project.org/package=gbm.

Hair, J. F., Hult, G., Ringle, C. M., & Sarstedt, M. (2013). *A primer on partial least squares structural equation modeling (PLS-SEM)*. Los Angeles: Sage.

Harlow, L. L., Mulaik, S. A., & Steiger, J. H. (1997). *What if there were no significance tests?* Mahwah, NJ: Psychology Press.

Harrell, F. (2015). *Regression modeling strategies* (2nd ed.). New York: Springer.

Hastie, T., & Tibshirani, R. (1995). *Generalized additive models*. London: Chapman & Hall.

Hastie, T., Tibshirani, R., & Friedman, J. H. (2009). *The elements of statistical learning: Data mining, inference, and prediction* (2nd ed.). New York: Springer.

Hoban, P. R., & Bucklin, R. E. (2014). Effects of internet display advertising in the purchase funnel: Model-based insights from a randomized field experiment. *Journal of Marketing Research, 52*(3), 375–393. http://doi.org/10.1509/jmr.13.0277.

Hochberg, Y., & Benjamini, Y. (1990). More powerful procedures for multiple significance testing. *Statistics in Medicine, 9*(7), 811–818. http://doi.org/10.1002/sim.478009071.

Holm, S. (1979). A simple sequentially rejective multiple test procedure. *Scandinavian Journal of Statistics*, *6*(2), 65–70.

Hosmer, D. W., Lemeshow, S., & Sturdivant, R. X. (2013). *Applied logistic regression* (3rd ed.). New York: Wiley.

Ioannidis, J. P. A. (2005). Why most published research findings are false. *PLoS Med*, *2*(8), e124. http://doi.org/10.1371/journal.pmed.0020124.

Ishwaran, H., & Rao, J. (2005). Spike and slab variable selection: Frequentists and Bayesian strategies. *Annals of Statistics*, *33*(2), 730–773.

James, G., Witten, D., Hastie, T., & Tibshirani, R. (2013). *An Introduction to statistical learning* (Corr. 5th printing 2015 ed.). New York: Springer.

Jöreskog, K. G., & Wold, H. (1982). The ML and PLS techniques for modeling with latent variables: Historical and comparative aspects. In K. G. Jöreskog & H. Wold (Eds.), *Systems under indirect observation: Causality – structure – prediction* (Vol. I, pp. 263–270). Amsterdam: North-Holland.

Kuhn, M. (2017). *Caret: Classification and regression training*. Retrieved from https://CRAN.R-project.org/package=caret.

Kuhn, M., & Johnson, K. (2013). *Applied predictive modeling*. New York: Springer.

Laird, N. M., & Ware, J. H. (1982). Random-effects models for longitudinal data. *Biometrics*, *38*, 963–974.

Leisch, F., Hornik, K., & Ripley, B. D. (2017). *MDA: Mixture and flexible discriminant analysis*. Retrieved from https://CRAN.R-project.org/package=mda.

Mandic, S., Barra, S. L. de la, Bengoechea, E. G., Stevens, E., Flaherty, C., Moore, A., . . . Skidmore, P. (2015). Personal, social and environmental correlates of active transport to school among adolescents in Otago, New Zealand. *Journal of Science and Medicine in Sport*, *18*(4), 432–437.

Mandic, S., Williams, J., Moore, A., Hopkins, D., Flaherty, C., Wilson, G., . . . Spence, J. C. (2016). Built environment and active transport to school (BEATS) study: Protocol for a cross-sectional study. *BMJ Open*, *6*(5), e011196.

McCullagh, P., & Nelder, J. A. (1983). *Generalized linear models*. London: Chapman & Hall.

McCullagh, P., & Nelder, J. A. (1989). *Generalized linear models* (2nd ed.). London: Chapman & Hall.

Meehl, P. E. (1978). Theoretical risks and tabular asterisks: Sir Karl, Sir Ronald, and the slow progress of soft psychology. *Journal of Consulting and Clinical Psychology*, *46*(4), 806–834.

Meyer, R. J. (2015). Editorial: A field guide to publishing in an era of doubt. *Journal of Marketing Research*, *52*(5), 577–579. http://doi.org/10.1509/jmr.52.5.577.

Milborrow, S. (2019). *Earth: Multivariate adaptive regression splines*. Retrieved from https://CRAN.R-project.org/package=earth.

Petersen, A., Witten, D., & Simon, N. (2016). Fused lasso additive model. *Journal of Computational and Graphical Statistics*, *25*(4), 1005–1025. http://doi.org/10.1080/10618600.2015.1073155.

Pinheiro, J., & Bates, D. (2000). *Mixed effects models in S and S-plus*. New York: Springer.

Rozeboom, W. W. (1960). The fallacy of the null-hypothesis significance test. *Psychological Bulletin*, *57*(5), 416–428.

Scheipl, F., Fahrmeir, L., & Kneib, T. (2012). Spike-and-slab priors for function selection in structured additive regression models. *Journal of the American Statistical Association*, *107*(500), 1518–1532.

Taylor, J., & Tibshirani, R. J. (2015). Statistical learning and selective inference. *Proceedings of the National Academy of Sciences*, *112*(25), 7629–7634. http://doi.org/10.1073/pnas.1507583112.

Therneau, T., & Atkinson, B. (2018). *Rpart: Recursive partitioning and regression trees*. Retrieved from https://CRAN.R-project.org/package=rpart.

Tibshirani, R. (1996). Regression shrinkage and selection via the lasso. *Journal of the Royal Statistical Society. Series B (Methodological)*, *58*(1), 267–288.

Tibshirani, R. (2011). Regression shrinkage and selection via the lasso: A retrospective. *Journal of the Royal Statistical Society, Series B (Statistical Methodology)*, *73*(3), 273–282.

Trafimow, D., & Marks, M. (2015). Editorial. *Basic and Applied Social Psychology*, *37*(1), 1–2. http://doi.org/10.1080/01973533.2015.1012991.

Tukey, J. W. (1969). Analyzing data: Sanctification or detective work? *American Psychologist*, *24*, 83–91.

Wasserstein, R. L., & Lazar, N. A. (2016). The ASA's statement on p-values: Context, process, and purpose. *The American Statistician*, *70*(2), 129–133. http://doi.org/10.1080/0 0031305.2016.1154108.

Williams, J. (2013). Clustering household electricity use profiles. In J. Deng (Ed.), *Proceedings of workshop on machine learning for sensory data analysis* (pp. 19–26). New York: ACM. http://doi.org/10.1145/2542652.2542656.

Williams, J. (2014). Some pitfalls of statistical analysis and the progress of knowledge accumulation in marketing. In S. Rundle-Thiele, K. Kubacki, & D. Arli (Eds.), *Proceedings of the Australian and New Zealand Marketing Academy (ANZMAC) annual conference: Agents of change* (pp. 742–748). Brisbane: ANZMAC.

Xie, Y. (2016). *Bookdown: Authoring books and technical documents with R markdown*. Boca Raton, FL: Chapman & Hall/CRC. Retrieved from https://github.com/rstudio/book down.

Xie, Y. (2018). *Bookdown: Authoring books and technical documents with R markdown*. Retrieved from https://github.com/rstudio/bookdown.

Zhao, Z., & Gene Hwang, J. T. (2012). Empirical Bayes false coverage rate controlling confidence intervals. *Journal of the Royal Statistical Society, Series B (Statistical Methodology)*, *74*(5), 871–891. http://doi.org/10.1111/j.1467-9868.2012.01033.x.

5. Meta-analysis: deconstructing marketing knowledge
İlayda İpek and Nilay Bıçakcıoğlu-Peynirci

INTRODUCTION

Meta-analysis is a method that helps incorporate multiple prior research results into a single study (Glass 1976), and can be considered a quantitative composition of aggregated research findings (Geyskens et al. 2009). Furthermore, meta-analysis gives absolute estimations about certain relationships by virtue of its enhanced statistical power and provides moderation effects of different factors (Hunter & Schmidt 2004; Zhao et al. 2004). However, when conducting meta-analytic research there are several issues that should be considered carefully so as to avoid controversial and misleading results, such as study inclusion criteria, publication bias, and heterogeneity of the methods (Schmidt & Hunter 2015; Stone & Rosopa 2017).

The meta-analytic approach has attracted significant attention from scholars in social science fields including finance, management, and marketing, etc. (Hunter & Schmidt 2004). Notably, the body of research on marketing has recorded valuable examples of meta-analysis containing various interesting research topics (Kirca & Yaprak 2010). Specifically, in the extant marketing literature, meta-analytic studies have offered useful insights into such areas of research as consumer behaviour (e.g., Szymanski & Henard 2001; Toufaily et al. 2013), services marketing (Carrillat et al. 2009; Orsingher et al. 2010), marketing communications (Eisend 2017; Lodish et al. 1995), and international marketing (Crouch 1996; Leonidou et al. 2014).

Building on the aforementioned issues, this chapter endeavours to contribute to the stream of marketing research pursuing the meta-analytic perspective. In particular, the main purpose of this chapter is twofold: (a) to throw light on the basic tenets of meta-analysis by concentrating on its nature, brief history, and important stages to conduct a good meta-analytic study; and (b) to investigate the influence of export market orientation on export performance through a meta-analytic research.

1.   META-ANALYSIS

1.1   What Is Meta-Analysis?

Meta-analysis is a quantitative review approach that combines all results from previous independent studies and presents statistical quantification by comparing findings for the purpose of integrating results and generating new theoretical propositions (Glass 1976; Kirca & Yaprak 2010). Also, the term 'research synthesis' is often used interchangeably with meta-analysis in the relevant literature (Cooper et al. 2009). On the other hand, a literature review (i.e., narrative reviews) can be defined as an integration of relevant literature on a specific subject with the help of classifying studies regarding importance levels. Meta-analysis, however, moves a step further than narrative reviews by concentrating on study outcomes, assigning weight to the studies with respect to the mathematical criteria, synthesizing the results of primary research in systematic and quantitative ways, and drawing conclusions (Borenstein et al. 2009; Farley & Lehmann 2001; Kirca & Yaprak 2010).

In reference to the advantages of meta-analysis, integrating the findings of several studies provides more credible and precise results through clarifying inconsistencies in the extant literature and identifying both research trend patterns in data over time and moderators/mediators in the scope of the research (Borenstein et al. 2009; Cooper et al. 2009; Hedges 1987; Rosenthal 1978). Furthermore, the cumulative perspective of meta-analysis enables researchers to look at the whole picture and get a solid grasp of the phenomenon by establishing a certain familiarity with the relevant literature (Rosenthal & DiMatteo 2001). With regard to the criticisms of meta-analysis, since every meta-analytic review has been conducted with distinct inclusion criteria for the purpose of reviewing the relevant literature, there may be bias in sampling the findings which should be addressed, such as publication bias, or the 'file drawer problem' (Rosenthal 1979). For instance, some crucial remarks indicated that studies reporting significant effects are more likely to be published than studies finding insignificant results, which directly constitutes a good example of bias in sampling (Borenstein et al. 2009). Moreover, as meta-analysis combines effect sizes from distinct studies with non-overlapping samples, a study reporting more than one effect size should be treated separately for examination of moderators and subgroups (Rosenthal & Rubin 1986). In addition, another common criticism is mixing apples and oranges, which implies that meta-analysis contains distinct types of studies in the same analysis (Borenstein et al. 2009; Card 2012; Sharpe 1997) and could also be explained by providing broader generalization to the audience (Rosenthal & DiMatteo 2001).

1.2   A Brief History of Meta-Analysis

Meta-analysis dates back to the early 1900s, with the first attempt at combining correlation coefficients reported in 11 studies by Karl Pearson in 1904 to examine the relationship between immunity and mortality (Chalmers et al. 2002). Along with this initial application of the meta-analytic perspective, several efforts were made to advance the related methodology. However, in spite of these initiatives in different streams of research, meta-analysis did not attract adequate attention in the field of social sciences until the 1970s (Card 2012). The approach emerged in social sciences with the introduction of the 'meta-analysis' concept by Gene Glass in 1976 (Card 2012; Hunter & Schmidt 2004), which has been also identified as the start of the modern era of meta-analytic studies (Lipsey & Wilson 2001).

In addition to the seminal work by Glass, focusing on psychotherapy, in the following years other notable studies on meta-analysis were conducted by Smith and Glass (1977), Schmidt and Hunter (1977), Rosenthal and Rubin (1978), and Smith et al. (1980), which have been widely acknowledged as breakthroughs in the improvement of meta-analytic knowledge (Cheung 2015; Lipsey & Wilson 2001). Building on this, in the 1980s pioneering books were published on the subject (e.g., Glass et al. 1981; Hedges & Olkin 1985; Hunter et al. 1982; Rosenthal 1984), with the aim of highlighting the methodological and statistical foundations of meta-analysis (Card 2012; Cooper et al. 2009). Outstanding guidance accompanied by the requirement to synthesize the prior body of research has led to an increasing tendency towards meta-analytic studies in different fields of research such as health and educational sciences, but, in particular, social sciences (Card 2012; Cheung 2015; Rosenthal & DiMatteo 2001).

1.3   Meta-Analytic Research Process

The meta-analytic research process primarily involves five stages: (1) problem formulation, (2) literature search, (3) data assessment, (4) robustness tests, and (5) data analysis.

1.3.1   Problem formulation
During the scientific process of meta-analytic reviews, the identification of a problem statement constitutes the most challenging and primary

step as it consists of: (a) reading seminal works related to the subject; (b) defining crucial variables and operationalization of these constructs; (c) recognizing inconsistent results; and (d) determining the main aim of the study (Cooper & Hedges 1994; Kirca & Yaprak 2010). In fact, the problem statement produces a research question that needs to be answered in meta-analysis and assists researchers in the subsequent stages such as identification, coding and analysis of relevant studies (Lipsey & Wilson 2001). First, the topic needs to be chosen based on: whether it is a worthwhile area to conduct a meta-analysis with respect to the significance of the subject; the heterogeneity of the findings across studies in order to reveal possible mediators/moderators; the number of articles published in the extant literature; and the availability of a reasonable number of studies reporting appropriate effect size for the analysis (Cooper et al. 2009). Another important issue is to define variables and their conceptualizations, since narrow definitions reveal less information concerning the distinct context in which studies took place, while broader conceptualizations provide more contextual variations, thus drawing more credible conclusions (Kirca & Yaprak 2010; Cooper et al. 2009).

1.3.2 Literature search

On the basis of the research problem developed in the first stage, the next step in the meta-analytic research process includes the recognition of eligible studies on the pertinent subject. As the strategy formulated to find related studies has an enormous impact on the meta-analytic findings, the right inclusion criteria need to be set (Grewal et al. 2018; Hunter & Schmidt 2004). In this stage, mainly, relevant articles are traced in different databases using selected keywords; thereafter, the references in identified studies are manually checked to find additional studies on the topic of interest (Kirca & Yaprak 2010). As a critical point, in the case of studies which can be grouped into conceptually equal but statistically separate replications, each finding should be evaluated individually (e.g., studies investigating more than one consequence) (Grewal et al. 2018). Special attention be also devoted to literature searches containing unpublished work, since studies coming up with insignificant impacts are less likely to appear in academic publications, which may give way to publication bias or the 'file-drawer problem' (Lipsey & Wilson 2001; Rosenthal 1979). Correspondingly, exhaustive coverage in gathering the associated literature allows the elimination of any potential bias of meta-analytic findings (Card 2012; Cooper et al. 2009), which, in turn, enhances the overall excellence of the meta-analysis (Kirca & Yaprak 2010).

1.3.3 Data assessment

After the literature search for data collection, researchers need to make critical evaluations regarding the quality of collected studies and code them according to standardized procedures (Cooper et al. 2009). First, there are noteworthy points that can be perceived as important threats to assessing the quality of the studies: (a) evaluating the quality of research concerning their methodological quality rather than research findings or institutions of primary researchers; (b) the likelihood of making mistakes during the coding stage, recommending that at least two researchers code all the studies and assess inter-coder reliability; and (c) examining solutions for missing data (Lipsey & Wilson 2001; Mahoney 1977; Orwin 1994). Second, as the main aim of this step is to develop a database, preparing a coding protocol that includes study characteristics (e.g., substantial and methodological attributes such as sample size, scale reliability), appropriate effect size statistics (e.g., correlation coefficients) and potential relevant moderators (e.g., time period, industry, operationalization) is recommended to improve the reliability and validity of the meta-analysis (Cooper & Hedges 1994; Henard & Szymanski 2001; Judge et al. 2001; Kirca & Yaprak 2010).

1.3.4 Robustness tests

Robustness tests of meta-analysis basically encompass the evaluation of publication bias and sensitivity analysis.

Publication bias An important consideration in meta-analysis absent data, the most usual of which in meta-analytic research is missing studies (Pigott 2012). The missing studies, which constitute a *random* group of all related studies, may not have a considerable influence on the results of a meta-analysis; nevertheless; but, being *systematically* distinctive from the studies incorporated in the meta-analysis, their exclusion produces a biased sample (Borenstein et al. 2009). Because published studies with statistically significant effects are more likely to be covered in a meta-analysis, in cases of biased samples the meta-analytic findings will reveal this bias through the computation of a higher mean effect size (Borenstein et al. 2009; Card 2012). Broadly termed 'publication bias', this issue has been seen as one of the biggest risks to the validity of a meta-analytic study (Cooper et al. 2009). Accordingly, different graphical (e.g., funnel plot) and statistical techniques – such as Rosenthal's (1979) file-drawer method, Orwin's (1983) 'fail-safe N', and the 'trim-and-fill' method (Duval & Tweedie 2000) – have been proposed to check for publication bias in meta-analytic research (Palmatier et al. 2006; Pigott 2012).

Sensitivity analysis Sensitivity analysis is crucial for meta-analytic reviews in order to demonstrate the robustness of the study findings and help us understand whether the findings shift with the effect of change in inclusion criteria or assumptions of the studies (Borenstein et al. 2009). Detailed sensitivity analyses should be conducted to explore the effect of individual studies by omitting one study procedure and investigating whether its elimination would affect the results of the study, such as reflecting an increased homogeneity in the subgroups or significant inverse trend (e.g., Strazzullo et al. 2009; Wit et al. 2010). Moreover, when reporting a meta-analytic review, the analysis is expected to present a forest plot. This helps researchers interpret the statistics through visual plots intuitively by illustrating point estimates with confidence intervals (i.e., narrower interval can be interpreted as having better accuracy) and emphasizing anomalies emerging in the analysis (Borenstein et al. 2009).

1.3.5 Data analysis

Effect size calculation Symbolizing the findings of individual studies (Cheung 2015; Cooper et al. 2009), effect size is described as "a quantitative reflection of the magnitude of some phenomenon that is used for the purpose of addressing a question of interest" (Kelley & Preacher 2012, p. 137). In meta-analytic research, relying on the effect size synthesized from relevant studies, a summary effect is calculated; effect size therefore represents a critical component of meta-analysis (Borenstein et al. 2009). Vital concerns are associated with the choice of effect size – such as consistency of a selected effect size across studies to allow comparisons and interpretations – and relative independency of the measured effect size from the elements of research design (Cooper et al. 2009; Lipsey & Wilson 2001). Effect sizes may take various forms (e.g., depending on means, binary data, and correlations) based on the essence of the relationships within a study, which can be convertible from one type to another (Borenstein et al. 2009). Among these, correlation coefficient has been one of the most frequently employed effect sizes in the social sciences (Cheung 2015). However, the transformation of correlations into Fisher's z-coefficients has been widely suggested, since z-transformed correlations have some advantageous statistical characteristics, such as being nearly normally distributed (Geyskens et al. 2009).

Heterogeneity analysis After quantifying all studies with the help of standardized effect sizes, the collected data is prepared for synthesizing the results, which first requires heterogeneity analysis to reveal variations in effect sizes (Borenstein et al. 2009). There are several tests to analyse the distribution of effect size values, such as: Q statistics, referring to the sum of squared deviations; T^2 statistics, related to the variance of true effects; and I^2 statistics, which is the ratio of true variation to observed variation (Borenstein et al. 2009; Grewal et al. 2018). Furthermore, Geyskens et al. (2009) recommend using a combination of several heterogeneity tests for meta-analytic reviews. Afterwards, when the distribution of effect sizes is found to be heterogeneous, researchers need to determine whether this variation demonstrates a fixed-effects model or a random-effects model (Grewal et al. 2018). While the former assumes the existence of the same true effect size for all studies, the latter reflects its variation among studies (Pigott 2012). In addition, the choice of meta-analytical model should depend upon the study objective – i.e., generalizing to other populations with higher variation in effect sizes or sharing a common effect size for a specific identified population (Borenstein et al. 2009).

Outlier analysis   When heterogeneity exists in effect sizes based on the results of statistical tests, researchers should perform an outlier analysis in order to address heterogeneity in the data and ensure the robustness of the findings (Geyskens et al. 2009; Grewal et al. 2018). If meta-analytic results change with the removal of one outlier study, a precise examination of the analysis is required, and the results should be reported both with and without outliers included in the analysis (e.g., Compeau & Grewal 1998). However, it should be noted that the presence of outlier studies does not make the analysis unreliable or inaccurate. On the contrary, it leads to more precise results (Grewal et al. 2018). There appear to be two techniques that can be used to identify outliers in the analysis: traditional outlier detection techniques (i.e., schematic plot analyses) and sample-adjusted meta-analytic deviancy (SAMD) (Geyskens et al. 2009). While the former can be conducted through schematic plot analysis, it has been criticized for disregarding sample size (Grewal et al. 2018). Meanwhile the latter, which is commonly used in several meta-analytic reviews (e.g., Chang & Taylor 2016), takes sample size into account and over-identifies relatively small correlations as outliers (Huffcutt & Arthur 1995).

Correcting for measurement and sampling errors   Owing to the absence of complete reliability, measurement error is always embodied in a meta-analytic research (Hunter & Schmidt 2004). Critically, measurement error produces underestimated effect sizes; hence, it is vital to apply statistical remedies in an attempt to control for such error (Grewal et al. 2018). Construct reliabilities obtained from relevant studies enable us to adjust for measurement error, such that corrected effects are calculated by dividing correlation coefficient values by the square root of construct reliabilities (Hunter & Schmidt 2004).

As for sampling error, it has been argued that: "If the population correlation is assumed to be constant over studies, then the best estimate of that correlation is not the simple mean across studies but a weighted average in which each correlation is weighted by the number of persons in that study" (Hunter & Schmidt 2004, p. 81). The underlying reason behind this argument is attached to the notion that studies with larger sample sizes offer more rigorous results as to effect sizes compared to studies with smaller sample sizes because the sampling error in large-sample studies is lower in magnitude (Lipsey & Wilson 2001). Therefore, meta-analysis aims to reduce sampling error through weighting studies by sample size, which is in line with the approaches of Hedges and Olkin (1985) and Hunter and Schmidt (2004) (Cooper et al. 2009).

Moderator analysis Akin to the perspective pursued in primary studies, in a meta-analytic study it is possible to investigate the association between one or more covariates (moderators) and a dependent construct (Borenstein et al. 2009). Moderator analysis can be performed in both fixed-effects and random-effects models; but each should be used with caution due to certain statistical deficiencies of these effects (Geyskens et al. 2009). Notably, the evaluation of moderating impacts in a meta-analytic study differs significantly between subgroup analysis and meta-regression (Grewal et al. 2018). In terms of the former, meta-analysis is carried out to compare the mean effects of separate sets of studies, similar to analysis of variance in primary research. In regard to the latter, meta-analytic research is conducted to test the linkage between study-level moderators and effect size, which is similar to multiple regression in primary research (Borenstein et al. 2009; Grewal et al. 2018).

2. THE EFFECT OF EXPORT MARKET ORIENTATION ON EXPORT PERFORMANCE: A META-ANALYTIC APPLICATION

2.1 Problem Formulation

In this part of the chapter a meta-analysis is conducted with an example application in the marketing area. The aim is to systematically synthesize empirical findings based on a meta-analysis of relevant studies investigating the relationship between export market orientation and export performance. Based on seminal works in the extant literature (e.g., Cadogan et al. 1999; Kohli & Jaworski 1990; Narver & Slater 1990) and increased interest in the concept of export market orientation in contemporary studies of international marketing literature, it was decided to examine the relationship between export market orientation and export performance. In particular, export companies with greater market orientation perform better in their export operations as they quickly learn and adapt to unfamiliar environments (Boso et al. 2012; Chung 2012; He et al. 2018).

In this sense, crucial variables were identified to perform the meta-analysis – such as export market orientation (i.e., independent), export performance (i.e., dependent) and economic development level of countries (i.e., moderator) – with respect to the conceptualization and operationalization of the constructs. Furthermore, the last two decades have witnessed a wealth of studies analysing the link between export market orientation and export performance (e.g., Acosta et al. 2018; Cadogan et al. 2012; Chang & Fang 2015; Gerschewski et al. 2015; Navarro-García et al. 2014).

2.2   Literature Search

Relying on the critical relevance of establishing the right inclusion criteria to meta-analytic results (Grewal et al. 2018; Hunter & Schmidt 2004), four criteria were developed to find suitable studies on the subject: (a) to concentrate on examining the association between export market orientation and export performance; (b) to measure export market orientation on the basis of well-established scales involving MKTOR (Narver & Slater 1990), MARKOR (Kohli et al. 1993), the export market orientation scale developed by Cadogan et al. (1999), and the market orientation scale of Deshpandé et al. (1993); (c) to assess export performance with objective and/or subjective indicators; and (d) to be empirical research by using primary and/or secondary data and report Pearson's correlation coefficients or its variants between the variables of interest (Rosenthal 1994).

Relevant studies were identified through both manual and electronic search methods. Electronic databases (e.g., EBSCO, Elsevier, JSTOR) were searched using the keywords "market orient*" in combination with "export performance". The references in the relevant studies identified through online searches were checked. In total, 38 studies analysing the link between export market orientation and export performance were obtained; however, 12 of these were eliminated due to failure to satisfy the eligibility criteria. As a result, with an inclusion rate of 68.4 per cent (26 out of 38 studies), 49 effects of export market orientation on export performance were gathered from 28 independent samples included in the 26 studies ($N = 7428$). This is comparable to other meta-analytic studies on the pertinent subject (e.g., Ellis 2006; Grinstein 2008).

2.3 Data Assessment

Regarding quality, all respective studies were scrutinized according to the *Academic Journal Guide* for 2015, published by the Chartered Association of Business Schools (CABS), which has commonly served as an academic journal guide (e.g., Adams et al. 2016; Coombes & Nicholson 2013). In total, 26 papers covering the period 1998–2018 were coded for the meta-analysis; two independent coders recorded the data according to a specified schema including key study characteristics (i.e., study name, journal name, industry, country, firm size, sample size, sampling method, analytical approaches, conceptualization of dependent and independent constructs, reliabilities and available effect size estimates). The countries were coded according to economic development levels – i.e., low-income, middle-income and high-income economies (World Bank 2016). Also, all disagreements were solved at the end of discussions, and inter-coder reliability ranged from 90 to 95 per cent (Szymanski & Henard 2001).

2.4 Robustness Tests

To estimate the publication bias related to published studies, both graphical and statistical techniques were adopted. First, funnel plots were used to visually check for the possibility of publication bias; and, owing to the approximately symmetric distribution of the effect sizes around the mean, no evidence of publication bias was observed (Pigott 2012). Second, the three most frequently applied statistical techniques were employed to gauge whether the publication bias exists in this meta-analytic study (Geyskens et al. 2009; Grewal et al. 2018). Initially, the file-drawer method was followed in an effort to reveal the number of null effect studies required to replace the significant result with the non-significant one (Rosenthal 1979). In this sense, the file-drawer N number (20 132) proved that the meta-analytic results are resistant to the file-drawer problem. Next, Orwin's 'fail-safe N' (set to 0.05), representing the number of missing studies that would change the overall effect size to a particular non-zero level (Orwin 1983), also supported the low likelihood of publication bias. Finally, in line with the 'trim-and-fill' method of Duval and Tweedie (2000), the funnel plot illustrating the observed effects accompanied by the imputed effects was evaluated; this was drawn by trimming and filling the data. The 'trim-and-fill' procedure again showed that this meta-analysis was safe from publication bias.

Sensitivity analysis was also performed in order to check the robustness of the findings with the help of the 'one study removed' option. Since these results did not significantly differ from the previous ones, outliers were not excluded from the study for further meta-analyses. Furthermore, the statistics were also interpreted through forest plot analysis, reflecting any anomalies in the analysis with visual plots and confidence intervals. In this study, when examining the forest plot analysis, there exist few outliers, and the point estimates with confidence intervals can be interpreted as showing better accuracy as a large majority of the confidence intervals illustrate narrower ranges (Borenstein et al. 2009).

2.5   Data Analysis

Before integrating all results it is necessary to reveal the true variation in effect sizes and choose the right model for further analyses. In line with this, as suggested by Geyskens et al. (2009), we conducted several different heterogeneity tests. As a result, the random-effects model was adopted, representing a greater variation in effect sizes since the findings – (Q-value (48df) = 483.028 (p = 0.000), I-squared = 90.063) – reveal a significant and high amount of heterogeneity in the distributions of variance among the studies (Cooper et al. 2009). Also, the heterogeneity of the results indicates that there appears to be possible moderators and mediators across studies (Hunter & Schmidt 2004). Moreover, when the 95 per cent confidence interval does not involve zero, it also implies important clues about the heterogeneity of the results and reflects a significant relationship between independent and dependent variables (Finkelstein et al. 1995).

In a significant number of the studies (46.2 per cent) involved in the impact of export market orientation on export performance, the correlation coefficients were reported on the basis of the link between different market orientation dimensions (e.g., customer orientation, export market intelligence generation, etc.) and export performance outcomes. For these instances, the effect sizes across the dimensions of export market orientation were averaged to calculate a mean export performance score for overall export market orientation (Ellis 2006; Grinstein 2008). In terms of measurement error, corrected correlations were computed by dividing each effect size by the square root of the construct reliabilities (Hunter & Schmidt 2004). In cases of studies failing to present the reliabilities, the mean reliability of the export market orientation concept was substituted (Ellis 2006; Kirca et al. 2005); this was specifically estimated for each of the scales utilized to measure export market orientation (The mean reliability for the MKTOR scale was 0.842, for the MARKOR scale 0.802, for Cadogan et al.'s (1999) export market orientation scale 0.878, and for Deshpandé et al.'s (1993) market orientation scale 0.890.) Thereafter, the reliability-corrected correlations were converted into Fisher's z-coefficients, which were subsequently averaged, and then retransformed into correlation coefficients for interpretation (e.g., Grinstein 2008; Kirca et al. 2005).

In this meta-analytic study, the proposed relationship between export market orientation and export performance was tested by means of Comprehensive Meta-Analysis (CMA version 2.2.057) software. Table 5.1 summarizes the meta-analytic results, incorporating the direct impact of export market orientation on export performance and the moderator analysis. The meta-analytic findings reveal that, overall, export market orientation has a favourable influence on export performance ($r = 0.323$, $CI_{95\%}$ 0.279 to 0.366), which can be evaluated as above moderate (Cohen 1988). This is consistent with other meta-analytic studies on the market orientation–performance association in the domestic context (e.g., Ellis 2006; Kirca et al. 2005) and with the notion that export market orientation enables a better response to conditions in overseas markets, which, in turn, cultivates export success (Cadogan et al. 2012; Murray et al. 2007).

Regarding moderator analysis, the statistics prove that significant differences exist among low-income, middle-income, and high-income countries with respect to the correlation between export market orientation and export performance: Q-value (2df) = 6.302 ($p = 0.043$). The results suggest that the effect size for the export market orientation–export performance link is higher in countries with low income levels ($r = 0.621$, $CI_{95\%}$ 0.341 to 0.800) compared to middle- and high-income countries. This finding might be attributed to the fact that, owing to the lack of sufficient tangible resources (e.g., physical, human, and monetary assets), firms operating in low-income countries rely heavily on market-oriented strategies to outperform their rivals in export markets (Birru et al. 2018).

DISCUSSION

This chapter consists of two distinct parts. The first provided brief information about meta-analysis and its history, and outlined the key steps that should be followed in order to conduct a good meta-analysis: problem formulation; literature search; data assessment; robustness tests; and data analysis. The latter represents a real application of meta-analysis, examining the relationship between export market orientation and export performance through the use of CMA version 2.2.057 software. With the integration of seminal papers in the relevant research field, meta-analytic papers draw a big picture and become vital to enhancing understanding for both researchers and practitioners, since meta-analysis also provides comprehensive insights for future research studies and offers new theoretical perspectives to unexplored areas (Palmatier et al. 2018).

Furthermore, the last two decades have seen growing attention to meta-analytic studies, particularly in the field of marketing (e.g., Grinstein 2008;

Table 5.1 Summary of meta-analyses of links between export market orientation and export performance

Link	Effects (N)	Total sample size	Corrected r	Standard errorr	−95% LCL	+95% UCL
Overall export market orientation → export performance	49	7482	0.323	0.007	0.279	0.366
Effect of country's economic development level × export market orientation → export performance						
Low-income country	2	159	0.621	0.102	0.341	0.800
Middle-income country	21	2832	0.278	0.008	0.217	0.337
High-income country	26	4491	0.333	0.009	0.275	0.389

Kirca et al. 2005; Kirca & Yaprak 2010; Scheer et al. 2015). In sum, this chapter contributes significantly to the extant literature, and constitutes a meta-analysis guideline for both academics and practitioners since the method of meta-analysis has been comprehensively explained, both from the theoretical perspective and by illustrating a real application from the marketing field.

SUMMARY

Meta-analytic studies provide integrated and accumulated knowledge of key research findings in a specific domain via testing robustness of the findings, revealing inconsistent previous results, and identifying potential new insights for future studies (e.g., moderators, measures and approaches). However, meta-analysis should also be approached with caution considering its substantial assessments.

REFERENCES

Acosta, A.S., Crespo, Á.H. and Agudo, J.C. 2018. Effect of market orientation, network capability and entrepreneurial orientation on international performance of small and medium enterprises (SMEs). *International Business Review*. **27**(6), pp.1128–1140.

Adams, R., Jeanrenaud, S., Bessant, J., Denyer, D. and Overy, P. 2016. Sustainability-oriented innovation: A systematic review. *International Journal of Management Reviews*. **18**(2), pp.180–205.

Birru, W.T., Runhaar, P., Zaalberg, R., Lans, T. and Mulder, M. 2018. Explaining organizational export performance by single and combined international business competencies. *Journal of Small Business Management*. **57**(3), pp.1172–1192.

Borenstein, M., Hedges, L.V., Higgins, J.P. and Rothstein, H.R. 2009. *Introduction to meta-analysis*. Chichester: Wiley.

Boso, N., Cadogan, J.W. and Story, V.M. 2012. Complementary effect of entrepreneurial and market orientations on export new product success under differing levels of competitive intensity and financial capital. *International Business Review*. **21**(4), pp.667–681.

Cadogan, J.W., Diamantopoulos, A. and De Mortanges, C.P. 1999. A measure of export market orientation: Scale development and cross-cultural validation. *Journal of International Business Studies*. **30**(4), pp.689–707.

Cadogan, J.W., Sundqvist, S., Puumalainen, K. and Salminen, R.T. 2012. Strategic flexibilities and export performance: The moderating roles of export market-oriented behavior and the export environment. *European Journal of Marketing*. **46**(10), pp.1418–1452.

Card, N.A. 2012. *Applied meta-analysis for social science research*. New York: Guilford.

Carrillat, F.A., Jaramillo, F. and Mulki, J.P. 2009. Examining the impact of service quality: A meta-analysis of empirical evidence. *Journal of Marketing Theory and Practice*. **17**(2), pp.95–110.

Chalmers, I., Hedges, L.V. and Cooper, H. 2002. A brief history of research synthesis. *Evaluation and the Health Professions*. **25**(1), pp.12–37.

Chang, W. and Taylor, S.A. 2016. The effectiveness of customer participation in new product development: A meta-analysis. *Journal of Marketing*. **80**(1), pp.47–64.

Chang, Y.S. and Fang, S.R. 2015. Enhancing export performance for business markets: Effects of interorganizational relationships on export market orientation (EMO). *Journal of Business-to-Business Marketing.* **22**(3), pp.211–228.

Cheung, M.W.L. 2015. *Meta-analysis: A structural equation modeling approach.* Chichester: Wiley.

Chung, H.F. 2012. Export market orientation, managerial ties, and performance. *International Marketing Review.* **29**(4), pp.403–423.

Cohen, J. 1988. *Statistical power analysis for the behavioral sciences.* Hillsdale, NJ: Erlbaum.

Compeau, L.D. and Grewal, D. 1998. Comparative price advertising: An integrative review. *Journal of Public Policy & Marketing.* **17**(2), pp.257–273.

Coombes, P.H. and Nicholson, J.D. 2013. Business models and their relationship with marketing: A systematic literature review. *Industrial Marketing Management.* **42**(5), pp.656–664.

Cooper, H. and Hedges, L.V. (Eds.) 1994. *The handbook of research synthesis.* New York: Russell Sage Foundation.

Cooper, H., Hedges, L.V. and Valentine, J.C. (Eds.) 2009. *The handbook of research synthesis and meta-analysis.* New York: Russell Sage Foundation.

Crouch, G.I. 1996. Demand elasticities in international marketing: A meta-analytical application to tourism. *Journal of Business Research.* **36**(2), pp.117–136.

Deshpandé, R., Farley, J.U. and Webster Jr, F.E. 1993. Corporate culture, customer orientation, and innovativeness in Japanese firms: A quadrad analysis. *Journal of Marketing.* **57**(1), pp.23–37.

Duval, S. and Tweedie, R. 2000. A nonparametric 'trim and fill' method of accounting for publication bias in meta-analysis. *Journal of the American Statistical Association.* **95**(449), pp.89–98.

Eisend, M. 2017. The third-person effect in advertising: A meta-analysis. *Journal of Advertising.* **46**(3), pp.377–394.

Ellis, P.D. (2006). Market orientation and performance: A meta-analysis and cross-national comparisons. *Journal of Management Studies.* **43**(5), pp.1089–1107.

Farley, J.U. and Lehmann, D.R. 2001. The important role of meta-analysis in international research in marketing. *International Marketing Review.* **18**(1), pp.70–79.

Finkelstein, L.M., Burke, M.J. and Raju, M.S. 1995. Age discrimination in simulated employment contexts: An integrative analysis. *Journal of Applied Psychology.* **80**(6), pp.652–663.

Gerschewski, S., Rose, E.L. and Lindsay, V.J. 2015. Understanding the drivers of international performance for born global firms: An integrated perspective. *Journal of World Business.* **50**(3), pp.558–510.

Geyskens, I., Krishnan, R., Steenkamp, J.B.E. and Cunha, P.V. 2009. A review and evaluation of meta-analysis practices in management research. *Journal of Management.* **35**(2), pp.393–419.

Glass, G.V. 1976. Primary, secondary, and meta-analysis of research. *Educational Researcher.* **5**(10), pp.3–8.

Glass, G.V., McGraw, B. and Smith, M.L. 1981. *Meta-analysis in social research.* Thousand Oaks, CA: Sage.

Grewal, D., Puccinelli, N. and Monroe, K.B. 2018. Meta-analysis: Integrating accumulated knowledge. *Journal of the Academy of Marketing Science.* **46**(1), pp.9–30.

Grinstein, A. 2008. The effect of market orientation and its components on innovation consequences: A meta-analysis. *Journal of the Academy of Marketing Science.* **36**(2), pp.166–173.

He, X., Brouthers, K.D. and Filatotchev, I. 2018. Market orientation and export performance: The moderation of channel and institutional distance. *International Marketing Review.* **35**(2), pp.258–279.

Hedges, L.V. 1987. How hard is hard science, how soft is soft science? The empirical cumulativeness of research. *American Psychologist.* **42**(5), pp.443–455.

Hedges, L.V. and Olkin, I. 1985. *Statistical models for meta-analysis.* New York: Academic Press.

Henard, D.H. and Szymanski, D.M. 2001. Why some new products are more successful than others. *Journal of Marketing Research.* **38**(3), pp.362–375.

Huffcutt, A.I. and Arthur, W. 1995. Development of a new outlier statistic for meta-analytic data. *Journal of Applied Psychology.* **80**(2), pp.327–334.

Hunter, J.E. and Schmidt, F.L. 2004. *Methods of meta-analysis: Correcting error and bias in research findings.* Thousand Oaks, CA: Sage.

Hunter, J.E., Schmidt, F.L. and Jackson, G.B. 1982. *Meta-analysis: Cumulating research findings across studies.* Beverly Hills, CA: Sage.

Judge, T.A., Thoresen, C.J., Bono, J.E. and Patton, G.K. 2001. The job satisfaction–job performance relationship: A qualitative and quantitative review. *Psychological Bulletin.* **127**(3), pp.376–407.

Kelley, K. and Preacher, K.J. 2012. On effect size. *Psychological Methods.* **17**(2), pp.137–152.

Kirca, A.H. and Yaprak, A. 2010. The use of meta-analysis in international business research: Its current status and suggestions for better practice. *International Business Review.* **19**(3), pp.306–314.

Kirca, A.H., Jayachandran, S. and Bearden, W.O. 2005. Market orientation: A meta-analytic review and assessment of its antecedents and impact on performance. *Journal of Marketing.* **69**(2), pp.24–41.

Kohli, A.K. and Jaworski, B.J. 1990. Market orientation: The construct, research propositions, and managerial implications. *Journal of Marketing.* **54**(2), pp.1–18.

Kohli, A.K., Jaworski, B.J. and Kumar, A. 1993. MARKOR: A measure of market orientation. *Journal of Marketing Research.* **30**(4), pp.467–477.

Leonidou, L.C., Samiee, S., Aykol, B. and Talias, M.A. 2014. Antecedents and outcomes of exporter–importer relationship quality: Synthesis, meta-analysis, and directions for further research. *Journal of International Marketing.* **22**(2), pp.21–46.

Lipsey, M.W. and Wilson, D.B. 2001. *Practical meta-analysis.* Thousand Oaks, CA: Sage.

Lodish, L.M., Abraham, M., Kalmenson, S., Livelsberger, J., Lubetkin, B., Richardson, B. and Stevens, M.E. 1995. How T.V. advertising works: A meta-analysis of 389 real world split cable T.V. advertising experiments. *Journal of Marketing Research.* **32**(2), pp.125–139.

Mahoney, M.J. 1977. Some applied issues in self- monitoring. In: Cone, J.D. and Hawkins, R.P. ed. *Behavioral assessment: New directions in clinical psychology.* New York: Brunner/Mazel, pp.241–254.

Murray, J.Y., Gao, G.Y., Kotabe, M. and Zhou, N. 2007. Assessing measurement invariance of export market orientation: A study of Chinese and non-Chinese firms in China. *Journal of International Marketing.* **15**(4), pp.41–62.

Narver, J.C. and Slater, S.F. 1990. The effect of a market orientation on business profitability. *Journal of Marketing.* **54**(4), pp.20–35.

Navarro-García, A., Arenas-Gaitán, J. and Rondán-Cataluña, F.J. 2014. External environment and the moderating role of export market orientation. *Journal of Business Research.* **67**(5), pp.740–745.

Orsingher, C., Valentini, S. and de Angelis, M. 2010. A meta-analysis of satisfaction with complaint handling in services. *Journal of the Academy of Marketing Science.* **38**(2), pp.169–186.

Orwin, R.G. 1983. A fail-safe N for effect size in meta-analysis. *Journal of Educational Statistics.* **8**(2), pp.157–159.

Orwin, R.G. 1994. Evaluating coding decisions. In: Cooper, H. and Hedges, L.V. ed. *The handbook of research synthesis.* New York: Russell Sage Foundation, pp.139–161.

Palmatier, R.W., Dant, R.P., Grewal, D. and Evans, K.R. 2006. Factors influencing the effectiveness of relationship marketing: A meta-analysis. *Journal of Marketing.* **70**(4), pp.136–153.

Palmatier, R.W., Houston, M.B. and Hulland, J. 2018. Review articles: Purpose, process, and structure. *Journal of the Academy of Marketing Science.* **46**(1), pp.1–5.

Pigott, T.D. 2012. *Advances in meta-analysis: Statistics for social and behavioral sciences.* New York: Springer.

Rosenthal, R. 1978. Combining results of independent studies. *Psychological Bulletin.* **85**(1), pp.185–193.

Rosenthal, R. 1979. The file drawer problem and tolerance for null results. *Psychological Bulletin.* **86**(3), pp.638–641.

Rosenthal, R. 1984. *Meta-analytic procedures for social research.* Beverly Hills, CA: Sage.

Rosenthal, R. 1994. Parametric measures of effect size. In: Cooper, H. and Hedges, L.V. ed. *Handbook of research synthesis.* New York: Russell Sage Foundation, pp.231–244.

Rosenthal, R. and DiMatteo, M.R. 2001. Meta-analysis: Recent developments in quantitative methods for literature reviews. *Annual Review of Psychology.* **52**(1), pp.59–82.

Rosenthal, R. and Rubin, D.B. 1978. Interpersonal expectancy effects: The first 345 studies. *Behavioral and Brain Sciences.* **1**(3), pp.377–386.

Rosenthal, R. and Rubin, D.B. 1986. Meta-analytic procedures for combining studies with multiple effect sizes. *Psychological Bulletin.* **99**(3), pp.400–406.

Scheer, L.K., Miao, C.F. and Palmatier, R.W. 2015. Dependence and interdependence in marketing relationships: Meta-analytic insights. *Journal of the Academy of Marketing Science.* **43**(6), pp.694–712.

Schmidt, F.L. and Hunter, J.E. 1977. Development of a general solution to the problem of validity generalization. *Journal of Applied Psychology.* **62**(5), pp.529–540.

Schmidt, F.L. and Hunter, J.E. 2015. *Methods of meta-analysis: Correcting error and bias in research findings.* Thousand Oaks, CA: Sage.

Sharpe, D. 1997. Of apples and oranges, file drawers and garbage: Why validity issues in meta-analysis will not go away. *Clinical Psychology Review.* **17**(8), pp.881–901.

Smith, M.L. and Glass, G.V. 1977. Meta-analysis of psychotherapy outcome studies. *American Psychologist.* **32**(9), pp.752–760.

Smith, M.L., Glass, G.V. and Miller, T.I. 1980. *The benefits of psychotherapy.* Baltimore, MD: Johns Hopkins University Press.

Stone, D.L. and Rosopa, P.J. 2017. The advantages and limitations of using meta-analysis in human resource management research. *Human Resource Management Review.* **27**(1), pp.1–7.

Strazzullo, P., D'Elia, L., Kandala, N.B. and Cappuccio, F.P. 2009. Salt intake, stroke, and cardiovascular disease: Meta-analysis of prospective studies. *BMJ.* **339**, pp.1–9.

Szymanski, D.M. and Henard, D.H. 2001. Customer satisfaction: A meta-analysis of the empirical evidence. *Journal of the Academy of Marketing Science.* **29**(1), pp.16–35.

Toufaily, E., Ricard, L. and Perrien, J. 2013. Customer loyalty to a commercial website: Descriptive meta-analysis of the empirical literature and proposal of an integrative model. *Journal of Business Research.* **66**(9), pp.1436–1447.

Wit, L., Luppino, F., van Straten, A., Penninx, B., Zitman, F. and Cuijpers, P. 2010. Depression and obesity: A meta-analysis of community-based studies. *Psychiatry Research.* **178**(2), pp.230–235.

World Bank. 2016. World Bank data: Country classifications [by income]. Retrieved from: https://www.acpe-accredit.org/pdf/World_Bank_Data_CountryClassification.pdf.

Zhao, H., Luo, Y. and Suh, T. 2004. Transaction cost determinants and ownership-based entry mode choice: A meta-analytical review. *Journal of International Business Studies.* **35**(6), pp.524–544.

ANNOTATED FURTHER READING

For more details about meta-analytic research, see the seminal works of Borenstein et al. (2009), Cooper et al. (2009), and Hunter and Schmidt (2004).

6. Experimental design in marketing research

Sumeyra Duman

SUMMARY

This chapter aims to discuss experimental design in marketing research through a theoretical perspective by providing examples from scholarly articles. The chapter includes topics of causal analysis, validity (both internal and external), types of experimental designs, and ethical aspects of experimental designs in marketing research.

INTRODUCTION

Many marketing managers enjoy making causal statements such as, "The new advertising campaign has resulted in a 10 percent increase in sales" (Kinnear and Taylor, 1995). However, in marketing we can never prove causality; we can only infer a cause-and-effect relationship (Malhotra and Birks, 2003). There may be several other reasons for an increase in sales, such as changing economic conditions, more effective distribution channels, etc. Marketing managers and researchers should be very cautious about these types of causal statements. Experiments are the fundamental research tools used to help identify cause-and-effect relationships. Experimental design has received considerable attention from marketing researchers and is a highly debated topic in terms of reliability and validity. It is therefore of critical importance to know the procedural rules of experimental design before conducting any experiment.

This chapter endeavors to contribute to the marketing research literature and provide practical examples and recommendations for marketing managers in terms of experimental research. The chapter starts by explaining the meaning of and conditions needed for causality, and continues with the principles of experiments. Internal and external validity, which are critical aspects of experiments, are outlined with the focus on confounding factors. Categorization of experiments is then presented in detail with examples from the literature, and the chapter ends with ethical aspects of experimental research in marketing.

1.   CAUSALITY

The scientific notion of causality implies that we can never prove that X causes Y. At best, we can only infer that X is one of the causes of Y, in that it makes the occurrence of Y probable (Malhotra et al., 2017). Correlation does not prove causation. This is so because we may not know which variable came first or whether alternative explanations for the presumed effect exist (Shadish et al., 2002). The goal of experimental design is the confidence it gives the researcher that the experimental treatment is the cause of the effect measured (Banks, 1964).

Three conditions are required to talk about causality (Kinnear and Taylor, 1995; Malhotra and Birks, 2003):

1.   *Concomitant variation:* The extent to which a cause X and an effect Y occur or vary together in the way predicted by the hypothesis under consideration.
2.   *Time occurrence of variables:* One event cannot cause another if it occurs after the other event. The causing event must occur either before or simultaneously with the effect. However, it is possible for each event in a relationship to be both a cause and an effect of the other event(s). For example, customers who shop frequently in a particular supermarket are more likely to have a loyalty card for that supermarket. Similarly, customers who have a loyalty card for a supermarket are likely to shop there frequently.
3.   *Elimination of other possible causal factors:* The factor or variable being investigated should be the only possible causal explanation.

The fundamental research tool used to help identify causal relationships is *experimentation*. The strength of experimentation is its ability to highlight causal inference. The weakness of experimentation is the doubt about the extent to which that causal relationship generalizes (Shadish et al., 2002). According to Kinnear and Taylor (1995), experimentation has been used successfully to provide conclusive answers to questions such as:

- Can we increase profits by servicing small accounts by mail rather than from branch stores?
- Can we increase supermarket sales of our product by obtaining additional shelf space?
- Will the addition of stannous fluoride to our toothpaste reduce users' cavities?
- Is a given newspaper advertisement more effective in color than in black and white?

- Which of several promotional techniques is most effective in selling a particular product?

When searching for causal relationships in nonexperimental situations, the researcher must proceed ex post facto – that is, observe the effect and then search for a cause. In these circumstances, we can never be completely sure of the proper time order of the occurrence of variables and the effects of other possible independent variables that have been excluded from consideration. The superiority of experiments in this regard is absolute (Kinnear and Taylor, 1995).

The following defines important concepts used in experimental research (Kinnear and Taylor, 1995; Malhotra and Birks, 2003).

Experiment: An experiment is executed when one or more independent variables are consciously manipulated or controlled by the person running the experiment, and their effect on the dependent variable(s), while controlling for the effect of extraneous variables, is measured.

Independent variables: Independent variables, or treatments, are the alternatives that are manipulated and whose effects are measured (e.g. package design, price level). The levels of these variables are determined by the researcher.

Test units: Test units are individuals, organizations or other entities to whom (or to which) the treatments are presented, and whose response to the treatments is measured (e.g. consumers, stores).

Dependent variables: Dependent variables measure the effect of independent variables on the test units (e.g. sales, preferences, awareness).

Extraneous variables: Extraneous variables are all the variables other than the treatments that affect the test units' response to the treatments. These variables can confound dependent variable measures in a way that weakens or invalidates the results of the experiment. The researcher has three possible courses of action for extraneous variables (Kinnear and Taylor, 1995):

1.   An extraneous variable may be physically controlled (e.g. price).
2.   If physical control is not possible, the assignment of treatments to test units may be randomized (e.g. randomly assign prices to all buyers).
3.   Use of specific experimental designs that accomplish this purpose.

If none of these can be accomplished, then no causal statements are possible, in which case the extraneous variable will now be called a *confounding variable*.

Experimental design: This involves the specification of (1) treatments to be manipulated, (2) test units to be used, (3) dependent variables to be measured, and (4) procedures for dealing with extraneous variables.

Control groups: In practice, a control group is sometimes defined as the group that receives the current level of marketing activity, as opposed to a group that receives no treatment at all. The control group is defined in this way because it is difficult to reduce current marketing activities such as advertising and personal selling to zero (Malhotra and Birks, 2003).

There are two types of environments in which an experiment may be conducted. The first is a *laboratory environment*, where the researcher conducts the experiment in an artificial environment constructed for the purpose of the experiment. In contrast, a *field experiment* is conducted in actual market situations. Three criteria may be used to compare lab experiments with field experiments (Kinnear and Taylor, 1995):

- *Validity:* Laboratory environments offer the researcher maximum control over possible confounding variables, and therefore have higher internal validity. However, there is a loss of generalizability to more realistic situations. Field experiments have lower internal validity but higher external validity.
- *Cost:* Laboratory experiments are generally less expensive than field experiments. They tend to be smaller in size, shorter in duration, and much easier to administer.
- *Time:* Laboratory experiments require less time to execute.

The balance between internal validity and external validity depends on the researcher's objectives. If internal validity is more critical, a well-designed lab experiment will suffice. However, if generalizability has greater meaning, then field experiment is recommended. If both are needed, then a lab experiment followed by a field experiment may be conducted and the results should support each of the experimental designs (Gegez, 2014).

2.   INTERNAL VALIDITY

Internal validity is the minimum validity concern that must be present in an experiment before any conclusions about experimental effects are made. It refers to whether the manipulation of the independent variables or treatments actually caused the observed effects on the dependent variables (Malhotra and Birks, 2003).

2.1   Extraneous Variables

Relevant to internal validity, we can talk about seven classes of extraneous variables which, if not controlled in the experimental design, might produce effects confounded with the effect of the experimental stimulus. They represent the following effects (Campbell and Stanley, 1963; Kinnear and Taylor, 1995; Zikmund, 1998; Malhotra and Birks, 2003):

1. *History* – the specific events occurring between the first and second measurements in addition to the experimental variable. The greater the time interval between observations, the greater the chance of history's confounding an experiment of this type. A special case of history effects is the *cohort effect*, which refers to a change in the dependent variable that occurs because members of one experimental group experienced different historical situations than members of other experimental groups.
2. *Maturation* is similar to history but refers to changes in the experimental units themselves that occur through time, including growing older, growing hungrier, becoming more experienced, growing more tired, and the like. Tracking and market studies that span several months are vulnerable to maturation since it is difficult to know how respondents are changing over time.
3. *Testing* – the effects of taking one test on the scores of a second test. There are two kinds of testing effect. The first is the *direct* or *main testing effect*, which occurs when the first observation affects the second observation. For example, respondents completing a pretreatment questionnaire and asked to complete the same questionnaire after treatment may respond differently, which then compromises internal validity. The second testing effect is related to external validity and is called the *reactive* or *interactive testing effect*. Here, the test unit's pretreatment measurement affects the reaction to the treatment, which negatively affects generalizability. To avoid the effects of testing, an alternative form of measuring instrument may be applied posttest, which may result in instrumentation effect.
4. *Instrumentation*, in which changes to the measuring instrument or in the observers or scorers used may produce changes in the obtained measurements.

5. *Statistical regression* effects occur when test units with extreme scores move closer to the average during the course of the experiment. This has a confounding effect on the results because the observed effect may be attributable to statistical regression rather than to the treatment.
6. *Selection bias* – biases resulting in differential selection of respondents for the comparison groups; in other words, assigning test units to treatment groups in such a way that the groups differ on the dependent variable prior to the presentation of treatments. If test units self-select their own groups or are assigned to groups based on researcher judgment, the possibility of selection bias exists. Test units should be randomly assigned to treatment groups.
7. *Mortality*, or differential loss of respondents from comparison groups (i.e. test units withdrawing from the experiment while it is in progress). This may happen for several reasons, such as test units refusing to continue in the experiment.

These extraneous variables constitute rival hypotheses that the researcher is testing. The effects of these variables should be minimized to not confound the results. According to Malhotra and Birks (2003), there are four ways of controlling extraneous variables: randomization, matching, statistical control, and design control.

- *Randomization:* refers to the random assignment of test units to experimental groups by random numbers. Treatment conditions are also randomly assigned to experimental groups.
- *Matching:* involves comparing test units on a set of key background variables before assigning them to the treatment conditions.
- *Statistical control:* involves measuring the extraneous variables and adjusting for their effects through statistical analysis. Analysis of covariance (ANCOVA) can be used to statistically control the effects of the confounding variable on the dependent variable (Kinnear and Taylor, 1995). In ANCOVA, the effects of the extraneous variable on the dependent variable are removed by an adjustment of the dependent variable's mean value within each treatment condition (Malhotra and Birks, 2003).
- *Design control:* involves the use of experiments designed to control specific extraneous variables.

3.   EXTERNAL VALIDITY

External validity is concerned with the "generalizability" of experimental results (Kinnear and Taylor, 1995). Threats to external validity arise when the specific set of experimental conditions does not realistically take into account the interactions of other relevant variables in the real world (Malhotra and Birks, 2003). The factors jeopardizing external validity or representativeness are as follows (Campbell and Stanley, 1963):

1.   The *reactive* or *interaction effect* of testing, in which a pretest might increase or decrease the respondent's sensitivity or responsiveness to the experimental variable, and thus make the results obtained for a pretested population unrepresentative of the effects of the experimental variable for the unpretested universe from which the experimental respondents were selected.
2.   The *interaction* effects of *selection* biases and the *experimental variable*.
3.   *Reactive effects of experimental arrangements*, which would preclude generalization about the effect of the experimental variable upon persons being exposed to it in nonexperimental settings.
4.   *Multiple-treatment interference* is likely to occur whenever multiple treatments are applied to the same respondents. This is because the effects of prior treatments are not usually erasable.

3.1   Reliability

Experimental design reliability is the degree to which the design and its procedures can be replicated and achieve similar conclusions about hypothesized relationships (Hair et al., 2000). Internal reliability is hard to achieve in marketing research since the results of the experiment should be able to be generalized beyond the specific conditions of the initial experiment.

4.   EXPERIMENTAL DESIGNS

There is a set of symbols commonly used for experimental designs in marketing research (Kinnear and Taylor, 1995; Malhotra and Birks, 2003):

- *X:* exposure of a test group to an independent variable, treatment, or event whose effects are to be determined

- *O:* observation or measurement of the dependent variable on the test units
- *R:* the random assignment of test units or groups to separate treatments
- *E:* treatment effect.

In addition to the symbols themselves, their presentation also has specific meanings, for example:

- Movement from left to right indicates movement through time.
- Symbols that are horizontal refer to a specific treatment group.
- Symbols that are vertical to one another refer to activities or events that occur simultaneously (Kinnear and Taylor, 1995).

4.1 Classification of Experimental Designs

Experimental designs can be classified as *pre-experimental, true experimental, quasi-experimental, and statistical designs* (Figure 6.1).

Pre-experimental designs do not employ randomization procedures for extraneous factors. In true experimental designs, the researcher can randomly assign test units to experimental groups and treatments to experimental groups. Quasi-experimental designs result when the researcher is unable to achieve full manipulation scheduling or allocation of treatments to test units, but can still apply for some of the experimental procedure. Statistical design is a series of basic experiments that allow for statistical control and analysis of external variables (Malhotra and Birks, 2003).

4.1.1 Pre-experimental designs
Pre-experimental designs are characterized by an absence of randomization. There are three pre-experimental designs: the one-shot case study, the one-group pretest-posttest design, and the static-group design.

The one-shot case study The one-shot case study is symbolically represented as:

$$X \quad O_1$$

A single group of test units is first exposed to a treatment X, and then a measurement is taken on the dependent variables. There is no random assignment (R) of test units to the treatment group. Subjects or test units participate because of voluntary self-selection or arbitrary assignment (Zikmund, 1998). The level of O is the result of many uncontrolled

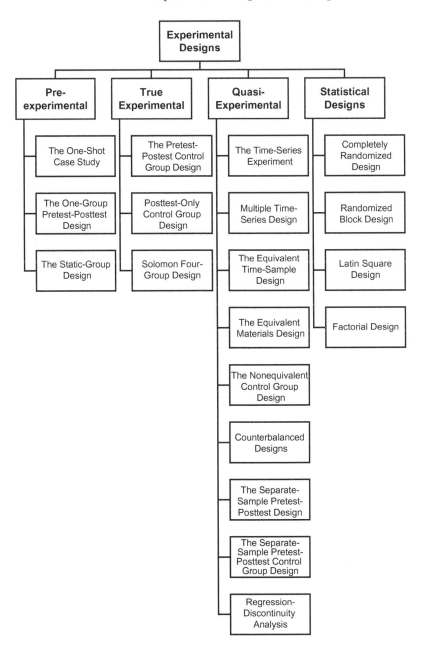

Source: Adapted from Malhotra and Birks (2003:269).

Figure 6.1   Classification of experimental designs

factors; thus history, maturation, selection, and mortality problems all cause this design to be internally invalid. For these reasons, the one-shot case study is more appropriate for exploratory than for conclusive research (Malhotra and Birks, 2003). An example of this design is managing the sales performance of salespeople after they have undertaken a new sales training program. In this type of measurement, performance after the training might be due to many uncontrolled conditions. Similarly, a new window design can be arranged in a store and, after a certain period, sales can be measured.

The one-group pretest-posttest design Here a pretest measurement is added to the one-shot case study design, and this design can be symbolized as:

$$O_1 \quad X \quad O_2$$

A number of extraneous variables could explain the difference $O_2 - O_1$. Even if the units were assigned to the treatments randomly, all sources of invalidity except selection would apply. As Leon and Cuesta (1993) articulated, seasonality may play a crucial role on performance for this type of design, and this design may even cause misleading results.

The static-group design In this design, a group which has experienced X is compared to one which has not, in order to establish the effect of X. Test units are not randomly assigned to groups (Campbell and Stanley, 1963; Kinnear and Taylor, 1995):

Experimental Group:	X	O_1
Control Group:		O_2

$$E = (O_1 - O_2)$$

An example is the comparison of school systems that require teachers to have a bachelor's degree (X) versus those which do not. This design instances no formal means of certifying that the groups would have been equivalent had it not been for X. This absence, indicated by the dashed line separating the two groups, provides the next factor needing control, i.e. selection. Another confounded variable for this design can be experimental mortality due to the differential drop-out of persons from the groups.

4.1.2   True experimental designs

The difference between pre-experimental designs and true experimental designs is that, in true experimental designs the researcher randomly assigns test units to experimental groups and treatments to experimental groups. True experimental designs include three designs: pretest-posttest control group design; posttest-only control group design; and Solomon four-group design.

Pretest-posttest control group design   In pretest-posttest control group design, test units are randomly assigned to either an experimental or a control group and a pretest measurement is taken on each group. Then, the treatment is applied to the experimental group and a posttest is measured for both groups (Malhotra and Birks, 2003). This design is presented symbolically as:

Experimental Group: R O_1 X O_2

Control Group: R O_3 O_4

$$E = (O_2 - O_1) - (O_4 - O_3)$$

This design calls for simultaneity of experimental and control sessions. If we actually run sessions simultaneously, then different experimenters must be used, and experimenter differences can become a form of intrasession history confounded with X. The optimal solution is a randomization of experimental occasions (Campbell and Stanley, 1963). The random assignment of test units to the treatment groups eliminates selection bias. All potential destroyers of internal validity are controlled by this design. The important point is that the experimenter does not care what extraneous variables are operative so long as they operate equally on all treatment and control groups (Kinnear and Taylor, 1995). A major difficulty with this design is the effect of the pretest measurement on the test's reaction to the treatment (the interactive testing effect), which creates doubts about generalizability (Kinnear and Taylor, 1995).

Beltramini and Bridge (2001) utilized this design to test the relationship between tobacco advertising and youth smoking by exploring the effectiveness of a single school-based antismoking intervention program. Another cause-related study (Pennings et al., 2014) – this time about the impact of an educational nutrition booklet on nutrition label-gazing using eye-tracker methodology – found significant results through this design.

Posttest-only control group design   This design is depicted as:

$$\text{Experimental Group:}\quad R\quad X\quad O_1$$

$$\text{Control Group:}\qquad\quad R\qquad\ O_2$$

$$E = (O_1 - O_2)$$

It is assumed that the two groups are similar in terms of pretreatment measures on the dependent variable because of the random assignment of test units to groups (Malhotra and Birks, 2003).

Since there is no pretest in this design, the interactive testing effect cannot occur (Kinnear and Taylor, 1995). This design is sensitive to selection bias and mortality, which can be controlled by carefully designed experimental procedures. Examination of individual cases is often not of interest. On the other hand, this design processes significant advantages in terms of time, cost, and sample size requirements. That is why this is the most popular design in marketing research (Malhotra and Birks, 2003).

Webster and Kinard (2014) used a randomized posttest-only control group design to explore the extent to which the priming of a consumer's regulatory orientation, or motivation toward promotion (to achieve positive outcomes) or prevention (to avoid negative outcomes), significantly affects their food portion size change intentions. Another example is Herrmann et al.'s (2016) posttest-only control group design to examine the awareness of fans and non-fans (of a soccer team) of the sponsorship link and their subsequent patronizing behaviors in response to a sponsor's promotional direct mail mentioning (or not) this sponsorship link.

Garnefeld et al. (2018) analyzed the effects of extension of sales promotions *ex post* through four experimental studies. One of these designs involved posttest-only control group design and showed that the extension did not stimulate customers' intention to repurchase.

Solomon four-group design   The Solomon four-group design (1949) combines the pretest-posttest control group and posttest-only control group designs, and is depicted as follows:

$$\text{Experimental group 1:}\quad R\quad O_1\quad X\quad O_2$$

$$\text{Control group 1:}\qquad\quad R\quad O_3\qquad\ O_4$$

$$\text{Experimental group 2:}\quad R\qquad\quad X\quad O_5$$

$$\text{Control group 2:}\qquad\quad R\qquad\qquad\ O_6$$

Treatment effect (E) could be judged by:

$$E = (O_2 - O_1)$$
$$E = (O_2 - O_4)$$
$$E = (O_5 - O_6)$$
$$E = (O_5 - O_3)$$
$$E = [(O_2 - O_1) - (O_4 - O_3)]$$

If all Es are similar, the cause-and-effect relationship is highly valid.

By paralleling the pretest-posttest control group design with experimental and control groups lacking the pretest, both the main effects of testing and the interaction of testing and X are determinable. In this way, not only is generalizability increased but, in addition, the effect of X is replicated in four different ways: $O_2 > O_1$, $O_2 > O_4$, $O_5 > O_6$, and $O_5 > O_3$ (Campbell and Stanley, 1963). The Solomon four-group design can determine the effect of pretest sensitization on posttest levels and, as such, provides a level of control for threats to validity (Walton Braver and Braver, 1988). Even though this design controls all extraneous variables and the interacting effect, it has practical limitations. It is expensive and time-consuming to implement, and therefore is not very widely used in marketing practice (Kinnear and Taylor, 1995; Malhotra and Birks, 2003).

When analyzing the literature, among the studies that utilized this design, Yin and Özdinç (2017) examined the influence of market practices targeting consumer budget and health-related motivation for food purchase in six Solomon four-group designs. The findings show that price discounts play a crucial role in the purchase intentions of normal-weight buyers. Beltramini (1992) measured the effectiveness of business gifts on customers' likelihood of contacting the donor company through a Solomon four-group design. Rutledge and Deshpande (2015) utilized Solomon four-group design to explain the effects of time orientation on consumer debt and saving behavior.

4.1.3 Quasi-experimental designs

A quasi-experimental design is one where the researcher has control over data collection procedures (e.g. the "when" and "to whom" of measurement) but lacks complete control over the scheduling of the treatments (e.g. the "when" and "to whom" of exposure) and also lacks the ability to randomize test units' exposure to treatments (Kinnear and Taylor, 1995). Quasi-experimental designs are useful because they can be employed in cases when true experimentation cannot be used, and because they are quicker and less expensive (Malhotra and Birks, 2003). Quasi-experimental designs include nine designs: time-series experiment, multiple time-series design, equivalent time-sample design, equivalent materials design, nonequivalent control group design, counterbalanced designs, separate-sample pretest-posttest design, separate-sample pretest-posttest control group design, and regression-discontinuity analysis.

Time-series experiment   This design undertakes periodic measurement of the dependent variables for some test units. The treatment is then introduced, and the periodic measurements are continued on the same test units in order to monitor the effects of the treatment (Kinnear and Taylor, 1995).

$$O_1 \qquad O_2 \qquad O_3 \quad X \quad O_4 \qquad O_5 \qquad O_6$$

An example of this type of design is consumer panels where the customer-purchasing pattern is analyzed. The fundamental weakness in this design is the experimenter's inability to control history. In addition, the interactive testing effect from repeated measures may cause the test units to become experts, thus making generalization more difficult (Kinnear and Taylor, 1995).

As an example of this design, we can look at Jue et al.'s (2012) study, which utilized a time-series experiment to examine the efficacy of five interventions (e.g. price discounts and novel presentations of calorie information) for shifting consumers toward zero-calorie beverages.

Multiple time-series design   In some studies utilizing time-series designs, another group of test units acting as a control group is added to the design:

Experimental Group:	O_1	O_2	O_3	X	O_4	O_5	O_6
Control Group:	O_7	O_8	O_9		O_{10}	O_{11}	O_{12}

The main problem with this design lies in the possibility of an interactive effect in the experimental group (Kinnear and Taylor, 1995). The experimental effect is in a sense demonstrated twice – once against the control and once against the pre-X values (Campbell and Stanley, 1963).

Murry et al. (1993) analyzed the impact of a mass media advertising campaign on anti-drinking and driving through multiple time-series design and found significant reduction in youth male drinking and driving behavior and traffic accidents. Wagenaar et al. (2005), through multiple time-series community trials, found that enforcement checks on alcohol outlets were significant in preventing alcohol sales to minors.

Equivalent time-sample design   The most usual form of experimental design employs an equivalent sample of people to provide a baseline against which to compare the effects of the experimental variable (Campbell and Stanley, 1963):

$$O \qquad X_1O \qquad X_0O \qquad X_1O \qquad X_0O$$

This design can be seen as a form of time-series experiment with the repeated introduction of the experimental variable (Campbell and Stanley, 1963). It serves as an alternative to finding a control group as the experimental group serves as its own control; for example, testing the effect of in-store conditions, such as music, on total purchases per customer. You can use a single store, whose customers make up the test units, and utilize equivalent sets of days with and without music over a period of time (Kinnear and Taylor, 1995).

Equivalent materials design   Similar to the equivalent time-sample design, this design bases its arguments on the equivalence of samples of materials to which the experimental variables being compared are applied (Campbell and Stanley, 1963):

$$M_aX_1O \qquad M_bX_0O \qquad M_cX_1O \qquad M_dX_0O \qquad \text{etc.}$$

Nonequivalent control group design   Here an experimental group and a control group are both given a pretest and a posttest, but the groups do not have pre-experimental sampling equivalence. Rather, the groups constitute naturally assembled collectives (such as classrooms) as similar as availability permits but not so similar that one can dispense with the pretest. The assignment of X to one group or the other is assumed to be random and under the experimenter's control (Campbell and Stanley, 1963). This design can be presented as:

$$
\begin{array}{lccc}
\text{Experimental Group:} & O_1 & X & O_2 \\
\text{Control Group:} & O_3 & & O_4
\end{array}
$$

This is a quasi-experimental design because the groups were not created by the random assignment of test units from a single population. In this design, the researcher has control over who is exposed to the treatment. If the groups are similar to each other, then this design can effectively control the effects of history, maturation, main attesting, instrumentation, selection, and test unit mortality.

Anand (1987) utilized this design to understand a franchisee's choice of attribution for their performance, and found that it is dependent on the behavior of other franchisees and their performance. Simester et al. (2000) adopted a nonequivalent control group design with nonequivalent dependent measures to test a multinational company's customer satisfaction improvement program in separate regions (the United States and China), and recommended this type of design for industrial use.

Counterbalanced designs   This heading encompasses all those designs in which experimental control is achieved or precision enhanced by entering all respondents (or settings) into all treatments (Campbell and Stanley, 1963). Half of the subjects are exposed to treatment A first and then to treatment B, while the other half receives treatment B first and then treatment A (Zikmund, 1998). Counterbalanced designs are depicted as:

X_1O	X_2O	X_3O	X_4O
X_2O	X_4O	X_1O	X_3O
X_3O	X_1O	X_4O	X_2O
X_4O	X_3O	X_2O	X_1O

Halford et al. (2007) conducted a within-subject counterbalanced design to investigate the effect of television food advertising on children's food intake. They stated that all children in the experimental group increased their consumption of high-fat and/or sweet, energy-dense snacks, and that the increase was largest for obese children. To examine the effects of brand metaphors on brand vividness, brand differentiation, and consumer preference, Noble et al. (2013) used a $3 \times 3 \times 3$ mixed factorial counterbalanced design – (form: human, animal, nonmetaphor) × (name: human, animal, nonmetaphor) × (logo: human, animal, nonmetaphor). They found that the consistency of brand metaphor application and the use of animal-based metaphors had a significant influence on key outcomes.

Separate-sample pretest-posttest design   For large populations one can exercise something like full experimental control over the when and to whom of the O, employing random assignment procedures (Campbell and Stanley, 1963). This design is depicted as:

R   O   (X)
R   X   O

The rows represent randomly equivalent subgroups, the parenthetical X standing for a presentation of X irrelevant to the argument. One sample is measured prior to X, and an equivalent one subsequent to X (Campbell and Stanley, 1963). The seminal study by Downs and Haynes (1984) used this design for retail image determinants. The study revealed that retail attributes such as store classification, quality of merchandise, assortment, store layout, and decor led to significant attitudinal changes for consumers.

Separate-sample pretest-posttest control group design   If there are comparable groups from which X can be withheld, then a control group can be added (Campbell and Stanley, 1963). This type of design is represented symbolically as:

Experimental Group:	R	O	(X)	
	R		X	O
Control Group:	R	O		
	R			O

This is similar to the nonequivalent control group design, except that the same specific persons are not retested, and thus the possible interaction of testing and X is avoided.

Regression-discontinuity analysis   Assignment in a regression-discontinuity (R-D) design is not random, and test units that receive treatment will differ systematically from those that do not. However, we have specific knowledge about the assignment rule that influences how persons are assigned to or selected for treatment. More specifically, the design requires that there is a known cut-off point in treatment assignment or in the probability of treatment receipt as a function of one or more continuous assignment variables, generating a discontinuity in the treatment receipt rate at that point (Van Der Klaauw, 2008). Hartmann et al. (2011) provide a comprehensive discussion on the usage of R-D analysis for causal marketing mix effects, and state that R-D methods are suitable for targeted marketing context.

4.1.4   Statistical designs
After examining the design procedures to make proper causal inferences, the issue of statistical significance in experimentation – more specifically

the procedures that allow determination when a measured effect is greater than that due to sampling error – will now be discussed (Kinnear and Taylor, 1995). Statistical designs offer the following advantages (Malhotra and Birks, 2003):

1. The effects of more than one independent variable can be measured.
2. Specific extraneous variables can be statistically controlled.
3. Economical designs can be formulated when each test unit is measured more than once.

The most widely used statistical designs are completely randomized design, randomized block design, Latin square design, and factorial design.

Completely randomized design   A completely randomized design is the simplest type of experiment and is useful when the researcher is investigating the effect of one independent variable. This independent variable should be a nominal scale, so that it may have categories. Each category will be a treatment. The test units are randomly assigned to each category (Kinnear and Taylor, 1995). This type of design may be suitable for an initial exploratory analysis (Schroeter et al., 2016).

Boisvert and Burton (2011) utilized this design to test and model the effect of parent brand salience, branding strategy, and extension innovativeness positioning on the extent of transfer of associations from parent brand to brand extension. They manipulated three factors – parent brand salience, product innovativeness, and branding strategy – and found that all three factors jointly influence the extent of transfer of associations from a parent brand to an extension.

Randomized block design   This design is built upon the principle of combining test units into blocks based on an external criterion variable. These blocks are formed with the anticipation that the test unit scores on the dependent variable within each block will be more homogeneous, in the absence of treatment, than those of test units selected at random from all test units (Kinnear and Taylor, 1995).

A randomized block design is useful when there is only one major external variable – such as sales, store size, or income of the respondents – that might influence the dependent variable (Malhotra and Birks, 2003).

The fundamental reason for doing blocking is to allow the researcher to obtain a measure of sampling error smaller than that which would result from a completely randomized design. The number of variables used to create a blocking factor can be extended beyond two. The problem is that the number of blocks required in the blocking factor increases as a multiplicative function of the number of categories in the external variables used. The other problem with blocking by using more than one external variable is that the researcher can measure only the overall effect of the blocking factor. The separate effects of the variables defining the blocking factor cannot be isolated. A possible partial solution to this problem is the Latin square design (Kinnear and Taylor, 1995).

Latin square design   In situations where the researcher wishes to control and measure the effects of two extraneous variables, the Latin square design may be used (Kinnear and Taylor, 1995).

Each external or blocking variable is divided into an equal number of blocks or levels. The independent variable is also divided into the same number of levels. The assignment rule is that each level of independent variable should appear only once in each level (Malhotra and Birks, 2003). The Latin square design provides more opportunity for reducing the residual error than the randomized blocks or completely randomized design, where there are at least two major sources of variation in the experiment not subject to direct control (Cox, 1964).

Even though the Latin square design is not widely used in marketing research, Hamlin (2005) states that this type of design is a technique of simplicity, elegance, accuracy, and matchless efficiency – especially for measuring the impact of packaging and other point-of-purchase cues on low involvement consumer evaluation and decision making.

Factorial design   Factorial design is used if the researcher is interested in examining two or more independent variables. Unlike the randomized block and the Latin square designs, factorial designs allow for interactions between variables (Malhotra and Birks, 2003).

In a factorial design, the categories of the independent variables are called levels. Each level of each independent variable appears with each level of all other independent variables. If we were running an experiment with four independent variables, with 2, 3, 3, and 4 levels, respectively we would have $2 \times 3 \times 3 \times 4 = 72$ cells in our design matrix. A factorial design allows us to measure the separate effects of each variable working alone (Kinnear and Taylor, 1995).

There is one other type of effect that is important in factorial designs. This effect is used to recognize that a number of independent variables working together often have a total effect greater than the straight sum of their main effects. This is called the *interaction effect*. Interaction occurs when the relationship between an independent variable and the dependent variable is different for different categories of another independent variable. The number of interactions increases as the number of independent variables increases (Kinnear and Taylor, 1995).

Bright and Daugherty (2012)'s study utilized factorial design of 2 × 2 × 3 to examine the effect of customization, desire for control, and type of advertising on consumer attitude toward advertising, content recognition, and behavioral intention of interacting with advertising. Another study, conducted by Keusch (2012), utilized full factorial between-subjects design to compare the effectiveness of different response-enhancing techniques in a list-based web survey. Keusch (2012) found that using a prenotification message and a female sender for contacting male sample members increases response rates; and that using an advanced questionnaire layout significantly reduces break-offs but does not influence total response.

In this section, the main experimental designs and the potential sources of invalidity of each design have been elaborated, and a summary is presented in Table 6.1.

5.   ETHICAL ISSUES IN EXPERIMENTAL DESIGN RESEARCH

Issues related to the subjects' right to be informed tend to be very prominent in experimental research. Research codes of conduct often suggest that experimental subjects should be fully informed and receive accurate information. However researchers may intentionally hide the true purpose of their experiments from the subjects and debrief the subjects after the experiment. Debriefing is the process of providing subjects with all the pertinent facts about the nature and purpose of the experiment after it has been completed (Zikmund, 1998). Briefly, the issues considered to be unethical in conducting experiments are as follows (Sekaran, 2003):

- Putting pressure on individuals to participate in experiments through coercion, or applying social pressure.
- Setting subjects mental tasks and asking demeaning questions that diminish their self-respect.
- Deceiving subjects by deliberately misleading them as to the true purpose of the research.
- Exposing participants to physical or mental stress.
- Not allowing subjects to withdraw from the research when they want to.
- Using the research results to disadvantage the participants, or for purposes not to their liking.

Table 6.1   Potential sources of invalidity of experimental designs

Design	History	Maturation	Testing	Instrumentation	Regression	Selection	Mortality	Interaction of testing and X	Interaction of selection and X	Reactive arrangements	Multiple-X interference
Pre-Experimental Designs											
One-Shot Case Study X O	–	–				–	–	–	–		
One-Group Pretest-Posttest Design O X O	–	–	–	–	?	+	+	–	–	?	
Static-Group Comparison X O O	+	?	+	+	+	–	–	–	–		
True Experimental Designs											
Pretest-Posttest Control Group R O X O R O O	+	+	+	+	+	+	+	–	?	?	
Posttest-only Control Group R X O R O	+	+	+	+	+	+	+	+	?	?	
Solomon Four-Group Design R O X O R O O R X O R O	+	+	+	+	+	+	+	+	?	?	
Quasi-Experimental Designs											
Time-Series O O O X O O O	–	+	+	?	+	+	+	–	?	?	
Multiple Time-Series O O O X O O O O O O O O O	+	+	+	+	+	+	+	–	–	?	
Equivalent Time-Sample O X_1O X_0O X_1O X_0O	+	+	+	+	+	+	+	–	?	–	–

165

(*Continued*)

Table 6.1 Continued

Design	Internal variables								External variables		
	History	Maturation	Testing	Instrumentation	Regression	Selection	Mortality	Interaction of testing and X	Interaction of selection and X	Reactive arrangements	Multiple-X interference
Equivalent Materials MaX_1O MbX_0O McX_1O MdX_0O etc.	+	+	+	+	+	+	+	−	?	?	−
Nonequivalent Control Group O_1 X O_2 O_3 O_4	+	+	+	+	?	+	+	−	?	?	
Counterbalanced Designs X_1O X_2O X_3O X_4O X_2O X_4O X_1O X_3O X_3O X_1O X_4O X_2O X_4O X_3O X_2O X_1O	+	+	+	+	+	+	+	?	?	?	−
Separate-Sample Pretest-Posttest R O (X) R X O	−	−	+	?	+	+	−	+	+	+	
Separate-Sample Pretest-Posttest Control Group R O (X) R X O R O R O	+	+	+	+	+	+	+	+	+	+	
Regression Discontinuity	+	+	+	?	+	+	?	+	−	+	+

Note: A minus sign indicates a definite weakness; a plus sign indicates that the factor is controlled; a question mark denotes a possible source of concern; and a blank means that the factor is not relevant.

Source: Adapted from Campbell and Stanley (1963).

166

- Not explaining the procedures to be followed in the experiment.
- Exposing respondents to hazardous and unsafe environments.
- Not debriefing participants fully and accurately after the experiment is over.
- Not preserving the privacy and confidentiality of the information given by the participants.
- Withholding benefits from control groups.

Many educational institutions require approval from a committee responsible for ensuring that any research is done within ethical frameworks. Researchers aiming to conduct experimental research must obey these ethical principles.

6. PERSONAL EXPERIENCE

Along with a colleague from the same university, we conducted a one-shot case study which aimed to analyze the applicability of Theory of Reasoned Action and mediating effect of intention to purchase three distinct types of Islamic brand; a true Islamic brand, an inbound Islamic brand, and a Turkish brand with a halal certificate (Ozgen and Duman Kurt, 2013). Since this was a preliminary study and exploratory in nature, this type of design suited the objective of the study; but, due to so many extraneous variables being valid for this design, the study cannot be interpreted as a satisfying causal research. Even though this was the first experimental study in the related field, this type of design does not include a control group, which jeopardizes validity. In addition, the test units (students) participated on a voluntary basis, which created a random sampling error. The fact that the experiment was conducted by us led to serious concerns about whether the test units were objectively responding to the research questions. This was because, first, the students were familiar with us as their instructors; and, second, the topic was highly sensitive and should have been measured in a more discreet way. This was a great opportunity for us to see how difficult it is to conduct experiments; in other words, the researcher should show foresight in designing the experiment by taking cognizance of the validity criteria for experimental designs.

7. DISCUSSION

Experimental research allows the researcher to test causal relationships among variables. The independent variable is manipulated to determine the effect on the dependent variable. In experimental designs, it is critical to consider internal and external validity. The extraneous variables should be controlled by the researcher in order to design a valid experiment.

There are many different types of experimental designs mentioned in this chapter. Therefore, researchers should be very cautious in choosing the type of experiment to be utilized. This decision may depend on several issues, such as the objective of the study, the nature of the test units, the applicability of the design, and the researcher's ability to control extraneous variables. Last but not least, ethical issues in conducting experiments should be strictly obeyed by the researcher.

This chapter aimed to provide a theoretical background on experimental design in marketing research using examples from scholarly articles. The advantages and disadvantages of various experimental designs are elucidated to present a guideline not only for researchers but also for marketing managers.

REFERENCES

Anand, P. 1987. Inducing franchisees to relinquish control: an attribution analysis. *Journal of Marketing Research*, **24**(2), pp.215–221.

Banks, S. 1964. Designing marketing research to increase validity. *Journal of Marketing*, **28**(4), pp.32–40.

Beltramini, R. F. 1992. Exploring the effectiveness of business gifts: a controlled field experiment. *Journal of the Academy of Marketing Science*, **20**(1), pp.87–91.

Beltramini, R. F. and Bridge, P. D. 2001. Relationship between tobacco advertising and youth smoking: assessing the effectiveness of a school-based antismoking intervention program. *Journal of Consumer Affairs*, **35**(2), pp.263–277.

Boisvert, J. and Burton, S. 2011. Towards a better understanding of factors affecting transfer of brand associations. *Journal of Consumer Marketing*, **28**(1), pp.57–66.

Bright, L. F. and Daugherty, T. 2012. Does customization impact advertising effectiveness? An exploratory study of consumer perceptions of advertising in customized online environments. *Journal of Marketing Communications*, **18**(1), pp.19–37.

Campbell, D. T. and Stanley, J. C. 1963. *Experimental and quasi-experimental designs for research*. Rand McNally: Chicago.

Cox, K. 1964. The responsiveness of food sales to shelf space changes in supermarkets. *Journal of Marketing Research*, **1**(2), pp.63–67.

Downs, P. E. and Haynes, J. B. 1984. Examining retail image before and after a repositioning strategy. *Journal of the Academy of Marketing Science*, **12**(4), pp.1–24.

Garnefeld, I., Böhm, E., Klimke, L. and Oestreich, A. 2018. I thought it was over, but now it is back: customer reactions to ex post time extensions of sales promotions. *Journal of the Academy of Marketing Science*, **46**(11), pp.1133–1147.

Gegez, E. 2014. *Pazarlama Araştırmaları*. Beta Basım: İstanbul.

Hair, J. F., Bush, R. P. and Ortinau, D. J. 2000. *Marketing research: a practical approach for the new millennium*. McGraw-Hill: Singapore.

Halford, J. C. G., Boyland, E. J., Hughes, G. M., Stacey, L., McKean, S. and Dovey, T. M. 2007. Beyond-brand effect of television food advertisements on food choice in children: the effects of weight status. *Public Health Nutrition*, **11**(9), pp.897–904.

Hamlin, R. P. 2005. The rise and fall of the Latin Square in marketing: a cautionary tale. *Journal of Marketing*, **39**(3/4), pp.328–350.

Hartmann, W., Nair, H. S. and Narayanan, S. 2011. Identifying causal marketing mix effects using a regression discontinuity design. *Marketing Science*, **30**(6), pp.1079–1097.

Herrmann, J. L., Kacha, M. and Derbaix, C. 2016. "I support your team, support me in turn!": the driving role of consumers' affiliation with the sponsored entity in explaining behavioral effects of sport sponsorship leveraging activities. *Journal of Business Research*, **69**(2), pp.604–612.

Jue, J. J., Press, M. J., McDonald, D., Volpp, K. G., Asch, D. A., Mitra, N., Stanowski, A. C. and Loewenstein, G. 2012. The impact of price discounts and calorie messaging on beverage consumption: a multi-site field study. *Preventive Medicine*, **55**(6), pp.629–633.

Keusch, F. 2012. How to increase response rates in list-based web survey samples. *Social Science Computer Review*, **30**(3), pp.380–388.

Kinnear, T. C. and Taylor, J. R. 1995. *Marketing research: an applied approach*. McGraw-Hill: New York.

Leon, F. R. and Cuesta, A. 1993. The need for quasi-experimental methodology to evaluate pricing effects. *Studies in Family Planning*, **24**(6), pp.375–381.

Malhotra, N. K. and Birks, D. 2003. *Marketing research: an applied approach*. Pearson: New York.

Malhotra, N. K., Nunan, D. and Birks, D. F. 2017. *Marketing research: an applied approach*. Pearson: New York.

Murry, J. P., Stam, A. and Lastovicka, J. L. (1993). Evaluating an anti-drinking and driving advertising campaign with a sample survey and time-series intervention analysis. *Journal of the American Statistical Association*, **88**(421), pp.50–56.

Noble, C. H., Bing, M. N. and Bogoviyeva, E. 2013. The effects of brand metaphors as design innovation: a test of congruency hypotheses. *Journal of Product Innovation Management*, **30**(S1), pp.126–141.

Ozgen, O. and Duman Kurt, S. 2013. Purchasing behavior of Islamic brands: an experimental research. *EMAC 42nd Annual Conference*. Istanbul, Turkey.

Pennings, M. C., Striano, T. and Oliverio, S. 2014. A picture tells a thousand words: impact of an educational nutrition booklet on nutrition label gazing. *Marketing Letters*, **25**, pp.355–360.

Rutledge, D. and Deshpande, S. (2015). The influence of time orientation on personal finance behaviours. In: Kubacki, K. (ed.) *Ideas in marketing: finding the new and polishing the old. Developments in marketing science: Proceedings of the Academy of Marketing Science*. Springer: Cham.

Schroeter, C., Ncholson, C. F. and Meloy, M. G. 2016. Consumer valuation of organic and conventional milk: does shelf life matter? *Journal of Food Distribution Research*, **47**(3), pp.118–133.

Sekaran, U. 2003. *Research methods for business: a skill building approach*. Wiley: New York.

Shadish, W. R., Cook, T. D. and Campbell, D. T. 2002. *Experimental and quasi-experimental designs for generalized causal inference*. Houghton Mifflin: Boston.

Simester, D. I., Hauser, J. R., Wernerfelt, B. and Rust, R. T. 2000. Implementing quality improvement programs designed to enhance customer satisfaction: quasi-experiments in the United States and Spain. *Journal of Marketing Research*, **37**(1), pp.102–112.

Solomon, R. L. 1949. An extension of control group design. *Psychological Bulletin*, **46**, pp.137–150.

Van Der Klaauw, W. 2008. Regression–discontinuity analysis: a survey of recent developments in economics. *Labour*, **22**(2), pp.219–245.

Wagenaar, A. C., Toomey, T. L. and Erickson, D. J. 2005. Preventing youth access to alcohol: outcomes from a multi-community time-series trial. *Addiction*, **100**(3), pp.335–345.

Walton Braver, M. C. and Braver, S. L. 1988. Statistical treatment of the Solomon four-group design: a meta-analytical approach. *Psychological Bulletin*, **104**(1), pp.150–154.

Webster, C. and Kinard, B. R. 2014. Explicit priming and eating behavior. *Marketing Management Association Spring 2014 Proceedings*, pp.175–179.

Yin, Y. and Özdinç, Y. 2017. Budget over health unless overweight: A Solomon four-group study. *International Journal of Consumer Studies*, **42**, pp.232–240.
Zikmund, W. C. 1998. *Essentials of marketing research*. Harcourt College Publishing: New York.

ANNOTATED FURTHER READING

For more details about experimental design in marketing research, see the seminal works of Campbell and Stanley (1963), Kinnear and Taylor (1995), and Malhotra and Birks (2003).

7. Partial Least Square Structural Equation Modelling (PLS-SEM) in marketing research

Soujata Rughoobur-Seetah, Robin Nunkoo and Viraiyan Teeroovengadum

INTRODUCTION

Research in the marketing and management areas has contributed immensely towards understanding and assessing human, customer, social media and travel dimensions, among others (e.g. French and Gordon, 2019; Landmark and Sjøbakk, 2017; Ramanathan et al., 2017; Alalwan et al., 2017; Camilleri, 2018). Most studies in these fields have adopted the positivist paradigm. The tendency for quantitative research in the marketing field prevailed for several decades before. It is interesting to note that studies in marketing emanate from diverse fields such as sociology, management, psychology and anthropology, among others. A more quantified and general approach to managing and analyzing data remains the first choice of researchers and scholars in the field. Additionally, the positivist approach is preferred as it allows the researcher to manage theoretical propositions through formal hypotheses which are tested to ensure verifiability and consistency with past empirical studies, providing explanations which help predict individuals' behavior (Neuman, 2003). The positivist approach provides a systematic way of mixing deductive reasoning with specific empirical explanations so as to provide confirmation of a series of cause-and-effect acts that might be used to predict human behavior (Neuman, 2003). According to Ulin et al. (2012), positivist researchers make use of validity, reliability, objectivity and generalizability in order to describe, forecast and confirm proposed empirical associations. These generalizations are necessary and probable, and the true causes of social scientific results can be tested for reliability and validity.

In short, the positivist approach makes use of theories for developing hypotheses that ultimately need to be tested so that they satisfy the theories' requirements to support the facts – that is: "fallibility of knowledge, indetermination of theory by fact, and a value-ladened [*sic*] inquiry process" (Sale et al., 2002, p.46). Therefore, the aim of adopting a positivist approach is to be able to measure and assess the cause-and-effect relationships among the proposed factors within a value-free framework (Denzin and Lincoln, 1994). Nevertheless, it should be recognized that scholars in the field of marketing management are diversifying in terms of the use of several other methodologies (e.g. Bilgin, 2017; Huang et al., 2019; Singh and Pathak, 2020). However, research using the positivist approach still dominates (Henseler et al., 2009; Hair et al., 2011a, 2011b, 2012b).

Despite studies in marketing management making extensive use of the quantitative approach, Structural Equation Modelling (SEM) is the covariance-based method mostly utilized by researchers in the field. Partial Least Square Structural Equation Modelling (PLS-SEM), although a new approach, is found not to be the preferred choice among such researchers. Only a few studies have used this approach to analyze their data. Among these are Hair et al. (2011a, 2011b), Shmueli et al. (2019) and Pant et al. (2020). It should be acknowledged that PLS-SEM offers a diverse range of advantages when it comes to data handling, the analysis and interpretation. The ability to handle small sample size data, formative indicators, and first- and second-order factors makes it unique in its usage. PLS-SEM also provides features such as mediation analysis using specific indirect effects providing better interpretation of the relationships among variables. Importance-Performance Map Analysis (IPMA) functionality is also a very interesting feature of PLS-SEM, where researchers are better able to evaluate the importance and performance of each variable vis-à-vis the dependent variable, which contributes to making the most appropriate recommendations. This chapter attempts to provide better guidance to upcoming scholars and researchers in the use of PLS-SEM, and to recognize the diverse features of this variance-based methodology. It has to be taken into consideration that this chapter is in no way trying to discourage the use of covariance-based methods as it only offers researchers and scholars other avenues to better manage and analyze data depending on the nature of their multidimensional frameworks.

PLS-SEM: COVARIANCE-BASED OR VARIANCE BASED

The social science literature shows considerable use of multivariate statistical techniques (Anderson and Gerbing, 1988; Nunkoo and Ramkissoon, 2012). Shook et al. (2004) defined SEM as a robust and complex analytical technique, and it is also known as a covariance-based SEM (CB-SEM). Shah and Goldstein (2006) are of the opinion that SEM is a mechanism utilized for the measurement of relationships among unobserved variables, and its use dates back to the early 20th century. According to Cheng (2001), SEM has been able to attract the attention of new scholars because it is able to create measurement and structural models. Hair et al. (1998) describe SEM as a very powerful technique that explains the study and also provides statistical efficacy for testing the model by making use of only one inclusive methodology. It is believed that SEM helps provide better explanation compared to regression models by including both dependent and independent variables. Studies in the marketing management field require multiple variables to be tested, and their inter-relationships established, in order to have a better understanding of the subject matter.

SEM comprises both observed and unobserved variables. The observed variables are known as measured variables (MVs) and the unobserved variables are referred as latent variables (LVs). The MVs act as a criterion to the LVs as the LVs cannot be measured directly (Nunkoo and Ramkissoon, 2012). These authors believe that, through the independent and dependent LVs, we can establish a linear relationship. In this view, SEM allows researchers and scholars to find explanations for the proposed relationships and inter-relationships among multiple variables, and it also takes into consideration the dependence and interdependence of the proposed relationships (Hair et al., 2006; Nunkoo and Ramkissoon, 2012). Cheng (2001) illustrated that, regarding the complexity of human and behavioral issues in management studies, SEM tries to find relationships between dependent and independent variables. SEM is said to have a very important role in terms of testing theoretical frameworks. For most scholars, SEM is similar to a covariance-based approach of testing models (Hair et al., 2014a), which is the most widespread method, especially for theory testing. Nevertheless, those authors believe that the variance-based PLS-SEM approach is also plausible as it can be related to a multiple regression analysis (Hair et al., 2011a, 2011b).

PLS-SEM was devised by Wold (1974) and is a causal modelling technique aimed at maximizing the explained variance of endogenous variables (Hair et al., 2011a, 2011b, 2014a). According to Ringle et al. (2009), PLS-SEM tends to provide better and more robust estimates of the structural model. PLS-SEM has received substantial attention in the field of strategic management (Hair et al., 2012a), marketing (Hair et al., 2012b) and strategic human resources management (Becker et al., 2012). Hulland (1999) believes that, due to the flexibility of PLS-SEM in terms of handling modelling issues, this approach has gained much popularity in research. This study is basically aimed at presenting and testing predictive powers of the model and further theory development; thus, according to Hair et al. (2011a, 2011b), PLS-SEM is the most suitable method for the same.

In addition, PLS-SEM also aims to better assess and analyze the data quality through confirmatory factor analysis (Hair et al., 2011a, 2011b). Those authors also believe that PLS-SEM provides better ways to address problems compared to covariance-based SEM. PLS-SEM is said to be able to better handle a broader range of sample sizes and cater for the density of the construct. Chin et al. (2003) argued that PLS-SEM is able to handle measurement error where the outcomes are reliable, and believed that PLS-SEM even caters for missing values and outliers. Hair et al. (2014a) argued that researchers tend to use PLS-SEM under the following conditions: first, if the data collected are non-normal, CB-SEM will tend to produce errors in terms of measurement indices (Lei and Lomax, 2005), whereas PLS-SEM tends to be less severe with non-normal data (Cassel et al., 1999; Ringle et al., 2010). Second, PLS-SEM allows for small sample size data even when the construct is very dense (Hair et al., 2014a; Ringle et al., 2010), unlike the CB-SEM. Third, PLS-SEM remains the best alternative when formative measures are involved. A number of studies have adopted PLS-SEM because of formative models (e.g. Becker et al., 2012; Hsu et al., 2006). This approach helps provide a better predictive model. Petter et al. (2007) argued that formative measures are measures that have formative indicators, which are joined for a better meaning of the LVs. Hair et al. (2014a) also pointed out that formative measures should be handled with caution as they follow more rigorous evaluation criteria when being assessed for validity of the same.

PLS-SEM AND THEORY DEVELOPMENT

PLS-SEM is said to have a very important role in testing theoretical frameworks. In particular, according to Lohmöller and Wold (1980, p.1): "PLS-SEM is primarily intended for research contexts that are simultaneously data-rich and theory skeletal ... In the process, the model extracts fresh knowledge from the data, thereby putting flesh on the theoretical bones." Bearing that in mind, PLS-SEM will facilitate the testing of proposed hypotheses, and their exploratory, confirmatory and predictive nature (Urbach and Ahlemann, 2010) will help link the empirical data to the theories. Therefore, it becomes very important to integrate proper theories in the model, which will result in better predictive power of the model. Theories acts to support the devised frameworks; therefore, it becomes very important for researchers to understand the theories and their role. This is because only through a proper understanding of these theories will the factors, the hypotheses and the data be well interpreted (Chin, 1998). Proper understanding of the theory also allows the researcher to interpret it as a set of models, and the factors are linked by the hypotheses. According to Wacker (1998, p.361), a theory must comprise the following attributes: "conceptual definitions, domain limitations, relationship-building, and predictions". Therefore, it can be postulated that the use of PLS-SEM will allow both theoretical and methodological contributions to research in the marketing management and management areas as a whole.

SmartPLS 3.0 (Ringle et al., 2015), a recognized technique for PLS-SEM, was used for the purpose of this study because it ensures that the proposed model meets the requirements of multidimensionality, validity and reliability. SmartPLS helps assess both measurement and structural models. Confirmatory factor analysis (CFA), second-order factor analysis and path analysis also form part of PLS-SEM. Davis and Weber (1985) argued that path analysis helps confirm the correlations of initial proposed relationships between dependent and independent variables. CFA, second-order factor analysis and the structural model will therefore be elaborated below.

CONFIRMATORY FACTOR ANALYSIS (CFA)

The confirmatory factor model is also referred to as the measurement model as it helps outline the items that comprise measurement of latent variables (Byrne, 1994). Observed variables are known as measured variables (MVs) and unobserved variables are referred as latent variables (LVs). Hoyle (2000) argued that CFA concerns the relationships between the measurement of constructs, indicators and factors. In order to conduct CFA, it is important to have a sound theoretical framework (Nunkoo and Ramkissoon, 2012).

According to Hair et al. (2006), there is a six-stage decision process in using SEM:

1. Defining individual hypotheses
2. Development of the overall measurement constructs
3. Formulating a study to create empirical outputs
4. An assessment of the validity of the measurement model
5. Specifying the structural model
6. Assessing the validity of the structural model.

SECOND-ORDER FACTOR ANALYSIS

Before testing the measurement model through CFA, it is important to carry out a second-order factor analysis based on the factor loadings obtained from an exploratory factor analysis (EFA). If the EFA demonstrates the presence of first- and second-order factors, a second-order factor analysis should be conducted. Jöreskog (1970) presented a second-order CFA (based on Thurstone's 1947 study), stipulating that each first-order factor should be influenced by two elements. According to Rindskopf and Rose (1988), in a second-order factor model there should be a linear relationship between at least one factor in the second order and the factors of the first order. Rindskopf and Rose (1988) also pointed out that each first-order factor should have a unique variable. Therefore, the objective of the second-order factor is to hypothesize to account for or provide an explanation in respect of the covariance among the first-order factors. In the simplest form, a second-order CFA is to confirm the construct of a study that loads into sub-constructs (Nunkoo et al., 2017). According to Chen et al. (2005), second-order models are mainly used in research frameworks where the measurement methodologies try to assess several constructs with multiple items and provide a more parsimonious and understandable model.

Past studies have strongly emphasized the advantages of second-order factor models (Chen et al., 2005). With second-order factor analysis, a better insight into the subject will be obtained as, despite hypotheses being presented in divergent ways, the related sub-constructs can be accounted for by an essential higher-order concept. Gustafsson and Balke (1993) argue that the second-order model formalized the covariance between first-order factors by explaining the covariance with lesser parameters. A second-order model helps split variance with regard to explicit factors from measurement error, thus contributing to a hypothetically error-free estimate of the variables (Nunkoo et al., 2017). Second-order factor models can be said to facilitate understanding of complex measurement structures (Eid et al., 2003). Nunkoo et al. (2017) postulated that a second-order factor analysis provides a better and clearer understanding compared to a single-factor model, and that second-order factor analysis has significant perspective in terms of promoting research on multidimensional concepts. Rindskopf and Rose (1988) also believed that the second-factor model helps in analyzing and assessing reliability and validity.

Although earlier studies made use of second-order factor analysis, several pointed out the need to better understand the level of analysis so as not to misinterpret the data collected (House et al., 1995; Klein et al., 1994, 1998; Rousseau, 1985; Vandenberg et al., 1999). After second-order factor analysis, Hair et al. (2006) prescribe following a six-stage model, the first four stages of which are covered by CFA. The authors specified that CFA is a way to test the extent to which the measured variables can be representative of a smaller number of constructs. Data obtained through CFA can demonstrate adequacy in terms of the specification of the variables with that of the actual data. Hair et al. (2006) reported that the CFA stages will offer the groundwork for further testing theories of the structural model through SEM. According to Musil et al. (1998), in CFA researchers have hypotheses that are being proposed earlier, which is in relation to LVs and other significant factors that make up the model.

According to Nunkoo and Ramkissoon (2012), the MVs selected by the researcher are a way to determine the LVs in the measurement model. The correlation of one MV to other MVs is a determining factor for correctly defining LVs. Poor correlation of the MVs will give rise to poor definition and understanding of the LVs. The link between the model and the indicators are also referred to as weights or formative indicators, and the model's link to the indicators in a reflective construct is referred to as loadings. In a formative construct, the indicators predict the LVs; that is, a causal relationship, whereas in a reflective model the LVs reflect the MVs. For this study, both formative and reflective measures will be utilized. Based on past theoretical and empirical findings, the researcher has established the hypotheses to be tested and the path coefficients (parameters) in the model.

Barclay et al. (1995) proposed the following criteria when considering sample size for PLS-SEM path modelling. Sample size is guided by the number of indicators in the scale items; it should be ten times the number of indicators of the selected scale with the greatest number of formative measures, or ten times the greatest number of structural paths leading to a specific construct in the inner model. Consequently, sample data will be used to test the model. PLS-SEM has always been considered as catering for missing values, and for this study all incomplete questionnaires were disregarded.

Cheng (2001) argued that if the proposed indicators cannot measure or are not trustworthy, the proposed model is subject to modification, that is, deletion of the indicator before the structural model is tested. Moreover, he specified that the deletion needs to be an incremental one in order to achieve the best fit model. Segars and Grover (1993) noted that any deletions should be done one after the other so as not to affect the overall model as deletion of indicators can have a significant impact on the proposed model. According to Cheng (2001), the model should be continuously subjected to modifications until the best fit is achieved. As a result, the best fit model would be able to give rise to goodness-of-fit indices and

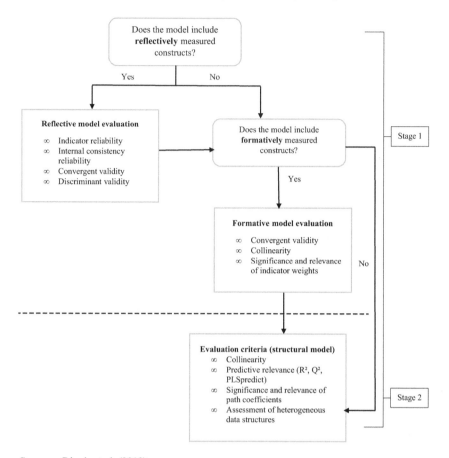

Source: Ringle et al. (2018).

Figure 7.1   Evaluation of the formative and reflective constructs

a measurement model which is theoretically sound. It is very important when analyzing the outer model (measurement model) for the researcher to be able to demarcate between reflective and formative variables (Ringle et al., 2011) as these two techniques require consideration of different concepts and measurement (Hair et al., 2014a). This study followed the pathways presented by Ringle et al. (2018), as shown in Figure 7.1.

The measurement model was further assessed based on its reliability and validity. According to Nunkoo et al. (2013), reliability is the degree to which the chosen measurements are free of errors which, as a result, will provide consistent results. Diamantopoulos and Winklhofer (2001) argued that the reflective indicators consist of an illustration of a set of all probable items of a construct. Hair et al. proposed that reliability and validity should be tested when evaluating reflective outer models: first, the internal consistency reliability should be measured through the composite reliability. Hair, Sarstedt et al. (2014, p.111) postulated that composite reliability "does not assume that all indicator loadings are equal in the population, which is in line with the working principle of the PLS-SEM algorithm that prioritizes the indicators based on their individual reliabilities during model estimation" – unlike Cronbach's alpha (Cronbach and Meehl, 1955). Through composite reliability, PLS-SEM is also able to cater for the differences that occur in the measurement loadings as well as sidestepping underestimation related to Cronbach's alpha (Hair, Gabriel et al., 2014). Hair et al. (2011a) considered a composite reliability score of greater than 0.70 to be acceptable. Nunnally and Bernstein (1994) argued that composite reliability is considered appropriate when exploratory research values lie between 0.60 and 0.70, while advanced research values should be between 0.70 and 0.90. Indicator reliability values are considered appropriate when each indicator's loadings are higher than 0.70. Consequently, according to Hair et al. (2011a), indicator loading values which are between 0.40 and 0.70 should be removed in order to enhance the composite reliability of the measurement scales of the recommended values.

CONVERGENT AND DISCRIMINANT VALIDITY

Nunkoo et al. (2013) stipulated that CFA validity is evaluated by convergent and discriminant validity. Convergent validity is calculated by the outer loadings of each indicator, which should be greater than 0.70 (Hair et al., 2014a), and by evaluating the average variance extracted (AVE), which specifies the latent variable through the amount of variance (Nunkoo et al., 2013). Hair et al. (2011a, p.145) believed that AVE should be greater than 0.50 in order to achieve convergent validity: that is, the LV provides explanation for "more than half of its indicators' variance". Hair et al. (2010) believed that an AVE of less than 0.5 indicates more errors in the observed variables compared to the explained variance by the LV on the construct.

Hair et al. (2010) also believed that discriminant validity is a means to ensure that the measurement of the construct is unique, that is, the construct is catching what other variables are not. Campbell (1960) also argued that it is important to take into consideration that a construct should not be too highly correlated with other variables and ultimately failing in terms of measurement of the construct. Farrell (2010) is of the opinion that discriminant validity is becoming more and more important when conducting SEM as proper establishment of discriminant validity helps the researcher establish proper relationships among constructs and reduce biases of results.

There are three ways to establish discriminant validity (Nunkoo et al., 2013). The first compares the squared correlation between paired constructs with that of the average variance extracted for both constructs (Fornell and Larcker, 1981). Nunkoo et al. (2013) argued that in order to find the discriminant validity it is important that, for each of the paired constructs, the squared correlation is lower than the average variance extracted values. Nunkoo et al. (2013, p.761) stated that "the second method examines the difference in the chi-square values between the unconstrained measurement model and the nested measurement model where the correlation between each pair of constructs is constrained to unity". Anderson and Gerbing (1988) believed that, for the unconstrained model, a relatively lower chi-square symbolizes the achievement of discriminant validity. Last but not least, according to Hair et al. (2011a), the third method involves examining the loadings of the indicators, which must be greater than the loadings of the other outstanding paradigms (Bagozzi and Yi, 2012).

With regard to analyzing discriminant validity, Ringle et al. (2018) believed that scholars should utilize the heterotrait–monotrait ratio (HTMT) instead of relying on poor results from the Fornell-Larcker criterion and cross loadings. Netemeyer et al. (2003) opined that the HTMT is an estimation of the correlation between constructs. Henseler et al. (2015) proposed that HTMT values should not be greater than 0.90 if the model includes constructs that are theoretically alike. For more differentiated constructs, Ringle et al. (2018) recommended an HTMT value of 0.85. They also recommended the bootstrapping approach in order to evaluate the HTMT value, which should be "statistically significantly lower than one" (2018, p.10).

For formative measures, convergent validity is required as it helps in determining whether an indicator is related to other indicators of the same construct (Hair et al., 2014a). Convergent validity is carried out by assessing the correlation between the formative measure and another reflective measure or single item measure (Hair et al., 2014a). A further step requires a test for collinearity, as high collinearity between two or more formative measures can lead to result bias (Hair et al., 2014a). The variance inflation factor (VIF) has been recommended by Ringle et al. (2018) to test collinearity. According to Hair et al. (2011a), the VIF value should be less than 5, while Kock (2015) suggested a value no greater than 3.3. The final step is to assess the importance and relevance of all the formative measures, and bootstrapping must be applied in order to evaluate the significance of the weight of each measure (Ringle et al., 2018). Ringle et al. (2018) argued that with larger sample size, the bootstrap samples should be as significantly high. It has also been proposed that the last analysis phase should be carried out using a minimum of 5000 bootstrap samples (Hair et al., 2011a).

THE STRUCTURAL MODEL

The structural model basically deals with assessment of the relationships between observed and latent variables (Hoyle, 2000). According to Cheng (2001), assessment is by simultaneous regression of the dependent variables in the structural model on their precursors. The results of the structural model might differ if the relationships between the observed and latent variables have no statistical significance or are significant in opposing directions. The model is subject to further modification until the recommended values are achieved. According to Nunkoo and Ramkissoon (2012), the structural model is a representation of the combined measurement model and the path model. The path coefficients help in establishing the relationships between the constructs (Cheng, 2001; Nunkoo and Ramkissoon, 2012). Ringle et al. (2018) argued that evaluation of the path coefficient is related to assessment of the regression coefficients.

The bootstrapping approach helps in calculating the relevance of each coefficient (Tenenhaus et al., 2005). Ringle et al. (2018) noted that studies in human resources management should also assess total effects as these will provide the calculation and comparison between the lower-order and higher-order constructs (Ringle et al., 2012). Henseler et al. (2009, p.304) argued that the total effect "copes with a frequent observation in PLS path modelling that the standardized inner path model coefficients decline with an increased number of indirect relationships, especially when mediating latent variables have a suppressor effect on the direct path." As a result, the direct relationships may become irrelevant when additional indirect relationships are included. Therefore, the authors recommend that the total effect should remain moderately constant and at significant level, which will result in better evaluation of the inner path model relationships.

The next step is to evaluate the values of R^2, which can be described as the proportion of variance in each endogenous LV. Chin (1998) recommends R^2 values of 0.67, 0.33 and 0.19 in PLS-SEM analysis as substantial, moderate and weak, respectively. Hair et al. (2011a) proposed values of 0.75, 0.50 and 0.25 for the same criteria. Henseler et al. (2009) believed that a "moderate" R^2 value is acceptable if an endogenous LV is explained by a few exogenous LVs; and if the endogenous LV is dependent on different exogenous LVs, the R^2 value should be a substantial one. The authors argued that a low R^2 value demonstrates that the theoretical foundation of the construct is poor, and that the construct is a poor illustration of the endogenous LVs. This study has followed the guidelines prescribed by Chin (1998) in assessing R^2 values. The use of Cohen's f^2 has been proposed to calculate the effect size in the path model (Henseler et al., 2009). Henseler and Fassott (2010) argued that the use of the f-test is to determine the strength of f^2 either by the addition or removal of a construct in an initially tested model. Henseler et al. (2009) believe that evaluation of f^2 is carried out as the increase in the R^2 value relative to the proportion of variance of the endogenous LV. Cohen (1988) recommended f^2 values of 0.02, 0.15 and 0.35 as small, medium and large respectively.

Following evaluation of the f^2 values, Q^2 values should be assessed in order to better evaluate the predictive power and predictive relevance of each effect of the proposed construct. Tenenhaus et al. (2005) suggested the blindfolding approach to evaluate the same. The Q^2 values are calculated by comparing the sum of the squares of prediction errors and the sum of the squares of original values. Q^2 provides better predictive power to the proposed construct (Ringle et al., 2018). According to Hair et al. (2011a), a Q^2 value greater than 0 indicates predictive power of the construct. Ringle et al. (2018) further recommend importance-performance map analysis (IPMA) as a consequent path way for PLS-SEM.

MEDIATION ANALYSIS

A mediating effect occurs when an antecedent factor influences a mediating factor which ultimately affects the dependent variable (Nitzl et al., 2016). According to Hadi et al. (2016), the bootstrap method is considered to be suitable as the mediation effects are calculated with precision. The majority of studies examined made use of Baron and Kenny's (1986) criteria to evaluate the mediation results between independent and dependent variables (Zhao et al., 2010). Yet, a lot of criticism was expressed for poor evaluation of the mediating criteria proposed by Baron and Kenny. According to Zhao et al. (2010, p.197), studies using the Baron and Kenny criteria were "terminated early in a research program or later in the review process because the data did not conform" to their proposed requirements.

PLS-SEM has provided a more detailed and in-depth understanding of the relationships that have not been supported when some hypotheses are tested. Hayes (2009) recommends a bootstrap of 5000 in order to guarantee empirical representation of the sample distribution. Hair et al. (2016) argued that a mediation effect usually occurs when a third variable/construct intercedes between two other related variables/constructs. In terms of effects, they believed that there are two types: direct effects, where two variables or constructs are linked with a single arrow; and indirect effects, when two or more direct effects are involved, which is related as the mediating effect. According to Chin (2010), the bootstrapping process with regard to indirect effect is important as information is obtained on the population distribution, which further helps to evaluate the hypotheses. Nitzl et al. (2016) reported that full mediation occurs when the indirect effect is significant (p value < 0.05) – that is, indirect effects through the mediator exist and the direct effect is not significant (p value > 0.05). According to Hair et al. (2016), partial mediation takes place when the mediator partially explains the relationship between an exogenous and an endogenous variable – that is, when both the direct and indirect effects are significant (p value < 0.05). Finally, a no effect occurs when neither direct nor indirect effects are significant (Hair et al., 2016).

Hair et al. (2016) believed that the mediation provides explanatory power of relationships between independent and dependent variables – that is, explaining the *whys* of the relationships. The mediator usually receives inputs from the independent variables and outputs from the dependent variables (Hair et al., 2014a). PLS-SEM not only takes into consideration the direct effects of the mediation; it also extends to assessing the indirect effects, particularly the specific indirect effects (Hair et al., 2017). The specific indirect effects contribute immensely to analyze the multiple mediating variables that tend to influence the relationships between two constructs (Hair et al., 2017). This led to better interpretation of the proposed relationships. The specific indirect effects have provided more understanding of the mediating factors and their significant impact on the proposed relationships. It is important to note that without the use of PLS-SEM, it would have been very difficult for researchers to assess the multiple mediating factors that influence certain proposed relationships in a given framework. Further to mediation analysis and its unique features that PLS-SEM provides, IPMA is an additional interesting feature that researchers and scholars can consider using.

IMPORTANCE-PERFORMANCE MAP ANALYSIS

Importance-performance map analysis (IPMA) has been described as an extension of the standard results of path coefficients through the addition of an element which takes into account the average values of LVs (Ringle and Sarstedt, 2016). IPMA has been found to be very rarely used in marketing management research. IPMA is a new feature that enables better evaluation of variables vis-à-vis the dependent variable, and it is mostly used for recommendation purposes. Ringle and Sarstedt (2016) noted that IPMA also compares total effects. Through the average scores of the LVs, IPMA can indicate the performance and importance of the antecedent constructs (Martilla and James, 1977). The main aim of IPMA is to detect those predecessors having both high and low average LV scores in order to evaluate their importance for the target model (Ringle and Sarstedt, 2016). Researchers have elaborated on the various advantages of using IPMA. For instance, Hock et al. (2010) pointed out that it provides an insight into the impact of the predecessor models and how management can utilize the results in order to implement better actions, thus improving management activities. The following steps prescribed by Ringle and Sarstedt (2016) can be considered a very simple and reliable method for conducting an IPMA.

1. Checking requirements
2. Computation of performance values
3. Computation of importance values
4. Creating the importance-performance map
5. Extending the IPMA on the indicator level.

Checking Requirements

The first step is to check whether all the LV values are rescaled on a range from 0 to 100 and all measures in the path model to utilize either a metric or quasi-metric measure (Sarstedt and Mooi, 2014). The coding of all the indicators is required to be in the same scale direction (Ringle and Sarstedt, 2016): the lowest score of the measure should represent the worst result and the highest score the best result.

According to Ringle and Sarstedt (2016), if the indicator coding has diverse direction compared to other indicators in the model, the indicator should be rescaled as the scores will not give the true performance. Furthermore, despite having formative or reflective measures, the outer weight scores should be positive. If the outer weights are reported to be negative, the LV values will lie in the range of −5 to 95. If the analysis reports a negative and significant outer weight, it is the researcher's responsibility to further investigate with regard to the measure and whether the direction of the scale should be reversed. If the negative outer weights are considered to be unimportant, they should be deleted. The authors also pointed out that having negative outer weights is also a result of high collinearity. Irrespective of being a reflective or formative construct, IPMA can be used on any PLS path constructs and the outer weights, especially the high weights, should be treated seriously as this gives rise to identification of managerial actions which will enhance the target model's performance (Hock et al., 2010; Ringle and Sarstedt, 2016). The processing of the reflective and formative models is conducted by linearly combining measures that formulate composite variables. The calculated composite variables are considered as inputs for processing IPMA (Ringle and Sarstedt, 2016).

Computation of Performance Values

Through the composite variables, calculation of performance values is carried out. IPMA is carried out at the construct and/or indicator level, and IPMA on the indicator level provides an average performance of the measure (Ringle and Sarstedt, 2016). IPMA allows rescaling of the scores obtained for the indicator ranging from 0 to 100, where 0 represents the lowest and 100 the highest performance (Hock et al., 2010; Ringle and Sarstedt, 2016). The scores obtained for the latent variables – either being reflective or formative which have been rescaled – is a linear arrangement of the rescaled measure and the rescaled outer weights (Ringle and Sarstedt, 2016). The rescaled weights are obtained by calculating the unstandardized weights by dividing the standardized weights by the standard deviation of its measure, and the standardized outer weights are automatically computed using a PLS path model.

Computation of Importance Values

In Step 3, the importance scores are calculated through the total effect of the established link between the constructs (Hock et al., 2010; Ringle and Sarstedt, 2016). The total effect is able to provide a better understanding in terms of whether the proposed model is comprised of other direct or indirect effects; that is, the total effect provides the sum of the direct and indirect effects. Through the IPMA importance facet, researchers are able to better analyze multifaceted constructs by adding (even several) mediating factors (Ringle and Sarstedt, 2016). Through analysis of the unstandardized effects, researchers can draw the conclusion that if the performance of a particular antecedent increases, this will lead to an increase in performance of the target construct (Hair et al., 2017). Furthermore, despite having an insignificant effect, the underlying construct needs to be retained as it may result in a substantial finding (Ringle and Sarstedt, 2016). Additionally, the path models with moderators are also supported by IPMA; however, based on the complexity of the interpretation of the total effects when including moderators, it is recommended that modera-tors not be included in the IPMA (Ringle and Sarstedt, 2016).

Creating the Importance-Performance Map

The target construct needs to be clearly defined when creating the importance-performance map. Before assessing the importance-performance map, the authors propose that researchers draw two addi-tional lines: a horizontal line to indicate the mean for performance value, and a vertical line for the mean importance value. The importance-performance map is analyzed by considering models: in the lower-right corner are those which can be considered to be improved, following by the top-right corner, lower-left corner and the top-left areas. The importance-performance map facilitates the understanding of the urgency of matters that need to be tackled at management level.

Extending the IPMA on the Indicator Level

In the final step, IPMA can be extended to assess measures as well as tap into new areas of improvement. It is proposed that the outer weights can help better explain the measure's contribution in creating the composite factor of the model. The importance-performance map is produced by the importance scores which resulted from the total effects of the measures and by the performance scores originated from the mean values of the measures (Ringle and Sarstedt, 2016).

CONCLUSION

PLS-SEM is a versatile and user-friendly approach to managing and testing data, and remains one of the most recommended methodologies for testing complex multidimensional frameworks. Since its use is con-sidered quite basic in marketing management, it is highly recommended for upcoming research in the field to use PLS-SEM – together with its additional features, such as in-depth mediation analysis – to better explain the relationships between variables. Mediation analysis, together with the component on direct, indirect and specific indirect effects, allows more comprehension of multidimensional frameworks and more theory development. Theory development as one of the fundamentals when dealing with complex models permits more contribution to the existing literature as scholars and researchers are able to extract and test theories from diverse fields. Furthermore, IPMA can be exploited by marketing management practitioners to assess to what extent one factor should be given due consideration when evaluating its relationship with the dependent variable. Finally, this chapter has attempted to explain the use of PLS-SEM step-wise and outline the many benefits of this methodology.

REFERENCES

Alalwan, A.A., Rana, N.P., Dwivedi, Y.K. and Algharabat, R., 2017. Social media in marketing: A review and analysis of the existing literature. *Telematics and Informatics*, *34*(7), pp.1177–1190.

Anderson, J.C. and Gerbing, D.W., 1988. Structural equation modeling in practice: A review and recommended two-step approach. *Psychological Bulletin*, *103*(3), pp.411–423.

Bagozzi, R.P. and Yi, Y., 2012. Specification, evaluation, and interpretation of structural equation models. *Journal of the Academy of Marketing Science*, *40*(1), pp.8–34.

Barclay, D., Higgins, C. and Thompson, R., 1995. The Partial Least Squares (PLS) approach to casual modeling: Personal computer adoption and use as an illustration. *Technology Studies*, *2*(2), pp.285–309.

Baron, R.M. and Kenny, D.A., 1986. The moderator–mediator variable distinction in social psychological research: Conceptual, strategic, and statistical considerations. *Journal of Personality and Social Psychology*, *51*(6), pp.1173–1182.

Becker, J.M., Klein, K. and Wetzels, M., 2012. Hierarchical latent variable models in PLS-SEM: Guidelines for using reflective-formative type models. *Long Range Planning*, *45*(5–6), pp.359–394.

Bilgin, Y., 2017. Qualitative method versus quantitative method in marketing research: An application example at Oba restaurant. In S. Oflazoglu (Ed.), *Qualitative versus quantitative research* (pp.1–28). Rijeka, Croatia: InTech.

Byrne, B.M., 1994. *Structural equation modeling with EQS and EQS/Windows*. Thousand Oaks, CA: Sage.

Camilleri, M.A., 2018. *Travel marketing, tourism economics and the airline product: An introduction to theory and practice*. Cham: Springer.

Campbell, D.T., 1960. Recommendations for APA test standards regarding construct, trait, or discriminant validity. *American Psychologist*, *15*, pp.546–553.

Cassel, C., Hackl, P. and Westlund, A.H., 1999. Robustness of partial least-squares method for estimating latent variable quality structures. *Journal of Applied Statistics*, *26*(4), pp.435–446.

Chen, F.F., Sousa, K.H. and West, S.G., 2005. Teacher's corner: Testing measurement invariance of second-order factor models. *Structural Equation Modeling*, *12*(3), pp.471–492.

Cheng, E.W.L., 2001. SEM being more effective than multiple regression in parsimonious model testing for management development research. *Journal of Management Development*, *20*(7), pp.650–667.

Chin, W.W., 1998. The partial least squares approach to structural equation modeling. In G. Marcoulides (Ed.), *Modern methods for business research* (pp.295–336). Mahwah, NJ: Lawrence Erlbaum.

Chin, W.W., 2010. How to write up and report PLS analyses. In V. Esposito Vinzi, W.W. Chin, J. Henseler and H. Wang (Eds.), *Handbook of partial least squares* (pp.655–690). Berlin: Springer.

Chin, W.W., Marcolin, B.L. and Newsted, P.R., 2003. A partial least squares latent variable modeling approach for measuring interaction effects: Results from a Monte Carlo simulation study and electronic mail emotion/adoption study. *Information Systems Research*, *14*(2), pp.189–217.

Cohen, J., 1988. *Statistical power analysis for the behavioral sciences*. Hillsdale, NJ: Lawrence Erlbaum.

Cronbach, L.J. and Meehl, P.E., 1955. Construct validity in psychological tests. *Psychological Bulletin*, *52*(4), pp.281–302.

Davis, J.A. and Weber, R.P., 1985. *The logic of causal order*. Beverly Hills, CA: Sage.

Denzin, N.K. and Lincoln, Y.S. (Eds.), 1994. *Handbook of qualitative research*. Thousand Oaks, CA: Sage.

Diamantopoulos, A. and Winklhofer, H.M., 2001. Index construction with formative indicators: An alternative to scale development. *Journal of Marketing Research*, *38*(2), pp.269–277.

Eid, M., Lischetzke, T., Nussbeck, F.W. and Trierweiler, L.I., 2003. Separating trait effects from trait-specific method effects in multitrait-multimethod models: A multiple-indicator CT-C (M-1) model. *Psychological Methods*, *8*(1), pp.38–60.

Farrell, A.M., 2010. Insufficient discriminant validity: A comment on Bove, Pervan, Beatty, and Shiu (2009). *Journal of Business Research*, *63*(3), pp.324–327.

Fornell, C. and Larcker, D.F., 1981. Evaluating structural equation models with unobservable variables and measurement error. *Journal of Marketing Research*, *18*(1), pp.39–50.

French, J. and Gordon, R., 2019. *Strategic social marketing: For behaviour and social change* (2nd ed.). Los Angeles: Sage.

Gustafsson, J.E. and Balke, G., 1993. General and specific abilities as predictors of school achievement. *Multivariate Behavioral Research*, *28*(4), pp.407–434.

Hadi, N.U., Abdullah, N. and Sentosa, I., 2016. Making sense of mediating analysis: A marketing perspective. *Review of Integrative Business and Economics Research*, *5*(2), pp.62–76.

Hair, J.F., Black, W.C., Babin, B.J. and Anderson, R.E., 2010. *Multivariate data analysis: A global perspective* (7th ed.). Upper Saddle River, NJ: Pearson.

Hair, J.F., Black, W.C., Babin, B.J., Anderson, R.E. and Tatham, R.L., 1998. *Multivariate data analysis*. Upper Saddle River, NJ: Prentice Hall.

Hair, J.F., Black, W.C., Babin, B.J., Anderson, R.E. and Tatham, R.L., 2006. *Multivariate data analysis* (6th ed.). Upper Saddle River, NJ: Pearson Prentice Hall.

Hair, J.F., Gabriel, M. and Patel, V., 2014a. AMOS covariance-based structural equation modeling (CB-SEM): Guidelines on its application as a marketing research tool. *Revista Brasileira de Marketing*, *13*(2), pp. 44–55.

Hair, J.F., Hult, G.T.M., Ringle, C. and Sarstedt, M., 2016. *A primer on partial least squares structural equation modeling (PLS-SEM)*. Thousand Oaks: Sage.

Hair, J.F., Matthews, L.M., Matthews, R.L. and Sarstedt, M., 2017. PLS-SEM or CB-SEM: Updated guidelines on which method to use. *International Journal of Multivariate Data Analysis*, *1*(2), pp.107–123.

Hair, J.F., Ringle, C.M. and Sarstedt, M., 2011a. PLS-SEM: Indeed a silver bullet. *Journal of Marketing Theory and Practice*, *19*(2), pp.139–152.

Hair, J.F., Ringle, C.M. and Sarstedt, M., 2011b. The use of partial least squares (PLS) to address marketing management topics. *Journal of Marketing Theory and Practice*, *19*(2), pp.135–138.

Hair, J.F., Sarstedt, M., Hopkins, L. and Kuppelwieser, V.G., 2014b. Partial least squares structural equation modeling (PLS-SEM): An emerging tool in business research. *European Business Review*, *26*(2), pp.106–121.

Hair, J.F., Sarstedt, M., Pieper, T.M. and Ringle, C.M., 2012a. The use of partial least squares structural equation modeling in strategic management research: A review of past practices and recommendations for future applications. *Long Range Planning*, *45*(5–6), pp.320–340.

Hair, J.F., Sarstedt, M., Ringle, C.M. and Mena, J.A., 2012b. An assessment of the use of partial least squares structural equation modeling in marketing research. *Journal of the Academy of Marketing Science*, *40*(3), pp.414–433.

Hayes, A.F., 2009. Beyond Baron and Kenny: Statistical mediation analysis in the new millennium. *Communication Monographs*, *76*(4), pp.408–420.

Henseler, J. and Fassott, G., 2010. Testing moderating effects in PLS path models: An illustration of available procedures. In V.E. Vinzi, W.W. Chin, J. Henseler and H. Wang

(Eds.), *Handbook of partial least squares: Concepts, methods and applications* (pp.713–735). Berlin: Springer.

Henseler, J., Ringle, C.M. and Sarstedt, M., 2015. A new criterion for assessing discriminant validity in variance-based structural equation modeling. *Journal of the Academy of Marketing Science*, *43*(1), pp.115–135.

Henseler, J., Ringle, C.M. and Sinkovics, R.R., 2009. The use of partial least squares path modeling in international marketing. In R.N. Sinkovics and P.N. Ghauri (Eds.), *New challenges to international marketing* (pp.277–320). Bingley: Emerald.

Hock, C., Ringle, C.M. and Sarstedt, M., 2010. Management of multi-purpose stadiums: Importance and performance measurement of service interfaces. *International Journal of Services Technology and Management*, *14*(2–3), pp.188–207.

House, R., Rousseau, D.M. and Thomas-Hunt, M., 1995. The meso paradigm: A framework for the integration of micro and macro organizational behavior. *Research in Organizational Behavior*, *17*, pp.71–114.

Hoyle, R.H., 2000. *Structural equation modeling: Concepts, issues, and applications.* Thousand Oaks, CA: Sage.

Hsu, S.H., Chen, W.H. and Hsieh, M.J., 2006. Robustness testing of PLS, LISREL, EQS and ANN-based SEM for measuring customer satisfaction. *Total Quality Management & Business Excellence*, *17*(3), pp.355–372.

Huang, L., Mou, J., See-To, E.W. and Kim, J., 2019. Consumer perceived value preferences for mobile marketing in China: A mixed method approach. *Journal of Retailing and Consumer Services*, *48*, pp.70–86.

Hulland, J., 1999. Use of partial least squares (PLS) in strategic management research: A review of four recent studies. *Strategic Management Journal*, *20*(2), pp.195–204.

Jöreskog, K.G., 1970. A general method for estimating a linear structural equation system. *ETS Research Bulletin Series*, *1970*(2), pp.i–41.

Klein, K.J., Dansereau, F. and Hall, R.J., 1994. Levels issues in theory development, data collection, and analysis. *Academy of Management Review*, *19*(2), pp.195–229.

Klein, K.J., Major, V.S. and Ralls, R.S., 1998. Worker participation: What, why, and whither. Unpublished manuscript, University of Maryland, College Park.

Kock, N., 2015. Common method bias in PLS-SEM: A full collinearity assessment approach. *International Journal of e-Collaboration (IJeC)*, *11*(4), pp.1–10.

Landmark, A.D. and Sjøbakk, B., 2017. Tracking customer behaviour in fashion retail using RFID. *International Journal of Retail & Distribution Management*, *45*(7–8), pp.844–858.

Lei, M. and Lomax, R.G., 2005. The effect of varying degrees of nonnormality in structural equation modeling. *Structural Equation Modeling*, *12*(1), pp.1–27.

Lohmöller, J.B. and Wold, H., 1980. *Three-mode path models with latent variables and partial least squares (PLS) parameter estimation.* Munich: Neubiberg.

Martilla, J.A. and James, J.C., 1977. Importance-performance analysis. *Journal of Marketing*, *41*(1), pp.77–79.

Musil, C.M., Jones, S.L. and Warner, C.D., 1998. Structural equation modeling and its relationship to multiple regression and factor analysis. *Research in Nursing and Health*, *21*, pp.271–281.

Netemeyer, R.G., Bearden, W.O. and Sharma, S., 2003. *Scaling procedures: Issues and applications.* Thousand Oaks, CA: Sage.

Neuman, W.L., 2003. *Social research methods: Qualitative and quantitative approaches* (5th ed.). Boston: Allyn and Bacon.

Nitzl, C., Roldan, J.L. and Cepeda, G., 2016. Mediation analysis in partial least squares path modeling: Helping researchers discuss more sophisticated models. *Industrial Management & Data Systems*, *116*(9), pp.1849–1864.

Nunkoo, R. and Ramkissoon, H., 2012. Structural equation modelling and regression analysis in tourism research. *Current Issues in Tourism*, *15*(8), pp.777–802.

Nunkoo, R., Ramkissoon, H. and Gursoy, D., 2013. Use of structural equation modeling in tourism research: Past, present, and future. *Journal of Travel Research*, *52*(6), pp.759–771.

Nunkoo, R., Teeroovengadum, V., Thomas, P. and Leonard, L., 2017. Integrating service quality as a second-order factor in a customer satisfaction and loyalty model. *International Journal of Contemporary Hospitality Management, 29*(12), pp.2978–3005.

Nunnally, J.C. and Bernstein, I., 1994. *Psychometric theory* (3rd ed.). New York: McGraw-Hill.

Pant, M., Virdi, A.S. and Chaubey, D.S., 2020. Examining the effect of marketing innovations on GPMA: A study using the PLS–SEM Approach. *Global Business Review, 21*(4), pp.1025–1036.

Petter, S., Straub, D.W. and Rai, A., 2007. Specifying formative constructs in information systems research. *MIS Quarterly, 31*(4), pp.623–656.

Ramanathan, U., Subramanian, N., Yu, W. and Vijaygopal, R., 2017. Impact of customer loyalty and service operations on customer behaviour and firm performance: Empirical evidence from UK retail sector. *Production Planning & Control, 28*(6–8), pp.478–488.

Rindskopf, D. and Rose, T., 1988. Some theory and applications of confirmatory second-order factor analysis. *Multivariate Behavioral Research, 23*(1), pp.51–67.

Ringle, C.M. and Sarstedt, M., 2016. Gain more insight from your PLS-SEM results: The importance-performance map analysis. *Industrial Management & Data Systems, 116*(9), pp.1865–1886.

Ringle, C.M., Götz, O., Wetzels, M. and Wilson, B., 2009. On the use of formative measurement specifications in structural equation modeling: A Monte Carlo simulation study to compare covariance-based and partial least squares model estimation methodologies. *METEOR Research Memoranda (RM/09/014).*

Ringle, C.M., Sarstedt, M. and Straub, D., 2012. A critical look at the use of PLS-SEM in *MIS Quarterly. MIS Quarterly, 36*(1), pp.iii–xiv.

Ringle, C.M., Sarstedt, M. and Zimmermann, L., 2011. Customer satisfaction with commercial airlines: The role of perceived safety and purpose of travel. *Journal of Marketing Theory and Practice, 19*(4), pp.459–472.

Ringle, C.M., Sarstedt, M., Mitchell, R. and Gudergan, S.P., 2018. Partial least squares structural equation modeling in HRM research. *International Journal of Human Resource Management*, pp.1–27.

Ringle, C.M., Wende, S. and Becker, J.M., 2015. *SmartPLS 3.* Boenningstedt: SmartPLS GmbH, http://www.smartpls.Com.

Ringle, C.M., Wende, S. and Will, A., 2010. Finite mixture partial least squares analysis: Methodology and numerical examples. In V.E. Vinzi, W.W. Chin, J. Henseler and H. Wang (Eds.), *Handbook of partial least squares: Concepts, methods and applications* (pp.195–218). Berlin: Springer.

Rousseau, D.M., 1985. Issues of level in organizational research: Multi-level and cross-level perspectives. *Research in Organizational Behavior, 7*(1), pp.1–37.

Sale, J.E., Lohfeld, L.H. and Brazil, K., 2002. Revisiting the quantitative-qualitative debate: Implications for mixed-methods research. *Quality and Quantity, 36*(1), pp.43–53.

Sarstedt, M. and Mooi, E., 2014. *A concise guide to market research: The process, data, and methods using IBM SPSS statistics.* Berlin: Springer.

Sarstedt, M., Ringle, C.M., Smith, D., Reams, R. and Hair, J.F. Jr, 2014. Partial least squares structural equation modeling (PLS-SEM): A useful tool for family business researchers. *Journal of Family Business Strategy, 5*(1), pp.105–115.

Segars, A.H. and Grover, V., 1993. Re-examining perceived ease of use and usefulness: A confirmatory factor analysis. *MIS Quarterly, 17*(4), pp.517–525.

Shah, R., and Goldstein, S.M. 2006. Use of structural equation modeling in operations management research: Looking back and forward. *Journal of Operations Management, 24*(2), pp.148–169.

Shmueli, G., Sarstedt, M., Hair, J.F., Cheah, J.H., Ting, H., Vaithilingam, S. and Ringle, C.M., 2019. Predictive model assessment in PLS-SEM: Guidelines for using PLSpredict. *European Journal of Marketing, 53*(11), pp.2322–2347.

Shook, C.L., Ketchen, D.J., Hult, T. and Kacmar, K.M., 2004. An assessment of the use of structural equation modeling in strategic management research. *Strategic Management Journal*, 25(4), pp.397–404.

Singh, A. and Pathak, G.S., 2020. The quest for consumer engagement via cause-related marketing: A mixed method study in an emerging economy. *Journal of Retailing and Consumer Services*, 55, p.102128.

Tenenhaus, M., Vinzi, V.E., Chatelin, Y.M. and Lauro, C., 2005. PLS path modeling. *Computational Statistics & Data Analysis*, 48(1), pp.159–205.

Thurstone, L.L., 1947. *Multiple-factor analysis*. Chicago: University of Chicago Press.

Ulin, P.R., Robinson, E.T. and Tolley, E.E., 2012. *Qualitative methods in public health: A field guide for applied research*. New York: Wiley.

Urbach, N. and Ahlemann, F., 2010. Structural equation modeling in information systems research using partial least squares. *Journal of Information Technology Theory and Application*, 11(2), pp.5–40.

Vandenberg, R.J., Richardson, H.A. and Eastman, L.J., 1999. The impact of high involvement work processes on organizational effectiveness: A second-order latent variable approach. *Group & Organization Management*, 24(3), pp.300–339.

Wacker, J.G., 1998. A definition of theory: Research guidelines for different theory-building research methods in operations management. *Journal of Operations Management*, 16(4), pp.361–385.

Wold, H., 1974. Causal flows with latent variables: Partings of the ways in the light of NIPALS modelling. *European Economic Review*, 5(1), pp.67–86.

Zhao, X., Lynch Jr, J.G. and Chen, Q., 2010. Reconsidering Baron and Kenny: Myths and truths about mediation analysis. *Journal of Consumer Research*, 37(2), pp.197–206.

PART II

QUALITATIVE
RESEARCH METHODS

8.   A guide to the successful use of case study in marketing management research
Edina Ajanovic and Beykan Çizel

SUMMARY

By following the leading textbooks and through a systematic literature review of concepts related to case studies, this chapter aims to derive an evaluation framework based on which positive examples of case study use will be defined together with common mistakes that occur during its application in the marketing management field.

INTRODUCTION

Although there has been increased use of case studies in marketing management research in recent years, the lack of methodological guidelines for their application is evident. As with other research methods, erroneous or poor management of the research process will probably lead to failure in conducting such studies. What can be hard for the novice researcher in the marketing management field is distinguishing business cases from case study research design. This conclusion may be based on sometimes confusing evidence and interpretations found in research that claims to use the case study method. In addition, it seems that the use of theory in case studies – whether or not one theoretical framework should be followed – is not sufficiently emphasized, which further raises the question of adequate reasoning choices and related generalizations made.

This chapter will propose the steps that need to be taken into consideration regarding the place of theory in case studies, as well as data collection methods, analysis and result reporting. Following the leading textbooks and through a literature review of the key concepts used in shaping and conducting case studies, this chapter aims to derive the framework based on which conducted case studies could be evaluated and show how some common mistakes that occur during its application can be avoided. Therefore, the main aim will be to introduce basic information on how to carry out high-quality case study research and highlight how confusion may be avoided in future marketing management studies.

The first part of the chapter provides definitions of case study research, reflecting on its initial use and the philosophical debates surrounding it. It will then describe how to shape a case study by providing detailed explanations on defining the case, choosing appropriate designs and using theory. This will be followed by an outline of the steps in conducting a case study in terms of data collection, analysis and reporting of the results. The chapter concludes with a summary of the key aspects of case study research design and reflections on how it can be used to prevent confusion in its application and to enhance its methodological contribution to marketing management research.

CASE STUDY RESEARCH

The main goal for researchers in all academic disciplines is to search for the truth. This is why they develop theories and search for proof that will allow them to understand and describe this truth. Case study research (CSR) refers to a design and framework where researchers search for evidence in different situations and environments in order to answer specific research questions. This evidence has to be abstracted and collated to get the best possible answers (Gillham, 2000, p. 1). Robert Stake (1998) claimed that for CSR it is not the research method that is the most important, but the condition or case itself. As a research design, case study is defined by the case(s) under investigation, rather than the research method used. Normally one case study concentrates on some past phenomena, while also including context and several variables and qualifications (Johansson, 2003).

CSR is useful in developing theories based on evidence. Like other qualitative methods, CSR can be used in situations where experimental and quantitative methods cannot be applied. It can be used to research situations that are less investigated in the available literature, and to explore the complexity beyond the scope of controlled approaches. This type of research allows for entering into a group or organization and discovering the truth in an informal way from the inside. The CSR approach provides significant benefits when it comes to examining the processes leading to the results, not the importance of the results themselves. Zonabend (1992) noted that CSR is carried out with special attention to the integrity of the analysis, by reconstructing and observing the cases. CSR is conducted in such a way as to include the views of "actors" in the examined case.

It is not such an easy task to define the term "case". Gillham (2000) defined it as: a settled unit of human activity in the real world; a concept that can operate and be understood in a certain context; a unit which is present here and now. One individual can be regarded as a case; but so too can groups such as family, classroom, office or hospital unit, organizations such as a school or factory, or a large-scale community such as a municipality, industry, profession, etc. These are all examples of a single case. However, more than one case can be investigated – for example several single parents, several schools, two different professions, and so on.

Case study was first used in anthropology at the beginning of the 19th century, when studies were mostly of an explanatory nature with the goal to systematically analyze other cultures and collect data through participative observation methods. After WWII rational positivism began to dominate in philosophy, with positivism and quantitative methods also being preferred by social scientists. In the years when statistical methods, surveys, experiments and semi-experiments were scientifically accepted, case study was being criticized as a qualitative method which was not considered scientific enough. In the second generation of case studies, "grounded theory" was used as the first inductive method, based on detailed procedures for analyzing data. The grounded theory concept, developed by Glaser and Strauss (1967), combined methods used in qualitative research with quantitative methods. In the following years, Robert Yin (1994) proposed a combination of experimental logic from the field of natural research and qualitative methods. At that time sociology was one of the fields strongly related to case study research. From today's perspective it should be noted that CSR is not part of the positivist philosophy which is a predominant paradigm in natural sciences. Positivist philosophers emphasize strongly that only those phenomena that can be observed and verified in their original form can be the subject of science, while excluding subjective phenomena and "unverifiable" theories (Johansson, 2003).

Researchers employing classical empirical positivist methods propose four main reasons for criticizing CSR (Woodside, 2010):

1. Most CSR reports do not show clear steps in creating and testing the theory. Therefore, some researchers are failing to conduct appropriate observation and provide adequate explanation of the phenomena under study, and thus inductively create the theory.
2. Defining processes in a specific context, which are presented in order to increase the accuracy of information found in case study reports, give chaotic complexity to researchers and readers of the study report.
3. Researchers criticizing case studies see variability in the multilingual interpretations of concise data, indicating that there is a weakness in the bold definitions.

4.   The practical suitability of a case study report to other contexts and normative practices can be questioned on the grounds that theory cannot always be extracted and data are collected in one or very few contexts.

CSR is criticized due to generalized findings in a single situation. Yin (1994) points out that the generalization of results obtained from single or multiple designs is made to populations, not theory. Copying the pattern matches in multiple cases will strengthen the results, and thus enhance the soundness of the theory. Case study assessments may include both the process and the results because they include both quantitative and qualitative data (Tellis, 1997a, 1997b). Case study research has gone beyond quantitative research by explaining the conditions of the situation from the point of view of the actors (Holder, 1987; Yin, 1994). Yin (1989) stated that the general applicability of case study results is possible due to the set of methodological qualities and rigorous approach to research procedures in conducting this type of study. In order to ensure the required methodological rigor, Yin provided detailed explanation of the case study procedures. Case study fulfills three conditions of the qualitative method: definition, understanding and explanation.

Another point in favor of case study is that researchers believe there is a lack of accuracy in the representation and prediction of key findings of researchers using classical empirical positivistic tools. A case study is an empirical inquiry made in the context of a single case or a small number of situations, with a close and in-depth sense of its own reality, especially when the boundaries between the phenomenon and the context are not clear. Case study research focuses on identifying, understanding and explaining the individual (for example, process, animal, person, house, organization, group, industry, culture or nationality). In addition, case study comprises systematic data collection and analysis processes. The findings are achieving wider application and contribution to the world's situations through analytical (not statistical) generalization.

SHAPING THE CASE STUDY

Yin (2012) defined three main steps in case studies: defining a case, selecting appropriate study designs, and the use of theory. Defining a case is the most important step in organizing this research approach. The basis of defining a case is the review of the literature and derivation of the research questions. Sometimes it is necessary to redefine the case situation during the research process and, in these cases, modifications to the reviewed literature and research questions are appropriate. The situation or concept defined as the case has the role of the basic analytical unit.

In the second step of case study it is necessary to choose one of four designs: single, multiple, holistic or embedded. These are explained in more detail in Yin's (2012) 2 × 2 matrix of four case studies. The last step determines whether theory will be used in defining research questions, selecting the cases and clarifying design, or in choosing basic methodological steps such as data collection and similar. It is easier to conduct a case study with a predefined theoretical framework. However, even though there is a risk, more experienced researchers may decide to avoid using any theory. It is assumed that they will approach the research phenomena without presuppositions or institutionally imposed biases. Studies conducted in this manner may be highly rewarding because it is when "limits are broken" that the full benefits and potential of case study emerge.

Generally, using theory as guidance for creating case study design and data collection is useful regardless of whether the case study is exploratory, explanatory or descriptive. Theoretical frameworks and connections will help in creating links with related literature and help researchers advance knowledge on certain topics from obtained results. The importance of theory for case study may be summarized in four statements (Yin, 2012):

- To determine what is going to be explored in exploratory study.
- To assist in defining the nature of the case(s), making them a part of the study.
- To make full and appropriate descriptions in the study.
- To define terms of opposite theories when conducting explanatory study.

Theory in case studies cannot be used to determine only cause-and-effect relationships. It is important to ensure proper use of theory in terms of defining case study design and the boundaries of the phenomena under study. In addition, theory will be beneficial to track and elaborate on the scientific contribution of the case study results through analytical generalization. Generally, researchers with less experience of conducting case studies will be more in need and will benefit more from using certain theoretical perspectives.

Structural validity in case study research was often criticized for researchers' potential subjectivity. In order to prevent this criticism, Yin (1994) proposed three remedies: using more than one data resource, creating data chains and having a case study report reviewed by key supporters. Pattern matching can be used to increase internal validity with causal or explanatory cases where often the problem of "inferences" occurs. Case study results should also be externally valid or applicable in the wider context. Reliability in a case study may be achieved through development of the case study protocol. Yin proposed the use of carefully composed case study protocols that should be followed as part of the research project. They should contain the following:

- An overview of the study – goals and topics of the case study.
- Field procedures – identification of data that should be collected, and access to the field.
- Questions – a list of research questions that should be available and used as guidance throughout the data collection phase.
- A guide to reporting case study results – a draft of how the results should be reported, taking into consideration the general case design and previously defined steps in the procedure (Yin, 1994, p. 64).

Triangulation is known as a research strategy in case studies. It was proposed that triangulation can be reached through the use of various data, theories, researchers and even methods. In order to ensure accuracy and explanation of the alternatives, Stake (1995) claimed that it is necessary to differentiate the protocols. Triangulation is used to verify the validity of the research process, which in case studies can be achieved by using various data sources (Yin, 1984). Case studies are multi-perspective analyses. This means that the researcher takes into account not only the words and perspective of the certain stakeholders under study, but also those of the whole group of participants, as well as their interactions. The main characteristic of case study is that the researcher seeks a holistic understanding of "cultural action systems" or sets of interrelated activities in a social situation by actors (Feagin et al., 1991). Therefore, this implies that definitions of appropriate design should determine the boundaries of case studies.

Case studies can be in the form of single or multiple designs. Single case study design can be used to validate or test a theory or represent unique or extreme situations (Yin, 1994). This design is ideal for situations where the researcher has access to phenomena which were previously unavailable and/or hard to reach. Single case studies can be holistic or embedded, which occurs when the same case study contains more than one unit of analysis. Rather than following the sampling principle by selecting from a population, multiple case studies follow replication logic.

Yin (1994, p. 20) defined five important elements of research design: (a) the study's questions; (b) its propositions, if any; (c) its unit(s) of analysis; (d) the logical linking of data to propositions; and (e) the criteria for interpreting the findings.

Most case study research questions are "how" and "why", and definitions are the first task of the researcher. Questions help the researcher to concentrate on the study goals. There is no need for recommendations in every study. Instead of recommendations, in exploratory study the goal or criteria will be defined. The unit of analysis defines the situation or case. These can be groups, organizations or countries. Campbell (1975) considered pattern matching to be a useful technique for linking data to propositions. He argued that pattern matching is a situation where a lot of information about the same situation may be related to some theoretical propositions.

STEPS IN CONDUCTING THE CASE STUDY RESEARCH PROCESS

The case study process consists of three steps: data collection, data analysis and reporting the results. Below is a brief summary of these phases.

Data Collection

Yin (1994) suggested that a case study should involve experiences and taking responsibility as a "senior researcher" throughout the data collection process. Prior to conducting the research, there should be a training period in which the research problem should be defined and case study design developed. However this may not be necessary if there is only one researcher. Training should provide the researcher with information on topics such as the purpose of the study, the type of data to be collected and what changes can be expected. This training can take the form of a discussion. Here it is advisable to use a case study protocol containing procedural and general rules.

There are different data collection methods for case study research. Stake (1995) and Yin (1994) defined at least six data sources: documents, archive records, interviews, direct observation, participant observation and physical proofs. Documents can refer to proof such as letters, notes, diaries, administrative documents, newspaper articles or investigation records. Following the goal of triangulation, it is useful to support material obtained from other sources (Tellis, 1997a, 1997b). Documents can be useful to get an insight into the phenomena under investigation. However, if approached and handled inappropriately, documents can be misleading as well. Items such as archive documents, service records, organization records, name lists, survey data and so on refer to communication between the parties in the study, while the investigator is only an observer. Case study research should therefore carefully assess the accuracy of collected documents.

As with the other qualitative research methods, interviews are considered one of the most important data collection methods in case study research. They may take the form of open-ended, focused and structured or surveyed interviews. Through open-ended questions critical case study participants are asked to provide their views and interpretations on the topic being researched. They can suggest solutions or provide insight into events while also providing support for evidence obtained from other sources. However, the researcher should avoid focusing on a single source of information, and instead search for data from various sources in order to better verify and increase the authenticity of the obtained data set. When a respondent has limited time for answering the questions, a focused interview with questions prepared in advance is used. This technique is useful when data collected from other sources should be validated. In structured interviews questions are prepared in advance (such as in a questionnaire), which is why this type of interview is also called surveyed.

When a field visit is made during the case study, direct observation takes place, where involvement of more than one observer is advisable for increased reliability. With this type of observation, the researcher should make sure not to intrude on the environment and processes under investigation (Glesne and Peshkin, 1992). On the other hand, through participant observation the researcher takes an active role in investigated activities and the environment, which allows extraordinary opportunities for data collection. This is especially useful in fieldwork with neighborhoods or specific groups. However, the researcher should be aware of their influence and power to change the course of events as part of the group, which may lead to misleading results and interpretations. Finally, physical forms of evidence are the tools and proof that can be collected during case study fieldwork. At the end of this exploration the researcher's perspective can be broadened.

Researchers should be able to manage the collection and handling of data from various resources as not all resources are suitable for all case studies (Yin, 1994). However, in certain situations alternative possibilities will present themselves. Data collection on the same topic(s) but through different methods is called a multi-method approach (Gillham, 2000). Each method has its own advantages and disadvantages. It is useful to be careful when basing findings, evaluations, comments and understanding of CSR on any data set. This does not mean that an obtained data set is wrong; but when we notice that the picture is more complex than expected, it may be wise to use different data collection methods.

Regardless of its data source, a case study may include both quantitative and qualitative data. The consistency of data from different sources must be continuously checked and evidence must be combined – a process also called triangulation. It is better to use different, more diverse resources than a single source. During data collection, researchers are advised to use case study protocols that include questions that guide the investigator to collect and combine data (Tellis, 1997a, 1997b).

Another important point in collecting data is to include opposing ideas and explanations. Case study researchers should be skeptical in that they should constantly question with opposing ideas the conducted literature review, events and actions as they appear, and whether the participants have given honest answers or not. This is an important strategy for eliminating researcher and participant bias. The last stage of the data collection process is to present the data in a way that the target audience can understand them clearly. Ideally, upon completion of this phase, results should be presented in the form of texts, tables, images, etc. The most critical point here is to combine numerical or textual evidence with adequate comments and interpretations. Confusing evidence and interpretations can imply that the researcher does not understand clearly the difference between the two, or does not know how to properly handle the data.

Data Analysis

Case study involves important issues related to data analysis. How are the findings verified? How to choose a case for the study? And how to make generalizations based on a single case? Triangulation may be considered as a useful strategy in increasing the validity of case study research. Normally, when triangulation is mentioned in this context it refers to diversification of data collection methods (many methods are combined); but it can also refer to diversification of data sources, theories or researchers (Denzin, 1978).

This aspect of CSR is the least explained in available textbooks on the use of case studies. As a basic guideline, analytical techniques proposed by Miles and Huberman (1994) – such as rearranging evidence, placing evidence in a category matrix, and creating flow charts – can be used. Identification of a case will have some important assumptions about analysis. For each case study type – descriptive, exploratory or explanatory – different analysis methods could be used. For example, the research pattern might start with an analysis of exploratory research questions. Collecting real data may sometimes require the researcher to make changes to the initial plan. However, having a plan to start with is better than having no plan at all.

The initial step in case study is establishing an analytical strategy that can lead to results. For general use Yin proposed two strategies. The first is to rely on the study's theoretical propositions and then analyze the evidence based on these propositions. The second is to develop a situation description that will be a framework for organizing the case study.

Pattern matching is considered as another important analysis style. This type of logic compares the predicted pattern with an empirical pattern. Internal validity increases when patterns overlap. With explanatory case studies patterns may be related to dependent or independent variables, while in descriptive cases the predicted model should be defined before data collection. Yin (1994) recommended the use of rival theoretical propositions in pattern matching with independent variables, as it is concerned with increasing the quality of the analysis.

Stake (1995) proposed categorical aggregation as another tool of analysis, and also proposed the development of protocols for this stage of the case study in order to improve the quality of the research. He recommended coding of data and other issues in the analysis phase. In order to improve the quality of the analysis, Yin (1994) proposed four principles: (a) assuring that analysis is based on all relevant data; (b) all rival theoretical propositions should be included in the analysis; (c) the most important aspects of case study should be addressed; and (d) the use of researcher and expert knowledge to advance research.

Having prejudices and expectations in the research process can be considered normal. However, the researcher should constantly ask himself/herself the following questions: *What am I hoping to find? What do I think this is about? Can these be my prejudices?* One may be right because prejudices are not always the wrong ones: there may be only insufficient proof. However, worse than prejudices are preferences, where the researcher finds only what he/she hopes and wants to find. At this point, the researcher should again constantly question himself/herself. It is not surprising that, when reading a research paper, one can see that people found what they were searching for. An absolute sense of "objectivity" may be impossible; but researchers must strive for a level of honesty when reflecting on their own position in the study and making judgments. Gillham (2000) proposes three strategies for this. The first is to assimilate culture. The value of being a participant observer is perhaps to be a temporary member of the environment, more likely to reach an informal reality. You can only find this by spending time with people in their environment. In a sense, every place has its own culture (language, ways of thinking and talking about life experience, etc.). It takes time to obtain this. When searching for evidence in the research, it is also necessary to look for and evaluate inconsistent data, contrary to the research goals and findings. As the research progresses, a lot of information is obtained and temporary explanations adhere to this. However, are there data that do not fit the "theory"? Negative, opposite or contradictory evidence, or searching for evidence that complicates our understanding, is essential for the credibility and integrity of the research.

The second important strategy is to combine data collected from various sources while trying to answer a research question. Consistency of data is important for the study's credibility (Gillham, 2000). Representative power of data is another important element. Representativeness differs from tri-angulation. You are listening to what people are saying to you, but are you listening only to certain people? In another words, if some people know you as an observer, are they willing to tell you their story? If people want to "help" you, you have to ask yourself why? Those who are more cautious can present you with a very different view on the phenomena. In this case, one should make sure that all the potential ideas are covered and represented in the data set. While listening to the study participants, it is necessary to listen carefully and pay equal attention to both those who are willing to share their views and those who are more reticent. Researchers should be very cautious and suspicious of those participants who are eager to be helpful. It is important to ensure that the opinion of everyone related to the case is addressed. Sometimes this is the case with documents and archive records, since some types of information are more accessible than others. Reasons for this should be investigated, and one needs to be suspicious.

Another important issue regarding data analysis in CSR is to check understandings and explanations with people sharing the culture of the scope of the research. In addition, interpretations of the case being inves-tigated should be checked through the thoughtful, experienced or com-mitted people who are experts in the research context. A peer counseling strategy is also useful and valuable in the analysis, and could include other students, other researchers and so on. In using a peer strategy, researchers should make sure to choose people who do the same thing as them, who are experts in the investigated area or in research methods (Gillham, 2000).

The search for negative evidence in data analysis is very important for the integrity and credibility of the research. Good researchers always test their assumptions, looking for evidence that complicates their understand-ing. Simply searching for verifiable evidence, evidence confirming what the researcher believes in or understands, is considered to be an indication of the inability to overcome subjectivity and bias.

Generalization represents one of the most critically approached issues in case study research. The main question that needs to be answered is how generalization can be made based on only one case (situation, group, organization, etc.). In order to explain generalization in case studies it is necessary to distinguish between two types: statistical and analytical.

Statistical generalization from sample to universe is the only way to generalize the findings from social science research. In contrast, analytic generalization depends on the use of the study's theoretical framework to create a logic that can be applied to other situations.

Case studies and experimental studies are similar to the two-step process for generalizing findings. The first step encompasses a conceptual claim in which researchers show how their findings reveal the relationship between a particular set of concepts, theoretical structure or event. The second step involves disseminating the same theoretical propositions, other than a completed case study, to similar situations, occurrences or other situations in which the sequence of events may be relevant. Making analytical generalizations, whether in situational or experimental work, requires meticulously formed claims. In summary, to the extent that any research is concerned about generalizing itself, case studies also tend to generalize to other situations (based on analytical claims).

Being analytical in nature implies that generalizations made from cases are based on cognitive reasoning. There are three principles of cognitive reasoning: deductive, inductive and abductive (Johansson, 2003). Generalizations from case studies may be based on the use of one or a combination of different cognitive reasoning types. When a generalization is based on the deduction principle, the procedure is similar to an experiment: a hypothesis is formulated and results are derived through deductive reasoning. It is possible to validate or disprove the theory by comparing the expected and empirically obtained findings derived after conducting the CSR. As a result, it is possible to define areas where the theory is more accurate. Conditions that are very important for the theory are selected. The test of a theory consists of emulating experimental methods in a natural environment. From a theory and the facts of a phenomenon, generalizations about the field of theory emerge. This model of how generalizations are drawn from a situation, was developed by Robert Yin (1994).

The second generalization mode is induction. In case studies, this is done by constructing or conceptualizing an inductive theory based on data in a state. The result is a theory that normally consists of a set of related concepts. According to Glaser and Strauss (1967), this is how generalizations are made in grounded theory. Finally, generalizations can be based on abductive reasoning principles. Inductive and deductive approaches are well known, but there are also increasing representations of and interest in abductive reasoning. According to the deductive principle, the result is necessarily valid for a situation and a rule. Deductive evidence proves that something must be true. With induction, we may derive a rule from one of the cases, which is actually active and in a similar situation. Abduction is the process of confronting an unexpected

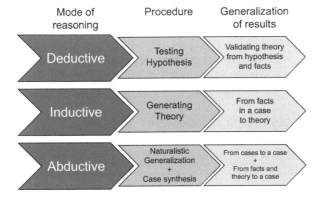

Source: Adapted from Johansson (2003, p.10).

Figure 8.1 Mode of reasoning and generalization of case study results

phenomenon, applying some rule(s) (already known or created for the situation), and introducing new concepts and ideas that may emerge as a result of the study. Modes of reasoning and generalization of case study results are illustrated in Figure 8.1.

Reporting the Results

Reporting the results of a CSR from the collected data is a challenging task. However the more organized the researcher and the whole process, the easier it will be. Reporting the research results implies not only making the collected material accessible, but also presenting the findings from the data in a structured manner. In the last stage of CSR, the researcher should strive to properly understand and interpret the data. There is no single way of preparing a research report. It can change based on the target audience, and vary in length and focus. However, there is usually a core report that contains every relevant issue of the study. The report should be viewed as providing a coherent, interpretive summary of what was discovered in the research. Writing a CSR report is challenging for the following reasons:

- Variety of different types of evidence obtained through various data collection methods
- Ability to turn this evidence into a coherent narrative
- The need to maintain focus and direction determined by general objectives and specific research questions
- The need to continually revise explanations or propose "theories".

Reporting results obtained in qualitative inquiry is not just a challenging task in case study designs, but may be considered problematic for other qualitative research methods as well. In their work on standards for reporting qualitative research, O'Brien et al. (2014) reflected that qualitative research is common in the medical and medical education fields, but guidelines are incomplete on how to report key elements of such studies. After a systematic review of studies on guidelines, reporting standards and critical appraisal criteria for qualitative research found in various academic databases, the authors proposed a set of standards for reporting qualitative research consisting of 21 items (pp. 1247–1248). These standards are consistent with ideas on how to conduct successful CSR proposed in this chapter. After formulating a research goal and deriving questions in the introduction part, issues explained earlier in this chapter – such as context, sampling strategy, data collection methods and instruments, units of study, data processing and analysis with reflections on trustworthiness issues – should be presented.

When reporting findings from CSR, O'Brien et al. (2014)'s standards may also be applicable in the context of marketing management research. Accordingly, results should be reported in a manner that describes the researcher's synthesis and interpretation. Researchers should ensure that the main findings are presented – whether in the form of interpretations, inferences, themes or categories. These results may include development of new theories and/or models, or they may be used as empirical contributions to prior research or theory. In addition, it is of great importance to show the clear link between interpretations and empirical data. Therefore, the inclusion of quotes, interview or text excerpts, photographs, and so on will provide firm support for the abstractions and interpretations made by the case study researcher(s). Any report on case study results should be followed by discussion on how the findings should be integrated with previous studies in the literature, or detail how they connect, support, elaborate, explain or contradict the existing theoretical frameworks found in the marketing and management literature. If new theories emerge, the significance of their contribution to the overall knowledge in the field should be put forward. Researchers should ensure that presented results should follow the principle of transferability or discuss dissemination of the current findings into broader theoretical and practical application. One should think of the current findings in terms of their suitability for future use in similar research contexts, and whether they can potentially be used as a basis for designing new case studies or stand as supportive or opposing points in future analysis and interpretations.

Writing a research report requires deep understanding and concentration on the part of the researcher. Yin (1989) stated that, for good reporting, temporary summary and registry records created throughout the research process may be very helpful. Basically, the researcher has to review all the evidence and procedures in order to draw up a general draft of what was found and what it can be used for. Especially, what the researcher should be looking for is to find and report different kinds of evidence about the same research topic. These diverse sources of evidence and data, which must be related to each other, represent what Yin calls a "chain of evidence", formed by the researcher's narratives and interpretations.

CONCLUSION

This chapter offered a detailed guide on how to shape and conduct successful case study research (CSR), which can also be used as an evaluative framework in analyzing current or future studies of this kind. With adequate use, researchers will be able to clearly distinguish between business cases and methodologically more complex CSR designs. Business cases are widely used in the field, and represent a very useful tool for students and novice researchers learning how to apply core managerial concepts in practice. Through various examples from business environments in different contexts, readers will be able to discuss and analyze the application and success of various managerial concepts that will lead to success in business environments. However, these types of business cases are often confused with case study research designs, and some researchers treat these two approaches as equal. What is often seen in practice is that most researchers claim that they used the case study approach in their work. This was based on the fact that they, as researchers, entered the environment in which they were researching the case and observed the business practices or interviewed the key stakeholders. Most of the time results lack deeper analysis and interpretations, and just represent reports of what was said by research participants. Based on propositions from the current chapter, it is important to adequately use the theoretical framework in shaping the research design, collecting the appropriate data, conducting the analysis and discussing findings through the lenses of the chosen theory. This does not mean it is compulsory to use theory when conducting a case study or that new theory cannot emerge from business cases; but the researcher's experience and skills to adequately interpret the case context and obtained results will be of great importance.

Case study is based on the principles and use of self-diversity in terms of a combination of method, theory and/or strategy at different technical levels. The skillful use of such combinations allows the case study to develop. Both qualitative and quantitative approaches are used in case studies. However, in qualitative research it is difficult to codify different quality standards in terms of applicability, consistency and impartiality. This implies that CSR is a rather comprehensive and complex design that should be approached carefully, with results that can be of great value to the overall knowledge of the phenomena under investigation.

Finally, the main discussion topic on case studies is how to make generalizations from the cases. In the current chapter reflections on different approaches to generalization were presented. It will be useful for potential case study researchers to address the adequate reasoning method according to the study's aim and choice of theoretical framework. All of these approaches have the potential for further development through the wider use by skillful case study researchers in the marketing management field.

REFERENCES

Campbell, D. (1975). Degrees of freedom and the case study. *Comparative Political Studies*, 8, 178–185.
Denzin, N. K. (1978). *The research act: A theoretical introduction to sociological methods* (2nd ed.). New York: McGraw-Hill.
Feagin, J. R., Orum, A. M. and Sjoberg, G., eds (1991). *A case for the case study*. Chapel Hill: University of North Carolina Press.
Gillham, B. (2000). *Case study research methods*. London: Continuum.
Glaser, B. and Strauss, A. (1967). *The discovery of grounded theory: Strategies for qualitative research*. Chicago: Aldine.
Glesne, C. and Peshkin, A. (1992). *Becoming qualitative researchers*. New York: Longman.
Holder, H. (1987). *Control issues in alcohol abuse prevention: Strategies for states and communities*. Greenwich, CT: JAI Press.
Johansson, R. (2003). Case study methodology. In *International Conference Methodologies in Housing Research*, Stockholm, Sweden, 22–24 September, pp. 1–14. Available at: http://www.psyking.net/HTMLobj-3839/Case_Study_Methodology-_Rolf_Johansson_ver_2.pdf.
Miles, M. B. and Huberman, A. M. (1994). *Qualitative data analysis: An expanded source book*. Thousand Oaks, CA: Sage.
O'Brien, B., Harris, I., Beckman, T., Reed, D. and Cook, D. (2014). Standards for reporting qualitative research: A synthesis of recommendations. *Academic Medicine*, 89, 1245–1251.
Stake, R. (1995). *The art of case study research*. Thousand Oaks, CA: Sage.
Stake, R. (1998). Case studies. In: N. Denzin and Y. Lincoln, ed., *Strategies of Qualitative Inquiry* (pp. 134–164). Thousand Oaks, CA: Sage.
Tellis, W. M. (1997a). Application of a case study methodology. *The Qualitative Report*, 3(3), 1–19. Retrieved from https://nsuworks.nova.edu/tqr/vol3/iss3/1.
Tellis, W. M. (1997b). Introduction to case study. *The Qualitative Report*, 3(2), 1–14. Retrieved from https://nsuworks.nova.edu/tqr/vol3/iss2/4.
Woodside, A. G. (2010). *Case study research: Theory, methods, practice*. Bingley: Emerald.
Yin, R. (1984). *Case study research: Design and methods*. Beverly Hills, CA: Sage.

Yin, R. (1989). *Case study research: Design and methods* (Rev. ed.). Beverly Hills, CA: Sage.

Yin, R. (1994). *Case study research: Design and methods* (2nd ed.). Beverly Hills, CA: Sage.

Yin, R. (2012). *Applications of case study research*. Thousand Oaks, CA: Sage.

Zonabend, F. (1992). The monograph in European ethnology. *Current Sociology*, 40(1), 49–60.

9. Visual research methods: volunteer-employed photography (VEP)
Brian Garrod and Nika Balomenou

SUMMARY

Visual methods have been criticised for an apparent lack of robustness with regard to their validity, reliability and practicality. This chapter argues that such methods can actually provide a realistic alternative to longer-established research methods such as surveys, interviews and observation. They also have additional advantages that are worth capturing.

INTRODUCTION

Visual materials, such as artworks, photographs and film, have often been considered inferior to the more familiar numbers, words and texts associated with the established canon of social research methods (Bell and Davison, 2013). While it is often said that the 'camera never lies', many social scientists have argued that the camera may lie – and, indeed, often does (Balomenou and Garrod, 2019). Visual images are polysemic by their very nature: they convey often complex, multi-layered meanings that are likely to be interpreted differently by different observers. This implies that the meanings the observer reads in the images are not necessarily those that were intended by the person creating the image, for example the photographer or the home film maker. Many researchers consider this to be a significant shortcoming, and conclude that visual methods are fundamentally unable to deliver results that match up to the standards of validity and reliability that can be achieved using more traditional methods such as questionnaires, interviews and observation (Linfield, 2011). In holding to this view, critics of visual methods are also implicitly promoting the argument that such weaknesses cannot realistically be addressed through careful research design and implementation, in the same way that such issues are dealt with when using traditional research methods.

Other researchers, meanwhile, have questioned the practicality of visual methods, particularly those that involve the analysis of a large number of visual items. Some have pointed to the practical difficulties involved in acquiring high-quality cameras to lend to research subjects (including the potential cost), while others would argue that the amount of time involved in analysing a large number of visual images renders visual methods too cumbersome to generate timely outcomes (Banks and Zeitlyn, 2015). Legal and ethical considerations have also been noted as potentially constraining factors (Bell and Davison, 2013).

Visual methods have therefore been used infrequently in social research. Notably, however, there has recently been an upsurge of interest in the use of visual methods in cultural studies, for example (Banks and Zeitlyn, 2015), and in tourism studies (Matteucci, 2013; Pennington-Gray et al., 2015). Management studies, however, of which marketing is a significant part, has been slow to adopt visual methods (Bell and Davison, 2013; Kozinets and Belk, 2007). This is difficult to understand given the strong visual dimension in much of marketing theory and practice. The relative lack of use of visual methods in marketing research also seems something of an anomaly given the power of such methods to analyse, explain and help understand subjects of great interest to marketers. Michaelidou et al. (2013), for example, point to significant dissonance between the imagery used by tourism destination marketers and those captured by the tourists themselves, which tend to reflect a more realistic, holistic, lived experience of the places they are visiting. Visual methods would enable destination marketers to distinguish between the two and address the gap.

Such potential cannot be realised if visual methods are, as their critics suggest, irretrievably flawed as research methods. The purpose of this chapter is to review the use of visual methods across the social sciences, focusing particularly on the use of volunteer-employed photography (VEP), which is a type of participant-generated image (PGI) method and one that arguably has some important methodological advantages. The chapter will then consider whether there is substance to the charge of unresolvable flaws. Indeed, if there are practical ways to address such concerns effectively through robust research design and implementation, the potential power of the visual methods can be unlocked. The chapter will then provide an example of how VEP has been used in the field of tourism marketing.

DESCRIPTION OF THE METHOD

Visual methods are defined as those that use pictorial images in the production of knowledge. Any medium may in theory be used to create such images, but the two most popular in social research have proven to be photography and film (Simpson, 2011; Pink, 2013). Such images may be used simply as a way of recording research results or presenting them to an intended audience. Their greater value is realised, however, when they are used as a means of gaining a greater understanding of a chosen phenomenon or issue.

In this respect, visual images have been used extensively in social research as stimuli to assist respondents in giving more effective and insightful answers to the questions that researchers put to them (Harper, 2002). This includes marketing research, where visual materials have often been employed as stimuli to assist in questioning people about their experiences, preferences and opinions (e.g. Heisley and Levy, 1991; Matteucci, 2013). Visual images may also contain valuable information about those creating them, which can be uncovered through the use of complementary methods of analysis. Creating a pictorial image involves making choices, be they explicit or implicit, about what the image represents. These choices can reveal information about people's opinions, beliefs, emotions, motivations and many other difficult-to-access variables that are of interest to marketers. This use of visual images is thus akin to the projective techniques that have long been used in marketing and market research (Haire, 1950).

This use of visual images in this manner is popularly known as photo-elicitation. One of the first studies to use photo-elicitation was undertaken by Collier (1957). In such studies, research subjects are shown items of visual media to help them reflect on the subject at hand and formulate more meaningful answers to questions that are typically difficult to answer. The difficulty could be due to the subject of the question being one of subconscious routine (such as the impulse purchase of a product), in which case a visual 'cue' may be useful to assist in memory recall. Alternatively, the question being asked may necessarily require deep introspection (such as why one tourism destination is preferred to another), in which case visual stimuli may help the research subject formulate his or her ideas and express them more effectively.

Within the photo-elicitation tradition there are two broad strands of research: researcher-driven photo-elicitation and PGI research (see Figure 9.1). The latter term was developed by Balomenou and Garrod (2016) with the aim of bringing together a field in which a very large number of names have been used for what is essentially the same technique. Researcher-driven photo-elicitation uses visual images that are collected by the researchers (perhaps photographs purchased from photo-stock websites or captured by the researchers themselves during fieldwork). PGI studies, in contrast, analyse visual images that have been created by the research subjects themselves. These images, which often

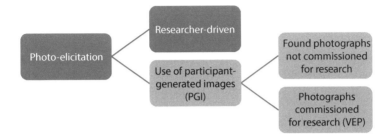

Figure 9.1   Strands of photo-elicitation

take the form of photographs, can then be analysed in a variety of ways to help answer the research questions set for the study.

It is then possible to divide PGI methods into two further sub-strands: those that use 'found' images and those that use 'commissioned' images. Again, the images in question are usually photographs, although in theory any form of visual image could be used. The former sub-strand involves taking samples of photos from databases, which can then be analysed by the researcher using a range of techniques. Such databases are increasingly digital and online in nature, including social media sites such as Instagram (e.g. Geurin-Eagleman and Burch, 2016), Flickr (e.g. Donaire et al., 2014) and even Facebook (Vilnai-Yavetz and Tifferet, 2015). The latter sub-strand involves asking research subjects to take photos, in context and in real time, that reflect their personal, lived experience of something or somewhere. Research subjects are typically asked to take a number of photographs that represent a theme of interest to the researchers, e.g. things research subjects like or do not like about a hotel room (Pullman and Robson, 2007) or a hospitality service (Venkatraman and Nelson, 2008). Even so, some studies have simply asked the research subjects to take photos of whatever appeals to them or catches their eye.

As noted above, PGI methods using commissioned photographs go under a variety of names, reflecting the many academic disciplines in which they have been adopted and the tendency for researchers within these traditions not to move far beyond them to identify when, where and how the techniques have been used before. Indeed, a systematic review of commissioned PGI studies by Balomenou and Garrod (2016) found that 35 names were used in nearly 300 studies over a 35-year period, implying that a new name for the technique has been coined on average once a year, every year, since it was first invented. As such, the method is known as visitor-employed photography, photovoice, autophotography and many other variants. Balomenou and Garrod (2016) therefore suggest that the term 'volunteer-employed photography' could be used to denote this group of methods: a more generic name that assumes neither who the research subjects may be (visitors to a site, residents of a local area, and so on) nor the research approach (as in photovoice); it is also one that uses an existing acronym (VEP, for visitor-employed photography) to provide a degree of continuity. The defining feature of VEP studies is that they place cameras in the hands of research participants who are given the task of taking photographs, over an agreed timespan, to represent their opinions, preferences or experiences of a product, event or place. The researchers then use these photographs as data to enable them to answer the research questions they have set for their study. A summary of the steps typically involved in a VEP study are shown in Figure 9.2.

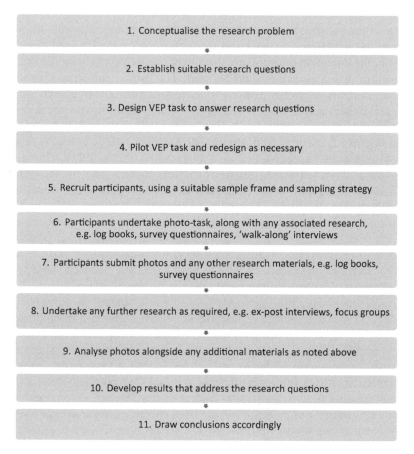

1. Conceptualise the research problem

2. Establish suitable research questions

3. Design VEP task to answer research questions

4. Pilot VEP task and redesign as necessary

5. Recruit participants, using a suitable sample frame and sampling strategy

6. Participants undertake photo-task, along with any associated research, e.g. log books, survey questionnaires, 'walk-along' interviews

7. Participants submit photos and any other research materials, e.g. log books, survey questionnaires

8. Undertake any further research as required, e.g. ex-post interviews, focus groups

9. Analyse photos alongside any additional materials as noted above

10. Develop results that address the research questions

11. Draw conclusions accordingly

Figure 9.2   Steps in a typical VEP study

HISTORY OF ITS USE

While PGI methods have had a shorter history of use than researcher-driven photo-elicitation methods, they have been applied across a variety of fields of academic study in a wide range of contexts. Turning specifically to methods using commissioned photographs, lack of awareness of previous uses of VEP has often meant that authors have assumed that their study is the first in the field (Balomenou and Garrod, 2016). This has often led to authors failing to report basic information such as sample size or method of data analysis: presumably in the belief that, being the first on the scene, they are free to write the rulebook as they go along.

The earliest papers using VEP were published in the 1970s under the name 'visitor-employed photography'. What is thought to be the earliest is a paper by Cherem and Traweek (1977), based on the second author's PhD thesis on interpretive planning. Chenoweth (1984) later used the method in the context of landscape assessment. While most of the subsequent studies sought to assess people's experience of natural areas, landscape, leisure and tourism, there have been exceptions. A study by Jenkins and Jenkins (1998), for example, examines community education and empowerment. This is a subject that would fit more readily into the group of studies called 'photovoice'.

With its roots in the 1980s, photovoice uses the same basic methods as visitor-employed photography studies. The differences lie in the uses to which the method has been put (most of the studies have been in the field of anthropology), the analytical techniques used (typically semiotics and content analysis) and the purpose of the study. With regard to the latter, photovoice studies have frequently sought to harness the knowledge of 'ordinary' people, who are viewed as the experts on their own everyday lives (Wang and Burris, 1997). In doing so it seeks to give a voice to groups that are under-empowered in society, using the power of visual images to promote their viewpoints, needs and aspirations. The participants used in such studies have tended to mirror this transformative aim, such as young people from poor backgrounds (Wilson et al., 2007), women living in deprived areas (e.g. Wang and Pies, 2004) and people with disabilities (e.g. Booth and Booth, 2003). Photovoice is probably the most common name given to VEP studies.

Another name by which such studies is often known is autophotography. This name was used initially by psychologists, the first study being by Ziller and Lewis (1981), who used PGIs to help them explore the concepts of self, social and environmental identity. Such concepts are widely considered to be difficult to verbalise, and it was hypothesised that visual methods could enable these concepts to be better communicated. Other studies in this field include Jones (2004) and Noland (2006). Some studies, meanwhile, have adopted a transformative or political purpose (e.g. Dodman, 2003). This purpose is, however, most often associated with photovoice, which again demonstrates the looseness of the use of terminology in the field.

This chapter does not seek to side with any one of these three variants of the VEP method. First, there are clearly many other variants in addition to these, each with their own claims to superiority. Second, the differences between these variants are minor in comparison to their similarities. It is important to focus instead on what binds these variants together, and that is the recruitment of participants to take photographs that are then used by the researcher as data to perform analyses intended to answer questions relating to the context in which the participants belong. This bestows such methods with several advantages over traditional, non-visual methods such as interviews, questionnaires and observation. This chapter argues that visual methods can address the same issues as the more traditional methods, but with additional advantages. What is important, then, is to ensure that concerns such as intent and timing are taken appropriately into account so that the methods deliver appropriately valid and reliable findings.

RESEARCH VALIDITY AND RELIABILITY

While PGI methods have often been criticised for a lack of reliability and validity, it is important to recognise that no research method can be considered truly free of such concerns (Prosser, 2005). Effective measures must *always* be taken in the application of any research method to ensure that it delivers as reliable and valid outcomes as possible. The crucial issue is therefore not whether visual methods are free from concerns about their reliability and validity, but whether there are measures available that can potentially address such concerns, and that these measures are known about and deployed to best effect. If this is the case, then there is no reason why visual methods cannot produce as reliable and valid results as any other research method. Visual methods also have some recognised advantages, which arguably give them superiority over other methods – a potential that will only be lost if such methods are dismissed out of hand. PGI methods may even be able to deliver greater reliability and validity in some respects, for example by enabling research questions to be answered more effectively and robustly, possibly even more so than methods in the traditional canon of social research methods.

Validity

Dealing first with issues of validity, it is important to bear in mind that visual methods are typically employed alongside more traditional research methods. Indeed, in the case of researcher-driven photo-elicitation, the purpose of using visual images is to enhance the validity of other research methods, interviews probably being the most common of these (Clark-Ibáñez, 2004). This enhancement usually takes the form of presenting visual images to research subjects as prompts or exhibits during interviews or surveys. These are used to help respondents recall memories, to think more deeply about the questions they are being asked, or to express thoughts, emotions or opinions they would otherwise find difficult to formulate. Indeed, as Harper (2002: 22–23) notes, photo-elicitation can help 'mine deeper shafts into a different part of human consciousness than do words-alone interviews'. Researcher-driven photo-elicitation may thus be able to deliver more valid research outcomes than the use of the accompanying traditional method alone. Provided that the method is itself properly designed and implemented, this enhancement may be a valuable one.

In PGI studies, various methods are used to enable visual images to be analysed, or 'read'. Some studies employ methods such as semiotics or manifest content analysis, which help the researchers 'read' the photos through a process of careful examination (MacKay and Couldwell, 2004). Others use complementary methods to assist in interpreting the images, such as surveys, interviews and observation, which allows the researcher to 'read' the photos more effectively than by examining them on their own, lending greater validity to the study.

PGI methods are equally open to the use of quantitative and qualitative methods: while studies employing qualitative methods appear to be more common (Wu and Pearce, 2014), many exist that use quantitative methods (Xie and Garner, 2009), including the use of statistical analysis (Naoi et al., 2011). Increasingly, however, a mixed-methods approach is being adopted (Balomenou and Garrod, 2016). This helps address the validity concerns associated with visual studies insofar as it enables triangulation to be undertaken. This approach can enhance the validity of a study by corroborating its findings. Triangulation is considered to be particularly effective when quantitative and qualitative methods are used alongside each other to address a given research question. The premise is that those findings that are consistent across different research methods are more likely to represent valid understandings of the issue or phenomenon being investigated (Jick, 1979).

It can also be argued that PGI methods have an advantage over researcher-driven photo-elicitation in terms of their ability to produce valid research outcomes: by definition, they employ visual images that have been produced by the research subjects. As genuine stakeholders in the problem domain, the images they create are more likely to provide valid perspectives on the research questions being addressed than images created by others, such as professional photographers or the researchers themselves. With VEP studies, it is possible to question the research subjects directly: for example, by interviewing them during or after they complete the task (Bennett and Dearden, 2013), or by asking them to complete a photo-diary or photo-log (e.g. Garrod, 2008). Survey methods can also be used to capture further information about the research subjects, be it demographic, psychographic or behavioural. This data can be useful in enabling correlations and associations to be established, which can help answer specific questions the research is aiming to address.

Another feature of VEP studies is that the research subjects are personally involved in the research: all VEP studies involve asking research subjects to undertake some form of photography task. In this way, the research subject effectively becomes a participant in the research. This unlocks further potential in the technique insofar as it serves as the basis for collaboration between the researcher and those whom the research is intended to serve or benefit (Harper, 2002). Collaborative research can be powerful in many regards (Dakin, 2003). For example, unlike research subjects, research participants can steer the direction of the research (Dodman, 2003), helping to shape its purpose, sharpen its process, and helping to ensure more accurate, focused, meaningful and thus valid outcomes (Packard, 2008).

Two further factors that may be said to enable VEP methods to deliver more valid answers to research questions than PGI methods that use 'found' photographs relate to *intent* and *timing* (Balomenou and Garrod, 2019). These require close attention in the design of VEP studies, and are therefore discussed in the following sub-section.

Issues of intent and timing

One of the potential advantages of VEP is that it can be more effective when it comes to establishing intent, i.e. understanding the 'story' the research subject was intending to tell through their photograph when it is being 'read' by the researcher. Intent can be crucial when it comes to establishing valid research outcomes (Goldstein, 2007). For example, a photo of a car is manifestly just that: a photo of a car. What is important, however, is what the photographer intended it to portray or mean: the car is (both metaphorically and literally) a vehicle for narrating the photo – a sign or symbol of something that the photographer wants to say in response to the task they have been set – but without further assistance the researcher may struggle to understand what that might be. VEP studies enable intent to be better understood because of the way they have been designed: the research subjects are usually asked to take photos to fulfil a specific task that the researchers have set them (Anglin, 2015; House et al., 2015). This task must be communicated clearly to the research subjects, however, and it must be one that they find easy enough to fulfil. It must be specific enough to enable the research question to be addressed, yet vague enough not to lead the research subjects into particular ways of thinking when taking their photos.

Another important issue relates to timing. It might be argued that it is possible to contact those who took the photos 'found' by researchers in that sub-strand of PGI research; but there is likely to be a time lapse between the photo being taken and it being interpreted by the photographer for the benefit of the researcher. This may be significant in that the research subject may not remember very well the thought processes that went into taking the picture. There is also a potential 'warm glow' effect that may alter the research subject's view of what they were trying to say: over time, even uncomfortable or unsatisfying experiences may be remembered in a better light (Balomenou and Garrod, 2019). Even more importantly, it might be possible that the photographer in a 'found' PGI study was not trying to make it say anything at all, taking the photo at a mere whim with no intention for it to 'mean' anything.

Timing is also important with respect to when the research subject is taking the photos. The research subject may, for example, be experiencing very different emotions when they first begin to use a product or arrive at an event – what might be called the 'puppy love' effect (Smith et al., 2015); but as time goes on emotions might become more neutral, or even negative. This implies that the message the research subject wants to tell – or, indeed, is able to tell – may depend on when they happened to have taken (or, in the case of VEP, are asked to take) their photographs. For example, following the typical build-up of anticipation about going on holiday (Vogt and Andereck, 2003), the research subject might be very pleased with the destination in the first few days after arrival. If the 'found' photographs are taken in this period, they might not represent the research subject's experience of their time in the destination as a whole. The same may, of course, be true with VEP studies: if the subjects are asked to complete the photo-task early in their holiday, it might produce rather different results than if it was conducted later on.

With VEP studies, however, such problems with timing are more easily overcome because the research has control over when the photos are taken. The researcher is also able to decide how long it will be after the photos are taken that complementary methods will be conducted with the research subjects. Indeed, it might be considered prudent for the researcher to be present when the research subject is undertaking the photo-task so the interviews (be they formal or informal), observation and even surveys can be undertaken at the same time as the photographs. It is also possible to control when the photos are taken during the course of the research subjects' experience: in the case of the holiday, how far into it they are and how many days they have left.

It might, meanwhile, be considered desirable to wait until the research subject's holiday is over – but again it is possible to time the use of complementary methods to ensure that the research subjects' memories are still fresh. It might even be desirable to undertake a series of interviews with research subjects at various points in the future to investigate how strong the 'warm glow effect' might be and how long it may last. The point is that this can be relatively easily achieved with VEP methods, while if the researcher is using 'found' images it could be considered to be a major impediment to the validity of the study.

Reliability

Moving on to the reliability of visual methods, critics have made much of the polysemic nature of visual images (meaning that they can have multiple meanings, interpretations or understandings, depending on who is charged with analysing them). These issues are, however, by no means unresolvable when implementing PGI research. The strategy employed to do so depends on whether the researcher is analysing the photographs directly or with the assistance of complementary methods such as interviews, surveys and observation.

In the first instance, where the researcher is analysing the photos directly, a semiotic or content analysis approach is frequently used. These methods do, of course, have the potential to produce unreliable results – but only if they are poorly designed and implemented. A robust semiotic approach, for example, will need to involve the researcher ensuring that the signs and symbols being drawn from the text (or in this case photographs) are well defined and properly documented. Continual triangulation within the semiotic coding scheme is also recommended (Stevenson, 2007). In content analysis, good practice may be considered to revolve around the use of multiple independent coders and the publication of high inter-coder reliability statistics (Balomenou and Garrod, 2014).

Other PGI studies employ complementary methods to assist in the interpretation of the photos that were either 'found' by the researchers or 'commissioned' from research participants. In these cases, the reliability of the entire approach depends largely on the good design and implementation of these methods. If the researcher chooses qualitative methods, then familiar issues such as taking appropriate steps to minimise researcher bias will come to the fore (Matteucci, 2013). If quantitative methods are chosen, the considerations will be quite different (albeit equally familiar), focusing on issues of sampling strategy, sample size, and so on. The important thing to note is that, in PGI studies, issues of reliability are not attached to the use of photographs but to the complementary methods used to assist in their interpretation. If these are poorly designed, then the study as a whole will produce unreliable results.

Practicality

Linked to the above, critics of VEP methods have sometimes suggested that they are essentially impractical to use (Taylor et al., 1995). Two of the most popular criticisms relate to the potential cost of acquiring cameras of suitable quality to give to the research subjects and the time it takes to develop the photographs inside the cameras, which may delay the use of ex-post complementary methods and even the timeliness of the study as a whole.

In the past there was certainly some value in these criticisms. Indeed, it used to be difficult to acquire cameras of suitable quality to lend to participants (Harper, 2010), for reasons including purchase cost (Halifax et al., 2008) and concern that equipment might be damaged, lost or not returned (Taylor et al., 1995). There are three arguments that can be made in response to this. The first is that participants can be provided with inexpensive single-use cameras, which nowadays take very high-quality photographs. Additionally, even if photographs taken on inexpensive cameras are of dubious quality, that does not mean they are unusable in the study. The combination of the photographic data alongside the complementary methods is what produces a very rich dataset. For example, a photograph taken for a study in St David's Peninsula, Wales (discussed in greater depth in the following section) was nearly black, with only a blurred view of a street and a house corner. However, complementary methods allowed the researchers to learn that the elderly participant purposely took this photo at 3am to prove that her village was safe. The poor quality of the photograph actually added to the point the participant was making, resulting in a more meaningful contribution to the study.

Second, although film and disposable cameras have been used as a matter of course in VEP studies since the 1990s, even during the 2000s they have become much more rarely used due to the widespread ownership of smartphones. Smartphone technology has also advanced significantly, in the last decade particularly, to the extent that criticisms about the quality of cameras built into mobile devices can no longer be justified. In cases where researchers need hard copies of photographs to be seen by participants straightaway or they need them as instant rewards, they might need to consider instant cameras, scanners and photo printers to ensure they are able to share the photographs with participants and keep a copy. However, in terms of cost, the price of instant cameras and film development is very low these days, with disposable cameras costing approximately £5 for 18 exposures, compared to £7 in 2008 and £8.50 for printing up to 27 exposures (including delivery).

It can therefore be argued that many of the criticisms about the practicality of VEP relate to the use of film-based cameras, which were the only realistic choice until perhaps 20 years ago. Such criticisms are no longer valid, however, due to widespread access to digital photography (Van House, 2011). Nowadays, rather than needing to provide study participants with cameras to sling around their necks, participants can almost be relied upon to be carrying their own camera-phones around with them in their pockets and bags. This has rendered photographic methods naturally accessible (Van House, 2011). Moreover, photography is now nearly universal as a skill. It is reported that preschool children learn to take photographs before they learn to write, while children and young adults are now considered 'digital natives' as taking and sharing digital photographs using email and social media platforms has become the new norm (Capistrán, 2016). Participants do not have to do anything new or difficult to be part of a VEP study; they need merely to follow their daily routine, of which photo-taking is a natural part.

AN EXAMPLE OF VEP IN ACTION

Case Study of St David's Peninsula, Pembrokeshire Coast National Park, Wales

This research study used VEP in a tourism destination context, with both user groups – locals and tourists – asked to participate. The outcomes of this study show how VEP can be an invaluable tool for destination management organisations (DMOs) to use across the broad spectrum of their marketing activities. VEP allows DMOs to focus on specific targets groups through the projected image of the destination likely to attract their attention.

The study took place at St David's Peninsula in Pembrokeshire Coast National Park, Wales, where the ratio of tourists to locals is more than 150 to 1, which can be considered very high (Balomenou and Garrod, 2014).

Due to there being a short tourist season from June to October, along with the very small size of the area (including St David's, the UK's smallest, city with fewer than 2000 inhabitants), the space is vigorously contested between the two main user groups. In order to appreciate what the two user groups like and dislike about the area, it was considered appropriate to ask them to show what they mean though photographs and diaries.

Participants were furnished with a camera, photo-diary, questionnaire and information letter, adapted after pilot studies to finalise the questionnaires and camera collection points. Participants were asked to return the camera and photo-diaries in designated boxes. Local participants were asked to take photographs of what gives them a sense of place and what detracts from their enjoyment of their area. Similarly, tourists were asked to show the researcher what they like about the area and what detracts from their enjoyment of the area. Complementary methods comprised asking them to give titles to the photographs and to write a brief summary of why they took each photograph.

After two weeks of sampling, 145 cameras were distributed to tourists and 54 to locals. The response rate was 78 per cent for the tourists and 45 per cent for the locals. Data was coded and stored in NVIVO, a software package that allows flexible interrogation and analysis without losing sight of the individual. The photos, diaries and questionnaires were analysed both thematically and statistically using canonical variate analysis. To illustrate this process, Figure 9.3 presents a very small part of the theme of 'sense of place' for local people and Figure 9.4 the theme of what is enjoyable about the participants' holiday, while Figure 9.5 represents the tourists' perception of the area and its value to them.

The most important result from this study is that the quality of the data is very rich. The participants' photos, in conjunction with the interviews and photo-diaries, provided a high-quality dataset which demonstrates the potential for VEP to assist in many different aspects of marketing management. In the context of tourism destination marketing, it can be seen that VEP makes it possible for DMOs to understand in great detail what visitors enjoy the most, and project relevant images in their marketing campaigns.

The general feeling of enjoyment and commitment to this kind of study has been identified in the literature by a number of researchers (Taylor et al., 1995). This proved to be very strong motivation in recruiting volunteers to this study, as a large number of participants commented on the enjoyment this project offered and wished the research team luck with the remainder of the study. Participants clearly engaged with the study, which can only serve to enhance its validity.

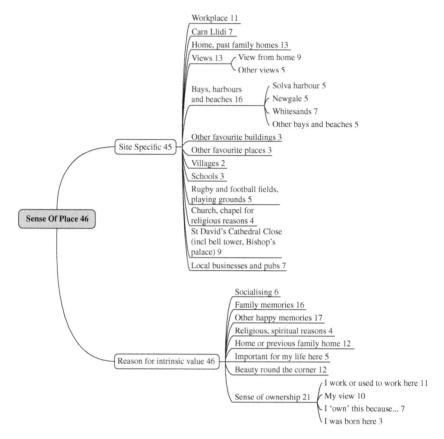

Figure 9.3   Sense of place for local community members

DISCUSSION

It is established in this chapter that photographs are polysemic in nature, and therefore it is surprising that the opportunities they offer have not been utilised more often by marketing researchers and DMOs to understand the best qualities their destination has to offer – ones that will appeal to the target groups of the DMO – and then to position their marketing offer accordingly. By using visual methods, VEP in particular, it can be argued that any dissonance between the images projected by DMOs through official channels and the lived experience projected in tourists' photographs can be overcome, resulting in marketing efforts that are more effective and efficient. Indeed, through the use of VEP, DMOs can

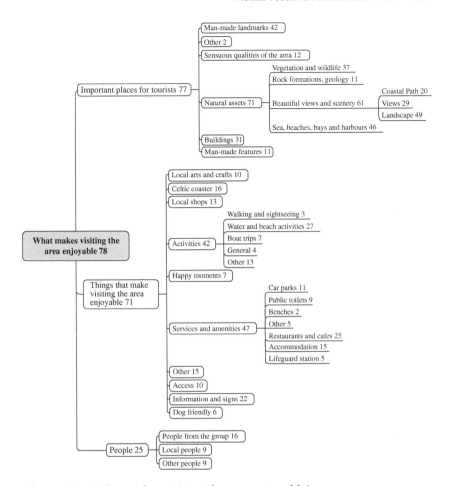

Figure 9.4 *What makes visiting the area enjoyable?*

gain a more in-depth understanding of how the destinations they promote are understood, experienced and remembered by visitors. A clear and detailed understanding of these experiences and memories can be useful in two main ways. First, it can help inform the visual elements of marketing campaigns that are needed to appeal to the destination's various target markets. Second, it can help shape the destination images of future tourists, whose expectations are, as a result, more likely to be fulfilled if these images are realistic and consistent. This may in turn create more positive word of mouth about the destination, resulting in further visits by new tourists in the future.

Figure 9.5   Mackerel fishing

There are good reasons to argue that photographs are subjective and difficult to interpret as stand-alone artefacts. However, to reject VEP on this basis is to dismiss the richness of information that participant-generated photographs can offer. Objections to VEP as a visual research method might have been reasonable in the 1970s and 1980s, but are not so today. On the contrary; the use of photography is nearly ubiquitous worldwide. Capturing and sharing photographs is not only the norm among people in the youngest generation (known as 'digital natives'), but is also widely used among people of older generations (even the oldest, sometimes called 'silver surfers'). Photo-taking is now used to achieve daily tasks, ranging from a snap to serve as an aide-memoir to where one parked one's car to a carefully curated series of artistic photographs of a beauty spot visited on holiday.

Concerns over lack of reliability can also be overcome in the research design process by deciding on appropriate complementary methods to accompany the photo-taking: ones that have a good fit with the context and the research question. There are ample complementary methods to choose from that are adaptable to different research approaches and allow participants to maintain the advantage VEP gives them. VEP puts participants in the driving seat to enable them to show the researcher their experience in real time, as it unfolds. By allowing participants to interpret their own photographs, researcher bias can be minimised, and the result is as close to a verbatim visual and verbal narrative as possible.

This chapter has also argued that VEP has a number of additional advantages over the traditional canon of marketing research methods. To capture these benefits, however, requires well-designed research. While there are no formal good-practice guidelines, much can be learned from reviewing the successes and shortcomings of previous research projects that have used the method. These lessons include the use of multiple coders, detailed sampling strategies and robust research frameworks to ensure the proper design and implementation of the VEP method. The so-called problems associated with VEP are not to be feared: good design and implementation of the method can successfully address them – and at the same time unlock the potential for VEP to make a revolutionary contribution to market and marketing research.

REFERENCES

Anglin, A. E. (2015). Voices from Costa Rica: Exploring youth perceptions of tourism and the influence of tourism on identity formation and cultural change. *Journal of Tourism and Cultural Change*, 13(3), 191–207.

Balomenou, N., & Garrod, B. (2014). Using volunteer-employed photography to inform tourism planning decisions: A study of St David's Peninsula, Wales. *Tourism Management*, 44, 126–139.

Balomenou, N., & Garrod, B. (2016). A review of participant-generated image methods in the social sciences. *Journal of Mixed Methods Research*, 10(4), 335–351.

Balomenou, N., & Garrod, B. (2019). Photographs in tourism research: Prejudice, power, performance and participant-generated images. *Tourism Management*, 70, 201–217.

Banks, M., & Zeitlyn, D. (2015). *Visual methods in social research*. London: Sage.

Bell, E., & Davison, J. (2013). Visual management studies: Empirical and theoretical approaches. *International Journal of Management Reviews*, 15(2), 167–184.

Bennett, N. J., & Dearden, P. (2013). A picture of change: Using photovoice to explore social and environmental change in coastal communities on the Andaman Coast of Thailand. *Local Environment*, 18(9), 983–1001.

Booth, T., & Booth, W. (2003). In the frame: Photovoice and mothers with learning difficulties. *Disability & Society*, 18, 431–442.

Capistrán, J. B. (2016). Mobile photography and social networks: Production, consumption, socialization and copyright practices among university students. *Journalism*, 6, 512–522.

Chenoweth, R. (1984). Visitor employed photography: A potential tool for landscape architecture. *Landscape Journal*, 3, 136–143.

Cherem, G. J., & Traweek, D. E. (1977). Visitor employed photography: A tool for interpretive planning on river environments. In *Proceedings of River Recreation Management and Research Symposium* (pp. 236–244). Washington, DC: USDA Forest Services.

Clark-Ibáñez, M. (2004). Framing the social world with photo-elicitation interviews. *American Behavioral Scientist*, 47(12), 1507–1527.

Collier, J., Jr. (1957). Photography in anthropology: A report on two experiments. *American Anthropologist*, 59, 843–859.

Dakin, S. (2003). There's more to landscape than meets the eye: Towards inclusive landscape assessment in resource and environmental management. *Canadian Geographer*, 47, 185–200.

Dodman, D. R. (2003). Shooting in the city: An autophotographic exploration of the urban environment in Kingston, Jamaica. *Area*, 35, 293–304.

Donaire, J. A., Camprubí, R., & Galí, N. (2014). Tourist clusters from Flickr travel photography. *Tourism Management Perspectives*, 11, 26–33.

Garrod, B. (2008). Exploring place perception: A photo-based analysis. *Annals of Tourism Research*, 35(2), 381–401.

Geurin-Eagleman, A. N., & Burch, L. M. (2016). Communicating via photographs: A gendered analysis of Olympic athletes' visual self-presentation on Instagram. *Sport Management Review*, 19(2), 133–145.

Goldstein, B. M. (2007). All photos lie: Images as data. In G. C. Stanczak (Ed.), *Visual research methods: Image, society, and representation* (pp. 61–81). Thousand Oaks. CA: Sage.

Haire, M. (1950). Projective techniques in marketing research. *Journal of Marketing*, 14(5), 649–656.

Halifax, D. N. V., Yurichuk, F., Meeks, J., & Khandor, E. (2008). Photovoice in a Toronto community partnership: Exploring the social determinants of health with homeless people progress in community health partnerships. *Research, Education, and Action*, 2, 129–136.

Harper, D. (2002). Talking about pictures: A case for photo elicitation. *Visual Studies*, 17(1), 13–26.

Harper, K. (2010). *Across the bridge: Using PhotoVoice to investigate environment and health in a Hungarian Romani (Gypsy) community*. European Association of Social Anthropologists (EASA). Maynooth, Ireland: Berkeley Electronic Press.

Heisley, D. D., & Levy, S. J. (1991). Autodriving: A photoelicitation technique. *Journal of Consumer Research*, 18(3), 257–272.

House, C., Samways, J., & Williams, A. (2015). Designing coastal management strategies for populations with distinct needs: The case of learning disabilities. *Coastal Management*, 43(6), 589–608.

Jenkins, D. I., & Jenkins, Q. A. L. (1998). Visions along the trail: Community action and visitor employed photography in two Native American communities. Paper presented at the annual meeting of the Rural Sociological Society, Portland, OR. Retrieved from http://0-files.eric.ed.gov.opac.msmc.edu/fulltext/ED425878.pdf.

Jick, T. D. (1979). Mixing qualitative and quantitative methods: Triangulation in action. *Administrative Science Quarterly*, 24(4), 602–611.

Jones, M. J. (2004). The effect of participation in the neighborhood academic program on the autophotographic self-concepts of inner-city adolescents. *Journal of Instructional Psychology*, 31, 188–201.

Kozinets, R. V., & Belk, R. W. (2007). Camcorder society: Quality videography in consumer and marketing research. In R. W. Belk (Ed.), *Handbook of qualitative research methods in marketing* (pp. 335–344). Cheltenham, UK and Northampton, MA, USA: Edward Elgar Publishing.

Linfield, S. (2011). *The cruel radiance: Photography and political violence*. Chicago: University of Chicago Press.

MacKay, K. J., & Couldwell, C. M. (2004). Using visitor-employed photography to investigate destination image. *Journal of Travel Research*, 42(4), 390–396.

Matteucci, X. (2013). Photo elicitation: Exploring tourist experiences with researcher-found images. *Tourism Management*, 35, 190–197.

Michaelidou, N., Siamagka, N. T., Moraes, C., & Micevski, M. (2013). Do marketers use visual representations of destinations that tourists value? Comparing visitors' image of a destination with marketer-controlled images online. *Journal of Travel Research*, 52(6), 789–804.

Naoi, T., Yamada, T., Iijima, S., & Kumazawa, T. (2011). Applying the caption evaluation method to studies of visitors' evaluation of historical districts. *Tourism Management*, 32(5), 1061–1074.

Noland, C. M. (2006). Auto-photography as research practice: Identity and self-esteem research. *Journal of Research Practice*, 2, M1.

Packard, J. (2008). 'I'm gonna show you what it's really like out here': The power and limitation of participatory visual methods. *Visual Studies*, 23(1), 63–77.

Pennington-Gray, L., Stepchenkova, S., & Schroeder, A. (2015). Using the lens of Flickr to decode emic meanings about the impact of Hurricane Sandy on a tourism destination: The Jersey shore. *International Journal of Tourism Anthropology*, 4(1), 89–109.

Pink, S. (2013). *Doing visual ethnography*. London: Sage.

Prosser, J. (2005). *Image-based research: A sourcebook for qualitative researchers*. Abingdon and New York: Routledge.

Pullman, M. E., & Robson, S. K. (2007). Visual methods: Using photographs to capture customers' experience with design. *Cornell Hotel and Restaurant Administration Quarterly*, 48(2), 121–144.

Simpson, P. (2011). 'So, as you can see . . .': Some reflections on the utility of video methodologies in the study of embodied practices. *Area*, 43(3), 343–352.

Smith, W. W., Li, X. R., Pan, B., Witte, M., & Doherty, S. T. (2015). Tracking destination image across the trip experience with smartphone technology. *Tourism Management*, 48, 113–122.

Stevenson, N. (2007). Visualising the city: An analysis of photographic images of London using semiotics and visual anthropology. Conference on Glancing, Glimpsing and Gazing: Tourists and Tourism in a Visual World. Eastbourne.

Taylor, J. G., Czarnowski, K. J., Sexton, N. R., & Flick, S. (1995). The importance of water to Rocky Mountain National Park visitors: An adaptation of visitor-employed photography to natural resources management. *Journal of Applied Recreation Research*, 20(1), 61–85.

Van House, N. A. (2011). Personal photography, digital technologies and the uses of the visual. *Visual Studies*, 26, 125–134.

Venkatraman, M., & Nelson, T. (2008). From servicescape to consumptionscape: A photo-elicitation study of Starbucks in the New China. *Journal of International Business Studies*, 39(6), 1010–1026.

Vilnai-Yavetz, I., & Tifferet, S. (2015). A picture is worth a thousand words: Segmenting consumers by Facebook profile images. *Journal of Interactive Marketing*, 32, 53–69.

Vogt, C. A., & Andereck, K. L. (2003). Destination perceptions across a vacation. *Journal of Travel Research*, 41(4), 348–354.

Wang, C., & Burris, M. A. (1997). Photovoice: Concept, methodology, and use for participatory needs assessment. *Health Education & Behavior*, 24, 369–387.

Wang, C. C., & Pies, C. A. (2004). Family, maternal, and child health through photovoice. *Maternal and Child Health Journal*, 8, 95–102.

Wilson, N., Dasho, S., Martin, A. C., Wallerstein, N., Wang, C. C., & Minkler, M. (2007). Engaging young adolescents in social action through photovoice: The Youth Empowerment Strategies (YES!) project. *Journal of Early Adolescence*, 27, 241–261.

Wu, M.-Y., & Pearce, P. L. (2014). Asset-based community development as applied to tourism in Tibet. *Tourism Geographies*, 16(3), 438–456.

Xie, P. F., & Garner, K. (2009). An analysis of students' photos of the novelty space on a field trip. *Journal of Teaching in Travel & Tourism*, 9(3–4), 176–192.

Ziller, R. C., & Lewis, D. (1981). Orientations: Self, social, and environmental percepts through auto-photography. *Personality and Social Psychology Bulletin*, 7, 338–343.

ANNOTATED READING

Balomenou, N., & Garrod, B. (2014). Using volunteer-employed photography to inform tourism planning decisions: A study of St David's Peninsula, Wales. *Tourism Management*, 44, 126–139. This study uses VEP to analyse the attitudes of residents and tourists at a busy tourism destination in the UK, demonstrating the considerable potential of VEP to analyse land-use planning issues.

Balomenou, N., & Garrod, B. (2016). **A review of participant-generated image methods in the social sciences.** *Journal of Mixed Methods Research,* **10(4), 335–351**. Undertakes a systematic review of nearly 300 academic papers and reports published between 1977 and 2012, identifying 35 names by which PGI methods are known and making recommendations for the reporting of basic information on data collection and analysis to assist in the development of best practice in the use of PGIs.

Balomenou, N., & Garrod, B. (2019). **Photographs in tourism research: Prejudice, power, performance and participant-generated images.** *Tourism Management,* **70, 201–217**. Presents a review of the use of photographs in social research and identifies how the prejudices social scientists have shown towards visual methods might best be overcome in order to harness their inherent methodological strengths.

10. Phenomenology: prospects and challenges for marketing research
Mine Inanc and Metin Kozak

INTRODUCTION

The paradigm of different disciplines has become an important focal point for businesses in order to provide competition and continuity in marketing. In general, positivism is the main paradigm of marketing, a quantitative method based on determinism and causation. Despite all these paradigmatic transformations, the positivist methods used in the field of marketing – e.g. experiments and statistics – have retained their popularity. Marketing studies are heavily biased towards using quantitative methods that simply report the outputs of primary data without deeper analysis. Considering the structure and effectiveness of the period there is a shift to quantitative research methods (Jamali, 2018), but there is a growing emphasis on promoting the usefulness of qualitative methods while mainly understanding human nature.

The dynamic nature of marketing has led to a paradigm shift in research methods. With this transformation, qualitative studies have become more important to explore the cause and effects of human behaviour in natural and objective settings (Goulding, 2005). Phenomenology, a qualitative research design, is a method that focuses on assessing individual lived experiences in the context of a particular phenomenon (Thompson et al., 1989) or travel or vacations in a tourism context (Wassler & Schuckert, 2017). This is one of the research methods that provide inferences appropriate to the content and structural transformation of marketing research (Hines & Ardley, 2011; Wilson, 2012). As a result, this chapter aims to address the methodologies of phenomenology in the context of the purpose served by marketing research. The chapter also offers the benefits to yield better results in marketing research through understanding consumer experiences and perceptions.

WHAT IS PHENOMENOLOGY?

Recently, post-positivist approaches have emerged as alternatives to positivist paradigms instead of generalizing social behaviour of social phenomena (Alvesson & Sköldberg, 2000; Law & Urry, 2004). The basic idea is that an event/situation can be understood by dimensions within its own boundaries. There is a kind of observation that social sciences are increasingly an attempt to benefit more from the advantages of qualitative methods. When we look at this paradigmatic transformation of marketing in terms of research methods, in particular, consumption in the consumer society is more difficult to predict and generalization of behaviour (such as the positivist approach) becomes difficult. Therefore, it is possible to understand and interpret consumer behaviour and consumption processes from a wider perspective by presenting more effective tools through a qualitative approach on an interpretive basis. For instance, using an interpretive phenomenological approach, the study by Alfakhri et al. (2018) concludes that aesthetics and design are likely to influence consumer experiences with a more specific focus on spending patterns, word-of-mouth recommendation and repeat visitation intentions in a hotel scape.

There is a common feeling that individuals assign different meaning to the same events, even if they are in the same culture or environment. Although phenomenology was developed as a science under Edmund Husserl (Richardson, 1999), it was described by Immanuel Kant (1764) as a reaction to the tension in science and ideas (Jasper, 1994). Husserl is recognized as the founder of the philosophical tradition of phenomenology. He argued that the methods used by the natural sciences are not suitable for studying the behaviour and experiences of human beings, and that there is a requirement to discover new methods to focus on things in their own settings. Husserl also aimed to provide a solid foundation for different disciplines by revealing the meaning of the most basic concepts (Ashworth, 2003). Giorgi and Giorgi (2008) state that psychology studies carried out with the help of phenomenology aim at discovering and describing the situations in which people live their daily life.

A number of things happen in our daily life, and perhaps we may immediately dismiss some of them or have trouble recalling some others even in the same day. In a similar sense, as potential consumers, we are surrounded by the large number of advertising campaigns through in/direct channels, even though we may have no idea about the functions or features of the majority of these products. Phenomenology is the detailed observation of the phenomena that the researcher is aware of but lacks in-depth knowledge about. The basis of this chapter is to illustrate the meaning of the phenomenon investigated. In other words, it is a research method that deals with what individuals perceive and understand about the meaning of their experiences in the universe/daily life. These phenomena can be lived experiences, concepts and perceptions of all kinds (Polidore et al., 2010).

BENEFITS AND CHALLENGES

As stated above, phenomenology-based empirical studies in psychology, instead of reducing a phenomenon to objective variables, aim to reveal the situations experienced by human beings in routine life. In other words, phenomenology allows the first-hand access to the identification of individuals' experiences of a phenomenon in order to discover that particular phenomenon. Giorgi (2006) questions the appropriateness of positivist research methods that have dominated the field of psychology and the objective knowledge produced by this approach. He argues that the model of natural sciences is designed to study physical objects in natural sciences, and is thus limited when applied to social sciences. However, the world is vital for all; therefore, all research in psychology should be based on a connection with phenomenology (Giorgi, 1997).

Becker (1992) argues that the phenomenological approach is driven by the idea that experience is considered to be both a valid and efficient source of knowledge. Phenomenological research has a dynamic process whose purpose is to examine as much as possible experienced by the researcher and the participants. Phenomenological research focuses on explaining what the common points are when participants experience a phenomenon (Creswell, 2013), such as how we know the world as human beings by questioning the way we experience the world (Van Manen, 1990, p.5).

According to Willig, going back to events and conveying varying human perceptions is the starting point of phenomenology. He describes phenomenology as "focusing on the content of consciousness and the individuals" (Willig, 2001, p.52). Van Manen (1990) considers the phenomenon as an "object of human experience" (p.163) and phenomenology as the "grasp of the very natural of the thing" (p.177). As such, phenomenology is driven to explore the causes of individual human experiences in a natural or objective setting, e.g. the lived experiences of a tourist joining a safari in Africa, staying at an all-inclusive resort in Turkey or enjoying a spa experience in Thailand.

As to the possible challenges that may result from the unstable nature of human perceptions and experiences, several points can be suggested. As stated above, these are the detailed observations about the phenomena we are aware of but do not have in-depth knowledge of. In other words, it is a research method that deals with what individuals perceive and understand about the meaning of their experiences in the universe/daily life. These phenomena can be any kind of experience, concept or perception. The phenomenological approach aims to explore how the research participants perceive their social and personal worlds and examine their personal perceptions of the situation in detail. Such perceptions may lead to creating the subjectivity in messages delivered by marketing campaigns or stereotypes set in one's mind by the influence of other consumers' own experiences.

APPLICATIONS IN MARKETING RESEARCH

As emphasized occasionally (e.g. Pine & Gilmore, 1998, 1999), the new century is likely to become the centre of experiences that will in/directly have an influence on changing the nature of habits, desires, expectations and lifestyle in one's personal, social, political and economic life. Thus, understanding human behaviour has already become more important as well as more difficult because this is a more dynamic process that is very sensitive to internal and external factors. Such dynamism is unlikely to be studied by statistics and metrics that are all produced as a consequence of quantitative methods. Quantitative data remains unhelpful in predicting the future of human behaviour as it has become more irrational (Bhaskar, 1998). For example, predictions estimate that people with higher income levels tend to buy more expensive products. However, today, we see many people with the lowest income levels who enjoy using expensive goods such as smart phones or iPads.

As opposed to the research world that is more quantitative-dominant, phenomenology is directly concerned with understanding human behaviour driven by individual perceptions, experiences or expectations. Kotler (1972) considers psychology to be at the core of marketing. Psychology conflates human beings with individuals, whereas marketing considers individuals as consumers. As these two terms work on humans and their experiences, the association of marketing with psychology brings out the term "consumer behaviour" (Gunter & Furnham, 2014). In this respect, due to its problem or mission that lies in how the real experience can or should be investigated, phenomenology offers a more stable platform to successfully conduct marketing research:

- *Purposeful* [WHY] – Each person as a consumer attributes a meaning to any object or subject they interact with or experience. Such meaning is valuable for each consumer as they consider it a personalized or individualized experience. In other words, consumers think that such an experience can be offered only to them, and that others may not have the same feeling. For instance, the production, promotion and consumption of individualized (personalized) products have become central to today's modern marketing strategies because such products pamper consumers; they maximize comfort, making each consumer feel that they are special and totally different from others. This refers to the importance of product differentiation and marketing segmentation in the context of luxury consumption, which is more likely to generate greater profits despite the risks during possible economic crisis.

- *Noema* [WHAT] – This refers to the thing, object or subject itself that is experienced – e.g. food in a restaurant, drinks in a pub, a Turkish night at a wedding, a spa in a hotel, business class on a flight.
- *Noesis* [HOW] – This concerns how the thing/object/subject is perceived, and is more emotional or subjective. This subjective or emotional nature of travel/vacation forms the background of the tourist experience with any travel parties.

The purpose of marketing research is to investigate how consumer behaviour is likely to be influenced by changes in elements of the marketing mix such as product, price, place and promotion (Alfakhri et al., 2018). With new products created either by the same business or its competitors, any increase or decrease in their price levels can somehow influence consumers' intentions to purchase certain products but not to purchase some others. As to the changing nature of places and promotion, there are new trends in locations and promotions for consumers to make purchases at shopping malls or from online platforms, which have become the centre of shopping places for today's dynamic and impulsive consumers.

In qualitative studies, researchers collect data in the form of words and analyse this data by using common themes to identify events (Creswell, 2007; Denzin & Lincoln, 2005). In interpretive phenomenological analysis, it is recommended that the sample should be consistent with the orientation of the qualitative paradigms and the orientation of the interpretive phenomenological analysis in general (Smith et al., 2009). Giorgi (1985) recommends that the written explanations of the phenomenon to be investigated are used as data for the analysis of these definitions. According to him, these written forms of data should have as much detail and experience as possible. Interpretation of the findings and preparation of the research report are particularly important steps to be taken into consideration. Possible explanations should be made regarding the results obtained.

PROCEDURES TO APPLY IN MARKETING RESEARCH

As a qualitative research method, phenomenology is suitable for studies aiming to investigate phenomena that we are aware of but do not fully understand (e.g. Berdychevsky & Gibson, 2015; Wassler & Schuckert, 2017; Willson et al., 2013). The method aims to reveal and interpret individual perceptions of a case or experience (Giorgi, 1997). In other words, it aims to describe, interpret and understand an individual's perceptions of the facts. The focus of this chapter is to reveal individuals' perceptions about consumption. Consumption patterns are suggested because they allow a description of phenomenology and the explanation of facts. In this context, the purpose is to reach the primary source based on the methodology applied. Phenomenological research involves three major steps – the topic, the research group and data collection – as outlined below.

Research Topic

What is to be investigated? Let's say it's how the consumer experience is formed and how likely it is to contribute to consumer satisfaction in the end. The logic of empirical studies lies in the fact that there should be a cause-and-effect relationship between the dependent and independent variables. Unlike traditional applications, the effect itself can stand as an empirically unsupportive way of carrying out studies. Having said that, one phenomenon may be considered the reason behind the occurrence of another. For example, any dissatisfaction with a vacation experience is an effect and dependent on the explanation of other variables. The cause may vary – from bad weather or poor facilities to food poisoning or being overcharged by shopkeepers. Despite the fact that a solid experiential design can easily and technically be established to explain the causes of effects using quantitative methods, there is still room for any type of qualitative method to offer more solid implications. Unlike quantitative methods, phenomenology is not dependent on cause–effect relationships and subjective explanations; instead, understanding consumer experiences with more objective and detailed interpretations becomes more important. Phenomenology is formed by finding answers to the questions who, how, what, why, where and when?

Research Group

Who is to be investigated? Denzin and Lincoln (2005, p.3) describe qualitative research as an "interpretative, naturalistic approach to the world". De Vos and Fouché (1998) state the advantages of grounded theory in different research designs in qualitative methods such as ethnography and phenomenology. Of these, phenomenological research emphasizes understanding the experiences of individuals through interviews and/or one's own experiences (Alfakhri et al., 2018; Patton, 2002; Hycner, 1985). From this point of view, phenomenology is a key method for understanding the truth about the world as a qualitative approach in social sciences. As a result, consumers in a travel/vacation situation can be the target group. Participants who will form the research sample should be selected from individuals who can provide a clear perspective on the phenomenon to be investigated and can access it (Wassler & Schuckert, 2017).

Data Collection

This procedure embodies several steps to be followed in answering the major questions: How, What, Why, Where, When? (Meister, 2010). Any form of interview with consumers is a tool of data collection (*How*). Phenomenology is the pattern of the research design. In this context, it aims to obtain the empirical data (*What*). Based on the study objectives, data is collected through observation in order to obtain the appropriate answers to the questions constituting the research problem (*Why*). Data is collected through one-to-one interviews by reaching out to consumers of a specific product group, such as clothes, cars or computers, through a brand recently purchased and perceived as premium or luxury. In order to reach other people with similar characteristics, the plan is to use snowballing, e.g. asking whether there are other people who are likely to have familiar consumption habits (Wassler & Schuckert, 2017). The sample is composed of people living in certain locations or affiliated with certain institutions in order to reach them in the places they are (*Where*) at certain times of the day or year (*When*).

While carrying out phenomenological analysis, the research process has a dynamic character: the researcher aims to reach the participants' experiences as much as possible. However, it is never possible to entirely complete this process. Experience in phenomenological research revolves around the subjective point of view, and from this point of view the purpose of the analysis is to make sense of experiences rather than make generalizations. In other words, the aim is to reach the group's in-depth perceptions, rather than proposing general statements.

Interviews are the main data collection method in phenomenological research (Alfakhri et al., 2018; Hycner, 1985). From this point of view, rather than the quantitative volume of the sample, the participants would be able to allow (reflect) the perspective appropriate to the subject being investigated. In other words, participants should reflect the quality of information obtained rather than the quantity. The number of participants should be controllable. Since in-depth interviews are conducted in phenomenological studies, and are not limited to single interviews, it is natural to limit the number of participants. For example, in a study to investigate the case of x in tourism marketing, the sample can be composed of individuals with x cases. For this purpose, x can be determined through observation by the researcher. In this respect, criterion sampling or snowball sampling can be suitable for this type of study.

In interpretive phenomenological studies, the process of analysis first conveys the personal experiences of participants (Giorgi, 1997; Polidore et al., 2010). For instance, there has been increasing attention in tourism studies on exploring the experiences of visitors during domestic or international vacations (e.g. Berdychevsky & Gibson, 2015; Desforges, 2000; Wassler & Schuckert, 2017; Willson et al., 2013). Second, it consists of a two-stage process in which the researcher tries to understand and convey the meanings that the researcher has imposed in various events (Smith & Osborn, 2003). Beyond just asking questions in the negotiation process, the researcher, who also helps elucidate rich narratives, should employ a collaborative process.

Creswell and Poth emphasize the importance of collecting comprehensive information about each participant in a phenomenological study. Choosing a large sample adversely affects this process (Sanders, 1982). According to Creswell and Poth (2017), small sample sizes make it easier for the researcher to collect comprehensive information about each participant. Sprenkle and Moon (1996) recommend that participants meet in their natural environment. On the other hand, the research sample should include individuals with a clear perspective on the phenomenon to be investigated and access to it.

In-depth verbal and/or semi-structured interviews with individuals need particular attention. It is important to examine the phenomenon investigated by the researcher and the flexibility and intense interaction. Participants prefer to feel comfortable, so it is important that the surroundings are based on trust in terms of both researchers and participants, for example, meeting in the latter's natural environment as recommended by Sprenkle and Moon (1996). The researcher should ensure that the individuals' perceptions and experiences are reported in detail. The main purpose in data analysis is to reveal experiences and meanings: content analysis is made on the data obtained, the description of the experiences in the analysis of the data, the discovery of perceptions/experiences, the conceptualization of the data and the themes revealed. The results are explained within the framework of the themes. Based on these written reports, data should be understood if interpreted and resolved. The results should be defined within the framework of the themes investigated in the report.

In addition to interviews etc., observation-based data collection can be used to support negotiations in phenomenological research (Bryman &

Bell, 2011; Denzin & Lincoln, 2005). For example, in an empirical study of the purchasing or consumption behaviour of x, it may be necessary to observe the researcher's interaction with x, y and z. Therefore, the use of observation techniques as the basis for support or negotiations at this point may underlie the questions the researcher considers asking – e.g. observing family members in their natural setting (that is, the household) to investigate their food purchases or their attitudes to recycling (paper, plastic, glass, etc.).

CONCLUSION

An individual or situation-based approach can be adopted in data analysis and in obtaining results, as in case studies. For example, with the participation of five marketing managers in a study on how to estimate future trends on the demand side, the data obtained from these managers can be analysed separately for each manager to allow comparison of the findings. This method is an individual-based data analysis, and aims to interpret the findings about the characteristics of the related individuals. Even though it may be difficult to be open to generalization, the results may still be valid to develop marketing strategies, at least for niche or specific markets in certain production units or industries.

In this approach, the experiences and opinions of the individuals involved in the research are important. For example, during in-depth interviews in the case investigated, key points are understanding consumers' experiences and how they make sense of these experiences or phenomena. In this way, consumer experiences and perceptions are expressed at the cognitive level. Especially with this paradigm, based on consumer perceptions of both personality traits and phenomena, strategies for brand positioning and market segmentation can be easily developed. Again, consumer behaviours and consumption preferences with the same values can be predicted.

As a final remark, the current study suggests using phenomenology in the context of marketing research. To help readers easily understand their importance, phenomenological studies do not produce definitive results that can be generalized in accordance with the nature of qualitative research. However, by providing more detailed and meaningful explanations of the case being studied, phenomenology can make significant contributions to the literature and practice by linking the emerging meanings related to the phenomenon investigated with the support of theories in the field.

REFERENCES

Alfakhri, D., Harness, D., Nicholson, J., & Harness, T. (2018). The role of aesthetics and design in hotelscape: A phenomenological investigation of cosmopolitan consumers. *Journal of Business Research*, 85, 523–531.

Alvesson, M., & Sköldberg, K. (2000). *Reflexive Methodology: New Vistas for Qualitative Research*. London: Sage.

Ashworth, P. (2003). An approach to phenomenological psychology: The contingencies of the lifeworld. *Journal of Phenomenological Psychology*, 34(2), 145–156.

Becker, C. S. (1992). *Living and Relating: An Introduction to Phenomenology*. Thousand Oaks, CA: Sage.

Berdychevsky, L., & Gibson, H. J. (2015). Phenomenology of young women's sexual risk-taking in tourism. *Tourism Management*, 46, 299–310.

Bhaskar, R. (1998). *The Possibility of Naturalism*. Abingdon: Routledge.

Bryman, A., & Bell, E. (2011). *Business Research Methods* (3rd ed.). Oxford: Oxford University Press.

Creswell, J. W. (2007). *Qualitative Inquiry and Research Design: Choosing among Five Approaches* (2nd ed.). Thousand Oaks, CA: Sage.

Creswell, J. W. (2013). *Qualitative Inquiry and Research Design: Choosing among Five Approaches* (3rd ed.). Thousand Oaks, CA: Sage.

Creswell, J. W., & Poth, C. N. (2017). *Qualitative Inquiry and Research Design: Choosing among Five Approaches* (4th ed.). Thousand Oaks, CA: Sage.

De Vos, A. S., & Fouché, C. B. (1998). General introduction to research design, data collection methods and data analysis. In A. S. De Vos (Ed.), *Research at Grass Roots: A Primer for the Caring Professions*. Pretoria: Van Schaik.

Denzin, N. K., & Lincoln, Y. S. (2005). Introduction: The discipline and practice of qualitative research. In N. K. Denzin & Y. S. Lincoln (Eds.), *The Sage Handbook of Qualitative Research* (pp. 1–32). Thousand Oaks, CA: Sage.

Desforges, L. (2000). Traveling the world: Identity and travel biography. *Annals of Tourism Research*, 27(4), 926–945.

Giorgi, A. (1985). Sketch of a psychological phenomenological method. In A. Giorgi (Ed.), *Phenomenology and Psychological Research* (pp. 8–22). Pittsburgh, PA: Duquesne University Press.

Giorgi, A. (1997). The theory, practice, and evaluation of the phenomenological method as a qualitative research procedure. *Journal of Phenomenological Psychology*, 28(2), 235–260.

Giorgi, A. (2006). Concerning variations in the application of the phenomenological method. *The Humanistic Psychologist*, 34(4), 305–319.

Giorgi, A. P., & Giorgi, B. (2008). Phenomenological psychology. In C. Willig & W. Stainton-Rogers (Eds.), *The SAGE Handbook of Qualitative Research in Psychology*. London: Sage (e-book pp. 3–29, print pp. 165–179).

Goulding, C. (2005). Grounded theory, ethnography and phenomenology: A comparative analysis of three qualitative strategies for marketing research. *European Journal of Marketing*, 39(3/4), 294–308.

Gunter, B., & Furnham, A. (2014). *Consumer Profiles (RLE Consumer Behavior): An Introduction to Psychographics*. London: Routledge.

Hines, A. A., & Ardley, B. (2011). Marketing theory and critical phenomenology: Exploring the human side of management practice. *Marketing Intelligence & Planning*, 29(7), 628–642.

Hycner, R. H. (1985). Some guidelines for the phenomenological analysis of interview data. *Human Studies*, 8, 279–303.

Jamali, H. (2018). Does research using qualitative methods (grounded theory, ethnography, and phenomenology) have more impact? *Library and Information Science Research*, 40, 201–207.

Jasper, M. A. (1994). Issues in phenomenology for researchers of nursing. *Journal of Advanced Nursing*, 19, 309–314.

Kant, I. (1764). *Observations on the Feeling of the Beautiful and Sublime.* Los Angeles: University of California Press.

Kotler, P. (1972). A generic concept of marketing. *Journal of Marketing*, 36, 46–54.

Law, J., & Urry, J. (2004). Enacting the social. *Economy and Society*, 33(3), 390–410.

Meister, D. G. (2010). Experienced secondary teachers' perceptions of engagement and effectiveness: A guide for professional development. *The Qualitative Report*, 15(4), 880–898.

Patton, M. Q. (2002). *Qualitative Research and Evaluation Methods.* Thousand Oaks, CA: Sage.

Pine, B. J., & Gilmore, J. H. (1998). Welcome to the experience economy. *Harvard Business Review*, July–August, 98–105.

Pine, B. J., & Gilmore, J. H. (1999). *The Experience Economy: Work Is Theatre and Every Business a Stage.* Boston, MA: Harvard Business School Press.

Polidore, E., Edmonson, S. L., & Slate, J. R. (2010). Teaching experiences of African American educators in the rural south. *The Qualitative Report*, 15(3), 568–599.

Richardson, J. T. E. (1999). The concepts and methods of phenomenographic research. *Review of Educational Research*, 69(1), 53–82.

Sanders, P. (1982). Phenomenology: A new way of viewing organizational research. *Academy of Management Review*, 7(3), 353–360.

Smith, J. A., & Osborn, M. (2003). Interpretative phenomenological analysis. In J. A. Smith (Ed.), *Qualitative Psychology: A Practical Guide to Methods* (pp. 53–80). London: Sage.

Smith, J. A., Flowers, P., & Larkin, M. (2009). *Interpretative Phenomenological Analysis: Theory, Method and Research.* Thousand Oaks, CA: Sage.

Sprenkle, D., & Moon, S. (1996). Toward pluralism in family therapy research. In D. Sprenkle & S. Moon (Eds.), *Research Methods in Family Therapy* (pp. 3–19). New York: Guilford.

Thompson, C. J., Locander, W. B., & Pollio, H. R. (1989). Putting consumer experience back into consumer research: The philosophy and method of existential-phenomenology. *Journal of Consumer Research*, 16(2), 133–146.

Van Manen, M. (1990). *Researching Lived Experience: Human Science for an Action Sensitive Pedagogy.* Albany: State University of New York Press.

Wassler, P., & Schuckert, M. (2017). The lived travel experience to North Korea. *Tourism Management*, 63, 123–134.

Willig, C. (2001). *Introducing Qualitative Research in Psychology: Adventures in Theory and Method*, Buckingham: Open University Press.

Willson, G. B., McIntosh, A. J., & Zahra, A. L. (2013). Tourism and spirituality: A phenomenological analysis. *Annals of Tourism Research*, 42, 150–168.

Wilson, T. (2012). What can phenomenology offer the consumer? Marketing research as philosophical, method conceptual. *Qualitative Market Research: An International Journal*, 16(3), 230–241.

11. Mobile ethnography: a customer experience research method for innovation

Birgit Bosio, Katharina Rainer and Marc Stickdorn

SUMMARY

This chapter introduces the emerging research method of mobile ethnography, which integrates customers as active researchers with mobile devices. This user-centred approach collects cross-channel feedback in situ and in real time, and helps organizations improve customer experience.

INTRODUCTION

In times of increasing importance of social media in people's everyday lives, it has become much easier for customers to access information and share their own knowledge and experience with others (Geser and Markus, 2008; Holloway, 2004; Schweda, 2004). Therefore, managing customer experience has become an important success factor for companies; in order to remain competitive it has become crucial to constantly research and improve products and services to provide value to customers and solve critical experience incidents (Peppers and Rogers, 2016; Pine and Gilmore, 2011; Stickdorn and Schneider, 2010).

Customer experience describes a customer's "interaction with a firm's goods, services, and 'atmospheric' stimuli" (Haeckel et al., 2003, p. 18), both at direct and indirect contact points (Klaus and Maklan, 2012). Customer experience was found to influence marketing outcomes such as customer satisfaction, loyalty and word-of-mouth behaviour and, hence, to influence marketing metrics, financial metrics and ultimately company success (Grewal et al., 2009; Klaus and Maklan, 2013). Visualizing customer experience is expected to help reduce costs and enable better decisions about investments to be made (Zehrer, 2009).

However, marketing research has long focused mainly on service quality and customer satisfaction (Parasuraman et al., 1988; Verhoef et al., 2007). In addition, the methods applied in marketing research are mainly based on these constructs, even though they often fall short. However, thanks to technological developments, today new methods are available to tackle this issue. One of these is mobile ethnography, a research method rooted in classic ethnography extended by making use of technology.

In this chapter, we illustrate how marketing research can enable companies to get closer to customers and learn more about their experience with products, services or brands. A typical research process is further outlined, also reflecting on existing mobile ethnography projects. This review should help marketers successfully apply the method and point out critical aspects of customer experience that should be taken into consideration in the further development of the product or service. Finally, limitations of the method are presented, along with a conclusion.

CUSTOMER EXPERIENCE AS THE NEW COMPETITIVE ADVANTAGE

Customer experience has become what companies are competing for – companies start to focus on offering superior experiences as a main competitive advantage (Hsieh, 2010). As research and advisory company Gartner puts it, "Customer experience (CX) is the new marketing battlefront" (Pemberton, 2018). According to the Gartner Customer Experience in Marketing Survey, 81 per cent say their companies will "be competing mostly or completely on the basis of CX" in two years (Pemberton, 2018).

Putting the customer at the centre of activities is a challenge for many companies. All relevant events have to be analysed, including both touchpoints and moments without direct or indirect contact with the company. As Katzan (2011, p. 54) states, "a touchpoint is a contact point between the service provider and a customer; it is sometimes known as a 'service interface'". However, this definition does not consider that not every step a customer takes in the use of a service is a touchpoint; for example, when users become aware of a need for the first time, they might not even be in contact with the product, service or brand at all. Still, this kind of moment should be considered during the research.

With the rise of customer experience, subjectivity of both cognition and emotions is gaining more interest in marketing research (Gentile et al., 2007). However, traditional research methods such as surveys or interviews frequently fall short in assessing these as they focus on objective and cognitive dimensions with hindsight, and barely capture the emotional or subjective dimensions of customer experience (Meyer and Schwager, 2007; Schwarz, 2007). Companies and organizations need to apply a more open approach to understand not just *what* customers experience, but also *why* they experience it the way they do (Stickdorn and Zehrer, 2009). In this run, the approach of service design becomes more and more common to tackle this issue and is applied by both academics and industry (Silvestro and Silvestro, 2003).

THE SERVICE DESIGN APPROACH

Companies need to become aware of the importance of customer experience assessment and create the necessary culture. Products and services need to be developed and improved according to what customers are looking for and need to solve their problems (Grewal et al., 2009; Kotler and Armstrong, 2014). This approach nowadays has many different names, including design thinking, service design, user-centred design, experience design, human-centred design or new marketing (Stickdorn et al., 2018). What all these approaches have in common is putting the customer or user at the centre of attention. While there are many definitions of service design, the one presented by Miller (2015) is among the most commonly used:

> Service design helps organizations see their services from a customer perspective. It is an approach to designing services that balance the needs of the customer with the needs of the business, aiming to create seamless and quality service experiences. Service design is rooted in design thinking, and brings a creative, human-centered process to service improvement and designing new services. Through collaborative methods that engage both customers and service delivery teams, service design helps organization gain true, end-to-end understanding of their services, enabling holistic and meaningful improvements.

Within a service design process, the problem stage focuses on understanding the critical incidents of customers and how they experience interactions with a product, service or brand – from informing themselves, through the decision-making process, onboarding (the pre-service period) and consumption (service period), to making an evaluation or telling others about their experience (post-service period) (Stickdorn and Zehrer, 2010).

Service designers often follow a model that includes the four phases of Discover, Define, Develop and Deliver (UK Design Council, 2005). During the discovery phase, an open approach is necessary to gather insights (divergent thinking) before narrowing down the number of problems, prioritizing them and identifying the one that matters most in the defining stage (convergent thinking). In the second phase, solutions or concepts are created by prototyping and testing, applying an iterative approach during the development stage. During delivery, the final product or service is then produced or launched.

RESEARCH METHODS FOR DEFINING THE PROBLEM WITHIN THE PROBLEM SPACE

Companies do not only have to find the best solution to customer problems; they must also make sure they do not end up solving the wrong problem because they base their decisions solely on assumptions, biased by their own point of view (Stickdorn et al., 2018). This is why research conducted during the discovery phase is crucial for product or service development. Traditional research methods used in service design include desk research, observation, interviews and self-ethnographic or other ethnographic approaches (Segelström et al., 2009; Stickdorn and Schneider, 2010). However, to understand customer experience, researchers must go beyond traditional approaches to find out what problems or challenges customers face when using a particular product or service. Big data might help companies in doing so; but, even if it turns out that something had a negative impact on the customer experience, the company might still be unaware of the reasons. To learn more about the why, this quantitative data needs to be backed by insights from qualitative research.

Traditional qualitative research methods imply several problems. First, many methods often capture experiences only after they have taken place. This retrospective evaluation may include a strong bias as customers might not remember every detail, referred to as recall bias (Poynter et al., 2014; Schwarz, 2007). This becomes especially urgent when it concerns recalling extended periods of time (Schwarz, 2007) or emotions, which are known to be volatile (Gerrig and Zimbardo, 2008). In addition, according to the Critical Incident Theory, customers tend to remember only the most important moments of their experience (Flanagan, 1954). Finally, experiences are closely related to the context in which they happen (Haeckel et al., 2003).

Therefore, in service design, ethnography is becoming an increasingly common research method for understanding the current and future use of a product or service through becoming part of individuals' lives and experiences – one of the most valuable aspects of ethnography is its research depth (Myers, 1999; Williams and Pollock, 2011). The different approaches of ethnography have in common that researchers try to see things from the point of view of the subject they are studying, rather than imposing their own cultural or political background. The aim is to generate insights on the motivations, dreams, concerns and practices of the people being studied. Classic ethnography uses methods such as photo observation, observation protocols, storytelling or video recordings in order to listen to people's stories (Arnould and Wallendorf, 1994; Fetterman, 2005; Goulding, 2005; Hooley et al., 2012; MacDonald, 2001; Segelström et al., 2009).

However, most traditional methods imply spatial migration as researchers have to follow the study object over a longer period, which is rather cost-, labour- and time-consuming (Alter, 2004; Myers, 1999; Walsham, 2006; Williams and Pollock, 2011). The close involvement of the researcher might also cause people to feel observed, and thus act less openly and honestly; and researchers involved might be biased as they socialize with the study object (Walsham, 2006).

MOBILE ETHNOGRAPHY AS A RESEARCH METHOD

Using mobile devices as research tools feels like a natural development as they have become part of people's daily life. In 2018, 36 per cent of the total world population possessed a smartphone, a figure predicted to reach 40 per cent by 2021 (Statista, 2019a). However, the smartphone user penetration rate differs strongly by country. For example, in 2018, 73 per cent of people in the UK owned a smartphone, 71 per cent in Germany, 70 per cent in the US, 69 per cent in France, 63 per cent in Spain, 60 per cent in Italy and 50 per cent in China. China, of course, has a much higher total number of smartphone users than European countries (Statista, 2018a, 2018b). Predictions for 2021 show a further increase in all these countries.

Age is another major factor influencing smartphone usage. For example, in 2016 the share of smartphone users under 25 in Germany was 96 per cent, but within the 55+ age group, only 44 per cent possessed a smartphone. However, this number showed high growth rates compared to 2012 (14 per cent) (Statista, 2019b).

The increase in smartphone usage also implies an increasing potential of mobile ethnography. The *GreenBook Research Industry Trends Report* (GRIT, 2016) lists mobile ethnography as an emerging research method, with more than one-third of researchers already applying it and a further 27 per cent considering using it.

In mobile ethnography projects, customers decide for themselves what event is relevant and what details they consider important to document. Depending on the project setup, they can collect reports consisting of detailed descriptions and other evidence, including photos, videos and audio reports, on their own. This open approach leads researchers to detect service gaps which are unknown to companies, and therefore would be missing in a survey (Bosio and Prunthaller, 2018; Koschel, 2018; Stickdorn et al., 2014).

AREAS OF APPLICATION OF MOBILE ETHNOGRAPHY

Mobile ethnography can be applied to a diverse set of contexts and industries. It has been chosen as a research method for studies in the field of health care (Connelly et al., 2006; Logan et al., 2007; Rodgers et al., 2005), retail (Koschel, 2018; Kourouthanassis et al., 2007), government (STBY, 2017), tourism (Bosio and Prunthaller, 2018; Bosio et al., 2017; Dimanche and Gibbs, 2016; Dimanche et al., 2014; Frischhut et al., 2012; Muskat et al., 2013; Stickdorn and Zehrer, 2010), mobility (Spinney, 2011) and education (Beddall-Hill et al., 2011). As Vargo and Lusch (2004) state, products should also be treated as services and, hence, customer centricity becomes relevant for any kind of industry. Thus, coming from customer experience research, the approach is increasingly relevant for other stakeholders other than customers. For example, recent projects put employees at the centre of attention, allowing companies to better understand their employees' experience (Bosio et al., 2017). In times of high competition for talent, employee experience is essential for company success.

Mobile ethnography is less cost-intensive than, for example, classic ethnography as researchers do not have to physically follow customers. However, preparatory work – such as the acquisition of participants and their induction to the tool, as well as support during the study – ties up resources and is crucial for the success of such projects (SIS International Research, 2015; Stickdorn and Frischhut, 2012). Finally, by collecting data in situ and in real time, mobile ethnography allows deeper evaluation (GRIT, 2016; Poynter et al., 2014; Stickdorn et al., 2014). Emotional and cognitive factors can be collected simultaneously (Urry, 2007), and researcher bias can be minimized (Hulkko et al., 2004) as the mobile device serves as a "protective barrier" (Beaulieu, 2004, p. 146).

Mobile ethnography projects are often combined with other research methods in order to allow method triangulation (von Bergner, 2014; Koschel, 2018). Participants might be interviewed before or after data collection or can be asked to fill out a questionnaire. Experience reports collected in mobile ethnography studies could serve as the basis for contextual interviews. By so doing, "researchers can improve the accuracy and richness of their research by using different methods to collect data on the same phenomenon" (Stickdorn et al., 2018, p. 107). This also allows for data triangulation as participants can provide various kinds of quali-tative and quantitative information (Frischhut et al., 2012; Segelström and Holmlid, 2012; Stickdorn et al., 2014). Furthermore, as various researchers can collaborate on mobile ethnography projects, they can decide together how participants are selected and how data is analysed. Therefore, mobile ethnography also allows for investigator triangulation, and thus minimizes potential bias (Denzin, 1978; Stickdorn et al., 2014).

SET-UP OF A MOBILE ETHNOGRAPHY PROJECT

Here we outline a typical approach to conducting a mobile ethnography project, as followed in diverse studies (Bosio and Prunthaller, 2018; Bosio et al., 2017; Dimanche and Gibbs, 2016; Dimanche et al., 2014; Muskat et al., 2013; Stickdorn and Frischhut, 2012; Stickdorn et al., 2014; Stickdorn and Zehrer, 2010). Still, readers should keep in mind that the setup of each project always depends on the project itself, on the research question and on the context. Data evaluation will vary from case to case. Our goal here is therefore to offer guidance on how to conduct a research project by including learning from past studies.

1.   Setting Up the Research Project

As in any other research project, in a mobile ethnography study the research question must be defined, including: what needs to be analysed; who should be part of the sample; what kind of data should be collected during the study; and what kind of data (e.g. interviews) should be assessed before or after the study. Researchers need to decide whether or not participation will be anonymous, and how they plan to interact with participants. A crucial question to address is what kind of data needs to be collected, e.g. whether participants should be able to share videos or whether GPS data is required. Scales and wording also need to be defined. Some apps include a small participant survey to gather more information on the participants.

2.   Participant Recruitment

Participant recruitment and motivation are crucial success factors (Bosio et al., 2017; Stickdorn and Frischhut, 2012; Stickdorn et al., 2014). Practice has shown that this step can become challenging (Hulkko et al., 2004; Koschel, 2018), and sometimes the dropout rates of people who are willing to participate in the first run might be quite high. While two mobile ethnography studies reported no-show rates of 57 per cent – only 130 out of 300 registered participants uploaded data (Bosio et al., 2017) and 50 per cent (Stickdorn et al., 2014) – other projects resulted in dropout rates of only 25 and 33 per cent (Bosio and Prunthaller, 2018). According to Koschel (2018), this might be because participants perceive downloading the relevant app and logging in to a project as too much effort. However, when comparing these numbers to the dropout rates of traditional methods, they don't differ a lot. Baruch and Holtom (2008) found an average survey response rate of 53 per cent for data collected by individuals and 36 per cent for data collected from organizations.

Participation greatly depends on personal motivation: intrinsic motivation results from the task itself being perceived as satisfying, while extrinsic motivation is driven by external incentives, e.g. rewards (Amabile et al., 1994; Ke and Zhang, 2009). Some people like to share their opinion on a product, service or brand, and enjoy the fact that someone is listening to them. For example, a person with a disability might have a high intrinsic motivation to participate in a museum's project about how to make its facilities accessible for all (Stickdorn and Frischhut, 2012). For the latter case, extrinsic motivation, incentives such as monetary compensation, vouchers, lotteries or other tangible incentives – have proven to work quite well for motivating people to participate (Bonner and Sprinkle, 2002; Rainer, 2016).

Mobile ethnography follows a qualitative approach; therefore, it involves a lower number of participants than quantitative research approaches. By limiting the project to a few participants, one can learn about different views and individual differences, gain insights by analysing the data in depth, easily motivate all participants by offering extensive support and valuable incentives, and follow up with other methods such as interviews or workshops (Bosio and Prunthaller, 2018).

3.   Instructing Participants before Data Collection

Before participants start collecting data, they must be given instructions on what the company or organization expects them to do (Koschel, 2018). Some researchers follow a very open approach and let customers decide themselves what they document. In contrast, others give participants rather concrete tasks to fulfil (Koschel, 2018; STBY, 2017), specific topics to focus on (e.g. interactions with employees) or specific times when they should report on experiences (e.g. the first three days of using a product). Giving detailed instructions and making sure participants have understood them is crucial for the collection of high-quality data. Another issue might be training, especially because people vary in terms of technology readiness (Parasuraman, 2000). This can be done either with flyers, or handouts, or in person. Personal introductions proved to be especially necessary for participants who show a rather low technology readiness (Parasuraman, 2000). Although not always necessary, it might be useful in some cases to meet participants in person before they start data collection so they can test the app and make sure they know how it works and what is expected of them (Stickdorn et al., 2014).

4.   Data Collection

Once participants have accessed the mobile ethnography tool, they can individually start collecting data by themselves and document experiences whenever and wherever they want. Some software tools offer the possibility to interact with users during this research phase – for example to remind them, clarify details, ask questions or motivate them to create reports on specific questions. One of the advantages of this method is that research can be done whether experiences happen online or offline. Even though digitalization is driving and changing our daily lives, researchers should not forget to track offline experiences; only by including a cross-channel approach is a holistic view on the customer journey possible (Rawson et al., 2013; Stickdorn and Frischhut, 2012).

5.   Data Analysis

Researchers can review the data through back-end software, depending on the software used, even in real time. Different back-end systems enable different ways of analysing data. For example, categorizing or tagging helps make sense of the data, discover patterns and define critical touchpoints. Furthermore, GPS data can identify hotspots where experiences were documented, or even hotspots of very positive or negative experiences. Data can also be exported for further (qualitative) analysis using software such as NVivo, ATLAS.ti or MAXQDA.

DISCUSSION

Compared to traditional research methods, mobile ethnography offers some interesting advantages. First, as data analysis can be done in real time it allows companies to react to customers' pain points straight away. Another advantage is its geographical independence. Further is the openness of the approach: the in situ data collection with own personal devices enables researchers to collect critical incidents (Koschel, 2018) as well as comprehensive insights of the customer's experience (Bosio and Prunthaller, 2018). Thus making use of digital technology, mobile ethnography manages to include experiences, no matter through which channel they occur, in order to get a holistic view of the customer journey. Additionally, it allows including a higher number of participants at lower costs compared to classic ethnography. Koschel (2018) points out that based on qualitative consumer panels, long-term consumption observations can be carried out simultaneously in various countries, and thus reach a wider geographical range. However, studies have also shown that a smaller number of participants can provide rich insights (Bosio and Prunthaller, 2018). It is therefore essential to select participants carefully and consider what will motivate them to deliver high-quality research insights. Another main advantage is GPS tracking, which is especially useful for tracking services in a wider geographical range (Koschel, 2018; Muskat et al., 2013; Stickdorn and Frischhut, 2012; Stickdorn et al., 2014).

As stated in GRIT (2016, p. 37), "Communities, mobile ethnography, and mobile 'in the moment' surveys can generate extraordinary insights into people's everyday life experiences. These can provide the rich ingredients needed to build stories and create change in executives' thinking." With this rich and high-quality data, mobile ethnography helps improve experiences (Bosio and Prunthaller, 2018; Dimanche and Gibbs, 2016; Stickdorn and Frischhut, 2012). However, not only critical incidents are collected. For example, a mobile ethnography study in an alpine destination proved that 89 per cent of data collected reached modest evaluation of −1 to +1, while extreme evaluations of −2 or +2 were only recorded by 11 per cent of participants (Stickdorn et al., 2014). Other studies also came to the same conclusion (Bosio and Prunthaller, 2018; Bosio et al., 2017). Thus, mobile ethnography collects "data beyond extreme experiences and therefore overcome[s] some of the major criticisms of the CIT" (Stickdorn et al., 2014, p. 497). Rainer (2016) and Bosio and Prunthaller (2018) stated that, through using the mobile ethnography tool, participants' holiday experience became even more intense.

Mobile ethnography has also proved to have limitations. The active participation of customers in the research process might bias the data collected and distort the findings (Rainer, 2016; Segelström and Holmlid, 2012). Another prerequisite is possession of a smartphone and a certain level of technology readiness (von Bergner, 2014; Bosio et al., 2017; Koschel, 2018; Stickdorn et al., 2014). However, figures show that smartphone use is on the rise across all age groups (Poushter et al., 2018; Statista, 2019b), and studies have shown that mobile ethnography also works for elderly customers (Bosio and Prunthaller, 2018; Plesner and

Claworthy, 2012). In addition to age group, the country and social status of participants must be taken into account when conducting a mobile ethnography study so as to limit bias through smartphone usage (Bosio et al., 2017).

Wireless internet is at some point a technical requirement, which might turn out to be a critical success factor (von Bergner, 2014; Stickdorn and Frischhut, 2012). Depending on the app, participants need to be connected to the internet to start the project, collect data and upload it. In some cases, though, data collection can also be done offline. Another technical issue might arise from dealing with huge amounts of data concerning storage, processing and analysis, both for the participant's mobile device and for the back-end software (Koschel, 2018).

A further challenge to this method is the documentation of touchpoints during the pre-service period. An example might be inviting hotel guests who have completed their booking in order to find out what information they might need before arriving at the hotel or how the hotel could positively influence their arrival experience – e.g. giving information on possible traffic problems, construction sites, interesting sights to visit on the way, weather conditions, etc. (Bosio et al., 2017; Stickdorn et al., 2014). However, participants can often only be recruited to a mobile ethnography study once they have made their decision and bought or consumed the product or service, which makes it difficult to obtain data for the pre-service period (Bosio et al., 2017). However, a mixed-methods approach might help to include these touchpoints for the research project. Furthermore, many projects do not consider the post-service period and only focus on the service period itself. As already shown, the post-service period is crucial as customers can evaluate their experience both off- and online. By doing so, they can influence new potential customers, and thus also the beginning of a new pre-service period.

Furthermore, the evaluation of shorter service periods (such as an event lasting 1–3 hours) proved difficult with mobile ethnography as participants do not have enough time to enjoy the event and can become rather stressed documenting their experiences (Stickdorn and Frischhut, 2012), while this was not the case for longer service periods (Bosio and Prunthaller, 2018).

Studies have shown that data varies in quality and quantity (Bosio and Prunthaller, 2018; Bosio et al., 2017; Stickdorn and Frischhut, 2012; Stickdorn et al., 2014). Besides the dropout rate of participants, sometimes the whole experience was documented within a single touchpoint rather than splitting it into various touchpoints in greater depth. In other cases it turned out to be hard to interpret data collected by customers (Bosio et al., 2017).

While customers are more likely to share negative experiences than positive ones on social media (65 vs. 25 per cent) (Dixon et al., 2010; IUBH, 2011), more data on positive than negative experiences is collected through mobile ethnography projects (Stickdorn et al., 2014; Bosio and Prunthaller, 2018). Sometimes, negative touchpoints are also described in more detail than positive ones (Stickdorn and Frischhut, 2012).

In order to overcome at least some of these limitations, various aspects need to be considered to make a mobile ethnography project successful. These include:

- considering the share of smartphone users within the target group of participants;
- choosing the right participants for the research projects and offering them an incentive to keep them motivated throughout the research process;
- putting a strong focus on the training of participants and clearly communicating the research goal and, thus, what data they should document (e.g. defining the minimum number of touchpoints that should be collected by each participant);
- making sure that participants have internet access with sufficient speed;
- providing a contact who stays in touch with participants and helps them with any problems regarding both technology and content (especially participants with lower technology readiness);
- making use of method, data and investigator triangulation to minimize various kinds of bias.

Mobile ethnography has already proven to be an effective research tool for studying customer experience (Dimanche and Gibbs, 2016; GRIT, 2016; Koschel, 2018; Muskat et al., 2013), allowing for more "co-participatory research" (Bosio and Prunthaller, 2018, p. 14). However, further research is necessary to evaluate this qualitative method in more detail. Current studies often use only mobile ethnography. However, a mixed-methods approach has various advantages, such as increased reliability and validity (Bosio and Prunthaller, 2018; Koschel, 2018; Stickdorn et al., 2014). Also, combining both frontstage customer experience and backspace employee experience would help companies and organizations design even better products and services. It might be interesting to combine customer and employee experiences, bring both stakeholder groups together and let them develop prototypes together. Even though the topic of employee experience is of rising interest, further research is necessary to identify which advantages the mobile ethnography approach could have in this field of study.

Many mobile ethnography studies are limited in time. However, it would be interesting to collect data over longer periods (von Bergner, 2014). By doing so, improvements to services or products based on the results of former mobile ethnography studies could be tested. This would allow for an iterative research process following one of the main principles of service design. More research should also be carried out on motivation and which incentives might work best for involving participants throughout the whole project (Bosio et al., 2017; Koschel, 2018; Stickdorn et al., 2014).

CONCLUSION

Experiences are the new currency in marketing (Kirillova et al., 2017; Pine and Gilmore, 2014; Smilansky, 2017). In order to better understand customers' needs and problems, it is therefore crucial to slip into their shoes. Products and services nowadays need to solve customers' problems in the easiest possible way in order to be successful. Therefore the design of services, as well as co-creation, is becoming vital in an environment of growing competition for customer experiences (Beltagui et al., 2016; De Jong, 2014; Pemberton, 2018).

By involving customers as active participants, mobile ethnography can serve as a research method for the problem area of a design process to gain real and in situ data. By transforming customers into researchers, this not only saves time and costs but also provides immediate evaluation of experiences in greater depth and of better quality. As participants can self-structure evaluations according to their own service experience, they capture and document emotions, moods and sensory impressions in everyday contexts. Thus, there is no bias caused by a researcher being directly present. "Consequently, mobile ethnography might [be] deem[ed] as an appropriate research method in the scholarly context of service orientation, service-dominant logic, experience co-creation and service (experience) blueprinting, as well as human-centred design, participatory design, product design, interaction design, and service design" (Stickdorn et al., 2014, p. 500).

The focus of service design processes on research-based data helps organizations or companies solve the right customer problems rather than just building on assumptions. Thus, concentrating on the customer's needs and pain points during the problem stage is essential for developing new products or services that are relevant and meaningful for them in order to make a strategic difference.

REFERENCES

Alter, S. (2004), "Possibilities for cross-fertilization between interpretive approaches and other methods for analyzing information systems", *European Journal of Information Systems*, Vol. 13 No. 3, pp. 173–185.

Amabile, T.M., Hill, K.G., Hennessey, B.A. and Tighe, E.M. (1994), "The Work Preference Inventory: Assessing intrinsic and extrinsic motivational orientations", *Journal of Personality and Social Psychology*, Vol. 66 No. 5, pp. 950–967.

Arnould, E. and Wallendorf, M. (1994), "Market-oriented ethnography: Interpretation building and marketing strategy formulation", *Journal of Marketing Research*, Vol. 31 No. 4, pp. 484–504.

Baruch, Y. and Holtom, B.C. (2008), "Survey response rate levels and trends in organizational research", *Human Relations*, Vol. 61 No. 8, pp. 1139–1160.

Beaulieu, A. (2004), "Mediating ethnography: Objectivity and the making of ethnographies of the internet", *Social Epistemology*, Vol. 18 No. 2–3, pp. 139–163.

Beddall-Hill, N., Jabbar, A. and Al Shehri, S. (2011), "Social mobile devices as tools for qualitative research in education: iPhones and iPads in ethnography, interviewing, and design-based research", *Journal of the Research Center for Educational Technology*, Vol. 7 No. 1, pp. 67–90.

Beltagui, A., Candi, M. and Riedel, J.C.K.H. (2016), "Setting the stage for service experience: Design strategies for functional services", *Journal of Service Management*, Vol. 27 No. 5, pp. 751–772.

Bonner, S.E. and Sprinkle, G.B. (2002), "The effects of monetary incentives on effort and task performance: Theories, evidence, and a framework for research", *Accounting Organizations and Society*, Vol. 27 No. 4, pp. 303–345.

Bosio, B. and Prunthaller, S. (2018), "Mobile ethnography as an innovative tool for customer experience research in tourism: A case of the tourism destination Upper Austria", *ARA Journal of Tourism Research*, Vol. 8 No. 2, pp. 7–24.

Bosio, B., Rainer, K. and Stickdorn, M. (2017), "Customer experience research with mobile ethnography: A case study of the Alpine destination Serfaus-Fiss-Ladis", In: Belk, R.W. (Ed.) *Qualitative Consumer Research*. Emerald, pp. 111–137.

Connelly, K.H., Faber, A.M., Rogers, Y., Siek, K.A. and Toscos, T. (2006), "Mobile applications that empower people to monitor their personal health", *e & i Elektrotechnik und Informationstechnik*, Vol. 123 No. 4, pp. 124–128.

De Jong, M.E. (2014), "Service design for libraries: An introduction", In: Woodsworth, A. and Penniman, W.D. (Eds.) *Advances in Librarianship*. Emerald, pp. 137–151.

Denzin, N.K. (1978), "Triangulation: A case for methodological evaluation and combination", In: Denzin, N.K. (Ed.) *Sociological Methods: A Sourcebook*. Routledge, pp. 339–357.

Dimanche, F. and Gibbs, C. (2016), "Improving service experiences with mobile ethnography: The case of two attractions in Toronto". [online] TTRA Canada 2016 Conference. Available from https://scholarworks.umass.edu/ttracanada_2016_conference/2 [Accessed 30 January 2019].

Dimanche, F., Prayag, G. and Keup, M. (2014), "Le service design dans le tourisme: Une approche ethnographique mobile [Service design in tourism: A mobile ethnographic approach]", *Mondes du Tourisme Hors-Série*, pp. 32–42.

Dixon, M., Freeman, K. and Toman, N. (2010), "Stop trying to delight your customers", *Harvard Business Review*, Vol. 88 No. 7/8, pp. 116–122.

Fetterman, D. (2005), *Encyclopedia of Evaluations*. Sage.

Flanagan, J.C. (1954), "The critical incident technique", *Psychological Bulletin*, Vol. 51 No. 4, pp. 327–358.

Frischhut, B., Stickdorn, M. and Zehrer, A. (2012), "Mobile ethnography as a new research tool for customer-driven destination management: A case study of applied service design in St. Anton/Austria", In: *CAUTHE 2012: The New Golden Age of Tourism and*

Hospitality, Book 2: Proceedings of the 22nd Annual Conference. Council for Australasian Tourism and Hospitality Education/La Trobe University, pp. 160–166.

Gentile, C., Spiller, N. and Noci, G. (2007), "How to sustain the customer experience: An overview of experience components that co-create value with the customer", *European Management Journal*, Vol. 25 No. 5, pp. 395–410.

Gerrig, R.J. and Zimbardo, P. (2008), *Psychologie* (18th ed.). Pearson Deutschland.

Geser, G. and Markus, M. (2008), *Prosumer im Tourismus*. ITD-Verlag.

Goulding, C. (2005), "Grounded theory, ethnography and phenomenology: A comparative analysis of three qualitative strategies for marketing research", *European Journal of Marketing*, Vol. 39 No. 3, pp. 294–308.

Grewal, D., Levy, M. and Kumar, V. (2009), "Customer experience management in retailing: An organizing framework", *Journal of Retailing*, Vol. 85 No. 1, pp. 1–14.

GRIT (2016), *GreenBook Research Industry Trends (GRIT) Report 2016, Q1–Q2 Edition*. GreenBook. Available from https://www.greenbook.org/GRIT_Q1-Q2-2016.html [Accessed 24 January 2019].

Haeckel, S.H., Carbone, L.P. and Berry, L.L. (2003), "How to lead the customer experience", *Marketing Management*, Vol. 12 No. 1, pp. 18–23.

Holloway, J.C. (2004), *Marketing for Tourism*. Pearson.

Hooley, T., Marriott, J. and Wellens, J. (2012), *What is Online Research? Using the Internet for Social Science Research*. Bloomsbury.

Hsieh, T. (2010), *Delivering Happiness: A Path to Profits, Passion, and Purpose*. Business Plus.

Hulkko, S., Mattelmäki, T., Virtanen, K. and Keinonen, T. (2004), "Mobile probes", In: *Proceedings of the Third Nordic Conference on Human–Computer Interaction*. Association for Computing Machinery (ACM), pp. 43–51.

IUBH. (2011), "Untersuchung der Bedeutung und Glaubwürdigkeit von Bewertungen auf Internetportalen [Analysis of the importance and credibility of online reviews]". [online] VIR Verband Internet Reisevertrieb. Available from https://v-i-r.de/wp-content/uploads/2016/02/Studie_Hotelbewertungen_iubh.pdf [Accessed 10 January 2019].

Katzan, H. (2011), "Essentials of service design", *Journal of Service Science*, Vol. 4 No. 2, pp. 43–60.

Ke, W. and Zhang, P. (2009), "Motivations in open source software communities: The mediating role of effort intensity and goal commitment", *International Journal of Electronic Commerce*, Vol. 13 No. 4, pp. 39–66.

Kirillova, K., Lehto, X.Y. and Cai, L. (2017), "Existential authenticity and anxiety as outcomes: The tourist in the experience economy", *International Journal of Tourism Research*, Vol. 19 No. 1, pp. 13–26.

Klaus, P. and Maklan, S. (2012), "EXQ: A multiple-item scale for assessing service experience", *Journal of Service Management*, Vol. 23 No. 1, pp. 5–33.

Klaus, P.P. and Maklan, S. (2013), "Towards a better measure of customer experience", *International Journal of Market Research*, Vol. 55 No. 2, pp. 227–246.

Koschel, K.V. (2018), "Mobile Ethnographie in der qualitativen Markt- und Konsumforschung", In: Theobald, A. (Ed.) *Mobile Research. Grundlagen und Zukunftsaussichten für die Mobile Marktforschung*. Springer Gabler, pp. 131–144.

Kotler, P. and Armstrong, G. (2014), *Principles of Marketing*. Pearson.

Kourouthanassis, P.E., Giaglis, G.M. and Vrechopoulos, A.P. (2007), "Enhancing user experience through pervasive information systems: The case of pervasive retailing", *International Journal of Information Management*, Vol. 27 No. 5, pp. 319–335.

Logan, A.G., McIsaac, W.J., Tisler, A., Irvine, M.J., Saunders, A. and Dunai, A. (2007), "Mobile phone-based remote patient monitoring system for management of hypertension in diabetic patients", *American Journal of Hypertension*, Vol. 20 No. 9, pp. 942–948.

MacDonald, S. (2001), "British social anthropology", In: Atkinson, P., Coffey, A., Delamont, S., Lofland, J. and Lofland, L. (Eds.) *Handbook of Ethnography*. Sage, pp. 60–79.

Meyer, C. and Schwager, A. (2007), "Understanding customer experience", *Harvard Business Review*, Vol. 85 No. 2, pp. 116–126.

Miller, M.E. (2015), "How many service designers does it take to define service design?", *Practical Service Design*, 15 December. https://blog.practicalservicedesign.com/how-many-service-designers-does-it-take-to-define-service-design-6f87af060ce9#.yt300rpys.

Muskat, M., Muskat, B., Zehrer, A. and Johns, R. (2013), "Mobile ethnography as an emerging research method", In: *BAM 2013 Conference Proceedings*. British Academy of Management.

Myers, M.D. (1999), "Ethnographic research methods in information systems". [online] ISWorld Net Virtual Meeting Center at Temple University. Available from http://interact.cis.temple.edu/~vmc [Accessed 10 January 2019].

Parasuraman, A. (2000), "Technology Readiness Index (TRI): A multiple-item scale to measure readiness to embrace new technologies", *Journal of Service Research*, Vol. 2 No. 4, pp. 307–320.

Parasuraman, A., Zeithaml, V. and Berry, L. (1988), "SERVQUAL: A multiple-item scale for measuring consumer perceptions of service quality", *Journal of Retailing*, Vol. 64 No. 1, pp. 12–40.

Pemberton, C. (2018), "Key findings from the Gartner Customer Experience Survey". [online]. Available from https://www.gartner.com/smarterwithgartner/key-findings-from-the-gartner-customer-experience-survey/ [Accessed 9 January 2019].

Peppers, D. and Rogers, M. (2016), *Managing Customer Experience and Relationships: A Strategic Framework*. Wiley.

Pine, J.B. and Gilmore, J.H. (2011), *The Experience Economy* (Updated edition). Harvard Business Review Press.

Pine, J.B. and Gilmore, J.H. (2014), "A leader's guide to innovation in the experience economy", *Strategy & Leadership*, Vol. 42 No. 1, pp. 24–29.

Plesner, A. and Claworthy, S. (2012), "Hurtigruten/Norway", In: Stickdorn, M. and Frischhut, B. (Eds.) *Case Studies of Applied Research Projects on Mobile Ethnography for Tourism Destinations*. Books on Demand, pp. 104–109.

Poushter, J., Bishop, C. and Chwe, H. (2018), "Social media use continues to rise in developing countries but plateaus across developed ones". Pew Research Center. [online]. Available from http://www.pewglobal.org/wp-content/uploads/sites/2/2018/06/Pew-Research-Center-Global-Tech-Social-Media-Use-2018.06.19.pdf [Accessed 19 January 2019].

Poynter, R., Williams, N. and York, S. (2014), *The Handbook of Mobile Market Research: Tools and Techniques for Market Researchers*. Wiley.

Rainer, K. (2016), *The Relevance of Real-Time Customer Experience Evaluation for Organizations and Customers* (unpublished masters thesis). University of Innsbruck.

Rawson, A., Duncan, E. and Jones, C. (2013), "Touchpoints matter, but it's the full journey that really counts", *Harvard Business Review*, Vol. 91 No. 9, pp. 90–98.

Rodgers, A., Corbett, T., Bramley, D., Riddell, T., Wills, M. and Lin, R.B. (2005), "Do u smoke after txt? Results of a randomised trial of smoking cessation using mobile phone text messaging", *Tobacco Control*, Vol. 14 No. 4, pp. 255–261.

Schwarz, N. (2007), "Retrospective and concurrent self-reports: The rationale for real-time data capture", In: Stone, A., Shiffman, S., Atienza, A. and Nebeling, L. (Eds.) *The Science of Real-Time Data Capture: Self-Reports in Health Research*. Oxford University Press, pp. 11–26.

Schweda, A. (2004), "Independent international traveller evaluations of traditional and interactive holiday information sources along temporal and utility dimensions", In: Frew, A. (Ed.) *Information and Communication Technologies in Tourism 2004*. Springer, pp. 151–160.

Segelström, F. and Holmlid, S. (2012), "One case, three ethnographic styles: Exploring different ethnographic approaches to the same broad brief", In: *Ethnographic Praxis in Industry Conference Proceedings, EPIC 2012*, pp. 48–62.

Segelström, F., Raijmakers, B. and Holmlid, S. (2009) "Thinking and doing ethnography in service design". *Proceedings of International Association of Societies of Design Research (IASDR) 2009*. [online] Available from http://www.iasdr2009.org/ap/Papers/Special%20

Session/Adopting%20rigor%20in%20Service%20Design%20Research/Thinking%20and%20Doing%20Ethnography%20in%20Service%20Design.pdf [Accessed 10 January 2019].

Silvestro, R. and Silvestro, C. (2003), "New service design in the NHS: An evaluation of the strategic alignment of NHS Direct", *International Journal of Operations & Production Management*, Vol. 23 No. 4, pp. 401–417.

SIS International Research (2015), "Mobile ethnographic approaches". [online]. Available from http://www.sisinternational.com/solutions/innovation/%20mobile-ethnography/ [Accessed 14 January 2019].

Smilansky, S. (2017), *Experiential Marketing: A Practical Guide to Interactive Brand Experiences*. Kogan Page.

Spinney, J. (2011), "A chance to catch a breath: Using mobile video ethnography in cycling research", *Mobilities*, Vol. 6 No. 2, pp. 161–182.

Statista (2018a), "Smartphone market in China dossier". [online] Available from https://www.statista.com/study/14315/smartphone-market-in-china-statista-dossier/ [Accessed 16 January 2019].

Statista (2018b), "Smartphones in the U.S. dossier". [online] Available from https://www.statista.com/study/26643/smartphones-in-the-us-statista-dossier/ [Accessed 16 January 2019].

Statista (2019a), "Prognose zum Anteil der Smartphone Nutzer weltweit". [online] Available from https://de.statista.com/statistik/daten/studie/321204/umfrage/prognose-zum-anteil-der-smartphone-nutzer-weltweit/ [Accessed 16 January 2019].

Statista (2019b), "Share of smartphone users in Germany from 2012 to 2016, by age". [online] Available from https://www.statista.com/statistics/732504/germany-smartphone-users-by-age/ [Accessed 16 January 2019].

STBY (2017), "Plants, protein and plastic: Sustainability in food". [online] Available from https://www.stby.eu/2017/06/30/sustainability_food/ [Accessed 22 January 2019].

Stickdorn, M. and Frischhut, B. (2012), *Case Studies of Applied Research Projects on Mobile Ethnography for Tourism Destinations*. Books on Demand.

Stickdorn, M. and Schneider, J. (2010), *This Is Service Design Thinking*. BIS Publishers.

Stickdorn, M. and Zehrer, A. (2009), "Service design in tourism: Customer experience driven destination management". *Proceedings of the First Nordic Conference on Service Design and Service Innovation*. [online] Available from www.aho.no/servicedesign09 [Accessed 6 January 2019].

Stickdorn, M. and Zehrer, A. (2010), "Mobile ethnography: How service design aids the tourism industry to cope with the behavioral change of social media", *Touchpoint: Journal of Service Design*, Vol. 2 No. 1, pp. 82–85.

Stickdorn, M., Frischhut, B. and Schmid, J. (2014), "Mobile ethnography: A pioneering research approach for customer-centred destination management", *Tourism Analysis*, Vol. 19 No. 4, pp. 491–504.

Stickdorn, M., Hormess, M., Lawrence, A. and Schneider, J. (2018), *This Is Service Design Doing*. O'Reilly Media.

UK Design Council (2005), *The Design Process*. UK Design Council.

Urry, J. (2007), *Mobilities*. Polity Press.

Vargo, S.L. and Lusch, R.F. (2004), "Evolving to a new dominant logic for marketing", *Journal of Marketing*, Vol. 68 No. 1, pp. 1–17.

Verhoef, P.C., Langerak, F. and Donkers, B. (2007), "Understanding brand and dealer retention in the new car market: The moderating role of brand tier", *Journal of Retailing*, Vol. 83 No. 1, pp. 97–113.

von Bergner, M. (2014), *Future Challenges for Global Tourism* (unpublished doctoral thesis). Leuphana University Lüneburg.

Walsham, G. (2006), "Doing interpretive research", *European Journal of Information Systems*, Vol. 15 No. 3, pp. 320–330.

Williams, R. and Pollock, N. (2011), "Moving beyond the single site implementation study: How (and why) we should study the biography of packaged enterprise solutions", *Information Systems Research*, Vol. 23 No. 1, pp. 1–22.

Zehrer, A. (2009), "Service experience and service design: Concepts and application in tourism SMEs", *Managing Service Quality: An International Journal*, Vol. 19 No. 3, pp. 332–349.

ANNOTATED FURTHER READING

Bosio, B., Rainer, K. and Stickdorn, M. (2017), "Customer experience research with mobile ethnography: A case study of the Alpine destination Serfaus-Fiss-Ladis", In: Belk, R.W. (Ed.) *Qualitative Consumer Research*. Emerald, pp. 111–137.

This study shows how mobile ethnography was applied in an alpine Austrian destination, including strengths and limitations of the research method.

Klaus, P.P. and Maklan, S. (2013), "Towards a better measure of customer experience", *International Journal of Market Research*, Vol. 55 No. 2, pp. 227–246.

In this article, Klaus and Maklan present a new approach to measuring customer experience with the customer experience quality (EXQ) in comparison to, for example, customer satisfaction.

PART III

MIXED-METHODS RESEARCH

12. Mixed methods in agricultural marketing research: building trust amongst participants
Rachel Hay

SUMMARY

This chapter draws from an agricultural marketing project to describe a mixed methods approach (face-to-face interviews and an online survey) to research surrounding technology adoption by women in agriculture.

INTRODUCTION

The research project investigated technology adoption by women in agriculture, particularly in the beef cattle industry in Queensland (QLD), Australia. Raising cattle for beef production involves collecting data on animals, pasture and/or weather using remote technologies (e.g. remote cameras and weather stations, walk-over scales, satellite imagery and GPS collars and other technology). Considerations such as an increasing trend for the consumption of animal products and potential perils to food security may see productivity in the beef industry boosted. This, coupled with an ageing rural workforce, may see Queensland cattle producers consider using remote livestock management systems to optimise beef production. To do so involves introducing new technologies, which require the grazier (traditionally male) to manage the technology from the station homestead, potentially keeping the grazier from performing outside operations. The research considered that male graziers may not want to forego paddock and stock work and station maintenance to complete computer-based technology operation from within the homestead. As such, the research anticipated that remote livestock management technology systems operation may fall to the women in the pastoral partnership (Pannell and Vanclay, 2011). The aim of the study was to establish the extent to which rural women use technology, and their views on their role in managing emerging livestock management tools.

This chapter outlines a mixed method approach to data collection within the beef cattle production industry. Typically graziers lack trust in researchers and other agencies. The mixed method approach includes a media campaign aimed at raising awareness of the research project and at building trust of the researcher amongst participants.

METHOD/ISSUE

This chapter draws from an agricultural marketing project to describe a mixed methods approach (face-to-face interviews and online survey) to research surrounding technology adoption by women in agriculture. Descriptive research is designed to "portray an accurate profile of persons, events or situations" (Saunders et al., 2009). The results of descriptive analysis may derive from either exploratory or explanatory research. However, it is necessary to have a clear picture of what is being researched. Extensive research should be undertaken to ensure that all areas of the topic are familiar. An emic (insider) approach was adopted to capture rich and descriptive data from conversational interviews and to seek meaningful patterns from key participants (Gubrium and Holstein, 2001). Theoretical sampling of the interview transcripts (to generate and develop theoretical ideas) defined gaps in the data, which facilitated questions for an online survey. The methodology was supported by a media campaign which aimed to build trust amongst participants. Hearing about the survey prior to the data collection event helps establish trust before interviews commence, enabling the researcher to recruit participants more readily (Saunders et al., 2009). Non-standardised interview techniques – often criticised for being unreliable due to interviewer effect and response bias (Gray, 2004; Gubrium and Holstein, 2001) – are considered in this chapter. This method has been successful when dealing with farmers in the beef and sugar industries in Australia, and may be extended to other participants who may be cautious around researchers.

Mixed Method Approach

A two-phase mixed method approach (conversational interviews and online survey) allowed the researcher to invoke a highly evaluated and trusted study (Saunders et al., 2009). Mixed methods use quantitative and qualitative data collection techniques and analysis. Qualitative and quantitative data was analysed individually, at the same time or sequentially, which is common in mixed method research (Saunders et al., 2009). Conversational interviews used in the first phase of data collection explored key issues about women's and men's views on technology use and adoption. These key issues, identified from the interview transcripts, facilitated questions for the second phase of the research, an online survey. The online survey explored the aims of the study, and complemented the rich and descriptive data from the first phase. A mixed method approach allowed the researcher to triangulate the data and corroborate findings within the study.

Triangulation refers to the use of multiple methods or data sources in qualitative research to develop a comprehensive understanding of phenomena under study (Patton, 1999). It facilitates validation (Carter et al., 2014), tests the consistency of findings through different instruments and helps identify and control threats (e.g. bias) that may influence the results of a study (BetterEvaluation, 2018). Methodological validation (Denzin, 1989), where more than one method was used to collect data (in this case interviews and survey), was employed in this study. While triangulation of the data assists with validation, it also allows a deeper and more meaningful understanding of human behaviour that adds value to the research outcomes (Nunkoo, 2018).

Conversational Interviews

Interviewing has been used since ancient times, when rulers gathered such information about people as age, gender and where they lived (Gubrium and Holstein, 2001). In recent times, the conversational interview has been used to gain deeper and more meaningful data from a respondent (Lavrakas, 2008b). Conversational interviews allow deviations from techniques such as standardised interviews where the respondent answers a list of predetermined questions (Roulston, 2008). In this model, the agenda for the interview is established interactively. A recursive process is used in which the interviewer's questions build on responses to previous questions and responses from other participants (Burgess-Limerick and Burgess-Limerick, 1998). Interviewers are allowed to ask whether or not respondents understand the question; and they can provide unscripted feedback to clarify meaning or glean deeper or more meaningful responses from participants (Lavrakas, 2008b; Gray, 2004; Gubrium and Holstein, 2001).

Conversational interviews do not require the participant to interpret the question exclusively. The researcher can provide any additional information needed to help the respondent map the specific terms in a question, or whenever they perceive that the respondent requires assistance (Lavrakas, 2008b). The interviewer must become an active listener; they must "suspend their own perspective and focus on what the interviewee [respondent] has to say" (Lillrank, 2012). The aim is to learn the respondent's reasons for doing or believing in something: clarifying the meaning makes the technique more flexible and improves response accuracy; and, in turn, the reliability of the data is improved (Kerlinger and Lee, 1992).

A fixed set of questions guides the interviewer through themes (previously identified in a review of extant literature) that the researcher wishes to explore. Questions in qualitative research are generally "open-ended, evolving and non-directional" (Onwuegbuzie and Leech, 2006); they are written broadly, but are specific to the research topic to allow the interviewer to seek, discover, describe and explore the respondent's experiences (Onwuegbuzie and Leech, 2006). Questions should be phrased clearly so that the respondent can understand them, and they should be asked in a neutral tone. While conversational interviews allow some probing, the open-ended questions should be broad yet concise enough to allow the researcher to explore the topic while avoiding bias (e.g. interviewer bias). Changing the order of the questions and asking spontaneous questions as an interview progresses enables rich and meaningful data to be extracted from the respondents, and also avoids data saturation (Saunders et al., 2009).

Conversational interviews are typically criticised because they are viewed as a non-standardised interview technique, which is used to undermine their reliability. To overcome these criticisms, the researcher must complete an exhaustive search of the literature on topics related to the study to ensure a high knowledge level of the topics (Hay, 2018). In this case that involved technology adoption and barriers to adoption, and women's role in agriculture and technology, which extended to include social capital, empowerment, leadership and social exclusion, as well as adaptive capacity and the psychology of change in both female and male producers. This can help a researcher convey confidence and purpose whilst conducting interviews.

Conversational interviews allow a large amount of information to be obtained from a relatively large population. Whilst expensive to implement, the amount of accurate, high-quality information achieved creates a balance in many cases (Kerlinger and Lee, 1992). Nevertheless, sampling errors can occur. Purposive sampling was used to help avoid sampling error (Gray, 2004). Subjective judgement was used to approach participants. To avoid inadvertently omitting a subject based on a vital characteristic, two filter questions were used to confirm suitability. The questions confirmed the participants' use of technology, and their fit within the scope of the study (i.e. that they lived and/or worked on cattle-producing properties), thus avoiding problems of both under-coverage and over-coverage. Equal numbers of males and females were selected as the interviewees were accompanied by their partners in the rural relationship.

Information received does not usually penetrate very deeply below the surface (Kerlinger and Lee, 1992). Depth in conversational interviews can be achieved by digging deeper, clarifying answers and changing the order of the questions. The aim of the conversational interview is to listen to stories, reconstruct them, censor them and convey them to others. However, limitations can occur when "different researchers construct different understandings from interviewing the same participant" (Burgess-Limerick and Burgess-Limerick, 1998). To avoid data collection error field notes were transcribed directly after completing the interview, again later the same evening, and again repeatedly during the week after the field days until the researcher's recall was exhausted. Missing data was ignored due to its relative insignificance and low importance.

Online Survey

The second method of data collection used an online survey with a mix of open, intuitive and semi-structured questions (Dillman et al., 2009; Gubrium and Holstein, 2001; Floyd and Fowler, 1995). The online survey method was chosen in this case because, geographically, the participants were widely spread and because online surveys are less expensive than face-to-face methods (Cantrell and Lupinacci, 2007; Dillman et al., 2009). In addition, the study's technology-using participants belong to an online membership group, so are assumed to have internet access. Furthermore, online surveys reduce the opportunity for distortion of the respondent's answers; sample sizes can be quite large; and there is increased accuracy and efficiency of data entry analysis when using online surveys (Saunders et al., 2009).

The online survey was open to women and men over the age of 18. However, only women responded to the survey, despite its open access. When conducting the conversational interviews many of the men commented that they were not interested in learning to use the technology, or perceived they were unable or not motivated to learn about or use it. Non-responses in this study produce the limitation of not knowing the views of the men who did not respond.

Version 2013 of Qualtrics Research Suite survey software was used to produce and implement the online self-administered surveys (www.qual trics.com). Using electronic survey software increases interactivity and reduces the chance of implementation error (Biemer, 2010). In addition, the software allows the researcher to present the questions in an attractive manner, to use consistent layouts, and to collect and manage responses (Dillman et al., 2009). Data can also be exported to programs such as IBM SPSS for analysis.

Recruiting Participants and Survey Delivery

When recruiting participants for a study, the purpose of the research and the research question must be considered. Participants should meet criteria relevant to the topic to be included in the study – such as age, gender, region and other information relevant to the research topic. For example, in this study participants must live and/or work on a cattle station. They must be accessible to the researcher, and be willing to participate and/ or suggest others who might like to participate. Before contacting participants, the project must meet research ethics approval. Research ethics approval ensures that the research meets moral and responsible criteria related to access to respondents, data collection, data analysis, process and storage of data, and the production of written outcomes of the findings (Saunders et al., 2009). Ethical considerations in qualitative work are very important because personal information is recorded, and confidentiality of records and information must be kept secure (Gray, 2004; Kerlinger and Lee, 1992; Saunders et al., 2009).

Sampling Strategy

A sampling strategy allows a researcher to break a population down into a more manageable size. Collecting data from a sub-group (i.e. a sample) enables the researcher to reduce the amount of data to be collected and, in turn, reduce the time and cost of both data collection and data analysis. To maximise generalisability (the extent to which research findings can be applied to settings other than that in which it was originally tested) it is important to define the parameters of the sample to ensure the research measures what it is supposed to measure.

There are two main types of sampling – probability and non-probability, as illustrated in Figure 12.1. Probability sampling relies on random selection, where the "chance or probability of each case being selected from the population is known and is equal for all cases" (Saunders et al., 2009, p. 213). Non-probability sampling is where the probability of each case being selected from the total population is not known, the chance of being selected is not equal, and the selection of participants relies on the subjective judgement of the researcher (Saunders et al., 2009).

In this study, for example, to seek out "respondents who are likely to epitomise the study's analytical criteria" (Gubrium and Holstein, 2001) the population was divided into mutually exclusive sub-groups of women aged 18–35, those aged 36 and older, and their accompanying men. The respondents, due to the nature of the environment where the data was collected (i.e. an agricultural field day), were most likely to fit the scope

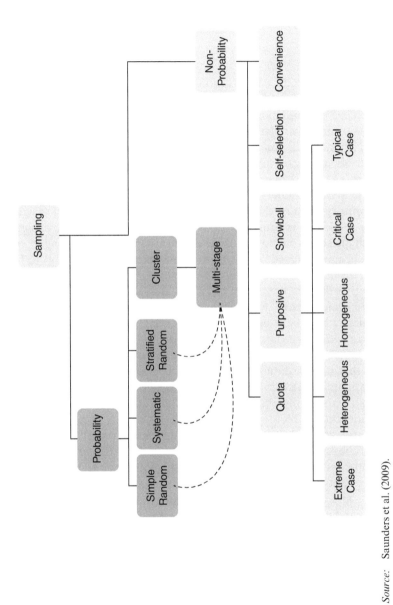

Source: Saunders et al. (2009).

Figure 12.1 Sampling techniques

of the research in that they live and/or work on cattle-producing properties, therefore increasing the generalisability of the results to women in
agriculture.

Data Analysis

The first and second study, conversational interviews, were analysed quali-
tatively using Leximancer content analysis tools (Smith and Humphreys,
2006) to achieve rich and meaningful technology and management experience data as a narrative. The online surveys used quantitative data, which
was coded numerically and analysed descriptively using frequencies,
means analysis and cross-tabulations to achieve an accurate profile of
rural women's use and management of emerging livestock management
tools (Gray, 2004; Saunders et al., 2009). The conversational interviews
were exploratory in nature and provided the researcher with an insight
into key issues. Using multiple methods allowed the researcher to answer
the research questions with a high level of trust in the data, allowing inferences (conclusions reached on the basis of evidence and reasoning) to be
made from the data (Saunders et al., 2009).

Quantitative data is based on meanings that are derived from data
that can be standardised. Analysis is carried out using "graphs, charts
and statistics, which help us to explore, present, describe and examine
relationships within our data" (Saunders et al., 2009, p. 414). Qualitative
research, on the other hand, is more flexible than quantitative research. It
recognises that not all data can be quantified into numerical findings; it
is naturalistic, participatory and interpretive, allowing the researcher to
make adjustments during observations (Nunkoo, 2018; Kerlinger and Lee,
1992; Saunders et al., 2009).

A qualitative methodology is unobtrusive to the point that "the natural
blending of the researcher into the environment reduces the amount of dis-
ruption in the setting and group under study" (Kerlinger and Lee, 1992).
While the qualitative methodology is a good match for conversational
interviews – and despite its flexibility – criticism has led researchers to be
careful to avoid experimenter bias by taking care not to view the research
situation with personal bias (Kerlinger and Lee, 1992).

RESEARCH VALIDITY AND CAVEATS

Validity and reliability are important considerations of conversational
interviews. Validity in qualitative research is challenging because of the
need to incorporate rigour and subjectivity into the scientific process.

Using mixed methods systematically aims to improve the plausibility and legitimacy of research validity (Whittemore et al., 2001). "Validity is not an inherent property of a particular method, but pertains to the data, accounts, or conclusions reached by using that method in a particular context for a particular purpose" (Maxwell, 1996, p. 284). In addition, method alone is not an assurance of validity (Whittemore et al., 2001). While grounded theory typically follows a sequential set of steps, the nature of this research, i.e. relying on informants to guide the research through conversational interviews and an online survey, cannot rely on a rigid sequence, or else it may miss out on the rich and meaningful data – the important stuff – as contributed by the participants of the study (Kevin, 2015).

Validity

Validity is concerned with the instrument measuring what it is supposed to measure (Gray, 2004). Internal validity is achieved through using interviewing techniques that build rapport and trust with the respondent, giving them scope to express themselves. Conversational interviews address concerns of internal validity by prompting the participants to expand on initial responses. A ten-minute conversation is long enough to encourage insightful answers to a set of predetermined questions that guide the broad focus of themes the researcher wishes to explore. External validity, which allows the findings to be generalised, was gained through the use of a selective group of participants who met the criteria for the scope of the study, that is, they lived and/or worked on a cattle-producing property. In addition, the larger the sample size, the more it enables different perspectives to be represented establishing generalisability (Gray, 2004).

Reliability

Reliability is the result of a measurement, calculation or specification that can be depended upon to be accurate (Gubrium and Holstein, 2001). In conversational interviews, reliability is concerned with whether more than one researcher would reveal similar information. Reliability may be affected by interviewer bias, where the interviewer's comments, tone or non-verbal behaviour creates bias in the way the participant is responding to the questions (Saunders et al., 2009). Interviewer bias can be avoided by interviewers being careful in their responses, asking probing questions to gain rich and meaningful data without leading the participant to take the interviewer's view. Likewise, response bias might see the participant answering in a way that portrays them in a socially desirable role, or in a way that they think the researcher wants them to respond (Saunders et al., 2009).

In an effort to avoid response bias, the researcher must "enter the conversational interview with an open mind and keep it that way" (Gray, 2004). If a socially desirable response is given, the researcher should re-frame the question to dig deeper for the participant's personal response.

Non-standardised interview techniques are often criticised, which undermines reliability (Gray, 2004; Gubrium and Holstein, 2001). To overcome this criticism the researcher must complete an exhaustive search of literature on topics related to their study to ensure a high level of knowledge. In this case, topics include precision agriculture, women in rural environments, technology adoption, psychology, research methods and analysis. As already mentioned, knowing the topic well helps the researcher convey confidence and purpose when conducting interviews.

Interviewer Effect

Building trust amongst participants, media campaign
Hearing about the survey prior to the data collection event helps establish a level of trust before the interviews commence, enabling the researcher to recruit participants more readily (Saunders et al., 2009). Participants in this case were alerted to the proposed study through an extended media campaign prior to the event. The campaign consisted of a media release, written by the researcher that described the research and the survey (i.e. duration, expectations, how the results will be used); it also introduced the researcher, allowing participants to form a relationship with both the purpose of the study and the person behind it.

In addition, to limit the interviewer effect, an emic (insider) approach was adopted to capture rich and descriptive data from respondents and to seek meaningful patterns from key participants (Gubrium and Holstein, 2001). The insider approach asked the researcher to wear similar clothing to the event as attendees and to maintain a natural conversational tone. The researcher dressed accordingly (as the event was an agricultural field day, jeans, a university t-shirt and boots were appropriate), allowing the researcher to blend into the environment. A conversational tone was kept during the interviews, and tactics such as not showing emotion or changing facial expression during the interviews were employed (Gray, 2004; Gubrium and Holstein, 2001).

HISTORY OF USE

This method was first used in 2014, in a research project that aimed to establish how rural women view and make decisions with regard to remote livestock management technology. The findings from the project were published in the *Journal of Rural Studies* in a paper entitled "Technology adoption by rural women in Queensland, Australia: Women driving technology from the homestead for the paddock" (Hay and Pearce, 2014). The method was used again in 2015 and 2016 after it was further developed and changes made in response to initial limitations – e.g. using Rossiter's (2002) now heavily criticised C-OAR-SE method of analysis. The second study consisted of three aims:

1. To understand the women producer's motives, actions and intentions in terms of technology use and management.
2. To investigate how technology can make the family property more attractive to workers and returning children.
3. To investigate whether and how the female producer using technology affects the well-being of the male producer in the producer partnership.

The findings from the second study are presented in an unpublished thesis "The engagement of women and technology in agriculture" (Hay, 2018), with several papers under development.

PERSONAL EXPERIENCE

Mixed Method Approach

The first study (Hay and Pearce, 2014) was completed in Queensland, Australia's foremost cattle-producing state. The research methodology used a mixed method data collection strategy (Dillman et al., 2009, Saunders et al., 2009): first, through conversational interviews with attendees of the Ag-Grow QMIX Field Day (a three-day agricultural event held in Emerald in the Central Highlands of Queensland); and, second, through an online survey completed by members of the Queensland Isolated Children's and Parents' Association (ICPA). The ICPA is "a voluntary, not for profit, apolitical organization of parents and individuals working together for access to quality education services for isolated students" (www.icpa.com.au).

Conversational Interviews

Phase one in both studies, through conversational interviews (N=60), explored key issues about women's and men's views on technology adoption. Key issues included: the women's role in terms of technology; their role in the decision to use technology, and in what way the technology is helpful in the cattle-production business; the women's views on technology management; and how the male graziers view the women's role when managing farming technology.

Interviewers were able to ask if respondents did not understand a question. They provided unscripted feedback to clarify meaning or to glean deeper and more meaningful responses from participants (Gray, 2004; Gubrium and Holstein, 2001; Lavrakas, 2008a; Roulston, 2008). Conversational interviews did not require the participant to interpret the question exclusively; the researcher was able to provide any additional information needed to help the respondent map the specific terms in a question, or whenever they perceived that the respondent required assistance (Lavrakas, 2008a). The aim was to learn the respondents' reasons for doing or believing in something, as clarifying meaning made the technique more flexible and improved response accuracy (Kerlinger and Lee, 1992).

Traditionally interviews are recorded using tape or video recorders to ensure that each individual's comments have been clearly captured (Krueger and Casey, 2015). In addition, the recording becomes a tool to detect problems and review progress and for evaluation. However, in this study conversational interviews were not recorded as the study considered the personality traits of the producer (Shrapnel and Davie, 2001). As noted by Shrapnel and Davie, producers are very private and reserved, they dislike pretension, and are cautious and alert to criticism. Therefore, they are unlikely to be open and honest within the context of a recorded interview. This theory was tested at one agricultural field day by recording a respondent to confirm the findings in the literature. The recording device altered the ensuing conversation and created a different context in which the respondent may have answered if the interview was not being recorded (Gubrium and Holstein, 2001). Recording allowed the interviewee to respond on or off the record. Typically this occurs for two reasons: "the respondent wants to talk about their own experiences or . . . the respondent does not want to talk about issues on the record for fear of retribution" (Gubrium and Holstein, 2001). It was clear from the following transcript that "fear of retribution" was uppermost in the mind of one participant.

> I can answer this question but I will just have to check with John, can you turn the recorder off for a minute. (Interview No. 10)

The researcher was confident in choosing not to record the interviews, as supported by Gubrium and Holstein (2001, p. 92), who state "it is a hallmark of quantitative interviewing that 'unrecorded' data are as important as those derived from tape recordings" as it was far more important to gain the trust of the interviewee than record the interview.

Each participant was given a gift bag containing promotional material from the university conducting the research (including a pen, notebook, research literature, information sheet, and a lip balm) on completion of the interview. The information sheet contained the contact numbers for the researcher, the supervisor and the University Ethics Department. In addition, participants were required to sign a consent form prior to the interview, which clearly stated that their responses would remain confidential. Notes were immediately recorded post-interview to ensure the accuracy of recorded answers.

Online Survey

Phase two in both studies, the online survey, explored three main questions:

- Is the technology useful at personal or practical levels?
- What value does it afford the woman graziers?
- Will adopting farming technology improve business for the family units?

In both studies, participants lived and/or worked on cattle-producing properties. Ethics approval for the research was obtained through university procedures. The online survey was emailed to the Isolated Children and Parents Association database (www.icpa.com.au) via the association's secretary. Members of the ICPA promoted survey distribution, and producers were invited to participate through extensive media coverage.

A limitation of online survey use in this study may be due to reduced internet access because of data shaping. Data shaping occurs when a user exceeds their contracted data allowance; the service provider lowers (shapes) the connectivity speed and the user's access to the internet is restricted (Kidman, 2016). As the demand for internet access in rural areas increases, accessibility and speeds are affected. Many of the members of the ICPA, whose database was used for the online component of the study, had their internet data allowances shaped. This was overcome by providing the survey as a fillable PDF form which could be completed by the respondent and returned to the researcher. However, while the dropout rate was approximately 20 per cent, none of the respondents requested a PDF. Rather, 36 per cent of respondents persisted with slow connections, taking between 30 minutes and three hours to complete the survey online.

The study by Hay and Pearce (2014), while aimed at both genders, found that men did not respond to the online survey; instead, women responded on their behalf. This is most likely because rural men approached in the study perceived that they were incapable of or uninterested in learning about and adopting technology (Hay, 2013). The perceptions of rural men surrounding technology were purposely managed in the second study (Hay, 2018) and, as a result, slightly more men responded to the survey. However, the response rate from men was still low. Therefore, in future studies of men's use of technology, either face-to-face or telephone interviews may be more successful.

The online survey used a mix of list questions and rating questions. In the first study (Hay and Pearce, 2014) the responses were limited to two items (agree/disagree) to enable analysis using the C-OARS-E method (Rossiter, 2010). The limitation aimed to allow the participant to see and easily choose one answer alternative that fit the main possible answers they could make. However, the validity of Rossiter's C-OAR-SE method has been highly criticised (Ahuvia et al., 2014; Boshoff and Theron, 2015; Diamantopoulos, 2015). The second study (Hay, 2018) therefore used a four-point Likert-scale response set with anchor points of 1 (strongly agree) and 4 (strongly disagree): first to allow comparison with the first study, which used the agree/disagree dichotomy; and, second, to avoid a response set or halo effect potentially produced by a mid-point (Change, 1994). A pilot study was used to test reliability of the survey. Six unrelated participants within the scope of the study (i.e. living and/or working on cattle-producing properties) tested the online survey to identify and allow for correction of any problems related to implementation procedures.

The survey was open for three weeks, with weekly emails sent to remind participants to complete it (Dillman et al., 2009). Each participant received a letter of introduction explaining the aims of the research, what was required of the participant, an ethics approval notice and information on how to contact the researcher if they needed assistance. The introductory letter gave clear instructions about who could complete the survey (men and women over 18 years old), and indicated that it would take approximately 5–10 minutes to complete. Implementation of the survey was managed using Dillman's Tailored Design Method for Internet, Mail and Mixed-Mode Surveys (Dillman et al., 2009). Participants had a reasonable expectation of receiving an online survey because a relationship existed previously between the researcher and the President of the ICPA Queensland, as is required by the Council of American Survey Research Organizations (CASRO) "code of standards" (as cited in Dillman et al., 2009). This relationship was strengthened through the use of a media campaign. The success of the campaign was measured by the large number of participants who were seeking out the researcher to become involved in the study.

Recruiting Participants and Survey Delivery: Sampling Strategy

Queensland as the population
Queensland is the foremost cattle-producing state in Australia. According to the state's website (www.qld.gov.au), it covers approximately 1.7 million square kilometres and managed 11.1 million head of cattle in 2017 (Meat and Livestock Australia, 2018). As such, studying the technology adoption views of graziers in Queensland provides a basis for addressing the topic as a major cattle-producing region of national importance.

Attendees of the Emerald Ag-Grow QMIX Field Day as participants
The Emerald Ag-Grow QMIX Field Day is a sponsored annual event held over three days that incorporates activities such as the Queensland Working Cattle Dog Championships, the Queensland Superior Beef Bull Sale, the Ag-Grow Invitation Horse Sale, Open and Ringer's Horsemanship Challenge and Open Cutting. The event attracts around 6000 attendees and highlights new technology and equipment to the agricultural and mining industries in Central Western Queensland. The Ag-Grow QMIX event is a good fit for the study because it is "recognised as one of the largest field days on the Australian national circuit, and as a social event for the surrounding regions" (Ag-Grow, 2013) that is well attended by rural women. Additionally it is held in Queensland.

Queensland ICPA members as participants
The Isolated Children's and Parents' Association of Australia is a voluntary, not-for-profit, apolitical organisation of parents and individuals working together to access quality education services for students from less populated regions. It has 47 branches across Queensland (Figure 12.2a). According to Andrew Pegler (then QLD ICPA President), the value of using the Queensland ICPA members as participants is that they are remote technology users, and primarily owners and/or staff of isolated cattle-producing properties (personal communication, 3 July 2013). The close relationship between Queensland's ICPA membership branches (as shown in Figure 12.2a) and the state's cattle density clusters (Figure 12.2b) supports Queensland ICPA members as a good sample source for this study, making the selection more representative of the intended population (Saunders et al., 2009).

Three types of sampling technique were included in this study: conversational interviews, online survey and snowball sampling.

ICPA Branches - Queensland

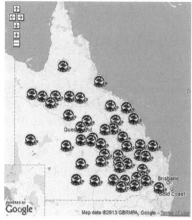

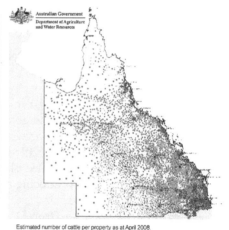

(a) ICPA Branches
   Queensland (ICPA, 2013). Each marker represents
   a membership branch of Queensland's ICPA.

(b) Cattle Density in Queensland, 2008 (DAFF, 2013).
   The darker shading represents areas with less than
   1000 heads of cattle/property; the lighter shading
   represents properties with 1000–5000 heads of cattle;
   and the other markers depict where there are >5000
   heads of cattle/property.

Notes: (a) Each marker represents a branch.
(b) Darker shading – areas with <1000 head of cattle per property; lighter shading –
properties with 1000–5000 cattle; other markers – areas with >5000 cattle per property.

Source: https://icpa.com.au; DAFF (2013).

Figure 12.2   *Relationship between ICPA membership branches (a) and
                 cattle density (b) in Queensland*

Conversational Interviews

Quota sampling was chosen for the Ag-Grow QMIX Field Days because
of the short lead time to the event and its expected large attendance
(Saunders et al., 2009). To seek out "respondents who are likely to epitomise the study's analytical criteria" (Gubrium and Holstein, 2001), the
population was divided into mutually exclusive sub-groups of women
aged 18–35 and 36 years and older, and their accompanying men. The
respondents, due to the nature of the field day, are most likely to fit the
research scope of living and/or working on cattle-producing properties.
Respondents were asked to complete an informed consent statement
prior to being interviewed. A respondent's suitability for the survey was
confirmed using filter questions about what sort of technology they use
and what type of livestock they breed. The researcher then used purposive

(or judgemental) sampling to select target participants non-randomly (Saunders et al., 2009). The researcher was careful to avoid researcher bias and give equal chances of selection to participants by consciously selecting them according to the proposed strata, rather than simply selecting those who were nearby or who looked the most friendly and inviting (Gray, 2004; Saunders et al., 2009). Participants were given an information sheet and a gift bag (an incentive to complete the survey) on completion of the interview.

Online Survey

Cluster sampling is a sampling technique where the entire population is divided into groups, or clusters, and a random sample of these clusters are selected. This technique is both practical and economical. All observations in the selected clusters are included in the sample (Saunders et al., 2009; Boslaugh and McNutt, 2008; Gray, 2004). This technique was selected because the Queensland ICPA membership base is widely spread throughout the state. The vast geographical spread presented some difficulty when trying to sample the population as a whole. Classifying the membership into ICPA branches is a simple and convenient way to organise the Queensland ICPA group, and avoids the geographical limitation. All observations from approximately 47 branch clusters (about 1200 members) were included in the sample.

Snowball Sampling

Snowball sampling asks initial participants to nominate other participants who meet the study criteria, in order to increase the size of the sample. Snowball sampling is a purposive technique used when there is no obvious source for locating participants from the population of interest (Gray, 2004; Gubrium and Holstein, 2001). Snowball sampling naturally occurred in this study. A diverse range of participants was recruited from the Queensland ICPA membership branches. Two participants in the survey requested permission to share the study with their extended contacts, enabling the study to reach different segments of the population. These additional participants were suitable because they remained within the scope of the study, in that they lived and/or worked on cattle-producing properties, which is representative of the population and an important aspect of avoiding a biased subset (Morgan, 2008).

Data Analysis

Descriptive research is designed to "portray an accurate profile of persons, events or situations" (Saunders et al., 2009), which makes it suitable for this study. The results of descriptive analysis may derive from either exploratory or explanatory research. However, it is necessary to have a clear picture of what is being researched. The researcher had undertaken extensive research to ensure that all areas of the topic were familiar. The study aimed to establish a causal relationship between poor rural digital technology adoption and barriers to adoption that are specific to producers.

Frequency analysis was used to show the number of occurrences for each response chosen by the respondents. Means analysis was then used to statistically measure the results, and cross-tabulation allowed the researcher to compare one response set to another to draw conclusions from the data. A chi-square test for independence with Yates's correction for continuity, which compensated for an overestimation of the chi-square value when using dichotomous data in 2×2 tables, was used to test the relationship between variables in the first and second study (Pallant, 2016).

Results from the first study showed a relationship between women and technology. It highlighted women as decision makers, and found that they are driving technology from the homestead for the paddock, highlighting a shift away from men as sole decision makers in the business and more towards women playing a larger role in farming diversification and productive partnerships (Hay and Pearce, 2014). Results from the second study confirmed that women are using technology more than men. Specifically, technology used by women relates to both management practices and social connection. Both management practices and social connection are leading to less isolation in terms of having better access to business management and communication tools. Women are using technology to research and improve production, manage accounting practices, and improve communication to create opportunity for and within their family business (Hay, 2018).

DISCUSSION

The contribution of this chapter is in the application of a mixed method approach to research involving difficult-to-reach participants. In-depth knowledge of the research topic, the participants and the use of media to build trust with the research team prior to data collection contributes to rich and meaningful outcomes. Triangulation allows for a deeper and more meaningful understanding of the outcomes, and adds validation and robustness of the mixed method approach. The methodology used has a greater relevance to research in the broader agricultural industry and in other industries where participants lack trust.

Information and communication technology extends into almost every aspect of life. Use of home computers, for example, has given widespread access to information and products that have transformed the way we live, changing many aspects of life within a large and growing share of the world's population (Deichmann et al., 2016). Today, information technology (the tools we use in different ways to increase efficiency) is rapidly transforming lifestyles in rural, regional and remote areas of Australia as well as in many developing countries. The widespread availability of fixed and mobile networks is connecting remote communities and opening up new opportunities in finance, marketing, health and lifestyle on a scale that was hitherto unimaginable (Charmley et al., 2016; Bishop-Hurley et al., 2016). While there are a large number of agricultural technology products available and access to the internet is improving, uptake rates of different forms of agricultural technology have been inconsistent across the industry (Charmley et al., 2016; Lamb et al., 2008; Mooty, 2001; Rango et al., 2011; Alford et al., 2008).

The inconsistent uptake of technology in agriculture is most often attributed to a lack of internet connectivity and high entry prices (Hay, 2016; Curtin, 2001); but it is also due to information fatigue (So et al., 2017), regulatory depletion (fatigue from resistance to impulses and desires in spending) (Wagner et al., 2013; Wan et al., 2010) and distraction from other tasks. Traditional barriers include arguments surrounding perceived cost–benefit and demographic factors such as age and education as well as farm size (Daberkow and McBride, 2003; Feder and Umali, 1993; Fountas et al., 2006; Kutter et al., 2011). However, whilst sales and marketing of agricultural technology are traditionally directed at men, women have been identified as important decision makers and users of technology in rural households and the producer men self-identified as incapable of or uninterested in learning technology (Hay, 2013). Furthermore, the extant literature focuses on women's role in agriculture as traditionally associated with duties related to the homestead (Alston and Wilkinson, 1998; Bryant and Pini, 2006; Little, 2009; Whatmore, 1991). In contrast, women are increasingly playing a more important role in decisions regarding whether or not to adopt technology, and thus in the diffusion of selected technological products (Hay and Pearce, 2014). Therefore a marketer's success when advertising agricultural technology to men may be hindered by the inability of the male producer to leverage that technology to their own benefit (Deichmann et al., 2016; Tey and Brindal, 2012).

280 Handbook of research methods for marketing management

REFERENCES

Ag-Grow. 2013. About Ag-Grow [Online]. Available: http://www.aggrow.com.au/agsite/about.html [Accessed 26 June 2013].

Ahuvia, A., Bagozzi, R. P. & Batra, R. 2014. Psychometric vs. C-OAR-SE measures of brand love: A reply to Rossiter. *Marketing Letters*, 25, 235–243.

Alford, A. R., Clark, R. A. & Griffith, G. R. 2008. The Measurement, Monitoring and Evaluation Strategy. *Australian Farm Business Management Journal*, 5, Paper 10.

Alston, M. & Wilkinson, J. 1998. Australian farm women: Shut out or fenced in? The lack of women in agricultural leadership. *Sociologia Ruralis*, 38, 391–408.

BetterEvaluation. 2018. Triangulation [Online]. Available: https://www.betterevaluation. org/en/evaluation-options/triangulation [Accessed 28 January 2019].

Biemer, P. P. 2010. Total survey error: Design, implementation, and evaluation. *Public Opinion Quarterly*, 74, 817–848.

Bishop-Hurley, G. J., Charmley, E., Mills, S., Atkinson, I., Hay, R. & Atkinson, M. 2016. The Digital Homestead assists rangeland managers to make timely and informed decisions. *In:* Iwaasa, A., Lardner, H. A. B., Schellenberg, M., Willms, W. & Larson, K. (eds.) *Proceedings of the 10th International Rangelands Congress.* Saskatoon, SK, 10th International Rangelands Congress.

Boshoff, C. & Theron, C. 2015. Why you must use my C-OAR-SE method, by John Rossiter: Review and commentary. *Australasian Marketing Journal*, 23, 263–264.

Boslaugh, S. & McNutt, L.-A. 2008. *Sampling Techniques.* Thousand Oaks, CA, Sage.

Bryant, L. & Pini, B. 2006. Towards an understanding of gender and capital in constituting biotechnologies in agriculture. *Sociologia Ruralis*, 46, 261–279.

Burgess-Limerick, T. & Burgess-Limerick, R. 1998. Conversational interviews and multiple-case research in psychology. *Australian Journal of Psychology*, 50, 63–70.

Cantrell, M. A. & Lupinacci, P. 2007. Methodological issues in online data collection. *Journal of Advanced Nursing*, 60, 544–549.

Carter, N., Bryant-Lukosius, D., Dicenso, A., Blythe, J. & Neville, A. J. 2014. The use of triangulation in qualitative research. *Oncology Nursing Forum*, 41, 545–547.

Change, L. 1994. A psychometric evaluation of 4-point and 6-point Likert-type scales in relation to reliability and validity. *Applied Psychological Measurement*, 18, 205–215.

Charmley, E., Hay, R. & Bishop-Hurley, G. 2016. Impact of communication technologies on pastoralist societies. *In:* Iwaasa, A., Lardner, H. A. B., Schellenberg, M., Willms, W. & Larson, K. (eds.) *Proceedings of the 10th International Rangelands Congress.* Saskatoon, SK, International Rangelands Congress.

Curtin, J. D. 2001. A digital divide in rural and regional Australia? *Current Issues Brief* [Online]. Available: http://www.aph.gov.au/About_Parliament/Parliamentary_Departments/Parliamentary_Library/Publications_Archive/CIB/cib0102/02CIB01 [Accessed 3 January 2017].

Daberkow, S. & McBride, W. 2003. Farm and operator characteristics affecting the awareness and adoption of precision agriculture technologies in the US. *Precision Agriculture*, 4, 163–177.

DAFF. 2013. Cattle density in Queensland. Department of Agriculture, Fisheries and Forestry: Animals. [Online]. Available: http://www.daff.Queensland.gov.au/27_10260.htm [Accessed 3 June 2013].

Deichmann, U., Goyal, A. & Mishra, D. 2016. Will digital technologies transform agriculture in developing countries? World Bank Policy Research Working Paper 7669. http://documents.worldbank.org/curated/en/481581468194054206/Will-digital-technologies-transform-agriculture-in-developing-countries.

Denzin, N. 1989. *The Research Act: A Theoretical Introduction to Sociological Methods.* Englewood Cliffs, NJ, Prentice Hall.

Diamantopoulos, A. 2015. The C-OAR-SE procedure for scale development in marketing: A comment. *International Journal of Research in Marketing*, 22, 1–9.

Dillman, D. A., Smyth, J. D. & Christian, L. M. 2009. *Internet, Mail, and Mixed-Mode Surveys: The Tailored Design Method.* Hoboken, NJ, Wiley.

Feder, G. & Umali, D. I. 1993. The adoption of agricultural innovations: A review. *Technological Forecasting and Social Change*, 43, 215–239.

Floyd, J. & Fowler, J. 1995. *Improving Survey Questions: Design and Evaluation*. Thousand Oaks, CA, Sage.

Fountas, S., Wulfsohn, D., Blackmore, B. S., Jacobsen, H. L. & Pedersen, S. M. 2006. A model of decision-making and information flows for information-intensive agriculture. *Agricultural Systems*, 87, 192–210.

Gray, D. E. 2004. *Doing Research in the Real World*. London, Sage.

Gubrium, J. F. & Holstein, J. A. (eds.) 2001. *Handbook of Interview Research: Context and Method*. Thousand Oaks, CA, Sage.

Hay, R. 2013. *Technology Adoption by Rural Women in Queensland, Australia: Women Driving Technology from the Homestead for the Paddock*. Bachelor's thesis, James Cook University.

Hay, R. (ed.) 2016. *Better Internet for Rural, Regional And Remote Australia (BIRRR): Regional Internet Access Survey Results, 2016*. Townsville, James Cook University. https://birrraus.files.wordpress.com/2016/05/birrr-report-2016-survey-results-final.pdf.

Hay, R. 2018. *The Engagement of Women and Technology in Agriculture*. PhD thesis, James Cook University.

Hay, R. & Pearce, P. 2014. Technology adoption by rural women in Queensland, Australia: Women driving technology from the homestead for the paddock. *Journal of Rural Studies*, 36, 318–327.

Kerlinger, F. N. & Lee, H. B. 1992. *Foundations of Behavioural Research*. Belmont, CA, Cengage Learning.

Kevin, G. C. 2015. A commentary on "What grounded theory is . . .": Engaging a phenomenon from the perspective of those living it. *Organizational Research Methods*, 18, 600–605.

Kidman, A. 2016. NBN: Who gets the most Sky Muster satellite coverage? Available: https://www.finder.com.au/nbn-who-gets-the-most-sky-muster-satellite-coverage [Accessed 13 April 2018].

Krueger, R. A. & Casey, M. A. 2015. *Focus Groups: A Practical Guide for Applied Research*, Los Angeles, Sage Publications.

Kutter, T., Tiemann, S., Siebert, R. & Fountas, S. 2011. The role of communication and co-operation in the adoption of precision farming. *Precision Agriculture*, 12, 2–17.

Lamb, D. W., Frazier, P. & Adams, P. 2008. Improving pathways to adoption: Putting the right P's in precision agriculture. *Computers and Electronics in Agriculture*, 61, 4–9.

Lavrakas, P., J. 2008a. Research design. *In:* Lavrakas, P. J. (ed.) *Encyclopedia of Survey Research Methods*. Thousand Oaks, CA, Sage Publications.

Lavrakas, P. J. 2008b. Conversational interviewing. *In:* Lavrakas, P. J. (ed.) *Encyclopedia of Survey Research Methods*. Thousand Oaks, CA, Sage Publications.

Lillrank, A. 2012. Managing the interviewer self. *In:* Gubrium, J. F., Holstein, J. A. & Marvasti, A. B. (eds.) *The SAGE Handbook of Interview Research: The Complexity of the Craft*. 2 ed. Thousand Oaks, CA, Sage Publications.

Little, J. 2009. Gender and rurality. *In:* Rob, K. & Nigel, T. (eds.) *International Encyclopedia of Human Geography*. Oxford, Elsevier.

Maxwell, J. A. 1996. *Qualitative Research Design: An Interactive Approach*. Thousand Oaks, CA, Sage Publications.

Meat and Livestock Australia. 2018. Fast facts: Australia's beef industry. https://www.mla.com.au/globalassets/mla-corporate/prices--markets/documents/trends--analysis/fast-facts--maps/mla_beef-fast-facts-2018.pdf.

Mooty, K. 2001. Beef breeding blends technology and agriculture. Talk Business and Politics, 23 July. https://talkbusiness.net/2001/07/beef-breeding-blends-technology-and-agriculture.

Morgan, D. L. 2008. Snowball sampling. *In:* Given, L. M. (ed.) *The SAGE Encyclopedia of Qualitative Research Methods*. Thousand Oaks, CA, Sage Publications.

Nunkoo, R. (ed.) 2018. *Handbook of Research Methods for Tourism and Hospitality Management*. Cheltenham, UK and Northampton, MA, USA, Edward Elgar Publishing.

Onwuegbuzie, A. J. & Leech, N. L. 2006. Linking research questions to mixed methods data analysis procedures. *Qualitative Report*, 11, 474–498.
Pallant, J. 2016. *SPSS Survival Manual*. Crows Nest, NSW, Allen & Unwin.
Pannell, D. & Vanclay, F. (eds) 2011. *Changing Land Management: Adoption of New Practices by Rural Landholders*. Collingwood, Vic: CSIRO.
Patton, M. Q. 1999. Enhancing the quality and credibility of qualitative analysis. *Health Services Research*, 34, 1189–1208.
Rango, A., Havstad, K. & Estell, R. 2011. The utilization of historical data and geospatial technology advances at the Jornada Experimental Range to support Western America ranching culture. *Remote Sensing*, 3, 2089–2109.
Rossiter, J. R. 2002. The C-OAR-SE procedure for scale development in marketing. *International Journal of Research in Marketing*, 19, 305–335.
Rossiter, J. R. 2010. *Measurement for the Social Sciences*. New York, Springer.
Roulston, K. J. 2008. Conversational interviewing. *In:* Given, L. M. (ed.) *The SAGE Encyclopedia of Qualitative Research Methods*. Thousand Oaks, CA, Sage Publications.
Saunders, M., Lewis, P. & Thornhill, A. 2009. *Research Methods for Business Students*. Harlow, Pearson.
Shrapnel, M. & Davie, J. 2001. The influence of personality in determining farmer responsiveness to risk. *Journal of Agricultural Education and Extension*, 7, 167–178.
Smith, A. & Humphreys, M. 2006. Evaluation of unsupervised semantic mapping of natural language with Leximancer concept mapping. *Behavior Research Methods*, 38, 262–279.
So, J., Kim, S. & Cohen, H. 2017. Message fatigue: Conceptual definition, operationalization, and correlates. *Communication Monographs*, 84, 5–29.
Tey, Y. & Brindal, M. 2012. Factors influencing the adoption of precision agricultural technologies: A review for policy implications. *Precision Agriculture*, 13, 713–730.
Wagner, D. D., Altman, M., Boswell, R. G., Kelley, W. M. & Heatherton, T. F. 2013. Self-regulatory depletion enhances neural responses to rewards and impairs top-down control. *Psychological Science*, 24, 2262–2271.
Wan, E. W., Rucker, D. D., Tormala, Z. L. & Clarkson, J. J. 2010. The effect of regulatory depletion on attitude certainty. *Journal of Marketing Research*, 47, 531–541.
Whatmore, S. 1991. Life cycle or patriarchy? Gender divisions in family farming. *Journal of Rural Studies*, 7, 71–76.
Whittemore, R., Chase, S. K. & Mandle, C. L. 2001. Validity in qualitative research. *Qualitative Health Research*, 11, 522–537.

ANNOTATED FURTHER READING

Dillman, D. A., Smyth, J. D. & Christian, L. M. 2009. *Internet, Mail, and Mixed-Mode Surveys: The Tailored Design Method*. Hoboken, NJ, Wiley. A tried and tested resource for mixed mode survey delivery methods.
Gubrium, J. F. & Holstein, J. A. (eds) 2001. *Handbook of Interview Research: Context and Method*, Thousand Oaks, CA, Sage. Getting a bit older now, but an invaluable resource for research using conversational interviews.
Venkatesh, V., Brown, S. A. & Sullivan, Y. W. 2016. Guidelines for conducting mixed-methods research: An extension and illustration. *Journal of the Association for Information Systems*, 17, 435–494. A relevant set of guidelines, which is a great starting point for mixed methods research.

13. Multi-methods in the measurement of emotion in tourism marketing
Arghavan Hadinejad, Noel Scott, Anna Kralj and Brent Moyle

INTRODUCTION

Tourism shares six characteristics with other services, specifically intangibility, inseparability, variability, perishability, customer participation and a lack of ownership (Rao, 2007). An important implication of these characteristics for tourism is that potential visitors experience difficulty in understanding a destination's attributes prior to travel. Consequently, the attitude people have to a destination advertisement prior to travel plays a vital role in destination choice (Morgan & Pritchard, 2012). Prior research has revealed that emotional responses evoked by tourism advertisement affect individuals' attitudes (Li et al., 2016). The current literature in tourism tends to apply self-report measures to assess emotional responses towards advertisement.

The self-report approach is simple and inexpensive to capture individuals' emotional responses (Poels & Dewitte, 2006). This approach is based on respondents' recollected emotional experiences. The self-report method cannot capture individuals' moment-to-moment emotions (Li et al., 2016), and thus is not an appropriate tool for continuous measurement of emotions in real time. The self-report surveys have been criticized for allowing retrospective reflection (Li et al., 2015), which might not reflect actual emotions. Recently, scholars have emphasized the application of physiological measurements combined with the self-report approach to assess emotional responses in tourism (Kim & Fesenmaier, 2015).

EMOTION MEASUREMENT IN TOURISM

Researchers in the marketing and tourism fields use two main approaches to investigate emotions, known as basic and dimensional approaches (Li et al., 2015). The basic emotion approach, otherwise known as the categorical approach or discrete approach, is based on all work that proposes six or more basic emotions – including happiness, sadness, anger, fear, disgust, and surprise (Darwin, 1872). Several scales in psychology belong to the basic emotion approach, such as the Differential Emotions Scale (DES) (Izard, 1977), the circular model of emotions (Plutchik, 1980) and the Consumption Emotions Set (CES) (Richins, 1997). There is a lack of consensus on the number of emotions listed in these scales. For instance, the DES identifies ten basic emotions, the circular model of emotions presented recognizes eight, and the CES, which is related to consumption experiences, identifies 16 emotions (Ma, 2013).

The dimensional or continuous approach to emotion attempts to identify two or more dimensions to differentiate emotions from one another (Shen & Morris, 2016). According to Mehrabian and Russell (1974), people show different emotions based on their environmental perceptions, and thus react positively or negatively. The two major dimensions used to distinguish emotions are valence and arousal. Valence indicates pleasantness (positive or negative) and arousal refers to the activation of an emotion (active or passive) (Kim & Fesenmaier, 2015). The circumplex model of emotion (Watson & Tellegen, 1985), the pleasure-arousal-dominance (P-A-D) model of emotion (Mehrabian and Russell, 1974) and the positive affect negative affect schedule (PANAS) (Watson et al., 1988) are dimensional approaches that have been used in consumer behaviour.

Tourism scholars have applied self-report methods to study emotions through either a basic or dimensional approach (Hadinejad et al., 2019). However, a number of physiological techniques as alternatives to self-report measurement of emotion have been introduced, such as Electro-dermal analysis (EDA), Heart rate response (HR), Facial electromyography (EMG), and the Facial Action Coding System (FACS) (Teixeira et al., 2012; Bastiaansen et al., 2016). EDA measures the conductance of the skin in response to a marketing stimulus (Riedl & Léger, 2016, pp. 47–72). HR is used to measure the number of heart beats per unit of time, commonly applying electrocardiography (ECG) (Turpin, 1986). EMG measures the electrical activity of facial muscle contraction (Mauss & Robinson, 2009). FACS measures emotions in terms of basic emotions (Terzis et al., 2013). FaceReader™ functions based on FACS, which analyses six basic emotions (plus neutral), emotional arousal and valence of emotions (Zaman & Shrimpton-Smith, 2006).

In response to criticism of the application of self-report surveys, this chapter applied FaceReader™ and Skin Conductance Response (SCR) to capture individuals' emotional responses (emotional arousal and valence in particular) in response to the Switzerland destination promotional video (DPV) project.

METHODOLOGY

In the study, 37 Australians (16 males and 21 females) watched the Switzerland DPV on a computer. The total of 37 was assumed to be adequate as studies with physiological measures usually contain small samples (e.g. Gakhal & Senior, 2008; Somervuori & Ravaja, 2013). Upon arrival at the lab, participants were recommended to read and sign the consent form. In order to better detect facial movement for FaceReader™ analysis, participants were asked to sit in front of a window (Hetland et al., 2016). Skin Conductance data collection and subsequent analysis were conducted using Biopac™ hardware (transmitter), Biopac™ data logger and Acq*Knowledge*® (psychophysiological software). The researchers attached two standard electrodes to the index and middle fingertips of the non-dominant hand of each participant to collect Skin Conductance data. The electrodes were connected to a transmitter which sent Skin Conductance signals to the Biopac™ data logger. The sampling rate for Skin Conductance data collection was 2000Hz. The researchers allowed five minutes between attaching the electrodes to participants' fingers and collecting data to check the quality of Skin Conductance data (Braithwaite et al., 2013). After watching the advertising stimulus, the electrodes were removed from the participants. Data collection with FaceReader™ and Skin Conductance was done simultaneously.

After watching the Switzerland DPV, participants were asked to complete the Self-Assessment Manikin (SAM) (Lang, 1980) indicating their valence and arousal levels. This was followed by a brief interview in which participants were asked to explain how they felt while watching the advertisement.

Data Analysis

Both data collection and analysis were conducted via a computer and laptop running FaceReader™ and Acq*Knowledge*®. FaceReader™ data was calibrated to have more accurate information. FaceReader™ exported data as a video analysis detailed log containing information about a participant's emotional arousal, valence and facial expressions, as well as gender, age and ethnicity. This information was then exported to an Excel sheet for further analysis. Since FaceReader™ provides data points per decisecond, the researchers aggregated and averaged data across one-second intervals. That said, 90 data points (one-second interval) were provided. In order to calculate the FaceReader™ mean score, each participant's data was aggregated and averaged. For Skin Conductance analysis, the frequency and amplitude of Skin Conductance Response (SCR), two common indicators of phasic Skin Conductance data, were calculated (Boucsein, 2012; Braithwaite et al., 2013). This analysis was conducted within Acq*Knowledge*® software. The mean scores for SCR frequency and amplitude were calculated based on the aggregated and averaged data (per person). Participants' real-time emotional arousal and valence obtained from Skin Conductance and FaceReader™ were standardized based on a z-score to analyse fluctuations of emotion. The z-score is used to average and standardize data across time to identify spikes in physiological measures (Biocca et al., 1994).

Results

SCR frequency and amplitude

Figures 13.1 and 13.2 illustrate the frequency of SCR (M = 3.8), SCR amplitude (M = 1.1), and participants' real-time emotional responses to the DPV. Participants' real-time emotional arousal obtained from Skin Conductance data were standardized based on a z-score. Consistent with prior research, only scores greater than 1.96 were identified as peaks (Li et al., 2016). Real-time emotional arousal in Figure 13.2 indicated four peaks. The first occurred at the beginning of the video, when participants did not report any particular emotion. The next occurred between 01:15 and 01:17, when an old man in the video rolls up his sleeves and shows his tattoo to some girls in a club. Participants explained their emotions regarding these moments as: "happy that the farmer was clubbing, dancing, and meeting women without his wife"; "I felt very comical when

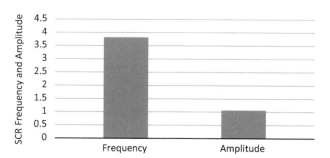

Note: N = 37 in all figures.

Source: All figures in this chapter were created by the authors.

Figure 13.1   Frequency and amplitude of SCR in response to the Switzerland DPV

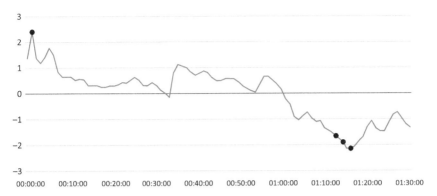

Figure 13.2   Moment-to-moment Skin Conductance data (z-score) for the Switzerland DPV

the old man was showing his tattoo"; or "laughing inside by the clubbing section". These findings suggest that the Switzerland DPV created emotional arousal in Australians.

Emotional arousal and valence

Participants' emotional arousal (M = 0.3) and valence (M = 0.08) captured by FaceReader™ are illustrated in Figure 13.3. The moment-to-moment data based on emotional arousal and valence is then demonstrated in Figures 13.4 and 13.5. Similar to Skin Conductance data, only the z-scores greater than 1.96 were identified as peaks. For both emotional arousal and valence graphs, peaks occurred in the first ten seconds of the advertisement, when two rural men enter a city in Switzerland. Participants reported their emotions regarding the first scenes of the video as "I was

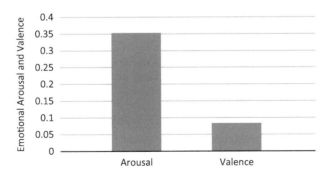

Figure 13.3   Emotional arousal and valence of FaceReader™ in response to the Switzerland DPV

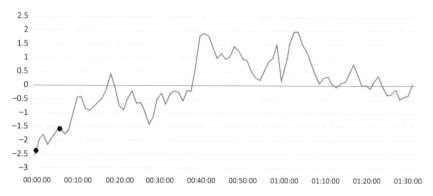

Figure 13.4 Moment-to-moment FaceReader™ valence data (z-score) for the Switzerland DPV

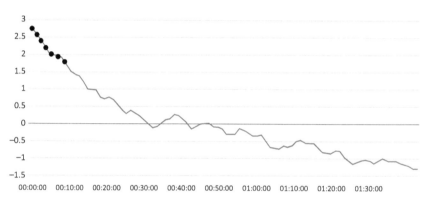

Figure 13.5 Moment-to-moment FaceReader™ arousal data (z-score) for the Switzerland DPV

happy at first, it was a little surprising and then it just seemed really weird!" or "Happy first but confused about what the video was for". These findings indicate that the Switzerland DPV created emotional arousal and positive emotions in Australians.

Mean of emotional arousal and valence in self-report measures
In order to capture self-reported emotional responses, participants were asked to rate their emotions using the SAM on a five-point scale. According to their reported emotional responses, the Switzerland DPV created a relatively high level of positive emotions (M = 4.3) and a moderate level of arousal (M = 3.5), as illustrated in Figure 13.6. The findings

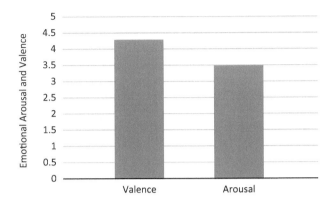

Figure 13.6   Means of emotional arousal and valence based on the self-reported data

from self-report surveys are consistent with the post hoc interviews. For instance, participants described the advertisement in terms such as "felt warmth, happiness"; "fun, humour, happiness"; and "intrigued, laughing at the humour in the ad". In total, 31 participants used the term "happiness", "laugh" or "fun" to describe their emotions.

CONCLUSION

This chapter provides readers with an insight into the application of physiological and self-report methods to measure emotions. The findings of Skin Conductance Response revealed that participants in the study showed emotional responses while viewing the Switzerland DPV. The moments when participants had high emotional arousal (e.g. an old man showing girls his tattoo) is in accord with prior research (Li et al., 2016). The Skin Conductance moment-to-moment data is similar to the FaceReader™ graph as both indicate that the Switzerland DPV elicited greater emotional arousal at the start and fluctuated at a low level at the end of the advertisement. The findings from FaceReader™ showed that participants' positive emotions fluctuated at a low level at the start of the DPV and increased in the middle to the end, which is in line with previous research (Li et al., 2016). In addition, the findings from the self-report surveys confirmed the FaceReader™ results as participants generated higher positive emotions rather than emotional arousal.

This chapter contributes to the body of literature by its novel application of FaceReader™ and Skin Conductance, along with self-report surveys and post hoc interviews, to measure emotions elicited from tourism advertisements. From a practical perspective, the present study will provide valuable feedback for destination managers and marketers. A potential limitation of this study is that the content of the Switzerland DPV is humorous. Therefore, future research needs to assess participants' emotions to other kinds of DPV. This chapter's study was conducted only on Australians. That said, different nationalities might differ in their emotional responses. It is suggested that future research employs other nationalities to explore the difference in emotional responses.

REFERENCES

Bastiaansen, M., Straatman, S., Driessen, E., Mitas, O., Stekelenburg, J., & Wang, L. (2016). My destination in your brain: A novel neuromarketing approach for evaluating the effectiveness of destination marketing. *Journal of Destination Marketing & Management*, 7, 76–88.

Biocca, F., David, P., & West, M. (1994). Continuous response measurement (CRM): A computerized tool for research on the cognitive processing of communication messages. In A. Lang (Ed.), *Measuring psychological responses to media messages* (pp. 15–64). Hillsdale, NJ: Lawrence Erlbaum.

Boucsein, W. (2012). *Electrodermal activity*. New York: Springer.

Braithwaite, J. J., Watson, D. G., Jones, R., & Rowe, M. (2013). A guide for analysing electrodermal activity (EDA) and skin conductance responses (SCRs) for psychological experiments. *Psychophysiology*, 49, 1017–1034.

Darwin, C. (1872). *The expression of the emotions in man and animals*. London: John Murray.

Gakhal, B., & Senior, C. (2008). Examining the influence of fame in the presence of beauty: An electrodermal "neuromarketing" study. *Journal of Consumer Behaviour*, 7(4–5), 331–341.

Hadinejad, A., Moyle, B. D., Scott, N., & Kralj, A. (2019). Emotional responses to tourism advertisements: The application of FaceReader™. *Tourism Recreation Research*, 44(1), 131–135.

Hetland, A., Vittersø, J., Fagermo, K., Øvervoll, M., & Dahl, T. I. (2016). Visual excitement: Analyzing the effects of three Norwegian tourism films on emotions and behavioral intentions. *Scandinavian Journal of Hospitality and Tourism*, 16(4), 528–547.

Izard, C. E. (1977). *Human emotions*. New York: Plenum Press.

Kim, J. J., & Fesenmaier, D. R. (2015). Measuring emotions in real time: Implications for tourism experience design. *Journal of Travel Research*, 54(4), 419–429.

Lang, P. J. (1980). Behavioral treatment and bio-behavioral assessment: Computer applications. In J. B. Sidowski, J. H. Johnson, & T. A. Williams (Eds.), *Technology in mental health care delivery systems* (pp. 119–167). Norwood, NJ: Ablex.

Li, S., Scott, N., & Walters, G. (2015). Current and potential methods for measuring emotion in tourism experiences: A review. *Current Issues in Tourism*, 18(9), 805–827.

Li, S., Walters, G., Packer, J., & Scott, N. (2016). Using skin conductance and facial electromyography to measure emotional responses to tourism advertising. *Current Issues in Tourism*, August, 1–23.

Ma, J. (2013). *Emotions derived from theme park experiences: The antecedents and consequences of customer delight*. PhD thesis, University of Queensland, Australia.

Mauss, I. B., & Robinson, M. D. (2009). Measures of emotion: A review. *Cognition and Emotion*, 23(2), 209–237.

Mehrabian, A., & Russell, J. A. (1974). *An approach to environmental psychology*. Cambridge, MA: MIT Press.

Morgan, N., & Pritchard, A. (2012). *Advertising in tourism and leisure*. Oxford: Butterworth-Heinemann.

Plutchik, R. (1980). *Emotion: A psychoevolutionary synthesis*. New York: Harper & Row.

Poels, K., & Dewitte, S. (2006). How to capture the heart? Reviewing 20 years of emotion measurement in advertising. *Journal of Advertising Research*, 46(1), 18–37.

Rao, K. R. M. (2007). *Services marketing*. Delhi: Dorling Kindersley.

Richins, M. L. (1997). Measuring emotions in the consumption experience. *Journal of Consumer Research*, 24(2), 127–146.

Riedl, R., & Léger, P.-M. (2016). *Fundamentals of NeuroIS*. Berlin: Springer.

Shen, F., & Morris, J. D. (2016). Decoding neural responses to emotion in television commercials. *Journal of Advertising Research*, 56(2), 193–204.

Somervuori, O., & Ravaja, N. (2013). Purchase behavior and psychophysiological responses to different price levels. *Psychology & Marketing*, 30(6), 479–489.

Teixeira, T., Wedel, M., & Pieters, R. (2012). Emotion-induced engagement in internet video advertisements. *Journal of Marketing Research*, 49(2), 144–159.

Terzis, V., Moridis, C. N., & Economides, A. A. (2013). Measuring instant emotions based on facial expressions during computer-based assessment. *Personal and Ubiquitous Computing*, 17(1), 43–52.

Turpin, G. (1986). Effects of stimulus intensity on autonomic responding: The problem of differentiating orienting and defense reflexes. *Psychophysiology*, 23(1), 1–14.

Watson, D., & Tellegen, A. (1985). Toward a consensual structure of mood. *Psychological Bulletin*, 98(2), 219–235.

Watson, D., Clark, L. A., & Tellegen, A. (1988). Development and validation of brief measures of positive and negative affect: The PANAS scales. *Journal of Personality and Social Psychology*, 54(6), 1063–1070.

Zaman, B., & Shrimpton-Smith, T. (2006). The FaceReader: Measuring instant fun of use. In *Proceedings of the 4th Nordic conference on human–computer interaction: Changing roles (NordiCHI '06)* (pp. 457–460). New York: Association for Computing Machinery.

14. Using a mixed methods approach to develop a scale in the context of social media attachment
Shabanaz Baboo

INTRODUCTION

The mixed methods approach has been gaining ground among marketing researchers, and has been described as one of the most contemporary trends in social and applied research in marketing (Gobo, 2015). Since mixed methods research is considered as a distinct approach, it is useful to provide a basic definition here. This method is:

> an approach to inquiry involving collecting both quantitative and qualitative data, integrating the two forms of data, and using distinct designs that may involve philosophical assumptions and theoretical frameworks. The core assumption of this form of inquiry is that the combination of qualitative and quantitative approaches provides a more complete understanding of a research problem than either approach alone. (Creswell, 2014, p. 4)

The mixed methods approach is recognized as a third methodological movement by Creswell and Plano Clark (2007) and it is conducted from one of two paradigmatic standpoints (Johnson et al., 2007). Calls to integrate both quantitative and qualitative research methods by emphasizing the value and advantages of this approach have been made in several fields, including sociology, education and health sciences (Tashakkori & Teddlie, 2003).

This chapter focuses primarily on the use of mixed methods in the process of scale development mainly in the social media context. Using mixed methods to develop a new scale is not a new idea; but it is essential to highlight its logic and contributions in order to understand why and how this approach is implemented when developing new scales. To maximize the likelihood of creating an instrument with sound psychometric properties, the chapter aims to offer some procedural guidelines from the scale development and validation literature. The objective is to answer two main questions: why and how the mixed methods approach is used to develop and conduct validation analysis for new scales. The chapter describes the procedures to follow in scale development with essential analytical methods by providing a hands-on example of using a mixed methods design to develop a scale using a real data set. Illustrative examples are incorporated to shed light on the scale development process for a social media attachment construct.

THE EVOLUTION OF MIXED METHODS RESEARCH

Mixed methods has undergone six stages of development and evolution in the last 30 years: the formative stage (1980s and before), the paradigm stage (1980s to 1990s), the procedural stage (1980s to present), the advocacy stage (early 2000s to present), the reflective stage (2000s to present), and the expansion stage (2010s to present) (Creswell & Plano Clark, 2011; Tashakkori & Teddlie, 1998; Teddlie & Tashakkori, 2009). In more recent years, research on mixed methods' expansion focused on its applications in and adaptations to specific disciplines or topics, such as experiment intervention, program evaluation, longitudinal research, and instrument development (Glogowska, 2011; Karasz & Singelis, 2009; Kettles et al., 2011; Plano Clark & Wang, 2010; Shaw et al., 2010).

There have been many ongoing debates about the use of mixed methods. Its opponents unequivocally believe that the integration of the qualitative paradigm (i.e. constructivism) and the quantitative paradigm (post-positivism) is neither possible nor sensible. Proponents state that mixed methods research recognizes that there are many correct techniques that can be applied in a single study to collect and analyse data. Mixed methods research is believed to be the long-awaited response to the unproductive debate on the pros and cons of quantitative and qualitative methods (Teddlie & Tashakkori, 2009).

Pragmatists (e.g. Cook & Reichardt, 1979) argue that paradigm characteristics are independent, and can therefore be combined in accordance with the most appropriate methods that work best for the problem. They further argue that insights and techniques from both approaches, when put together, produce a superior product than mono-method studies. The goal of mixed methods research is to draw on the strengths and minimize the weaknesses of both in a single research study (Johnson & Onwuegbuzie, 2004; Johnson et al., 2007), hence offering the best opportunity to address the research questions. Comprehending the strengths and weaknesses of quantitative and qualitative research enables the researcher to collect multiple data samples using a combination of different strategies and methods, resulting in a mix of complementary strengths and non-overlapping weaknesses (Johnson et al., 2007). Scholars of numerous studies – such as Johnson et al. (2007) and Tashakkori and Teddlie (2003)

– have championed the mixed methods "wave" as an unrestrained form of research that often results in superior studies. Of late, mixed methods research has been thriving as scholars help advance its concepts with regular practice and numerous publications.

The overall purpose and central premise of mixed methods studies is that the use of quantitative and qualitative approaches in combination may provide a better understanding of research problems and complex phenomena that would not have been possible through one method on its own (Creswell & Plano Clark, 2007).

PURPOSES AND DESIGN OF MIXED METHODS RESEARCH

According to a theoretical review by Greene et al. (1989), mixed methods research has five purposes:

- triangulation (combining several research methods to study one thing);
- complementary (elaboration or clarification of the results from one method with the findings from another method);
- development (when the researcher uses the results from one method to help develop the use of another method);
- initiation (seeking paradoxes and contradiction, new framework perspectives, recasting questions or results from one method with questions or results from another method); and
- expansion (seeking to extend the breadth and range of inquiry by using different methods for different inquiry components).

A crucial aspect in this approach is how to design and perform a mixed methods study as there are different types of mixed methods design. The two main factors that help researchers design and conduct a mixed methods study are the implementation of data collection and priority (Morgan, 1998; Tashakkori & Teddlie, 1998). While implementation refers to the sequence the researcher uses to collect both qualitative and quantitative data, priority refers to the amount of priority given to both quantitative and qualitative data. Data gathering can be done at the same time – i.e. a concurrent, simultaneous or parallel design – or it can be done in phases – i.e. a sequential or two-phase design. In concurrent data collection, both forms of data (quantitative and qualitative) are collected and a comparison made to search for congruency (Creswell, 2013).

SCALE DEVELOPMENT

In social sciences and human behaviour, scholars usually found the need to develop new scales due to the lack of existing instruments in these fields. Traditionally, researchers referred to the psychometric literature on reliability and validity for item generation (Rowan & Wulff, 2007) and survey methodology for questionnaire design (May, 2011) when developing new scales. In recent years, researchers have realized that scale development was not merely a procedure within a research project, but a systematic study from research design level to implementation; and, accordingly, mixed methods has been applied to scale development (Bryman, 2006; Collins et al., 2006; Greene et al., 1989). A few methodologists have discussed the rationale of using mixed methods in scale development since the mid-2000s (Collins et al., 2006; Creswell & Plano Clark, 2011; Onwuegbuzie & Combs, 2010; Smolleck et al., 2006). For instance, Collins et al. (2006) explicated the necessity and appropriateness of using mixed methods to "assess the appropriateness and/or utility of existing instrument(s); create new instrument(s) and assess its appropriateness and/or utility".

Using Mixed Methods for Instrument/Scale Development

From the early 2000s, methodologists began discussing why mixed methods could help in developing reliable instruments, including the comprehensiveness of item generation and the rigorous validation of new items (Bryman, 2006; Collins et al., 2006). Researchers such as Creswell and Plano Clark (2011) discussed a sequential mixed methods research design for scale development, exploratory instrument design, which consisted of three phases: a qualitative phase defining the construct of the instrument; an instrument development phase including item generation and revision; and a confirming quantitative phase to test the instrument. Following their exploratory instrument design, other researchers have used mixed methods in scale construction (Crede & Borrego, 2013; Durham et al., 2011; Hitchcock et al., 2006; Nastasi et al., 2007).

Appropriateness of Using Mixed Methods for Instrument/Scale Validation Analysis

Many researchers misunderstood that validation analysis is required only after the scale development phase. In fact, instrument validation analysis started at the beginning of instrument development and involved the whole process. For instance, content analysis of literature and panel reviews for item generation usually assisted in the formulation of the systematized concept, and thus provided the content evidence of validity for the instrument (Luyt, 2012). Why did validation happen as early as item writing? To answer this question, we shall review the concepts of validity and validation. According to Messick (1989), validity was defined as "the degree to which empirical evidence and theoretical rationales support the adequacy and appropriateness of interpretations and actions based on test scores" (p. 6). Validation referred to an ongoing process of "developing a scientifically sound validity argument to support the intended interpretation of test scores and their relevance to the proposed use" (AERA et al., 1999, p. 9). In other words, validity was viewed as a property from an ontology perspective, whereas validation was the process of gathering evidence through philosophical, experimental, and statistical means to evaluate such property (Borsboom et al., 2004; Messick, 1989; Sireci & Sukin, 2013).

To gather evidence for validity, multiple types of data should be collected and mixed, including subjective judgment and statistical analysis (Hubley & Zumbo, 2011; Sireci, 2009). Accordingly, using different methods to collect and integrate different types of data could help with validation. That said, using mixed methods is appropriate to enhance the quality of instrument validation. According to Onwuegbuzie and Combs (2010), mixed methods could be used to provide content-related evidence for face validity, item validity, and sampling validity; and construct-related evidence for substantive validity, outcome validity, and generalizability. Taking validation analysis for content validity as an example, early in the 2000s researchers discussed multiple methods in instrument validation. For instance, Brod et al. (2009) stated that qualitative approaches (i.e. grounded theory) were best to support content validity, whereas Meurer et al. (2002) preferred a standardized and statistical method for content evidence of validity, such as surveying a panel of experts and calculating inter-rater agreement as well as the content validity index. More recently, researchers have suggested mixed methods as the most suitable for instrument validation. For instance, Newman et al. (2013) advocated an interactive model that allowed integration of qualitative and quantitative methods to collect content evidence of validity. They presented a table of specifications which were used to collect experts' views of the accuracy and sufficiency of a specific concept and to calculate the agreement between judges. According to Newman et al., when researchers attempted to estimate agreement by aligning these concepts (qualitative) empirically (quantitative), the process was inherently mixed method.

Moreover, the mixed methods approach has been used to collect different types of validity evidence. For instance, Lee and Greene (2007) showed how mixing qualitative and quantitative approaches provided evidence for the predictive validity of a test. Morell and Tan (2009) demonstrated how mixed methods could be implemented to gather internal validity evidence, and thus help form the validation argument. Hitchcock et al. (2006) used mixed methods to collect cross-cultural evidence for construct validity through ethnographic and factor analysis techniques. Ungar and Liebenberg (2011) mixed qualitative and quantitative approaches in the development of cultural-relevant measures for translation validity.

OVERVIEW OF RECOMMENDED PROCEDURES FOR SCALE DEVELOPMENT

There is clear guidance from numerous articles and books on how to develop a scale (e.g. Churchill, 1979; Clark & Watson, 1995; DeVellis, 1991; Haynes et al., 1999; Nunnally & Bernstein, 1994; Spector, 1992). Steps and procedures often vary from author to author based on the goals, purposes and context of the study and the measurement. However, most studies share a common set of guidelines for scale development. These include a phased approach starting with construct definition and context domain; then generating and judging measurement items; followed by designing and conducting studies to develop and refine the scale; and ending by finalizing the scale. Given the focus of this chapter, the steps and procedures used to guide the study are based on the research objectives and questions with regard to the construct of social media attachment.

DEVELOPING A SCALE FOR ATTACHMENT TO SOCIAL MEDIA

Developing a measurement scale that is valid and reliable is a challenging task in any research field as it takes time and reflection. This illustrative example of mixed methods explains how the concept and measurement scale of attachment to social media was developed. It describes several procedures that were applied in the scale development process for this context, namely: interdisciplinary literature review, interviews, expert opinions, a pilot study, and two large-scale studies with questionnaires and data analysis for assessing measure reliability and validity. Readers can have a grasp of the appropriate procedures and their sequence in the scale development process and the importance of the mixed method approach in a scale development process. By applying the scale development guidelines presented in this example, the reader will also be able to assess the appropriateness of scale development processes of existing measurement scales and develop their own measurement scale.

Attachment to Social Media

Attachment to social media is defined as the psychological connection consisting of both affective and cognitive bonds between a consumer and social media (VanMeter et al., 2015). A new direction is therefore being taken in social media research relating to marketing, with the aim of understanding the psychological connections consumers may be forming with social media. Researchers and scholars recognize that attachment to social media is a potential concept that more accurately predicts consumer behaviours, although evidence is inconclusive (VanMeter et al., 2015). However, despite the obvious importance of the construct, the conceptualization and measurement of attachment to social media are still at an early phase of development (VanMeter et al., 2015); and studies in this field are somewhat limited, and measurement seems inconsistent across studies (Chiu et al., 2015; Fiedler & Sarstedt, 2014; Kim et al., 2016; Park et al., 2019; Ren et al., 2012). Rigorous attention should be paid to the concept of attachment to social media since a more reliable and contextualized measure is needed in order to ensure its applicability to future studies (VanMeter et al., 2015). Therefore, this requires a rigorous scale development initiative that takes into account the context of social media, including the specifics and characteristics of this virtual world.

For the purpose of developing a parsimonious scale representative of the dimensions of social media attachment, the present example has followed the scale development process posited by Churchill (1979) and the guidelines of DeVellis (1991), Gerbing and Anderson (1988), Hair et al. (2010) and Nunnally and Bernstein (1994), which have been used in many scale development studies. The scale development process is outlined in Figure 14.1, and the different phases discussed in the following.

The present study used mixed methods research to develop a scale for attachment to social media. To make the procedures concrete, researchers first need to be clear about what they want to measure. More often than ever, researchers in marketing are dealing with unobservable, abstract concepts and human constructs such as love, happiness, motivation and, in this case, attachment. Theoretical foundations for those concepts are crucial and substantive literature review helps clarify what researchers wish to measure. It is important to refer to relevant theories before developing an instrument which can also serve as a guide for scale development (Cronbach & Meehl, 1955; DeVellis, 2012). Therefore, an extensive review of the literature to locate standardized measures of attachment in other

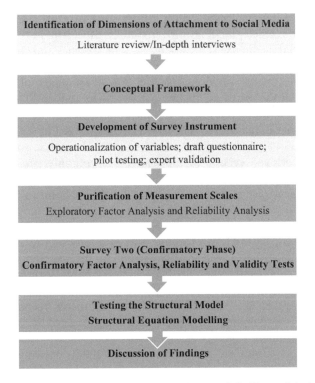

Source: Adapted from Churchill (1979), DeVellis (2003) and Gerbing and Anderson (1988).

Figure 14.1 Flowchart of the research process

fields was performed. The next step was the generation of an item pool. The study then carried on with an exploratory, qualitative first phase of interviews with heavy social media users.

Phase 1: Qualitative Phase

The adoption of mixed methods for a scale development process inevitably requires a phased research approach. Phase 1 of this research relates to the first research objective (RO1) and research question (RQ1), which aims at identifying the underlying dimensions of attachment to social media. As per the scale development and research process outlined above, a qualitative phase is the first step and is crucial in this study. The qualitative findings are pivotal in providing the dimensions of attachment to social media and adding insights to the existing literature. The qualitative findings helped the researcher uncover the dimensions of attachment to social media that have been lacking in past studies, especially in the digital era in which social media use is prevalent; and the specifics and characteristics of this virtual world are different from other contexts in which attachment scale was developed in previous research. The development of instruments as reflective of the social media context would subsequently allow for the generation of a highly relevant social media attachment survey in a quantitative manner in the subsequent phase 2 (Creswell & Plano Clark, 2007).

After a thorough literature review, it was clear that some authors created a shortened version of the scale measuring interpersonal attachment style, while others constructed scales explicitly to measure attachment to objects such as brands (Park et al., 2010; Thomson et al., 2005), service employees, firms (Mende & Bolton, 2012; Mende et al., 2013) and place (Ramkissoon et al., 2012, 2013). As a consequence, existing studies relied only on past literature to build survey questionnaires or made use of questionnaires developed in other contexts, such as non-virtual environments (Andangsari et al., 2013; Baek et al., 2014; Both & Best, 2017; Coulson et al., 2018; Hart et al., 2015; Levine & Stekel, 2016; Lim et al., 2014; Monacis et al., 2017; Shu et al., 2017), therefore neglecting the dimensions of attachment that are relevant to the specifics of the social media environment.

According to Johnson and Onwuegbuzie (2004), drawing exclusively on existing questionnaires, dimensions and scales from other contexts to measure online attachment risks producing limited and/or incongruous knowledge that may not reflect the underlying dimensions of attachment to social media. The researcher may overlook details arising on the phenomena. A qualitative approach provides in-depth understanding of an understudied phenomenon, thus increasing validity and reliability (Malterud, 2001; Mays & Pope, 2000). The users of social media were able to share their experiences of using social media and their attachment to social media that may have been missed out by prior studies, and such insights would enable the researcher to extract meaningful data from the participants' personal experience to develop survey items, thereby overcoming the weakness of using questionnaires and scales that rely on past studies. As per Greene et al. (1989), the qualitative results would then help the researcher develop and adapt the quantitative instruments as well as determining and validating relationship pathways between variables in a nomological network.

Sampling and recruitment
The sampling and recruitment of interviewees was based on the study's purpose and research questions. Here the qualitative goal was to procure

information-rich insights from social media users that would maximize understanding of the dimensions underlying attachment to social media. Therefore a purposive sampling technique was chosen to increase interpretive and descriptive validity of the study (Tashakkori & Teddlie, 2003). Of the various purposive sampling strategies available, this study used convenience sampling. The participants were chosen on the criterion that they were heavy users of social media. Suitable candidates were contacted based on referrals from colleagues, students, friends and experts in the field (Arnold & Reynolds, 2003).

Defining a sufficient sample size for a qualitative study is more challenging than for a quantitative study in which an adequate sample size is calculated statistically (Hair et al., 2010). In a qualitative study the right sample size is determined by theoretical saturation, as stated by Yin (2010). According to Neuman (2011), theoretical saturation is reached when a researcher believes that all relevant dimensions and relationships have been identified and there is little possibility that new insights will arise from continued sampling. Regarding sample size for qualitative studies (as per Creswell, 2012), when a researcher reaches this point it is a subjective assessment to ensure the saturation point; and, according to Lindloff and Taylor (2002), around 12 participants is the optimal sample size for qualitative research including interviews. Interviews were conducted with 20 social media users aged 18 and above (11 females, 9 males). The sample included undergraduate students and working individuals. Undergraduates are considered a frequently used and acceptable sample of respondents in consumer behaviour and communication studies (Reagan, 2006; Wimmer & Dominick, 2000). It is therefore acceptable to identify university students as part of a convenience sample for interviews.

In this study, the sample size was adequate for answering the research question concerning underlying attachment to social media, and theoretical saturation was reached within the first 15 interviews, after which no new concepts or ideas arose. However, the researcher continued interviews with the remaining five participants to establish more credible results. Interviews varied in length from 12 to 52 minutes (average 34 minutes), which falls within recommended limits (Lindloff & Taylor, 2002). All interviews were conducted in English and were recorded for later analysis of the data. Permission to digitally record the interviewees' voices was obtained in advance via emails sent to participants prior to the interviews. Data was analysed using content analysis, a method commonly used in qualitative research to examine trends and patterns (Cavanagh, 1997; Kyngäs & Elo, 2008). Keywords, concepts and sentences were distilled, with the aim of understanding and generating knowledge of the attachment to social media phenomenon (Cavanagh, 1997). The qualitative phase yielded quotes and keywords, and an instrument can be developed by using the quotes to write items; this method design is a useful procedure for moving from the qualitative data analysis to scale development (DeVellis, 2003).

After transcription, a preliminary pool of scale items was developed based on qualitative research and literature review (as explained above), and a pretest of the items was conducted. The instrument went through several refinements following rigorous instrument-scale development procedures. The key informant technique was applied to the improved pool of items as per Parasuraman et al. (2006). The pool of items was then presented separately to industry experts. In accordance with Li et al. (2002) and DeVellis (2003), the list was presented to a panel of expert judges in order to assess its content and face validity. The items finalized in the qualitative phase were assessed by a panel of ten experts consisting of two professors of marketing and consumer behaviour, two lecturers in psychology, two social media experts and four respondents. They all had more than three years' experience in their respective fields. The experts were given the definitions of the concept and instructed to retain items based on relevance and clarity of wording. The panel helped in eliminating redundant items further, refining and selecting items that had good face validity, thus ensuring that the newly developed measurement scale was correctly conceptualizing attachment to social media.

Phase 2: Quantitative Phase – Scale Development for Attachment to Social Media Using Exploratory Factor Analysis

After finalizing the list of items with potential to carry the research forward, the next phase was to conduct the quantitative research. A questionnaire for this phase was written in English and administered as paper-and-pencil surveys. The questionnaire was designed with clear written instructions given at the beginning of the survey. A brief statement described the background and objectives of the research, and the participants were assured that any information provided would remain confidential, thus reducing any apprehension. The demographic section asked the respondents to select the various social media platforms they used and indicate the amount of time spent per day on each platform. They were also instructed to indicate their level of agreement with the items in the survey on a 5-point Likert scale (1 = "Strongly disagree" to 5 = "Strongly agree").

After developing a set of items that conceptualize the construct of attachment to social media, the next step was to administer those items to respondents in an appropriate way and in the relevant research environment and context. Oppenheim (1992) and Fink (2010) explain that the validity, reliability and practicality of the survey instrument can be determined through pilot testing. Therefore, a pretest was conducted as part of paying considerable attention to common method variance with a sample of 24 social media users through convenience sampling before it was administered to an appropriate and larger sample for the main study (Malhotra et al., 2006; Podsakoff et al., 2003; Siemsen et al., 2010).

In addition to the relevance of the items, the clarity, length and flow of the questionnaire were also pretested. Such assessment was used to determine a scale and research instrument appropriate for this study. When the responses of the pretest sample were examined, it was clear that some respondents had issues with the attachment scale, especially the wording. Therefore, precautions were taken as suggested by authors such as Peterson (1999), Podsakoff et al. (2003) and Spector (1992) to further refine the items and questionnaire instructions in order to be focused, simple and without idiosyncrasies and unfamiliar colloquialisms, and to get rid of items that are verbose, obscure or confusing (Angleitner & Wiggins, 1986).

The finalized items developed to measure attachment to social media were then taken for further tests using a survey with social media users on a larger scale. Here sample size was guided by the requirements for exploratory factor analysis (EFA), a technique of factor loading into categories to extract principal latent variables. This method makes use of the data it generates, and involves combining observable variables on a single factor or a number of different factors (Hair et al., 2006).

After the qualitative phase and design and pilot testing of the questionnaire, an EFA is crucial in the scale development process in order to meet the research objectives. Item purification is an essential stage to ensure that the scale being developed is measuring what it is intended to measure and to further refine the pool of items (Bearden et al., 2001; Shimp & Sharma, 1987), and an EFA is conducted as part of the purification process. EFA is used to reduce data and refine a developing scale, identify latent constructs and reduce a large number of items to a few factors that explain co-variation between them (Hair et al., 2006; Tabachnick & Fidell, 2007). EFA also tests the uni-dimensionality of measurement scales, and is often used as a preliminary step for more advanced testing using structural equation modelling (SEM) (Hair et al., 2006). Since there was a newly developed scale for this study, it was important to reduce the number of items and identify the dimensionality of the construct for a parsimonious analysis.

An EFA allows a researcher to determine the nature of the constructs influencing a set of responses by statistically determining the number of common factors, sometimes referred to as dimensions, influencing a scale or set of measures (Hair et al., 2010). The aim of EFA is to maximize the percentage of variance explained by the model that it lays out. The researcher does not necessarily need to have a model in mind at the onset of EFA. Factors that are derived from the data are then interpreted by the researcher, and EFA helps determine the structure of the items. Therefore, an EFA was carried out for the newly developed items representing attachment to social media.

The raw data was gathered, coded and entered manually into a data file using IBM's Statistical Package for the Social Sciences (SPSS) Version 21 software. The data was then carefully inspected and amended for out-of-range values. Missing responses were detected and assessed as to whether they were a risk to the data set by using the steps recommended by Hair et al. (2006). Three respondents were dropped from a sample of 154 due to incomplete data, thus leaving 151 usable responses. This sample satisfied the stated minimum sample size required to successfully perform an EFA, namely 100 (Hair et al., 1998). After data cleaning – removing incomplete surveys, treating missing values (which is discussed in Chapter 5) – the data was then ready to be used for EFA.

SPSS 21 was used to perform the EFA on the finalized pool of items; the extraction method utilized was the principal component extraction method, and the rotation type was both varimax and oblimin to reveal the underlying factor structure of attachment to social media. Hair et al. (2006) suggested that researchers should use different rotation methods to find the most interpretable factor solution. Item deletion and/or retention was based on the size of the loadings of the items and some cross-loadings (Tabachnick & Fidell, 2001). It is customary to observe smaller loadings in social science studies and when newly developed scales are employed. More specifically, a loading of 0.40 or greater is acceptable in an exploratory study such as this. Any item that had substantial cross-loading (above 0.40) was dropped (Gorsuch, 1983; Hair et al., 2010; Yaremko et al., 1986). Factor loadings of less than 0.40 were deleted (Churchill, 1979). However, several items did not load significantly (0.40) on a factor and other items loaded on more than one factor, which meant they cross-loaded. This process is iterative; that is, the loadings and communalities change when items are eliminated and the final results come from multiple iterations of item deletions and analysis (Hair et al., 2010).

The study then followed Hair et al. (2010), who suggested using the Kaiser-Meyer-Olkin Measure of Sampling Adequacy (KMOMSA) to test adequacy of size and Bartlett's Test of Sphericity (BToS) to check the appropriateness of the data. All results obtained were in accordance with the criteria based on: (1) Eigenvalues over Kaiser's acceptable criteria of 1 (Kaiser, 1960; Field, 2009); (2) total variance explained above 60 per cent;

and (3) meaningfulness and easy interpretability. The reliability of each factor was then verified using Cronbach's alpha test (Cronbach & Meehl, 1955). Reliability testing is recommended even though the item measurements have been clearly and carefully defined during the development and preparation process in order to increase the accuracy of measurement and ensure that the data is robust (Straub et al., 2004). After analysing the final list of items under each factor extracted from the EFA, the dimensions were named accordingly.

Phase 3: Quantitative Phase – Scale Development for Attachment to Social Media Using CFA and SEM

The third phase of the study (i.e. the second part of the quantitative research) comprised of conducting a second survey on a larger scale and with a different sample, aimed at testing the measurement and structural model. This was done by both Confirmatory Factor Analysis (CFA) and Structural Equation Modelling (SEM) in order to confirm the scale and test the complete model with antecedents and consequences of attachment.

Sampling and recruitment
This phase consisted of a survey of social media users, and the study population was defined through snowball sampling. Through the snowball sampling approach, the investigator can approach respondents with greater variability in demographic characteristics, such as age, education and so on (Kau & Loh, 2006). Kline (1998) suggested a maximum sample size of 200 for SEM analyses. Out of a total of 405 questionnaires completed, four were eliminated due to more than 10 per cent missing values across the scales (Hair et al., 2006), resulting in a usable sample of 401 respondents – and therefore meeting the requirements for using SEM (Nunkoo et al., 2013). A further six responses that contained more than 10 per cent missing values were then removed as per Hair et al. (2006), leaving a sample of 400. The scale development process needs to follow good procedures for instrument design, and the steps for this include results such as item discrimination, construct validity and reliability estimates (DeVellis, 2003). To this end, IBM AMOS 21 statistical software was used to conduct a CFA. Given that the first objective of this study was to develop a scale to measure attachment to social media, the use of CFA was a prerequisite, as outlined in Figure 14.1.

Confirmatory factor analysis is a statistical method used to confirm hypothesized relationships between a set of indicators and their respective latent variables derived a priori (Kline, 2011). The aim of CFA is to investigate the extent to which the proposed relationships based on theory prevail in the data, and testing the validity of a construct is an essential requirement to be able to proceed with further testing of theory and development (Hair et al., 2006). The objective of CFA is therefore to refine and establish the preliminary item scale and to assess the new scale's latent structure, dimensionality, reliability and validity (Bassi, 2011). Since the present study consists of developing a new scale, it was of primary importance to use CFA.

The first-order factor model, comprising of the four dimensions of attachment to social media, displayed good fit indices (CMIN/DF = 2.325/98; CFI = 0.975; GFI = 0.933; AGFI = 0.907; NFI = 0.956; IFI = 0.975; RMSEA = 0.058; SRMR = 0.06) and was tested further for reliability and validity. Reliability was assessed by analysing the composite reliability (CR). Both CR and average variance extracted (AVE) values should be greater than 0.70 and 0.50 respectively (Hair et al., 2006; Nunkoo & Ramkissoon, 2012; Nunkoo et al., 2013). These conditions were met, evidencing reliability. AVE values greater than 0.50 for each dimension and statistically significant factor loadings also evidenced convergent validity. However, the model did not achieve discriminant validity.

However it is on the very basis of highly correlated factors that attachment to social media should potentially be considered as a second-order factor, where the first-order factors act as indicators of the second-order construct (Hair et al., 2006; Koufteros et al., 2009). Based on previous emotional attachment scale development research (Park et al., 2010; Thomson et al., 2005), a multi-dimensional second-order factor structure was predicted. This possibility was examined further, as discussed below. These outcomes were to be expected because, in a second-order factor model, one cannot demonstrate discriminant and convergent validity at the same time because of highly correlated factors. Therefore, for such a model, convergent validity takes precedence (Koufteros et al., 2009; Marsh & Hocevar, 1985). The next stage was carried out with the following objectives:

- Testing the proposed second-order structure of attachment to social media;
- Testing the proposed structure against competing measurement models;
- Demonstrating attachment to social media convergent and discriminant validity.

As stated by Marsh and Hocevar (1985), a model that hypothesizes a second-order factor can never produce a better fit than a model that proposes correlated first-order factors.

Structural Equation Modelling

Following the CFA, the data set was subjected to SEM using Analysis of Moment Structures (AMOS) software to fulfil the second objective of this research – that is, to test the structural model in order to achieve nomological validity. Structural models consist of the set of relationships between independent and dependent variables (Hair et al., 2006; Kline, 2011). SEM enables investigators to study real-life phenomena; it "provides a useful medium for sense making and in so doing link[s] philosophy of science to theoretical and empirical research" (Bagozzi & Yi, 2012, p. 12). SEM is regarded as the most widely used statistical technique for testing complex models which involve several dependent and independent variables, and has become prevalent in social and behavioural sciences (Heene et al., 2011; MacCallum & Austin, 2000).

Studies such as by Nunkoo and Ramkissoon (2012) and Nunkoo et al. (2013) identified the essential issues that must be taken into consideration by researchers when using SEM. These include a two-step approach, reliability and validity, model evaluation fit indices, multivariate normality, post hoc modifications, decomposition effects and sample size, among others. Sample size is determined in light of recommendations for SEM (Hair et al., 2006). Bagozzi and Yi (2012) stated that a sample of above 200 is acceptable. The two-step approach explained by Nunkoo and Ramkissoon (2012) has received considerable attention across several areas of research, and consists of a measurement and a structural model that are estimated separately (Nunkoo et al., 2013). It has also been suggested that a number of alternative models exist for any data set; therefore, before running a SEM analysis, it is imperative that researchers determine alternative models that can produce equally good fit to the theorized model.

Alternative models should be specified a priori in a robust SEM analysis, and it is suggested that the fit indices of the potential competing models are reported. As structural models are estimates of reality, not all hypotheses may be true; and, as a consequence, a number of fit indices that reflect the goodness or weakness of SEM have been developed. In order to ascertain whether the model fits the observed data, CMIN/df, p-value, comparative fit indices (CFI), goodness of fit index (GFI), adjusted goodness of fit (AGFI) and root mean square error of approximation (RMSEA) were calculated. The literature suggests the following values for the variables: CMIN/df < 3, AGFI > 0.80, CFI > 0.90, RMSEA < 0.06, p-value > 0.05, Tucker–Lewis Index (TLI), Normed Fit Index (NFI) > 0.90, Incremental Fit Index (IFI) > 0.90, (GFI) > 0.90, (AGFI) > 0.80, standardized root mean square residual (SRMR) < 0.90, and p of close fit (PCLOSE) value > 0.05 (Bagozzi & Yi, 2012; Bentler, 1990; Hair et al, 2010).

The overall measurement model showed a satisfactory level of fit (χ^2/df = 2.756; CFI = 0.941; TLI = 0.933; RMSEA = 0.056). It is crucial to check the validity and reliability of the scale. Cronbach's alpha and composite reliability (CR) were the two measures of reliability used to assess the level of internal consistency of the measurement scales. The cut-off point required for alpha scores is 0.7 (Nunnally, 1978) and 0.6 for composite reliability (Bagozzi & Yi, 1988). All the observable variables loaded significantly on their respective constructs, thus demonstrating evidence of convergent validity (Anderson & Gerbing, 1988; Hair et al., 2006). The standardized loadings and all the indicators had values greater than 0.50 (Hair et al., 2006; Kline, 2011). Discriminant validity was also confirmed among the constructs of the overall measurement model. According to the two-step approach recommended by Gerbing and Anderson (1988), Hair et al. (2006) and Nunkoo et al. (2013) to conduct structural equational modelling, the measurement model was first tested.

Confirmatory factor analysis was conducted to test the overall measurement model so as to determine the reliability and validity of the measurement scales. First, the model fit was undertaken for the overall measurement model; three forms of validity were then tested, namely convergent validity, discriminant validity and nomological validity. Finally, the reliability of each construct was also examined. The principal objective of the analysis was to test the measurement model developed (including the new scale) as well as the integrated structural model linking social media involvement, attachment to social media, social media satisfaction and attitude to social media marketing. All four hypotheses tested within the structural model were supported and found to be significant.

CONCLUSION

This chapter has outlined the phases for collectively employing quantitative and qualitative methods in instrument scale construction and validation. A number of quantitative and qualitative methods have been described and employed throughout the history of instrument development and validation. However, these methods are often used in isolation rather than fully integrated to inform evidence of scale validity. The present study can help researchers improve their understanding of mixed methods for scale development and use it appropriately. The illustrative example of the scale development and validation for attachment to social media is practical and useful for researchers seeking to develop a reliable scale. To address the need for detailed instructions for researchers aspiring to design a mixed methods study for instrument development, the present study proposed a mixed methods model that provided clear guidance on research design, integration phases, validation techniques and psychometric consideration involving scale development and validation. Readers get to know the appropriate procedures, their sequence in the scale development process and the importance of the mixed method approach in a scale development process. By applying the guidelines in this example, readers will also be able to assess the appropriateness of scale development processes of existing measurement scales and develop their own measurement scales. Hopefully, mixed methods will be adopted in practice by many researchers from a wide range of disciplines.

REFERENCES

American Educational Research Association [AERA], American Psychological Association [APA], & National Council on Measurement in Education [NCME]. (1999). *Standards for educational and psychological tests*. Washington, DC: AMA.

Andangsari, E. W., Gumilar, I., & Godwin, R. (2013). Social networking sites use and psychological attachment need among Indonesian young adults population. *International Journal of Social Science Studies*, *1*(2), 133–138. https://doi.org/10.11114/ijsss.v1i2.66.

Anderson, J. C., & Gerbing, D. W. (1988). Structural equation modeling in practice: A review and recommended two-step approach. *Psychological Bulletin*, *103*(3), 411–423.

Angleitner, A., & Wiggins, S. (1986). *Personality assessment via questionnaires: Current issues in theory and measurement*. New York: Springer.

Arnold, M. J., & Reynolds, K. E. (2003). Hedonic shopping motivations. *Journal of Retailing*, *79*(2), 77–95. https://doi.org/10.1016/S0022-4359(03)00007-1.

Baek, Y. M., Cho, Y., & Kim, H. (2014). Attachment style and its influence on the activities, motives, and consequences of SNS use. *Journal of Broadcasting & Electronic Media*, *58*(4), 522–541. https://doi.org/10.1080/08838151.2014.966362.

Bagozzi, R. P., & Yi, Y. (1988). On the evaluation of structural equation models. *Journal of the Academy of Marketing Science*, *16*(1), 74–94.

Bagozzi, R. P., & Yi, Y. (2012). Specification, evaluation, and interpretation of structural equation models. *Journal of the Academy of Marketing Science*, *40*(1), 8–34.

Bassi, F. (2011). Latent class analysis for marketing scale development. *International Journal of Market Research*, *53*(2), 209–230. Retrieved from http://www.scopus.com/inward/record.url?eid=2-s2.0-84859945577&partnerID=40&md5=404681bdf45aeb7d88a3730559df34b8.

Bearden, W. O., Hardesty, D. M., & Rose, R. L. (2001). Consumer self-confidence: Refinements in conceptualization and measurement. *Journal of Consumer Research*, *28*(1), 121–134. https://doi.org/10.1086/321951.

Bentler, P. M. (1990). Comparative fit indexes in structural models. *Psychological Bulletin*, *107*(2), 238–246.

Borsboom, D., Mellenbergh, G. J., & Van Heerden, J. (2004). The concept of validity. *Psychological Review*, *111*(4), 1061–1071.

Both, L. E., & Best, L. A. (2017). A comparison of two attachment measures in relation to personality factors and facets. *Personality and Individual Differences*, *112*, 1–5. https://doi.org/10.1016/j.paid.2017.02.040.

Brod, M., Tesler, L. E., & Christensen, T. L. (2009). Qualitative research and content validity: Developing best practices based on science and experience. *Quality of Life Research*, *18*(9), 1263–1278.

Bryman, A. (2006). Integrating quantitative and qualitative research: How is it done? *Qualitative Research, 6*(1), 97–113.

Cavanagh, S. (1997). Content analysis: Concepts, methods and applications. *Nurse Researcher, 4*(3), 5–13. https://doi.org/10.7748/nr1997.04.4.3.5.c5869.

Chiu, C. M., Fang, Y. H., & Wang, E. T. (2015). Building community citizenship behaviors: The relative role of attachment and satisfaction. *Journal of the Association for Information Systems, 16*(11), 947–979.

Churchill, G. A. (1979). A paradigm for developing better measures of marketing constructs. *Journal of Marketing Research, 16*(1), 64–73. https://doi.org/10.1016/j.tourman.2014.10.018.

Clark, L. A., & Watson, D. (1995). Constructing validity: Basic issues in objective scale development. *Psychological Assessment, 7*(3), 309–319. https://doi.org/10.1037/1040-3590.7.3.309.

Collins, K. M., Onwuegbuzie, A. J. and Jiao, Q. G. (2006). Prevalence of mixed-methods sampling designs in social science research. *Evaluation & Research in Education, 19*(2), 83–101.

Cook, T. D., & Reichardt, C. S. (1979). *Qualitative and quantitative methods in evaluation research* (Vol. 1). Beverly Hills, CA: Sage Publications.

Copes, H., Brown, A., & Tewksbury, R. (2011). A content analysis of ethnographic research published in top criminology and criminal justice journals from 2000 to 2009. *Journal of Criminal Justice Education, 22*(3), 341–359.

Coulson, M. C., Oskis, A., Meredith, J., & Gould, R. L. (2018). Attachment, attraction and communication in real and virtual worlds: A study of massively multiplayer online gamers. *Computers in Human Behavior, 87*, 49–57. https://doi.org/10.1016/j.chb.2018.05.017.

Crede, E., & Borrego, M. (2013). From ethnography to items: A mixed methods approach to developing a survey to examine graduate engineering student retention. *Journal of Mixed Methods Research, 7*(1), 62–80.

Creswell, J. W. (2012). *Planning, conducting, and evaluating quantitative and qualitative research* (4th ed.). Boston: Pearson.

Creswell, J. W. (2013). *Research design: Qualitative, quantitative, and mixed methods approaches* (4th ed.). Thousand Oaks, CA: Sage Publications.

Creswell, J. W. (2014). *Research design: Qualitative methods and mixed methods approaches* (4th ed.). Thousand Oaks, CA: Sage Publications.

Creswell, J. W., & Plano Clark, V. L. (2007). *Designing and conducting mixed methods research.* Thousand Oaks, CA: Sage Publications.

Creswell, J. W., & Plano Clark, V. L. (2011). *Designing and conducting mixed methods research* (2nd ed.). Thousand Oaks, CA: Sage Publications.

Cronbach, L. J., & Meehl, P. E. (1955). Construct validity in psychological tests. *Psychological Bulletin, 52*(4), 281–302.

DeVellis, R. F. (1991). *Scale development: Theory and applications.* Newbury Park, CA: Sage Publications.

DeVellis, R. F. (2003). *Scale development: Theory and applications* (2nd ed.). London: Sage Publications.

DeVellis, R. F. (2012). *Scale development: Theory and applications* (3rd ed.). Newbury Park, CA: Sage Publications.

Durham, J., Tan, B. K., & White, R. (2011). Utilizing mixed research methods to develop a quantitative assessment tool: An example from explosive remnants of a war clearance program. *Journal of Mixed Methods Research, 5*(3), 212–226.

Fiedler, M., & Sarstedt, M. (2014). Influence of community design on user behaviors in online communities. *Journal of Business Research, 67*(11), 2258–2268.

Field, A. (2009). *Discovering statistics using SPSS* (3rd ed.). London: Sage Publications.

Fink, A. (2010). Survey research methods. In P. Peterson, E. Baker, & B. McGaw (Eds.), *International encyclopedia of education* (pp. 152–160). Oxford: Elsevier.

Gerbing, D. W., & Anderson, J. C. (1988). An updated paradigm for scale development incorporating unidimensionality and its assessment. *Journal of Marketing Research, 25*(2), 186–192. https://doi.org/10.2307/3172650.

Glogowska, M. (2011). Paradigms, pragmatism and possibilities: Mixed-methods research in speech and language therapy. *International Journal of Language and Communication Disorders*, *46*(3), 251–260.

Gobo, G. (2015). The next challenge: From mixed to merged methods. *Qualitative Research in Organizations and Management: An International Journal*, *10*(4), 329–331.

Gorsuch, R. (1983). *Factor analysis* (2nd ed.). Hillsdale, NJ: Lawrence Erlbaum.

Greene, J., Caracelli, V. J., & Graham, W. F. (1989). Toward a conceptual framework for mixed method evaluation designs. *Educational Evaluation and Policy Analysis*, *11*(3), 255–274.

Hair, J. F., Anderson, R. E., & Tatham, R. (2010). *Multivariate data analysis* (7th ed.). Upper Saddle River, NJ: Pearson Prentice Hall.

Hair, J.F., Anderson, R. E., Tatham, R., & Black, W. (1998). *Multivariate data analysis* (5th ed.). Upper Saddle River, NJ: Prentice Hall.

Hair, J. F., Black, W., Babin, B., Anderson, R. E., & Tatham, R. (2006). *Multivariate data analysis* (6th ed.). Upper Saddle River, NJ: Pearson Prentice Hall.

Hart, J., Nailling, E., Bizer, G. Y., & Collins, C. K. (2015). Attachment theory as a framework for explaining engagement with Facebook. *Personality and Individual Differences*, *77*, 33–40. https://doi.org/10.1016/j.paid.2014.12.016.

Haynes, C. E., Wall, T. D., Bolden, R. I., Stride, C., & Rick, J. E. (1999). Measures of perceived work characteristics for health services research: Test of a measurement model and normative data. *British Journal of Health Psychology*, *4*(3), 257–275.

Heene, M., Hilbert, S., Draxler, C., Ziegler, M., & Bühner, M. (2011). Masking misfit in confirmatory factor analysis by increasing unique variances: A cautionary note on the usefulness of cut off values of fit indices. *Psychological Methods*, *16*(3), 319–336.

Hitchcock, J. H., Sarkar, S., Nastasi, B. K., Burkholder, G., Varjas, K., & Jayasena, A. (2006). Validating culture and gender-specific constructs: A mixed-method approach to advance assessment procedures in cross-cultural settings. *Journal of Applied School Psychology*, *22*(2), 13–33.

Hubley, A. M., & Zumbo, B. D. (2011). Validity and the consequences of test interpretation and use. *Social Indicators Research*, *103*(2), 219–230.

Johnson, R. B., & Onwuegbuzie, A. J. (2004). Mixed methods research: A research paradigm whose time has come. *Educational Researcher*, *33*(7), 14–26. https://doi.org/10.3102/0013189x033007014.

Johnson, R. B., Onwuegbuzie, A., & Turner, L. A. (2007). Toward a definition of mixed methods research. *Journal of Mixed Methods Research*, *1*(2), 112–133.

Kaiser, H. F. (1960). The application of electronic computers to factor analysis. *Educational and Psychological Measurement*, *20*(1), 141–151.

Karasz, A., & Singelis, T. M. (2009). Qualitative and mixed methods research in cross-cultural psychology. *Journal of Cross-Cultural Psychology*, *40*(6), 909–916. doi:10.1177/0022022109349172.

Kau, A., & Loh, E. (2006). The effects of service recovery on consumer satisfaction: A comparison between complainants and non-complainants. *Journal of Services Marketing*, *20*(2), 101–111. https://doi.org/10.1108/08876040610657039.

Kettles, A. M., Creswell, J. W., & Zhang, W. (2011). Mixed methods research in mental health nursing. *Journal of Psychiatric and Mental Health Nursing*, *18*(6), 535–542.

Kim, M. J., Lee, C. K., & Preis, M. W. (2016). Seniors' loyalty to social network sites: Effects of social capital and attachment. *International Journal of Information Management*, *36*(6), 1020–1032.

Kline, R. (1998). *Principles and practice of structural equation modeling*. New York: Guilford Press.

Kline, R. (2011). *Principles and practice of structural equation modeling* (3rd ed.). New York: Guilford Press.

Koufteros, X., Babbar, S., & Kaighobadi, M. (2009). A paradigm for examining second-order factor models employing structural equation modeling. *International Journal of Production Economics*, *120*(2), 633–652.

Kyngäs, H., & Elo, S. (2008). The qualitative content analysis process. *Journal of Advanced Nursing, 62*(1), 107–115. https://doi.org/10.1111/j.1365-2648.2007.04569.x.

Lee, Y. J., & Greene, J. (2007). The predictive validity of an ESL placement test: A mixed methods approach. *Journal of Mixed Methods Research, 1*(4), 366–389.

Levine, D. T., & Stekel, D. J. (2016). So why have you added me? Adolescent girls' technology-mediated attachments and relationships. *Computers in Human Behavior, 63*, 25–34. https://doi.org/10.1016/j.chb.2016.05.011.

Li, H., Edwards, S., & Lee, J. (2002). Measuring the intrusiveness of advertisements: Scale development and validation. *Journal of Advertising, 32*(2), 37–47.

Lim, E. T. K., Cyr, D., & Tan, C. (2014). Understanding members' attachment to social networking sites: An empirical investigation of three theories. In *2014 47th Hawaii International Conference on System Sciences* (pp. 614–623). IEEE. https://doi.org/10.1109/HICSS.2014.82.

Lindloff, T. R., & Taylor, B. C. (2002). *Qualitative communication research methods.* Thousand Oaks, CA: Sage Publications.

Luyt, R. (2012). A framework for mixing methods in quantitative measurement development, validation, and revision: A case study. *Journal of Mixed Methods Research, 6*(4), 294–316.

MacCallum, R. C., & Austin, J. T. (2000). Applications of structural equation modeling in psychological research. *Annual Review of Psychology, 51*(1), 201–226.

Malhotra, N. K., Sung, K. S., & Ashutosh, P. (2006). Common method variance in IS research: A comparison of alternative approaches and a reanalysis of past research. *Management Science, 52*(12), 1865–1883. https://doi.org/10.1287/mnsc.l060.0597.

Malterud, K. (2001). Qualitative research: Standards, challenges, and guidelines. *The Lancet, 358*(9280), 483–488. https://doi.org/10.1016/S0140-6736(01)05627-6.

Marsh, H. W., & Hocevar, D. (1985). Application of confirmatory factor analysis to the study of self-concept: First- and higher-order factor models and their invariance across groups. *Psychological Bulletin, 97*(3), 562–582.

May, T. (2011). *Social research: Issues, methods and process* (4th ed.). Maidenhead: Open University Press/McGraw-Hill.

Mays, N., & Pope, C. (2000). Assessing quality in qualitative research. *British Medical Journal, 320*(7226), 50–52. https://doi.org/10.1111/j.1743-6109.2010.02151.x.

Mende, M., & Bolton, R. N. (2012). Why attachment security matters: How customers' attachment styles influence their relationships with service firms and service employees. *Journal of Service Research, 14*(3), 285–301. https://doi.org/10.1177/1094670511411173.

Mende, M., Bolton, R. N., & Bitner, M. J. (2013). Decoding customer–firm relationships: How attachment styles help explain customers' preferences for closeness, repurchase intentions, and changes in relationship breadth. *Journal of Marketing Research, 50*(1), 125–142. https://doi.org/10.1509/jmr.10.0072.

Messick, S. (1989). Meaning and values in test validation: The science and ethics of assessment. *Educational Researcher, 18*(2), 5–11.

Meurer, S. J., Rubio, D. M., Counte, M. A., & Burroughs, T. (2002). Development of a healthcare quality improvement measurement tool: Results of a content validity study. *Hospital Topics, 80*(2), 7–13.

Monacis, L., De Palo, V., Griffiths, M. D., & Sinatra, M. (2017). Exploring individual differences in online addictions: The role of identity and attachment. *International Journal of Mental Health Addiction, 15*(4), 853–868. https://doi.org/10.1007/s11469-017-9768-5.

Morell, L., & Tan, R. J. B. (2009). Validating for use and interpretation: A mixed methods contribution illustrated. *Journal of Mixed Methods Research, 3*(3), 242–264.

Morgan, D. L. (1998). Practical strategies for combining qualitative and quantitative methods: Applications to health research. *Qualitative Health Research, 8*(3), 362–376.

Nastasi, B. K., Hitchcock, J., Sarkar, S., Burkholder, G., Varjas, K., & Jayasena, A. (2007). Mixed methods in intervention research: Theory to adaptation. *Journal of Mixed Methods Research, 1*(2), 164–182.

Neuman, W. L. (2011). *Social research methods: Qualitative and quantitative approaches* (7th ed.). Boston: Pearson.

Newman, I., Lim, J., & Pineda, F. (2013). Content validity using a mixed methods approach: Its application and development through the use of a table of specifications methodology. *Journal of Mixed Methods Research*, 7(3), 243–260.

Nunkoo, R., & Ramkissoon, H. (2012). Structural equation modelling and regression analysis in tourism research. *Current Issues in Tourism*, 15(8), 777–802.

Nunkoo, R., Ramkissoon, H., & Gursoy, D. (2013). Use of structural equation modeling in tourism research: Past, present, and future. *Journal of Travel Research*, 52(6), 759–771. https://doi.org/10.1177/0047287513478503.

Nunnally, J. C. (1978). *Psychometric theory* (2nd ed.). New York: McGraw-Hill.

Nunnally, J. C., & Bernstein, I. H. (1994). *Psychometric theory*. New York: McGraw-Hill.

Onwuegbuzie, A. J., & Combs, J. P. (2010). Emergent data analysis techniques in mixed methods research: A synthesis. In A. Tashakkori & C. Teddlie (Eds.), *SAGE handbook of mixed methods in social and behavioral research* (2nd ed., pp. 397–430). Thousand Oaks, CA: Sage Publications.

Oppenheim, A. N. (1992). *Questionnaire design, interviewing and attitude measurement*. London: Pinter.

Parasuraman, A., Grewal, D., & Krishnan, R. (2006). *Marketing research*. Boston: Houghton Mifflin.

Park, C. W., Macinnis, D. J., Priester, J., & Eisingerich, A. B. (2010). Brand attachment and brand attitude strength: Conceptual and empirical differentiation of two critical brand equity drivers. *Journal of Marketing*, 74(6), 1–17.

Park, M.-S., Shin, J. K., & Ju, Y. (2019). Attachment styles and electronic word of mouth (e-WOM) adoption on social networking sites. *Journal of Business Research*, 99, 398–404. http://dx.doi.org/10.1016/j.jbusres.2017.09.020.

Peterson, R. A. (1999). *Constructing effective questionnaires*. Thousand Oaks, CA: Sage Publications.

Plano Clark, V. L. (2010). The adoption and practice of mixed methods: US trends in federally funded health-related research. *Qualitative Inquiry*, 16(6), 428–440.

Plano Clark, V. L., Anderson, N., Wertz, J. A., Zhou, Y., Schumacher, K., & Miaskowski, C. (2015). Conceptualizing longitudinal mixed methods designs: A methodological review of health sciences research. *Journal of Mixed Methods Research*, 9(4), 297–319.

Podsakoff, P. M., MacKenzie, S. B., Lee, J.-Y., & Podsakoff, N. P. (2003). Common method bias in behavioral research: A critical review of the literature and recommended remedies. *Journal of Applied Psychology*, 88(5), 879–903.

Ramkissoon, H., Smith, L. D. G., & Weiler, B. (2012). Relationships between place attachment, place satisfaction and pro-environmental behaviour in an Australian national park. *Journal of Sustainable Tourism*, 21(February), 1–24. https://doi.org/10.1080/09669582.2012.708042.

Ramkissoon, H., Smith, L. D. G., & Weiler, B. (2013). Testing the dimensionality of place attachment and its relationships with place satisfaction and pro-environmental behaviours: A structural equation modelling approach. *Tourism Management*, 36, 552–566. https://doi.org/10.1016/j.tourman.2012.09.003.

Reagan, J. (2006). *Applied research methods for management*. Spokane, WA: Marquette Books.

Ren, Y., Harper, F. M., Drenner, S., Terveen, L., Kiesler, S., Riedl, J., & Kraut, R. E. (2012). Building member attachment in online communities: Applying theories of group identity and interpersonal bonds. *MIS Quarterly*, 36(3), 841–864.

Rowan, N., & Wulff, D. (2007). Using qualitative methods to inform scale development. *Qualitative Report*, 12(3), 450–466.

Shaw, J. A., Connelly, D. M., & Zecevic, A. A. (2010). Pragmatism in practice: Mixed methods research for physiotherapy. *Physiotherapy Theory and Practice*, 26(8), 510–518.

Shimp, T. A., & Sharma, S. (1987). Consumer ethnocentrism: Construction and validation of the CETSCALE. *Journal of Marketing Research*, 24(3), 280–289. https://doi.org/10.2307/3151638.

Shu, C., Hu, N., Zhang, X., Ma, Y., & Chen, X. (2017). Adult attachment and profile images on Chinese social networking sites: A comparative analysis of Sina Weibo and WeChat. *Computers in Human Behavior, 77*, 266–273. https://doi.org/10.1016/j.chb.2017.09.014.

Siemsen, E., Roth, A., & Oliveira, P. (2010). Common method bias in regression models with linear, quadratic, and interaction effects. *Organizational Research Methods, 13*(3), 456–476. https://doi.org/10.1177/1094428109351241.

Sireci, S. G. (2007). On validity theory and test validation. *Educational Researcher, 36*(8), 477–481. doi:10.3102/0013189X07311609.

Sireci, S. G. (2009). Packing and unpacking sources of validity evidence: History repeats itself again. In R. W. Lissitz (Ed.), *The concept of validity: Revisions, new directions and applications* (pp. 19–37). Charlotte, NC: Information Age.

Sireci, S. G., & Sukin, T. (2013). Test validity. In K. F. Geisinger & B. A. Bracken (Eds.), *APA handbook of testing and assessment in psychology, Vol. 1: Test theory and testing and assessment in industrial and organizational psychology* (pp. 61–84). Washington, DC: American Psychological Association.

Smolleck, L. D., Zembal-Saul, C., & Yoder, E. P. (2006). The development and validation of an instrument to measure preservice teachers' self-efficacy in regard to the teaching of science as inquiry. *Journal of Science Teacher Education, 17*(2), 137–163.

Spector, P. E. (1992). *Summated rating scale construction: An introduction*. Los Angeles: Sage Publications.

Straub, D., Boudreau, M. C., & Gefen, D. (2004). Validation guidelines for IS positivist research. *Communications of the Association for Information systems, 13*(1), 380–427.

Tabachnick, B., & Fidell, L. (2001). *Using multivariate statistics* (4th ed.). Boston, MA: Allyn and Bacon.

Tabachnick, B., & Fidell, L. (2007). *Using multivariate statistics* (5th ed.). Boston: Pearson/ Allyn and Bacon.

Tashakkori, A., & Teddlie, C. (1998). *Mixed methodology: Combining qualitative and quantitative approaches*. Thousand Oaks, CA: Sage Publications.

Tashakkori, A., & Teddlie, C. (2003). *Handbook of mixed methods in social and behavioral research*. Thousand Oaks, CA: Sage Publications.

Teddlie, C., & Tashakkori, A. (2009). *Foundations of mixed methods research: Integrating quantitative and qualitative approaches in the social and behavioral sciences*. Thousand Oaks, CA: Sage Publications.

Thomson, M., Macinnis, D. J., & Park, C. W. (2005). The ties that bind: Measuring the strength of consumers' emotional attachments to brands. *Journal of Consumer Psychology, 15*(1), 77–91.

Ungar, M., & Liebenberg, L. (2011). Assessing resilience across cultures using mixed methods: Construction of the child and youth resilience measure. *Journal of Mixed Methods Research, 5*(2), 126–149.

VanMeter, R. A., Grisaffe, D. B., & Chonko, L. B. (2015). Of "likes" and "pins": The effects of consumers' attachment to social media. *Journal of Interactive Marketing, 32*, 70–88. https://doi.org/10.1016/j.intmar.2015.09.001.

Wimmer, R. D., & Dominick, J. R. (2000). *Mass media research: An introduction* (6th ed.). Belmont, CA: Wadsworth.

Yaremko, R. M., Harari, H., Harrison, R. C., & Lynn, E. (1986). *Handbook of research and quantitative methods in psychology: For students and professionals*. Hillsdale, NJ: Erlbaum.

Yin, R. (2010). *Qualitative research from start to finish*. New York: Guilford Press.

PART IV

OTHER ISSUES IN MARKETING RESEARCH

15. New frontiers in marketing research methods: forensic marketing – using forensic science frameworks and methods in marketing research*

D. Anthony Miles

> Physical evidence cannot be intimidated. It does not forget. It sits there and waits to be detected, preserved, evaluated, and explained.
>
> *Herbert Leon MacDonell*

SUMMARY

The purpose of this chapter is to illustrate and discuss forensic marketing – a new investigative research model based on marketing dynamics. The chapter discusses the forensic science model and evidence framework, which includes evidence with regard to: industry position and competitors; law and policy; pricing and product line; brand offering; and distribution channels.

INTRODUCTION

Forensic science has long been prominent in the fields of criminology, medicine and science. More recently, forensics has also been used in accounting and economics. However, the practice of *forensic marketing* is quite different. Forensic marketing involves the application and focus of forensic investigation techniques and skills to marketing. This is what makes forensic marketing different from forensic accounting and forensic economics. Forensic marketing has thus emerged as an investigative practice and procedure.

This chapter discusses the characteristics of forensic marketing. The purpose is to demonstrate the theoretical framework for forensic investigation in the field of marketing. The chapter will first define and outline the history and characteristics of forensic marketing. It will then discuss matters such as how forensic marketing differs from forensic accounting and forensic economics. This chapter describes five methods that apply forensic science techniques to solve marketing problems, including the development of an investigative model to examine marketing problems in companies.

FORENSIC MARKETING: DEFINITION AND FOUNDATION

As its name suggests, in contrast to *forensic accounting* and *forensic economics*, *forensic marketing* is the application and focus of forensic investigation techniques and skills to marketing. Historically, forensic marketing has primarily been concerned with gaps in marketing performance, focusing mainly on three areas: (a) closing gaps in the marketing effectiveness of reaching customers; (b) addressing issues of marketing approach and products; and (c) closing gaps in approaches to responding to competition and environmental shifts (competitive intelligence and responding to competitors).

However, forensic marketing could approach examining marketing problems as a crime scene investigation (CSI). Bussière (2005) discussed the development of a forensic marketing method as this has been deficient in comparison with other forensic methods such as forensic accounting. The literature on forensic accounting is extensive because this is an established method in the field of accounting. However, forensic marketing is less established in the field of marketing or business compared with its predecessors.

The historical foundations of forensic marketing can be traced to the field of law and marketing. Forensic marketing is somewhat related to the investigation of fraud and product claims. However, most of the forensic marketing evidence centered on marketing and law. Anderson et al. (2008) provides further information on the development of forensic marketing.

A starting point could be the model proposed by Barrett (1996). However, this model had some prevailing inadequacies. First, it focused on one facet of marketing, marketing communications. Marketing has grown into a multifaceted field of study that is diverse and complex. Therefore Barrett's (one-dimensional) model – focusing only on communications – would not address some of the new emerging areas in marketing. Marketing has grown into a field of study that is comparable to the field of law, which has a notable number of complexities. There are so many subcategories of law that it cannot have a singular definition. Marketing, like the field of law, has become specialized. Last, marketing has been affected by the emergence of the Internet and digital marketing.

So, the model proposed by Barrett also would not address this new area of marketing. Although this model could have been valid at the time, it is lacking in the Internet age.

Compared to forensic accounting and forensic economics, and despite having been around for more than 20 years, forensic marketing has still not developed into a solid, formal investigative model. In other words, the practice of forensic marketing professionals is still in its infancy. Forensic marketing has been practiced with mergers and acquisitions. It has been used in counseling on business structures and structural changes, and it has also been used to provide legal expert testimony regarding product claims and false advertising. We will discuss this in more depth in the next section.

HOW FORENSIC MARKETING DIFFERS FROM ITS PREDECESSORS

Historically, *forensic marketing* primarily concerned gaps in performance in marketing effectiveness. Forensic marketing chiefly focuses on three key matters: (a) closing gaps in the marketing effectiveness of reaching the customer; (b) addressing issues with marketing approach and products; and (c) closing gaps in the approach to responding to competition and environmental shifts (competitive intelligence and responding to competitors). However, forensic marketing could approach examining marketing problems as a crime scene investigation.

Forensic marketing has opportunities to be established as a professional practice. There are two roles it can play in the investigation of marketing problems. First, it can encompass forensic accounting in fraud investigation that centers on aspects such as detection or prevention – for example, on fraud investigation with product claims. Forensic marketing also borrows some applications of forensic economics investigation such as financial damages in disputes over copyright infringement with product claims or branding. These are two roles forensic marketing can play as professional practice. On the legal side, the field of forensic marketing can be similar to the role of an accountant who serves in court as an expert witness in legal disputes.

What is fascinating about the investigative approach of forensic marketing is that it tends to be a hybrid of both forensic accounting and forensic economics. Nevertheless, the differences are acute with the investigation and evidence focus. Forensic marketing can be an investigation method for both fraud and economic damage in the context of marketing. The forensic method used in marketing is to evaluate and interpret evidence, reach conclusions, and present facts. This takes on a different nature with marketing problems. The differences between the three business forensic investigation frameworks are outlined in Table 15.1.

INVESTIGATION FOCUS AND ACTIVITIES

As discussed earlier, the practice of forensic marketing is used to investigate matters of marketing. Based on examination of research from other fields of study, forensic marketing would be most effective with a team of professionals – ideally a team of five forensic marketing analysts. Anderson et al. (2008) propose a five-point conceptual model of forensic marketing as a new, legitimate, and emerging functional area of marketing:

- Forensic marketing may be defined at first as dealing with the application of marketing facts and laws.
- It should be considered a distinct field of applied marketing (such as marketing research).
- It should be based on a distinct subject matter and body of knowledge, presently identified as business or commercial law, as applied to marketing and potential exchange fraud.
- Forensic marketing practice and areas of specialty should most logically be organized around the traditional four Ps to include product, place, price, and promotion investigative services and expert witness testimony.
- Forensic marketing should be practiced using a case study method as a means of organizing information and should be supported by a marketing audit method.

The term "forensic" – from the Latin *forensis* ("in open court, public"), i.e. "before the forum" – is effectively a synonym for "legal" or "related to courts." The term has practically become synonymous with the field of forensic science and, historically, has been associated with such fictional characters as Sherlock Holmes, Dick Tracy, and Perry Mason, as well as the most recent *Crime Scene Investigation* TV programs to produce what is known as the "CSI effect" in criminal investigations (Anderson et al., 2008). Again, the practice of forensic marketing could be used to investigate three general things: (a) gaps in marketing effectiveness in reaching the customer; (b) issues with marketing approach and products; (c) gaps in responding to competition and environmental shifts (see Table 15.1).

Table 15.1   Comparison of business forensics

Forensic Accounting	Forensic Economics	Forensic Marketing
Established		
Estimated to be 30 years old	Estimated to be 40 years old	Has not been established as a field of study; maybe 10 years
Investigative focus		
The investigation of fraud: mitigating internal control procedural risks (Brickner et al., 2010)	Investigates the impact of economic damage (Cotella & Ireland, 1998; Ireland, 2004)	Could be used to investigate: (a) closing gaps in marketing effectiveness in terms of reaching customers; (b) issues with marketing approach and products; (c) closing gaps in approach to responding to competition and environmental shifts (competitive intelligence and responding to competitors)
Evidence		
Financial: income statements, cashflow, balance sheets, etc. (Dorweiler &Yakhou, 2004)	Economic reports, industry reports, employment records, medical reports, financial other data (Abrams et al., 1996; Brookshire et al., 2004)	Data, sales, marketing financials, market reports, law and policy, and related material (Anderson et al., 2008; Barrett, 1996; Bussière, 2005; Miles, 2015, 2016)
Environment		
Tends to be an *internal* type of forensic analysis	Tends to be an *external* type of forensic analysis	Tends to be a hybrid of *forensic accounting* and *forensic economics*; both *internal and external* forensic analysis

Source: Miles (2015, 2016a, 2016b).

Investigation Plan and Evidence Research Strategy

To conduct a forensic marketing investigation, it is necessary to decide on budget, timeframe, and investigation team and tools. First and foremost, the budget needs to be discussed with the client. One of the most important

Table 15.2   Investigation plan and evidence research strategy framework

Budget	Timeframe	Investigation Team	Investigation Tools
Cost allocation	Year	Personnel	Software
Resources	Quarters	Internal	Intelligence
Fees	Few months	External	Licensing
Rentals	Month	Consultants	Databases
Storage	Weeks	Outside specialists/professionals	Devices
Litigation/legal	Days	Domestic/international travel	Hardware

Source: Miles (2015, 2016a, 2016b).

issues other than budget is the timeframe. Investigations can take a considerable amount of time, which all stakeholders should be aware of, and some sort of cost control has to be established by the investigator and investigative team. Third, an investigation team needs to be assembled. This could comprise internal and/or external people with access to evidence and resources. Last is assembling the investigation tool, which could also involve considerable cost. There are other things that might be needed such as software, hardware, devices, intelligence, databases, and other tools (see Table 15.2).

FORENSIC MARKETING INVESTIGATION MODEL AND FRAMEWORK

The investigation method used in forensic marketing at the crime scene can be somewhat similar to the crime scene in a criminal investigation, even though there is no "crime" as such. There are three general similarities: (1) surveying the crime scene; (2) documenting key evidence; and (3) presentation of the facts and theory. On the other hand, the differences are acute. Because forensic marketing is based not on "crime" but on determining the effectiveness of marketing efforts, the investigation model takes a different approach. For example, the task of compiling and combining evidence is unique in this practice. In forensic marketing this can be a Herculean task because evidence is both internal and external to the investigators (see Figure 15.1).

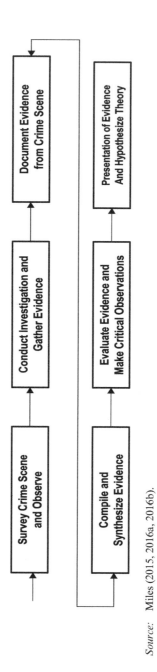

Source: Miles (2015, 2016a, 2016b).

Figure 15.1 Forensic marketing crime scene investigation model

INVESTIGATION FRAMEWORK AND EVIDENCE GATHERING

When you compare forensic marketing investigation to its predecessors, forensic accounting and forensic economics, again it is rather different but also similar in context. Following a five-point framework model, a forensic marketing investigation should focus on the following key activities: inquiry/awareness; planning; gathering evidence; analyzing the evidence; and presenting the findings (see Figure 15.2). When gathering evidence on market position, the focus should be on the business and industry the firm is in, and evidence should come from industry reports and industry insiders if possible. The goal is to gather evidence that can be used to identify the firm's market position and industry leaders, so an initial investigation may be needed.

In conducting a forensic marketing investigation, the focus should be on these key activities (methods): *evidence and information gathering;*

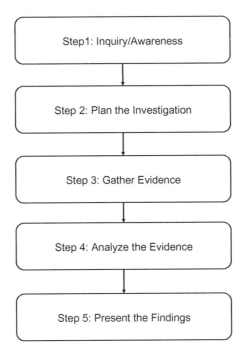

Source: Miles (2015, 2016a, 2016b).

Figure 15.2   The five-point forensic marketing investigation framework

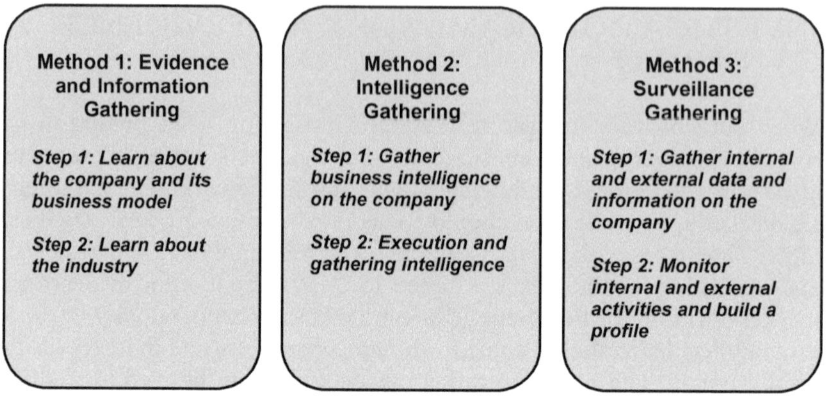

Method 1: Evidence and Information Gathering	Method 2: Intelligence Gathering	Method 3: Surveillance Gathering
Step 1: Learn about the company and its business model	*Step 1: Gather business intelligence on the company*	*Step 1: Gather internal and external data and information on the company*
Step 2: Learn about the industry	*Step 2: Execution and gathering intelligence*	*Step 2: Monitor internal and external activities and build a profile*

Source: Miles (2015, 2016a, 2016b).

Figure 15.3   Forensic marketing investigation framework and evidence gathering

intelligence gathering; and *surveillance gathering* (see Figure 15.3). The investigator wants to gather as much as possible, and these three methods are the cornerstone of forensic marketing. Also, the investigation must consider a lot of outside industry material because there are warning signs in the marketplace that will affect the client. The client should always be made aware of any outside influence and shifts in the marketplace as this could be critical to the decisions the client makes on those moves.

Here again, forensic marketing takes investigative techniques from forensic accounting and forensic economics and applies them to marketing. The key is to take something from both predecessors and apply it in the forensic marketing investigation (Figure 15.3).

Method 1: Evidence and Information Gathering

As stated above, forensic marketing investigation borrows from both forensic accounting and forensic economics. For evidence and information gathering this chapter borrowed three components (out of four) of Silverstone and Sheetz's (2007) framework used in forensic accounting – *intelligence gathering*, *surveillance*, and *database searches*.

As discussed earlier, forensic accounting is the investigation of fraud: mitigating internal control procedural risk. More so, forensic accounting is concerned with aspects such as accounting fraud, forensic auditing, compliance, diligence and risk assessment, financial misrepresentation, and financial statement fraud.

First and foremost, you must understand the company and its business, including the industry, the company's products/product lines, and its competitors. Understanding the business requires understanding of the business structure. Understanding the structure of the business will reveal who is behind the decisions that are being made. In addition, it will reveal the firm's procedures. Gaining some insight into a business will reveal many things about its marketing strategies and decisions.

After developing an understanding about the business, you need to study the industry. This is most obvious for forensic marketing investigators. This will include competitors, products, and other pertinent information. Industry reports are very important here. The industry will tell you a considerable amount about the competitors and product lines.

Method 2: Intelligence Gathering

Intelligence gathering is almost an undervalued endeavor, but it is a key component in the investigative process. There is certain information and evidence that should be examined when gathering evidence on the firm's position in the industry and market, and certain places hold that information. For forensic marketing investigation, intelligence gathering is comprised of two areas – surveillance gathering and database searching, both of which should be considered starting points.

There are three important eras of research in the history of marketing. Most of the research reviewed relates more to social issues and consumer protection issues rather than ethical decision making. Eras I and II (1900–1920, 1920–1950) focused on the marketing and society interface, with issues related to costs to consumers, efficiency of the marketing system, elements of the marketing system necessary for consumers, the role of advertising and sales methods, and fair pricing (Digabriele, 2008).

Method 3: Surveillance Gathering

Surveillance is critical to the foundation of an investigation, providing a wealth of information, evidence, and data on the client and their associates in the case. Surveillance gathering will uncover information on important aspects such as:

- the internal environment of the firm (key resources, personnel resources)
- the external environment of the firm (marketplace, market share, competitors)

- banking or financial institutions (marketing expenditures, revenue streams, budgets)
- the marketing portfolio of the firm (customer segments and relationships)
- the marketing relationships of the firm (vendors, partners, customer segments).

Forensic marketing investigators can assess a company's marketing stature during the investigation. They can investigate the firm's marketing financial situation and value while looking for signs of activity (Harris & Brown, 2000).

The areas of investigation in forensic marketing tend to be broad and include examination of: (a) marketing environment, (b) marketing strategy, (c) marketing organization, (d) product lines, (e) marketing alignment, (f) competitive and marketing intelligence, (g) marketing functions, and (h) integrated marketing communications (IMC) (Rothe et al., 1997; Kotler & Keller, 2011; Miles, 2016a, 2016b).

Database searching

Databases can provide a wealth of information to forensic marketing investigators. Data is all around us. We create, collect, and collate it. We use data for tracking people, predicting their buying preferences, and changing their behavior. We have so many uses for data. Data oftentimes is stored somewhere that was collected from some organizations. It is therefore natural for investigators to seek to tap into this wealth of personal information to try and piece together a picture of their target. Generally these databases may be divided into two categories: private and public.

Private databases   Private databases include both commercial and government sources. An example in the US is the restricted access to states' driver license information. Another example would be credit reporting services such as Experian or Equifax. Private databases are very powerful repositories of data and contain a broad range of often sensitive information. Access to some areas is therefore restricted to law enforcement personnel for legitimate law enforcement purposes. So it is difficult for private individuals such as marketing investigators to download page after page of information – although it may be possible for a fee.

Public databases   Public databases are usually free or accessible at low cost to the general public. For example, US property and tax assessment records are routinely available from county clerk offices; civil and criminal histories are often available on a county-by-county basis; and, in most states, corporate filings are only a mouse-click away. With public databases, some agencies charge a nominal copying fee for records, most will allow searches for free, and many also provide free downloads. However, the trade-off is convenience. Private commercial databases usually offer a one-stop approach to intelligence gathering. Public database searches, however, usually must proceed on an entity-by-entity basis.

World Wide Web

The World Wide Web (WWW) is really a database from which you can attain an unprecedented amount of information with a click of a button. We live in an information-rich world. Almost everyone uses the Internet, and there is vast amounts of social media and other content (photos, videos, etc.) offering valuable information on people's vacations and other intimate happenings. The Internet also offers access to other sources of information, such as industry reports and business periodicals:

- Industry reports allow access to information about companies and industries, and include sources such as D&B Hoovers, IBISWorld, Plunkett Research, etc.
- Useful business periodicals include the *Wall Street Journal*, *BusinessWeek*, *Fortune*, *Bloomberg*, etc.

Information from these sources is very important in determining a firm's position in the market. Again, these periodicals can offer free access or charge access fees. In terms of marketing terminology, this would be considered secondary information (see Figure 15.4).

SKILLS NEEDED FOR FORENSIC MARKETING INVESTIGATORS

There are specialized skills and technical abilities that forensic marketing practitioners require. First, they should have a strong background in the field of marketing, not just in public relations (PR) but in the actual field of marketing. They should also have some background in marketing and law, most specifically in the areas of copyright, trademarks, and intellectual property.

Second, forensic marketing practitioners should have developed some type of specialized investigative skills, including in theories, business analysis, methods, and investigative frameworks. These skills can be developed by studying, for example, the *Case Study Method* (Miles, 2011).

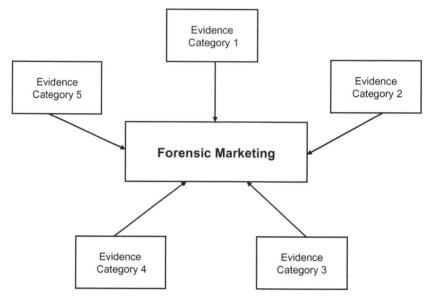

Source: Miles (2015, 2016a, 2016b).

Figure 15.4   Forensic marketing investigation conceptual model framework

Third, a successful forensic marketing practitioner must have strong analytical and critical thinking abilities. This is the ability to take information from many places and be able to synthesize this information and make it useful for management. The forensic marketing practitioner must also have strong written and verbal communication skills, a creative mindset, and business acumen. This also includes the skill of interviewing and eliciting information from both cooperative and uncooperative people across organizational levels.

Fourth, because forensic marketing is quite complex, the skill of reviewing and interpreting financial statements is also important. Practitioners should therefore be able to detect sales trends and investigate those trends.

Fifth, although not a critical requirement, a background in the field of psychology would certainly be useful as it helps forensic marketing practitioners understand the impulses and motivation behind marketing decisions, behavior, and actions. Such skills would be very important, for example, when investigating management competence. This can help address management competence in terms of: (a) interpersonal and communication skills that aid in disseminating information about the company's ethics; and (b) marketing background and cognitive abilities in marketing decisions of the management and staff.

Sixth, concerning educational background, the field of marketing is wide open to the forensic marketing practitioner because marketing has no formal certification. However, it would be good for a forensic marketing practitioner to have a graduate degree, preferably an MBA. A JD would also be a good foundation, although a PhD in business or specifically in marketing would be a great asset.

To recap, an effective forensic marketer must have an assortment of skills encompassing six critical areas: (1) competency in marketing and knowledge; (2) effective oral and written communication skills; (3) a level of familiarity with marketing principles and their relevance to law; (4) business acumen in sales and business development; (5) the ability to read and understand marketing financial and sales trends; and (6) some knowledge of statistics and research methods such as market research (quantitative skills), focus groups, and interviewing (qualitative skills) (Miles, 2015).

FORENSIC MARKETING EVIDENCE FRAMEWORK: THEORETICAL MODEL

The forensic marketing model investigation model proposed here is divided into five general evidence category classes. Because marketing is becoming increasingly complex, a new forensic marketing model has been developed to address new marketing problems. Building a forensic marketing framework for conducting a good investigation can be difficult. However, based on prior literature and studies on forensic marketing, a proposed framework is illustrated in Table 15.3. As indicated, there are five evidence categories, with specific concepts within each category to conduct a sound forensic marketing investigation. Each evidence category has distinct areas of focus that require specific investigation.

DISCUSSION

This chapter aimed to discuss and explain forensic marketing – its definition, foundation, and history, and the development of forensic marketing methodology. The chapter provides a background to law and marketing; the law as it applies to marketing and its effect on legal activities in the field of marketing.

This research is significant because it make a key contribution to the body of knowledge in marketing by demonstrating the importance of

Table 15.3   The five forensic marketing evidence categories theoretical model

Category 1: Industry Position and Competitors	Category 2: Law, Policy, and Customer Segment	Category 3: Pricing and Product Line	Category 4: Brand Offering and Brand	Category 5: Distribution Channels and Customer Relationship
Market position forensics Competitive intelligence forensics	Law and policy forensics (legal) Customer market segment forensics	Price forensics Product/ product line forensic	Brand forensics Value proposition/ brand offering forensics	Distribution channel forensics Customer relationship forensics

Source: Miles (2015, 2016a, 2016b).

forensic marketing as an investigative research tool. The chapter discussed how forensic marketing differs from forensic accounting and forensic economics, the forensic marketing investigation process, and the investigative framework of forensic marketing.

Managerial Implications

Today, there is a dearth in terms of business forensics. Forensic marketing has emerged as an investigative research model. Building on its predecessors, forensic economics and forensic accounting, forensic marketing thus focuses on investigating marketing problems. We need a business forensic investigative model that focuses on marketing problems. Practitioners, consultants, and managers as well as academics will recognize the importance and value of forensic marketing and its influence on decisions.

There is increasing demand for a forensic model to address marketing problems. To meet this demand managers need something more to investigate such problems, namely forensic marketing. It is important therefore to highlight the benefits of forensic marketing as it becomes an important tool for investigating marketing problems in companies.

NOTE

*   This chapter was previously published in Miles, D. Anthony (2020). *How to Get Away with Murder in Marketing: Forensic Marketing*. Bloomington, IN: Archway.

REFERENCES

Abrams, S., Welsch, D., & Jonas, B. (1996). Calculating expectations damages using forensic economics. *Ohio State Law Journal, 57*(3), 809–834.

Anderson, S., Volker, J., & Philips, M. (2008). The forensic marketing case study methods. *SAM Advanced Management Journal, 6*(3), 4–9.

Barrett, G. (1996). *Forensic Marketing: Optimizing Results from Marketing Communication: The Essential Guide.* New York: McGraw-Hill.

Brickner, D., Mahoney, L., & Moore, S. (2010). Providing an applied-learning exercise in teaching fraud detection: A case of academic partnering with IRS criminal investigation. *Issues in Accounting Education, 25*(4), 695–708. doi:10.2308/iace.2010.25.4.695

Brookshire, M. L., Luthy, M. R., & Slesnick, F. L. (2004). Forensic economists, their methods, and estimates of forecast variables: A 2003 survey. *Litigation Economics Review, 6*(2), 28–44.

Bussière, D. (2005). Forensic marketing: The use of the historical method in a capstone marketing course. *Journal of Marketing Education, 27*(1), 61–67. Retrieved from http://search.proquest.com/docview/204429148?accountid=35812

Cotella, J., & Ireland, T. (1998). Neutrality and advocacy: A challenge for forensic economics. *Journal of Legal Economics, 8*(1), 71–87.

Digabriele, J. (2008). An empirical investigation of the relevant skills of forensic accountants. *Journal of Education for Business, 83*(6), 331–338. doi:10.3200/JOEB.83.6.331-338

Dorweiler, V. P., & Yakhou, M. (2004). A forensic analysis of business scandals: Charges against scandalous companies. *Management Research News, 27*(10), 42–50. Retrieved from http://search.proquest.com/docview/223540432?accountid=35812.

Harris, C. K., & Brown, A. M. (2000). The qualities of a forensic accountant. *Pennsylvania CPA Journal, 71*, 2–3.

Ireland, T. (2004). Why Markov Process worklife expectancy tables are usually superior to the LPE method. *Journal of Legal Economics, 16*(2), 95–110.

Kotler, P., & Keller, K. (2011). *A Framework for Marketing Management* (5th ed.). New York: Pearson Prentice Hall.

Miles, D. A. (2011). Bridging the gap between theory and application: Using the Harvard Case Study Method to develop higher order thinking skills with college students. *Southwest Teaching and Learning Journal, 1*(1), 1–22.

Miles, D. A. (2015). *How to Get Away with Murder in Marketing? A Framework for Using Forensic Investigation Methods for Examining Marketing Problems.* Marketing session moderated by W. B. Valentine (Chair), symposium conducted at the meeting of the 2015 Academy of Business Research Conference in San Antonio, TX.

Miles, D. A. (2016a). *How to Get Away with Murder in Marketing Part 1: New Forensic Investigation Methods for Examining Marketing Problems.* Presented on the new field of forensic marketing. Session moderated by Makila Major (Chair), symposium conducted at the meeting of the 2016 Black Doctoral Network (BDN) Conference in Atlanta, GA.

Miles, D. A. (2016b). *How to Get Away with Murder in Marketing Part 2: Using Forensic Marketing Research Methods for Examining Marketing Problems in Firms.* In Junzhou Zhang (Chair), A Practitioner's Guide to the Marketing Research Galaxy session symposium conducted at the meeting of the 2016 Society of Marketing Advances (SMA) Conference in Atlanta, GA.

Rothe, J. T., Harvey, M. G., & Jackson, C. E. (1997). The marketing audit: Five decades later. *Journal of Marketing: Theory and Practice, 27*(1), 1–16.

Silverstone, J., & Sheetz, M. (2007). *Forensic Accounting and Fraud Investigation for Non Experts* (2nd ed.). Hoboken, NJ: Wiley.

16. An examination of the legal theories and research methods relevant to marketing research

Marie Valerie Uppiah and Roopanand Mahadew

SUMMARY

This chapter examines how legal theories and research methods can be relevant for marketing researchers. The chapter provides an overview of the different legal theories and legal research methods that can be used throughout a marketing research process. This multidisciplinary approach adds value to the outcome of research as it provides a multifaceted way of analysing, interpreting and implementing data collected.

INTRODUCTION

Many experts in the field of marketing agree that the subject entails a multi-disciplinary approach. Fields such as psychology, economics and sociology have, for years, contributed to research in the field of marketing. Analysing consumer behaviour, understanding how the market works to develop the best products or understanding the culture of a particular community in order to devise or adapt products that match their specificities, research in these areas include theories and methods that fall within and outside the realm of marketing. Law, it is argued, should not be an exception to this rule.

Research methods in law and legal theories are used to examine a legal state of affairs, and work towards providing solutions to legal problems (Taekema, 2018). They do not seek to explain why an event happened or try to find ways to satisfy the needs of individuals or groups. For example, a researcher in law analysing infringement of intellectual property rights will not investigate the motives behind a competitor's actions in copying a particular product. The task of the legal researcher is to examine and assess whether the laws related to intellectual property rights are efficient enough to address this particular case. If a law is inefficient, the researcher proposes changes to be made. In order to justify a change in law and propose a new one, the researcher will make use of legal theories and apply the relevant legal methods.

Applying legal theories and research methods in the field of marketing can contribute to providing high-impact research. Various legal theories and research approaches – such as Legal Positivism, social contract theory or socio-legal research – can assist a marketer in understanding the relationship between society and the legal frameworks that regulate actions within that society. This is particularly useful as the marketer can legally justify the reasons why they are (or are not) able to market a product or service in a country.

Furthermore, adopting this multidisciplinary approach of using law in marketing research can add value to the literature and analysis parts of the research. Most of the time, data analysed in law is not based on empirical evidence. The data examined is mainly based on normative frameworks that regulate a particular context. However, in marketing research, most data analysis is based on empirical data. When combining the normative data analysis used in law with the empirical data analysis methods used in marketing, it is argued that this can provide a broader way of analysing information that enriches the outcome of the research.

The purpose of this chapter is to examine how legal theories and legal research methods can be relevant for researchers in the field of marketing. It is divided into two parts. Part I elaborates on the legal theories and normative framework used in legal research. An analysis will be made of three legal theories: Natural Law Theory, Legal Positivism and Legal Formalism vs Legal Realism. How these theories can be useful for marketing research will be explained. Part II examines the different legal research methods that are often used to conduct research in law. Furthermore, the advantages of these legal research methods to marketing will be dealt with. The chapter concludes on the relevance for marketers to use legal theories and research methods in their own research.

PART I: LEGAL THEORIES

The study of the creation and evolution of legal theories is often known as "jurisprudence". According to Cornell Law School's Legal Information Institute (1992), the term comes from the Latin *juris prudentia*, meaning "the study, knowledge or science of law". Legal theories, jurisprudence, serve various purposes for legal researchers. First, they provide researchers with the basis to analyse and criticise bodies of law. Second, they allow researchers to compare law with other fields of study. Third, they help the researcher understand the moral, historical and cultural background for the existence of a law and finally, it assists in finding answers to more philosophical questions like "what is law?" or "why do laws exist?". It can be stated that the main role of jurisprudence in the legal arena is to help researchers understand the function of laws and examine their usefulness.

Throughout the centuries philosophers such as Thomas Aquinas, John Austin, Karl Marx and Thomas Hobbes have sought to understand the functions of law and explain its impact on society. These philosophers have developed their own schools of thought and theories to address their concerns. Today's legal researchers take inspiration from these schools of thought and theories to investigate the rationale behind the creation of a law and its impact. These theories are however not restricted to the legal domain. Other fields of knowledge such as economics, sociology and even marketing are influenced by these legal theories.

This section examines three leading legal theories: Natural Law Theory, Legal Positivism and Legal Formalism vs Legal Realism. Despite having a legal basis, these theories can be used in other fields of aiming to give to the research topic a multidisciplinary aspect.

Natural Law Theory

Natural Law Theory can be defined as a legal theory which associates law with morality. Morality is concerned with distinguishing between good and bad or right from wrong. Therefore, according to natural law theorists, law should be, and is, a reflection of those moral values. For example, the moral wrong of taking someone's belonging without their authorisation is sanctioned by the laws on larceny. Influential natural law theorists such as Lon L. Fuller (1969) argue that in order to understand a law, one should understand the moral values behind it.

Thomas Aquinas, one of the forefathers of Natural Law Theory, viewed this theory as comprising four main components: Eternal Law, Natural Law, Human Law and Divine Law. Eternal Law is linked to God and his plan for all things. Natural Law states that people should act according to reason and should pursue what is good and avoid what is bad. Human Law is mainly concerned with the laws that are made by human beings for human beings. Examples include financial regulation laws, Constitutional Law or Civil Law. Finally, Divine Law is the divine revelations that were given to humans and later codified, such as the Ten Commandments found in the Bible.

Making use of Natural Law Theory in marketing research can assist a marketer in understanding the moral rationale behind some laws in a country, and hence devise marketing strategies that will not hurt the sensitivities of the people of that country. For example, in some countries homosexuality is considered a moral wrong, and on that basis laws exist that criminalise it. Therefore, in those countries, marketers should be careful before developing marketing strategies that might appear LGBT friendly.

Legal Positivism

Legal Positivism is a school of thought developed by John Austin and Jeremy Bentham in the 18th and 19th centuries. This legal theory was then vulgarised by philosopher H.L.A. Hart in the 20th century. According to legal positivists, laws are made by superior bodies such as Parliament and to some extent the judiciary. Positivists adopt a completely different view from natural law theorists. They believe that laws should derive from an authority and not from nature or human values and morality (Hart, 1958).

According to legal positivists, law represents the will of a superior authority and is a concept that should not be assimilated with morality. For laws to exist, legal positivists state that three elements should be taken into consideration: political sovereignty, command and sanctions (Austin, 1832). Political sovereignty refers to the existence of an authority in which power was vested to make laws. Positivists argue that this power allows those who are in authority to make laws that serve the best interest of individuals and society. The political sovereignty, while making laws, should not consider the moral principles anchored to a particular society. Command relates to the duty this law imposes on individuals. As soon as a law is made, individuals have an obligation to follow the rules imposed by it. In case of any deviation from this law, sanctions are imposed.

Legal Positivism is a useful principle to be used in marketing research. Compared to Natural Law Theory, which explains the moral rationale behind the creation of a law, Legal Positivism shows another facet of law. Here, law represents the interests of society; but this does not necessarily mean it is a reflection of the moral values that society holds. For instance, in Mauritius individuals from various religious backgrounds and holding different moral values have reservations with regard to the consumption of pork or beef. Parliament, acknowledging these moral values and principles, has not forbidden, for instance, the consumption of these products in the country. The Mauritius Meat Act of 1974 regulates the sale of meat in the country, regardless of its animal source.

Hence, for marketing research, it is useful not to mix the moral principles present in a society and the legal framework that regulates them. Legal Positivism allows the researcher to demarcate legal reasoning from societal values and morality.

Legal Formalism vs Legal Realism

When analysing a law court judgment, two theories have been developed to examine the judges' methodology and procedures: Legal Formalism and Legal Realism (Tumonis, 2012). Formalists view law as a legal science which is rational, functional, mechanical and complete. This means that, since laws represent all these factors, judges should follow the law and legal procedures as the latter provide the structure and legal reasoning needed to make a court decision. Legal formalists are of the opinion that when judges make decisions, their primary objective is to look at the word and spirit of the law and apply them *stricto sensu*. During the decision-making phase, judges will refer solely to legal principles, doctrines and rules. They do not take into consideration any social or environmental factor that can impact the decision. For legal formalists, law and legal reasoning are the backbone of any decision-making process. Tumonis (2012) describes Legal Formalism as a "rule bound activity".

Compared to Legal Formalism, the judging theory of Legal Realism emphasises that judicial decision making is a twofold activity. First, the judges will consider any external mitigating factors associated with the case; these may be the social, political or ideological environment. Second, after assessing these mitigating factors and forming their own opinions, judges will find a legal rule to support these opinions and then submit their judicial decision (Tumonis, 2012).

For legal realists, in contrast to formalists, the process of judicial decision making should not focus exclusively on the application of the law *stricto sensu*. Indeed, realists acknowledge that applying the law to a judicial decision is a fundamental part of the decision. However, what they also advocate is that other social, political and environmental factors along with the law play a significant role in judges' decision-making process.

Both Legal Formalism and Legal Realism can contribute to enrich the literature in marketing research. Court decisions should always be the judging theories that judges have applied. These theories can be used in marketing research to explain the rationale and process that judges might use in court proceedings.

PART II: LEGAL RESEARCH METHODS

Legal research can be defined as the process of investigating a purely legal or socio-legal issue in order to identify the facts of the problem, concluding by providing the relevant legal solutions to the issue. Legal research aims at contributing and increasing knowledge in the field of law (Vibhutek and Aynalem, 2009).

Legal research serves the purpose of resolving several questions as to why a particular law exists. These questions are: What is this law trying to regulate? Is it able to achieve its purpose? To what extent does the law match the social reality in which it is evolving? In order to answer these questions, various techniques and research methods have been developed. The following provides an insight into the techniques used for legal investigation.

Doctrinal Research (Black Letter Research)

Black Letter research involves examination, critical analysis and evaluation of laws, legal principles, theories and rules. Through this technique, the researcher conducts what is known as legal reasoning. This provides for a review of the law, underlines its impact and effectiveness, and assesses the strengths and weaknesses of a law. This form of research is only concerned with the legal text, and does not take into consideration the social implications of the law.

Research in Theory

This involves assessment of the various legal theories. One aim of research in theory is to provide an intellectual framework to support empirical evidence obtained. Another aim of this method is to expose debate based on the literature concerning the research, and it provides a legal framework that supplements the Black Letter analysis of the law.

Empirical Investigation

Empirical investigations try to fill the gap between legal idealism and social realism (Vibhutek and Aynalem, 2009) as sometimes the law does not reflect social reality. In this method the researcher investigates the social, political and cultural environment in which the law evolves, and provides recommendations as to how the law should reflect reality.

Reform-Oriented Research

This form of research analyses the effectiveness of the law and provides amendments to the law. This method often supplements other techniques of legal investigation.

Legal research is a highly dynamic activity as the world in which laws evolve is in a state of constant change. For example, laws do not only regulate activities between individuals; they also regulate activities between individuals and their environment. In addition, with the rapid evolution of technology and other scientific discovery, the role of law in providing legal protection for all these as well as providing for a legal framework to regulate these activities, is very important nowadays. Hence, the role of legal research becomes crucial as it provides the background in which a law should either be developed or amended. Legal research also provides for an actual state of affairs as it shows gaps that exist between the law and reality. Through legal investigation and research solutions can be devised to solve these problems.

The technical aspects of conducting legal research involve three major stages, as put forward by Vibhutek and Aynalem (2009): planning, implementation and presenting findings. Planning involves identifying the legal issue(s) to be studied and choosing the research method to be used to get the best results. Implementation refers to the collection of data for the research. At this stage, the researcher analyses the data and sets out the findings of the research. Finally, when presenting the research findings, the language used should inform the reader about the nature and outcome of the results. The language should be informative, advisory, recommendatory or demanding. In line with the three stages of research, a legal researcher should adopt a suitable methodology in order to proceed with the subject of the investigation. Two main legal research methodologies can be used: doctrinal and non-doctrinal.

Doctrinal Legal Research

Doctrinal legal research involves systematic analysis of laws, doctrines, rules and legal principles and theories. It also involves examining scholarly cases and writing. The technique of legal reasoning is used to analyse the data collected in order to state whether a law is effective or not. The rationale behind doctrinal legal research is to develop new theories and legal principles. This method is also called "research in law".

This type of research is more theoretical in nature. Researchers adopting this methodology base themselves on legal propositions or hypothesis. An example of such a legal proposition might be: What would be the best rule or legal framework to protect consumers against unfair competition? In order to answer this proposition, the legal researcher will collect primary data. For doctrinal research, primary data is obtained by studying parliamentary debates in order to understand the intent behind passing a particular law. Researchers refer to existing conventions, statutes and court decisions. They refer to existing theories and legal principles to form their theoretical framework. The aim of doctrinal legal research is usually to provide a new law or amend an existing one, or to develop a new theory.

Doctrinal legal research offers advantages and opportunities not only for those in the legal field but also for researchers in other fields such as marketing. Doctrinal researchers have the capacity to compile all the required legal information about a particular legal issue. The fact that parliamentary debates have been summarised, and legal theories, principles and the laws explained, provides everyone with access to simplified and detailed information about a legal issue. The purpose of doctrinal legal research is to simplify law and make sure everyone understands it. Through this method, marketing researchers are able to understand the reasoning behind a particular law. This will enable them to develop marketing strategies in accordance with the legal environment they are working in.

By providing an in-depth analysis of a law through legal reasoning, doctrinal legal researchers can identify any loopholes that exist in the law. Although they provide way(s) to address these loopholes, doctrinal researchers also open the door for other researchers (not restricted to the legal field) to express their views on the topic. This opens up an opportunity for multidisciplinary research, which in turn contributes to increasing literature and knowledge.

Non-Doctrinal Legal Research

The scope of non-doctrinal research differs from that of doctrinal research. In the former, the scope of the research is not based on assessing the rationale behind a law. The aim of non-doctrinal legal research, or socio-legal research, is to examine the impact and consequences of law in society. In other words, this method focuses on the relationship between law and the environment in which law evolves. It studies the effects that laws have on human behaviour, and vice versa. Socio-legal research is also called "research about law" as it examines the effects that laws have on individuals. This type of research is more empirical in nature. The aim of the socio-legal approach is to test the theories developed through doctrinal legal research and identify their application in society.

In order to study the social dimension and social impact of law, researchers should address the following questions: Is the law working in the interest of society? What is the impact of the law on different stakeholders, for example, minority groups? Is there proper enforcement of the law? To address these questions, researchers will go through different steps. First, they will examine the legislative process to understand the intent of the legislature/Parliament in adopting a particular law. Then, they will undertake a social assimilation study to examine the impact of the law in society. This social assimilation study can be done through questionnaires, interviews or observation. By the end of the study the researcher will be able to demonstrate the extent to which legal idealism is being reflected in social reality. In the event that there is a gap between the law and its application in society, based on what was observed, the researcher will offer solutions to fill this gap.

The aim of non-doctrinal research is to show the law in action. Non-doctrinal legal research has the advantage of exposing any existing flaws in the application of the law. Compared to doctrinal legal research, where the law itself is questioned, in non-doctrinal legal research the application of the law is tested. This allows the researcher to identify any structural or institutional inaction that reflects why the law is not being applied as it should be. The purpose of non-doctrinal legal research is to address institutional inaction.

Another importance of socio-legal research is that it provides expert evidence of how the law is being applied. It shows the positive and negative aspects of application of the law. This will act as feedback to the legislature and show how the law it has passed is being properly implemented (or not) in reality. Taking this feedback into consideration, the legislature can then either amend the law to make it more effective or work with the executive to redress any institutional inaction that hinders the proper application of the law.

Socio-legal research, just like doctrinal research, provides for the opportunity of undertaking multidisciplinary research. For example, when analysing the impact of consumer-protection laws, it is important to understand what pushes people to consume more products and services. This is where understanding marketing strategies in legal research gets its importance. Based on that, the socio-legal researcher will be able to understand and examine that particular law in action.

CONCLUSION

This chapter examined how legal theories as well as legal research methods can be applied by marketers. Law is a versatile subject that can significantly contribute to any topic being researched. The concept of law does not necessarily mean a body of written rules and regulations that everyone has to abide to. Law also involves a set of theories, principles and research methods that, when combined, explain why the law exists.

The legal theories presented in this chapter – Natural Law Theory, Legal Positivism and Legal Formalism vs Legal Realism – are the most common in legal research. This chapter demonstrated how these theories can be relevant when undertaking marketing research. The marketer can use one of these theories to understand the moral and legal as well as judicial implications of promoting or devising a certain product or service in a particular country.

Legal research can take the form of doctrinal methods, i.e. research in law, and socio-legal methods, i.e. research about the law. Both of these methods, although having fundamental differences, allow researchers to undertake multidisciplinary research. Marketers can use the information obtained through doctrinal research in order to understand why a particular law exists. This will allow them to develop strategies according to the legal context they are in.

Both legal theories and research methods can add value to the outcome of a marketing research project. Marketers and legal researchers should put forward their comparative advantages by combining theories, principles and research methods that exist in their respective fields. This multidisciplinary approach will give a new perspective to the topic being studied and give more value to the outcome of the research.

REFERENCES

Austin, John, *The Province of Jurisprudence Determined* (London: John Murray, 1832).
Bentham, Jeremy, *An Introduction to the Principles of Morals and Legislation* (Oxford: Clarendon Press, 1781).
Boorstin, Daniel J, *The Mysterious Science of Law: An Essay on Blackstone's Commentaries* (Chicago: University of Chicago Press, 1996).
Finnis, John, *Natural Law and Natural Rights* (Oxford: Clarendon Press, 1980).
Fuller, Lon L, *The Morality of Law* (New Haven, CT: Yale University Press, 1969).
Hart, H L A, 1958, 'Positivism and the separation of law and morals', *Harvard Law Review*, Vol.71, No.4, pp. 593–629.
Legal Information Institute, 1992, 'Jurisprudence', accessed 12 January 2019, https://www.law.cornell.edu/wex/jurisprudence.
Paulson, S L P, 2011, 'The very idea of legal positivism', *Revisit Brasilia de Estudos Politicos*, No.102, pp. 139–165.
Stott, D, *Legal Research* (2nd edition, London: Cavendish, 1999).
Taekema, S, 2018, 'Theoretical and normative frameworks for legal research: Putting theory into practice', *Law and Method*, 14 February, doi:10.5553/REM/.000031. Available at SSRN: https://ssrn.com/abstract=3123667.
Tumonis, V, 2012, 'Legal realism and judicial decision making', *Jurisprudence*, Vol.19, No.4, pp. 1361–1382.
Vibhutek, K and Aynalem, F, 2009, *Legal Research Methods: Teaching Material*, Justice and Legal System Research Institute, accessed 24 January 2019, https://chilot.files.wordpress.com/2011/06/legal-research-methods.pdf.

17. Assessing the legal implications and parameters of marketing research
Roopanand Mahadew and Marie Valerie Uppiah

1. INTRODUCTION

While it can be a daunting task to define what market research is all about, an overview of its main components can provide a sound and reliable explanation. It has been explained as a process of gathering, analysing and interpreting information in relation to a market, product or service for sale in that market. It is the process of researching the past, present and potential customers of such products, with specific reference to the spending habits, characteristics, location and needs for the targeted market, the industry in general and the competitors in particular (Entrepreneur, 2019). It is thus clear that one important aspect of marketing research is to engage with people and obtain information from them (Hardey, 2009). This aspect raises an essential ethical question which has long dominated the discussion on ethical marketing research (Day, 1975). However, marketing research is not only restricted by ethics but also, and perhaps more importantly, by laws. Frey and Kinnear (1979) argued that there had been a body of legal constraints on research activities on marketing which had started to develop to replace industry self-regulation by enforceable laws. Over 40 years down the line, this body of legal constraints has witnessed considerable growth and change which has revolutionised the way marketing research is carried out within a prescribed ambit of the law.

This chapter makes a humble attempt to provide a legal framework governing marketing research with which all marketing researchers, whether from academia or industry, should be adequately acquainted. While marketing research can have multiple legal implications, it is generally agreed that the most direct ones relate to data collection, privacy, use and dissemination of information, misleading advertisement and pricing. The chapter focuses on this specific list and presents the legal framework on each as per international legal standards and domestic laws from a few selected jurisdictions. Its main aim is to act as a working tool and a soft reminder to researchers about the legal aspects of marketing research and parameters to observe while embarking on such research. This chapter discusses the above-mentioned aspects by drawing on examples and cases from various countries as well as from international normative and legal frameworks. It serves as a guide for a general understanding of critical issues in marketing that can have serious legal implications.

2. DATA COLLECTION AND PRIVACY

Data collection has been an integral part of marketing research, and its importance is often highlighted in the literature (McDonald and Adam, 2003). In this modern technological era, data collection has undergone drastic changes, with other methods, such as online data collection, coming to the fore which has required the development and teaching of data collection techniques (Malhotra, 2012). Often, marketing research requires the collection of information about the age, demography, spending habits, tastes and interests of the respondent or selected audience. It can be argued that as soon as a marketing researcher starts to cross these lines, it raises an important question of privacy.

Privacy has indeed been regarded as *a high-profile public policy issue that affects consumers and marketers* (Milne, 2000: 1). The emergence of online marketing has forced the scholastic community to re-think the concept of data collection and to exercise greater care with regard to privacy implications (Luo, 2002). Privacy has great importance not only in marketing but also from a legal perspective. It implies that the legal framework around the concept of privacy is well developed and highly enforceable and justiciable. It is therefore relevant and important for marketers and researchers in marketing to have a good grasp of the legal framework on privacy. Indeed, Acquisti et al. (2013) contend that understanding the value that individuals assign to the protection of their personal data is of great importance for business, law and public policy.

Privacy is regarded as an important element in the autonomy of an individual, and is related to what he says, does and even feels (McMenemy, 2016). Such is the importance of privacy that it is even regarded as a fundamental human right. Indeed, Article 17 of the United Nations International Covenant on Civil and Political Rights (ICCPR) provides that no one shall be subjected to arbitrary or unlawful interference with his privacy, family, home or correspondence, or to unlawful attacks on his honour and reputation. It also adds that everyone has the right to the protection of the law against such interference or attack. The European Convention on Human Rights (ECHR) provides further details in its corresponding article on the right to privacy by stating that everyone has the right to respect for their private and family life, home and correspondence.

The right to privacy entails the individual's right to protect their identity, intimacy, gender, name, honour, dignity, sexual orientation, feelings and appearance (Mahadew, 2018: 189). While the right to privacy is not an absolute right and can be limited, the United Nations Human Rights Committee has stated that such limitation or interference must be provided by law and must be reasonable. It states that 'any interference with privacy must be proportional to the end sought and be necessary in the circumstances of any given case' (*Toonan v Australia*, 1992).

It follows from the above that there is a co-relation between the collection of data by marketing researchers and how they may use same as there are direct implications on the right to privacy. Extrapolating from the decision of the Human Rights Committee mentioned above, marketers can only make use of data collected from people in a way which is proportionate to the end sought, and necessary in the circumstances. It should be highlighted here that the above-cited legal instruments are international instruments on human rights that act as the over-arching standards. Marketers must be aware that each country in which they operate has its own legal regime on the right to privacy that may draw inspiration from the international standard but be more detailed and contextualised.

One of the basic and primary sources of law for the right to privacy, and which the marketing researcher must verify, is the Constitution. Each country's written or unwritten constitution has a provision which enlightens on the definition, scope and meaning of the right to privacy. For example, the Mauritian Constitution protects the right to privacy of home and other property under Section 9, and privacy as a general and all-inclusive concept is covered by Article 22 of the Mauritian Civil Code. Other countries have Acts of Parliament specifically dedicated to privacy. For instance, Australia has the Privacy Act (1988), which regulates the handling of personal information. The Act defines personal information as 'information or an opinion, whether true or not, and whether recorded in a material form or not, about an identified individual, or an individual who is reasonably identifiable'. Some common examples of personal information include name, address, date of birth, signature, telephone number, medical records, bank account details, and a person's commentary and opinions (Office of the Australian Information Commissioner, 2019).

It is therefore imperative for a marketing researcher to proceed in a systematic way when dealing with data that can have implications on personal privacy. Such data must only be used for marketing purposes in a manner that is in line with the prescribed legal framework on the right to privacy. As such, the researcher must first have a good grasp of the right to privacy and its content from an international perspective as provided by international legal instruments on human rights. He should also acquaint himself with the domestic legal framework on the right to privacy by consulting the laws that provide for same. It is important for the content of privacy to be understood and how it can be limited – in other words, what can the marketing researcher do with information obtained that will limit the right to privacy of the person but not infringe it? Reference to case law on the right to privacy may be helpful as it will explain the parameters around privacy and what does and does not amount to violation. For example, the case of *Madhewoo v The State of Mauritius* (2015) provides an insightful overview of the scope, definition and application of the right to privacy under, in this case, the Mauritian Constitution.

It should be added that a dose of reasonableness and logic on behalf of the marketing researcher can also be helpful in dealing with personal data and privacy. Perhaps the best test is to ask oneself: *What would I like as private information of mine to be and not to be public?* Guidance can then be drawn from this self-monitoring principle, and the risk of infringing the privacy of the audience/public involved in marketing surveys can be reduced significantly. In addition, it is always advisable for researchers to clearly and explicitly request and obtain informed, prior and free consent from the audience to use their information and data. They must also be in a position to explain to their audience how this information will be stored, used and destroyed. Firms and organisations involved in marketing research sometimes come up with ethical and legal policies about people's privacy. For instance, British companies tend to be compatible and in harmony with directives and laws such as the EU General Data Protection Regulation (GDPR), the Data Protection Act 1998, the Market Research Society's (MRS) Code of Conduct, and the European Society for Opinion and Marketing Research International (ESCOMAR) Code on Market and Social Research. Indeed, it is highly recommended that organisations build up a data and privacy policy and adhere to it in a strict and consistent manner.

3. USE AND DISSEMINATION OF INFORMATION

The work of a marketing researcher is not limited to collecting information; more it involves disseminating said information to meet a specific marketing end (Maltz and Kohli, 1996). The mode of dissemination and delivery employed by researchers can range from door-to-door techniques to telemarketing to emails. It has been argued that such methods can sometimes be controversial and borderline illegal (Bush et al., 2000). It also involves a degree of annoyance which may sometimes result in civil suits and actions. The handling of information is therefore another important aspect that marketing researchers must be mindful of when conducting research and dealing with information.

Article 19 of the ICCPR provides for the right to information as a subset of the right to freedom of expression. It states that 'everyone shall have the right to freedom of expression; this right shall include freedom to seek, receive and impart information and ideas of all kinds, regardless of frontiers, either orally, in writing or in print, in the form of art, or through any other media of his choice'. A similar provision is provided by Article 10 of the ECHR. The African Charter on Human and Peoples' Rights grants an even broader right to information through Article 9: 'every individual shall have the right to receive information'. It implies therefore that marketing researchers have a legitimate right to seek, receive and impart information in the course of their duties and within the ambit of the law. However, there are special duties and responsibilities attached to the right to information. The ICCPR stipulates that 'the exercise of the rights provided for in paragraph 2 of this article carries with it special duties and responsibilities. It may therefore be subject to certain restrictions, but these shall only be such as are provided by law and are necessary'. This special provision is echoed by Article 10(2) of the ECHR.

General Comment No. 16 of the UN Human Rights Committee (1994) clearly states the parameters to be observed when gathering and holding information:

> The gathering and holding of personal information on computers, data banks and other devices, whether by public authorities or private individuals or bodies, must be regulated by law. Effective measures have to be taken by States to ensure that information concerning a person's private life does not reach the hands of persons who are not authorized by law to receive, process and use it, and is never used for purposes incompatible with the Covenant. In order to have the most effective protection of his private life, every individual should have the right to ascertain in an intelligible form, whether, and if so, what personal data is stored in automatic data files, and for what purposes. Every individual should also be able to ascertain which public authorities or private individuals or bodies control or may control their files. If such files contain incorrect personal data or have been collected or processed contrary to the provisions of the law, every individual should have the right to request rectification or elimination.

From the above, it is clear that marketing researchers and organisations are bound by the guiding parameters enunciated by the Human Rights Committee. Similar to the right to privacy, the right to information may be provided by domestic laws in the form of a constitution or Act of Parliament. For example, the Indian jurisdiction enacted the Right to Information Act 2005 setting out the legal regime on the right to information, while in Mauritius the right to information is to be indirectly found in the Constitution. Such laws, sometimes aided by case law, explain the scope, definition and various components of the right to information. It is contended that marketing researchers must be aware of such legal rules, especially with regard to the storage, dissemination and handling of sensitive information belonging to their audience. As a matter of practice, researchers and marketing organisations must have prescribed internal rules that must be clearly explained to the target audience, after which the research participants' consent must be explicitly obtained.

4. MISLEADING AND ILLEGAL ADVERTISEMENT

Advertising plays a major role in marketing, and takes various forms – from the usual modes to guerrilla advertising, which is a novel concept (Bigat, 2012). The main aim of advertising is to boost sales of goods and services, and companies often adopt short-term or long-term advertising campaigns to achieve this aim (Assmus et al., 1984). Advertisements are increasingly important in the marketing world today, so competing companies often spend a lot on advertising campaigns. There is indeed cutthroat competition at campaign level which sometimes may lead to the use of inaccurate, imprecise and misleading advertisements.

Misleading advertisements may have serious legal consequences that marketing researchers must be fully aware of. One example of a misleading advertisement can be for toothpaste with claims that 99 per cent of germs are destroyed or other such claims that can only be realised under clinical or laboratory conditions. A consumer who believes in such an advertisement, trusts that particular brand but eventually finds out that what was claimed may not be true can turn against the brand's company in legal suits. Marketing researchers must therefore be acquainted with the legal regime on civil actions or tortious actions as the case may be. The legal regime will depend on the type of jurisdiction the researcher is operating in. For example, a civil law country will mostly be regulated by the civil code, which provides specific articles for civil claims if a particular advertisement has prejudiced a client. A common law country will have a similar framework but its application may be slightly different from a strictly legalistic point of view, such as the application of the law of tort and the law of delict in the UK and France respectively. Under both systems, in essence, it should be understood that any act depicted in the advertisement that will cause prejudice, physical or moral, to a person will result in an action in claim or compensation against the advertising company which can also indirectly entail the responsibility of the marketing researcher.

Another critical aspect researchers must be aware of is the existence of legal and regulatory frameworks on advertising. For example, many European countries have strict legal frameworks regarding sexism in advertisements. Norway and Denmark prohibit the use of a model's body if it has no direct relevance to the product being advertised. The concept of human dignity is also used in countries such as France, Germany and Bulgaria in assessing the content of advertisements. According to the Public International Law & Policy Group (PILPG, 2015), in these countries degrading or demeaning depictions of women may violate advertising laws. UK authorities have also held advertisements as illegal where women are portrayed sexually.

The content, scope or purview of an advertisement should also not be discriminatory in nature. Thus, a marketing researcher must be familiar with the legal frameworks on discrimination that exist in the country of operation. Some countries have more comprehensive laws on advertising that encompass aspects of public health and safety and the environment. For example, Bulgarian media law provides that commercial communications must not (1) affect human dignity; (2) include or promote any discrimination on grounds such as sex, race or ethnic origin, nationality, religion or belief, disability, age or sexual orientation; (3) encourage behaviour that endangers public health or safety; (4) encourage behaviour grossly prejudicial to the protection of the environment (Article 75(5) Bulgarian Law on Radio and Television). In France, a similar law contains provisions for the respect of diversity, human dignity and women's rights (1986 Law no. 86-1067 on the Freedom of Communication), while in Germany advertising content is regulated by both the Constitution and general competition law. As per the Constitution, advertisements can be banned if they encroach on the concept of human dignity and women's personality. In addition, German competition law contains standards that regulate advertisements, especially those which degrade certain groups or persons on the basis of gender.

A marketing researcher must therefore have a sound knowledge of the laws on discrimination in general, and of specific regulations on advertising, before designing and finalising advertisement content. A particular advertisement that directly harms a person or group of persons will result in a civil suit for claims and compensations. On a different note, illegal and unauthorised advertising content can breach state laws and regulations, and may lead to criminal sanctions such as fines and/or imprisonment.

5.   PRICING

Pricing is a crucial stage of marketing, and is often considered as marketing strategy (Samiee, 1987). Gijsbrechts (1993) argues that 'it has increasingly been recognized that developing an appropriate pricing strategy is both crucial and highly complex'. To this complexity is added the need to take into account existing legal parameters and regulations on the concept of pricing. Every country has well-defined regulatory frameworks on pricing, with the aim of protecting customers. It is therefore apposite for marketing researchers who use pricing methods as a marketing strategy to be aware of existing legislation that covers pricing practices. Generally, most countries have legislation to protect consumers from unfair trading practices, for example the UK Consumer Protection from Unfair Trading Regulations 2008. The aim of this legislation is to ban traders from using any unfair commercial practices that would mislead customers and persuade them to buy goods and services they would not have otherwise bought.

Commercial practices imply any act of commission or omission that is directly linked to the supply of goods and services to members of the public. Marketing researchers should be acquainted with the several forms of ban that are imposed by legislation on unfair trading practices. For example, customers cannot be misled about the price of a good or service or the way in which that price is worked out. Neither must they be lured into buying a product upon false claims of a price advantage that does not exist – for example, being told that the price is lower than that of a direct competitor. Marketing researchers should also be aware that purposely omitting details of extra hidden costs (such as delivery charges, postal charges or taxes) is also prohibited by unfair trading practice laws. The UK also has a range of other legislation covering pricing practice, such as the Consumer Rights Act 2015 and the Consumer Credit Act 1974. If the customers are themselves other businesses, there is a specific law called the Business Protection from Misleading Marketing Regulations of 2008.

Price comparison is another way of conducting marketing for goods and services. By comparing its prices with its competitors', a business often tries to show that it is offering the best prices and deals to attract more customers. It should be noted that price comparison also has its own regulatory framework that must be abided by. For example, any price comparison must be justified, and claims of best prices or deals being made after such comparison must be accurate, valid and real. In addition, the comparison must be made with like products.

Australia also has legislation regarding price fixing, which is illegal. By definition, price fixing means an agreement, verbal or formal, among competitors to set agreed prices for products or services. Such practices are prohibited under the Competition and Consumer Act 2010, a law administered by the Australian Competition and Consumer Commission. The US also has specific laws regarding online prices, which can differ from prices for the same products bought in physical stores. The law requires that factors such as costs of overheads, shipping, sales tax and methods of payment be taken into account when determining online prices.

6.   CONCLUSION

Marketing is an area which is closely linked to people's lives in relation to private information and data that are taken and used from them. It has a considerable bearing on personal privacy and, equally, a financial impact when it comes to advertising and pricing. As a result, across the world, legislation has been created to ensure that the close interaction between the public and marketing researchers and their work is carried out within specific legal parameters. It has thus been argued that marketers and marketing researchers must be fully alive to the existence of such laws and work within the limitations of those laws. An individual marketer has the responsibility to learn about the laws on information and data handling and sharing, privacy, advertising and pricing, and to work and function accordingly. As for companies involved in marketing and related research, they must have clearly defined policies on these aspects, preferably vetted by qualified legal practitioners. Non-compliance with laws related to marketing may have serious and damaging effects on brand reputation and goodwill as well as on the body or individual responsible for marketing. It is therefore essential that there is sound understanding of the legal framework around the selected aspects of marketing discussed in this chapter.

REFERENCES

Books

Churchill, G.A. and Iacobucci, D., 2006. *Marketing research: Methodological foundations.* New York: Dryden Press.
Douglas, S.P. and Craig, C.S., 1983. *International marketing research.* Englewood Cliffs, NJ: Prentice Hall.
Malhotra, N.K., 2012. *Basic marketing research: Integration of social media.* Boston, MA: Pearson.
Malhotra, N.K., Hall, J., Shaw, M. and Oppenheim, P., 2006. *Marketing research: An applied orientation.* Frenchs Forest, NSW: Pearson Education Australia.

Rao, V.R. ed., 2009. *Handbook of pricing research in marketing*. Cheltenham, UK and Northampton, MA, USA: Edward Elgar Publishing.

Journal Articles

Acquisti, A., John, L.K. and Loewenstein, G., 2013. What is privacy worth? *Journal of Legal Studies*, 42(2), pp.249–274.

Assmus, G., Farley, J.U. and Lehmann, D.R., 1984. How advertising affects sales: Meta-analysis of econometric results. *Journal of Marketing Research*, 21(1), pp.65–74.

Bigat, E.C., 2012. Guerrilla advertisement and marketing. *Procedia: Social and Behavioral Sciences*, 51, pp.1022–1029.

Biswas, A., Wilson, E.J. and Licata, J.W., 1993. Reference pricing studies in marketing: A synthesis of research results. *Journal of Business Research*, 27(3), pp.239–256.

Bush, V.D., Venable, B.T. and Bush, A.J., 2000. Ethics and marketing on the internet: Practitioners' perceptions of societal, industry and company concerns. *Journal of Business Ethics*, 23(3), pp.237–248.

Day, R.L., 1975. A comment on 'Ethics in marketing research'. *Journal of Marketing Research*, 12(2), pp.232–233.

Frey, C.J. and Kinnear, T.C., 1979. Legal constraints and marketing research: Review and call to action. *Journal of Marketing Research*, 16(3), pp.295–302.

Gijsbrechts, E., 1993. Prices and pricing research in consumer marketing: Some recent developments. *International Journal of Research in Marketing*, 10(2), pp.115–151.

Hardey, M., 2009. Conference notes – the social context of online market research: An introduction to the sociability of social media. *International Journal of Market Research*, 51(4), pp.1–5.

Lal, R. and Rao, R., 1997. Supermarket competition: The case of every day low pricing. *Marketing Science*, 16(1), pp.60–80.

Luo, X., 2002. Trust production and privacy concerns on the internet: A framework based on relationship marketing and social exchange theory. *Industrial Marketing Management*, 31(2), pp.111–118.

Mahadew, R., 2018. Does the Mauritian Constitution protect the right to privacy? An insight from *Madhewoo v The State of Mauritius*. *African Human Rights Law Journal*, 18(1), pp.189–204.

Maltz, E. and Kohli, A.K., 1996. Market intelligence dissemination across functional boundaries. *Journal of Marketing Research*, 33(1), pp.47–61.

McDonald, H. and Adam, S., 2003. A comparison of online and postal data collection methods in marketing research. *Marketing Intelligence & Planning*, 21(2), pp.85–95.

Milne, G.R., 2000. Privacy and ethical issues in database/interactive marketing and public policy: A research framework and overview of the special issue. *Journal of Public Policy & Marketing*, 19(1), pp.1–6.

Rao, V.R., 1984. Pricing research in marketing: The state of the art. *Journal of Business*, 57(1), pp.S39–S60.

Samiee, S., 1987. Pricing in marketing strategies of US-and foreign-based companies. *Journal of Business Research*, 15(1), pp.17–30.

Papers

McMenemy, D. 2016. Rights to privacy and freedom of expression in public libraries: Squaring the circle. https://pureportal.strath.ac.uk/files-asset/54531639/McMenemy_ IFLA_2016_rights_to_privacy_and_freedom_of_expression_in_public_libraries.pdf.

PILPG, 2015. Legal frameworks regarding sexism in advertising: Comparison of national systems. https://pilpnjcm.nl/wp-content/uploads/2015/12/150609-PILP-sexism-compara tive-practice-memo.pdf.

UN Human Rights Committee. [1994]. CCPR General Comment No. 16: Article 17 (Right to Privacy). The right to respect of privacy, family, home and correspondence, and protection of honour and reputation. https://www.refworld.org/pdfid/453883f922.pdf.

Cases

Madhewoo v The State of Mauritius & Another, 2015 SCJ 177.
Toonan v Australia, 1992. Communication No. 488/1992, para. 8.3; see also No. 903/1999, para 7.3 and No. 1482/2006, paras. 10.1 and 10.2.

Websites

The Entrepreneur. 2019. Market research. https://www.entrepreneur.com/encyclopedia/market-research#.
Law on Radio and Television (Bulgaria, 1999). Available in Bulgarian at https://lex.bg/laws/ldoc/2135472223.
Office of the Australian Information Commissioner. https://www.oaic.gov.au/privacy-law/privacy-act/.

18. Ethical considerations in marketing research

Mridula Gungaphul and Mehraz Boolaky

SUMMARY

This chapter delves into ethical issues in marketing research, an area of direct relevance to consumers and stakeholders alike. It discusses the importance of upholding ethical standards throughout the marketing research process and provides some recommendations from a practical point of view.

INTRODUCTION

Research has always been directed by evolving ethical standards across time. Changes in the external and internal business environment – such as political/legal, economic/demographic, social/cultural and technological aspects – have necessitated revision of research ethics and practice.

The literature on 'ethics' provides diverse definitions. The concept of ethics can be viewed as an analysis of human acts to determine what is right or wrong measured by two criteria: truth and justice (Walton, 1977). Ethics also reflects moral obligations, social justice and responsibility. To put it simply, ethics can be seen as an attempt to make sense of what is good or bad, just or unjust, right or wrong (Steiner and Steiner, 1999). The problem, though, lies in the subjectivity of the concept. What one individual may view as good or right may be viewed as bad or wrong by another. Ethics tends to differ from individual to individual and business to business.

In the business arena, ethics is a set of criteria governing human actions to societal expectations, fair competition, aesthetics of advertising, the extent of consumer sovereignty and the handling of communications, amongst others (Walton, 1977). Ethics in marketing research involves assessing the actions of stakeholders in terms of what is right or wrong (Proctor and Jamieson, 2004), and the application of ethical practices in marketing activities is instrumental in developing sustainable marketing (Kotler and Armstrong, 2010).

353

With the upsurge of consumerism and equal rights legislation, consumers are more informed of their rights and are vigilant about the marketing practices of businesses. Indeed, many consumers do not hesitate to report unethical practices to the relevant authorities. In fact, the general public perceives that marketing is the area of business where unethical practices mostly happen (Malhotra and Miller, 1998). Laczniak and Murphy (1991) observe that from a 'marketing standpoint . . . professionals holding marketing positions are viewed to be the least ethical' (p. 261). Unfortunately, some research methods used in collecting marketing information are often manipulated or fabricated because of their high power of influence. If marketing managers are to make the right decisions for their organisations – both profit making and non-profit making, they need to have and convey the right information. Thus, ethical issues should be addressed in each step of the marketing research process, and due consideration should be given to the type of research being conducted and the population of interest. These steps are elaborated further in the next sections.

This chapter provides an overview of historical milestones and highlights the ethical issues in the research process. Some innovative techniques in marketing research are also highlighted, and guidelines for students and practitioners are provided to inspire them in adopting ethical practices while working on their dissertations and research projects.

HISTORICAL CONTEXT OF ETHICAL ISSUES IN MARKETING

The importance of ethics in marketing dates as far back as the 1960s, when marketing was considered more of an art; and, as such, it was assumed that practitioners could use different approaches while conducting research in marketing. The initiative was taken by Twedt (1963), who produced a 'code of ethics' that was based on three main aspects, namely:

1. the desire to maintain public confidence in marketing research procedures;
2. the need to self-regulate the discipline before outsiders decided marketing research needed regulation; and
3. the concern to maintain a positive public image of marketing in general.

Following that initiative, the first volume of the *Journal of Marketing Research* published an article addressing ethical concerns in marketing research. Since then numerous researchers have added to the debate with various views, and the converging view was that regulation was necessary as several vulnerable groups – such as children, sick persons, etc. – were being targeted by researchers for the latter's own benefit. Thus, it was felt important to restore the public image of the marketing field by both industry players and academia.

MARKETING RESEARCH CODE OF ETHICS

To this end, the American Marketing Association took the lead and published a code of ethics that was the outcome of a committee comprising various dignitaries, including consumers in marketing. The main purpose was to provide guidelines to members of the association and others on what to do when conducting research in the marketing area – the overall objective was to protect the public from misrepresentation and exploitation under the pretext of research. The protagonists in marketing research were identified as being the research practitioners, interviewers and users of research data.

Below is an outline of the code developed at that time to give an idea of what was discussed and agreed.

For Research Users, Practitioners and Interviewers

1. Marketing research must not be a pretext to sell products or services to persons contacted to participate in the research as respondents.
2. Anonymity of respondents must be ensured if promises are made that this would be the case.

For Research Practitioners

1. Research methods and results are to be made available to any party sponsoring the research project if these are requested. Due evidence that surveys have been conducted must also be presented to sponsors, etc.
2. Unless the research design requires the same, identities of sponsors or clients requesting the research must always be kept confidential. All information pertaining to the research project must be kept strictly confidential and must not be used for personal interests and/or made available to third parties unless authorised by clients or sponsors.
3. Research agencies must refrain from undertaking marketing studies for competitors, particularly when these could endanger the confidential nature of client–agency relationships.

For Users of Marketing Research

1. Users of marketing research must not share inconsistent findings of a given research project or service.
2. Original research designs not commonly used by other researchers must not be solicited from one agency to be executed by another agency for implementation and execution unless express permission is given by the design originator.

For Field Interviewers

1. All research specifications and materials received for the purpose of conducting a research project must be kept confidential by field interviewers. This applies to all information derived from respondents as well.
2. No data derived from a marketing research project are to be utilised for personal interest or advantage of the interviewer.
3. Interviews shall be conducted in strict accordance with specifications and instructions received.
4. Interviewers must not conduct two or more interviewing assignments at the same time unless due permission is given by parties concerned.

As may be noted, this code provides relevant guidelines to researchers for adopting ethical standards when engaging in research. The ethical dilemmas arising in the various stage of the research process are illustrated in the next section.

ETHICAL CONSIDERATIONS IN THE MARKETING RESEARCH PROCESS

Activities related to marketing research impact on four main stakeholders – i.e. the marketing researcher, the client, the public and the respondent – and in cases of conflict of interest, the behaviour of each of these stakeholders should be guided by a code of ethics (Malhotra and Peterson, 2001). As already mentioned, organisations such as the Marketing Research Association (2013) as well as the American Marketing Association provide codes of conduct in the ethical research behaviour domain to enable researchers in marketing to limit damage in the research process and uphold integrity in the research profession. The ethical issues in the research process are briefly illustrated next.

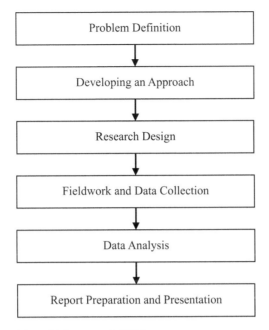

Source: Adapted from Malhotra et al. (1996).

Figure 18.1 Marketing research process

Marketing research is a six-step process (Malhotra et al., 1996) as shown in Figure 18.1, and ethical problems can stem from at least one if not all of the steps.

Step 1: Problem Definition

The first step of the marketing research process is the problem definition stage. It is widely recognised that this is the most significant stage in the whole process (Chapman, 1989) since management action depends on it (Drummond, 1992). If a problem is poorly defined, all of the subsequent steps in the marketing research process will be affected, resulting in conclusions being flawed or meaningless, with no or little contribution to a management decision. The main stakeholders involved in this stage are the client and the marketing researcher. Ethical dilemmas between these two parties in this stage could stem from personal interests or hidden agendas (Malhotra and Peterson, 2006).

An example to illustrate a case of ethical dilemma

A client approaches a marketing researcher to undertake some research to solve a marketing problem. After some discussions, both parties agree that it is a complicated problem and that thorough research has to be conducted. Considering the seriousness of the problem, both parties also agree on the fees to be paid.

However, when conducting an in-depth diagnosis of the problem the researcher realises that the problem is not as serious as initially thought, and could be solved much quicker and easier. What should the researcher do? If he informs the client this would mean considerable savings for the client. As for the researcher, he would be worse off since the fees will be lower than in the proposal.

The code of ethics indicates that the researcher should disclose the state of affairs to the client.

Step 2: Developing an Approach

In this stage of the marketing research process, an appropriate approach should be developed by the researcher. As proposed by Malhotra and Peterson (2006), this should include key components such as analytical framework and models, formulation of research questions as well as hypotheses and a description of specific information required.

Ethical problems can arise if the researcher adopts a similar approach to one he/she has previously used for another client. This type of situation may arise when the researcher carries out research for clients operating in the same sector/industry, for example hotels. The researcher might use the findings from his/her previous research to formulate research questions and develop hypotheses for his/her current client. This practice is unethical if the client has not given his/her consent.

Step 3: Research Design

Research design is a framework detailing the techniques that will be used to conduct the research and how it will be accomplished. The researcher should ensure that the research design selected will generate valid information that addresses the marketing problem identified in the problem formulation stage. The main components of this step include the type of design to be used (exploratory, descriptive or causal), the population of interest, sampling techniques, and instruments for data collection, measuring and scaling, amongst other relevant information. A sound research design should be one that is able to ensure that the research will be carried out effectively and efficiently.

Since various activities are involved in research design, ethical issues could stem from many sources. For instance, a researcher chooses and justifies a descriptive research simply because he/she is more experienced in this type of research, when in fact an exploratory research would have been more appropriate to the marketing problem. Another example of an unethical issue may occur when the client has approached more than one researcher to submit proposals for a specific marketing problem. If the client extracts information from other proposals which he/she has not paid for and passes it to the selected researcher, this practice is unethical. Ethical dilemma also occurs if the client makes unrealistic demands, for example, demanding the use of a specific research design which is time-consuming and expecting the researcher to submit the research report under severe time constraints.

Use of secondary data
Data collected in research can be of a primary or secondary nature, and often secondary data is collected prior to primary data as it can assist in generating new hypotheses or be used as a stepping stone to collect primary data. Secondary data refers to existing data collected and used for a different problem than the one at hand. The use of secondary data in marketing research raises some ethical concerns. Reusing respondents' data collected from previous studies for new/different research without their approval is an invasion of their privacy, especially when there is identifying information.

Another ethical issue arises when the researcher uses and relies only on secondary data when primary data should also have been used for the research problem. This practice may reduce costs for the researcher but is morally wrong if the client has paid for primary research to be conducted. Furthermore, with the increasing use and accessibility of technology, the availability of secondary data is paramount – and this raises another salient ethical concern. Information is gathered, stored, compiled and shared easily and rapidly, which could lead to breach of confidentiality and invasion of privacy. Many organisations – including airlines, super-markets, department stores and restaurants – issue loyalty cards to their customers. Personal information about the card holder is required when issuing the card, and each time the card is used, information about the products purchased and amount spent are stored. If this information is shared with other firms without the knowledge and consent of the shoppers, this is unethical practice.

In some instances primary data may not be necessary if the secondary data collected is sufficient to address the research problem. In this case, if the researcher fails to inform the client about this and knowingly collects unnecessary primary data, this raises ethical concerns.

Ethical issues in conducting qualitative and quantitative research

In the process of collecting qualitative and quantitative data, researchers are confronted with several ethical challenges. Among others, these challenges include informed consent, influence of researcher on respondents, anonymity, confidentiality and causing embarrassment and distress to respondents.

In qualitative research, the relationship that is built between the researcher and the respondents can lead to numerous ethical dilemmas (Sanjari et al., 2014). Hence, it is very important that researchers clearly indicate at the onset the purpose of the research, how data/information will be collected and used, the identity of the researcher, and the organisation for which the research is being conducted. It is the researcher's responsibility to spell out this information in simple terms and ensure that respondents have understood fully the information provided. The researcher should also provide any clarification sought by participants.

Unethical practices in qualitative research that may arise include the following situations:

Focus groups   In focus groups, moderators often use audio and/or video recording to gather information. If the participants are not informed that the discussion is being recorded, this raises an ethical concern. Furthermore, if the researcher invites the client to attend the focus group meeting and the true identity of the client is not revealed to the group's members, this is ethically wrong as the participants are being deceived. To address these unethical practices, if the discussions are being recorded, researchers should inform participants who will have access to and use the recording. If for some valid reasons participants are informed about the recording *after* the meeting, any request they make to be removed from the discussion should be accepted, and the recording edited accordingly.

In-depth interviews   Ethical issues may also pose a challenge in in-depth interviews. For instance, if such interviews are being carried out with sales people from the same organisation, confidentiality may be breached if the interviewer makes reference to a previous interviewee who could be identifiable to other people in that organisation, even if his/her identity is not revealed. This can cause harm to participants. Respondents can also experience discomfort if they feel pressurised to answer questions of a sensitive nature or are coerced to provide more information than they want to. Besides morally affecting the participants, the data collected may be flawed and impact the overall research.

Observation   Ethical issues in observation techniques are rooted in how the data collection is carried out. The researcher is very much involved in the phenomenon under study, either covertly or overtly over a period of time (Denzin and Lincoln, 2005). Information is gathered by observing the subjects in a planned or natural environment, for example, observing the shopping habits of customers in a retail outlet. The subjects under study are often not informed that they are being observed so as to allow them to behave more naturally. However, this practice raises ethical concerns relating to informed consent, invasion of privacy and deception (Oliver and Eales, 2008). With increasing internet use, website cookies also raise ethical concerns. Although cookies do not yet store personal information that can identify individuals, personal information can be linked to the information stored and is available from cookies. According to *Scientific American*, web servers use cookies to identify and track users as they browse websites without the users' knowledge. This practice constitutes an infringement of privacy.

To address these ethical concerns, permission should be sought from the respondents before data collection starts. Where observation techniques are used, and if there is a dedicated location for observing participants, notices should be placed in the designated location so that the subjects are informed that they will be observed for a specific purpose. This will give the subjects the choice of forming part of the research or not. In cases where covert observation is used, the subjects should be informed at the end of the observation session. If any participant does not give his/her consent to be part of the study, all records on that should be deleted from the recording.

In the context of quantitative research, similar ethical dilemmas to those addressed in qualitative research arise.

Survey   When sampling a large number of people, surveys are popular methods for collecting data. There are various methods of conducting surveys, e.g. face-to-face, telephone, mall intercept, mail interviews and electronic surveys. Irrespective of the method used, confidentiality and anonymity of respondents must be respected. The identity of the respondents should not be revealed even to the client if consent has not been obtained. Respondents should not be forced to continue with the survey if they do not wish to. For example, in recruiting for face-to-face interviews, the researcher should reassure potential respondents that the survey will take no more than ten minutes. However, if the survey is still not completed after 15 minutes and the respondent no longer wishes to participate, an ethical issue arises if the respondent is intimidated or pressured by the researcher to complete it. Some researchers also offer incentives, such as gifts, to recruit respondents. This also raises an ethical issue.

When conducting surveys with a vulnerable population, such as children, the consent of parents/guardians is imperative; otherwise this raises ethical concerns.

Questionnaires   If data collection is through questionnaires, the questions formulated should gather the data needed to meet the objectives set in the problem definition stage; they should be free of bias and not lead the respondent to answer in a specific way. If respondents have agreed to devote time to answering questions, the researcher is ethically obliged to ask questions that are easily understood and free of jargon. If questions of a sensitive nature are included in the questionnaire, extra care should be taken so as not to cause distress to the respondent. Researchers should avoid long questionnaires, and should only include items that are absolutely necessary for the problem being investigated.

Researchers should also consider the environment in which the questionnaire is to be administered to avoid ethical dilemmas. For instance, if the questionnaire is being administered online and respondents feel aggrieved about sensitive questions, the researcher will not know about the distress experienced; nor will he/she be able to respond ethically.

Prior to the start of fieldwork, the questionnaire should be pilot-tested to iron out any potential problems and lacunas and address ethical concerns that may crop up.

Sampling design   The researcher should ensure that the sample chosen should reflect the population of interest, that is, it must be representative. If this is not the case, the results obtained from the sample will impact negatively on the research findings. The researcher has a responsibility to the client to adopt an appropriate sampling design to take care of sampling and non-sampling errors (Malhotra and Peterson, 2001). Researchers should be honest with clients, not mislead them about the type of sampling used, and not pass on the use of non-probability sampling as probability sampling. Where the population is small and respondents are easily identifiable, the researcher should take care to protect the respondents' anonymity and not reveal their identity to any other stakeholder (Akaah, 1997).

Step 4: Fieldwork and Data Collection

Ethical standards should be consistently maintained in the data collection stage. Respondents should not be forced to participate, should have the right to be anonymous, and should not be deceived by fake sponsorship (Boyd et al., 1998). Fieldworkers should clearly explain the research purpose to respondents prior to the start of data collection. Issues of anonymity and confidentiality should be addressed with respondents to make them feel at ease about participating in the research. The expectations of the fieldworkers and respondents should be addressed. For example, the length of time the data collection is expected to last should be mentioned and respected. It is also important for researchers to train all fieldworkers involved so that the data collection process is consistent. The researcher should be ethical in documenting this process in detail and provide the information to the client.

Step 5: Data Analysis

Ethical concerns in data analysis could stem from various circumstances. Where a Likert scale is used in a questionnaire to gauge the extent of agreement or disagreement on a specific issue, say, for example, the respondent indicates neither agree/nor disagree throughout. How should the researcher treat this questionnaire? An ethical issue arises as to whether or not to remove this respondent from the analysis. Furthermore, if it is noticed that some respondents have not fully understood a few questions, should these participants be discarded? If discarded, this will affect the response rate; and if included, this will negatively impact the findings. Malhotra and Peterson (2006) argue that discarding respondents after the analysis phase is unethical, and that decisions to discard any respondent should be taken in the data preparation phase. Other ethical dilemmas emerge when data is discarded simply because the results derived from the analysis are not as the researcher expected. Thus results are manipulated.

Step 6: Report Preparation and Presentation

As with all the previous steps of the research process, ethical issues should also be addressed in preparing and presenting the final report in an appropriate format. This should include in detail the research approach used, the research design procedures, the fieldwork and other relevant information. Researchers should include all key findings and not selectively omit certain information when formulating final recommendations. For example, it is unethical not to reveal the response rate, especially when it is low. Any limitation encountered during the research process should also be revealed to the client (Malhotra and Peterson, 2006). Findings should be accurately reported and not misinterpreted to meet personal objectives. As for clients, they should be ethical in using the findings in all honesty and not hide any information which was not expected to come out in the research findings.

As can be seen, ethical issues can arise in all stages of the marketing research process. Ethical dilemmas can be more pronounced in the research design step due to the various activities involved and the various ways of gathering information. As technology evolves and more innovative research methods are adopted, researchers will be faced with new sets of ethical dilemmas. The next section focuses on some innovative techniques in marketing research and the ethical challenges in using technology in marketing research.

INNOVATION IN MARKETING RESEARCH AND ETHICAL CONSIDERATIONS

The digital revolution has transformed individuals' way of living and communicating. Similarly, the techniques used in research have evolved from those available during the 'offline' era. With these technological developments, researchers are now able to collect and analyse a huge amount of data, and recruit research participants relatively quickly and easily (Kuyumdzhieva, 2018). The increase in the number of online services continues to generate vast amounts of data, and marketing researchers are using analytics such as data mining to assist businesses in gaining a better understanding of their consumers (Dean et al., 2016).

The use of technology in marketing research can be beneficial to businesses as it provides in-depth knowledge of consumer behaviour, thereby enabling better marketing strategies to be devised. It, however, also raises some ethical concerns. For instance, consumers who do not want their personal information to be shared or used for any other purposes will feel let down by the organisation that does so.

Various new marketing research techniques are being used. Three of the most recent are highlighted below, followed by a brief discussion of where researchers ought to be careful to maintain ethical practices.

Behavioural Economics

Behavioural economics technology is now used by many e-commerce retailers, and is mainly based on data collection and observation by watching online behavioural patterns. This technology can point out which marketing strategies would be more appropriate to attract consumers, which marketing activities should be given priority, and which activities create pain points for customers. The technology used in behavioural economics helps provide researchers with in-depth explanations of consumer behaviour and how their behaviour impacts on what, where and when they buy.

Researchers usually integrate various research processes, such as cognitive computing, psychological research and machine learning (Hemsley, 2017).

Neuro-Research

There is growing interest in neuro-technology which explores, nonstop, the electrical reactions of the brain. With this technology, the researcher can observe the brainwaves of participants under study for memory encoding, engagement and emotional intensity (Hemsley, 2017). For instance, the findings could help in creating appropriate advertisements through knowledge of consumer emotions.

Sensory Research

Sensory research involves the use of technology such as eye-tracking devices, biometrics and other emotional intelligence technology to analyse consumers' senses (e.g. to monitor skin response, heart rate or facial responses) (Hemsley, 2017). Sensory research can be helpful to companies looking to get the most appropriate images for online advertisements or to analyse the effectiveness of their current television advertisements.

It should be noted, however, that no matter how innovative the research technique may be, researchers should always maintain ethical standards vis-à-vis respondents. To some extent, consumers of online services are aware that the organisation they are dealing with holds their personal information, but they might not know how or for what purposes the information is being used. In fact, consumers often raise concerns about their private information being used without their knowledge (Pearson, 2009). Although privacy policies are provided, in the majority of cases these are quite difficult to understand and often go unread by consumers.

From an ethical point of view, marketing researchers and businesses should ensure the maintenance and protection of personal information of respondents and consumers. Consent should be sought if their personal information is to be used and the purpose clearly explained. In cases where the customers are against their information being used, they should not be forced.

Another ethical dilemma in conducting online marketing research concerns minors. Minors are very active on social media and virtual communities, which makes them available to take part in surveys just like adults would. Since parental consent needs to be obtained for interviewing minors, an ethical issue arises if permission has not been sought (Krasonikolakis and Pouloudi, 2015).

The use of technology in data collection is very common nowadays, not only with organisations but also with students working on their research projects and dissertations. The next section provides some guidelines to address ethical dilemmas faced by students.

ETHICAL CONSIDERATIONS FOR DISSERTATIONS AND RESEARCH PROJECTS

Ethical considerations can be specified as one of the most important parts of such research. Dissertations and research projects may even be doomed to failure if a section is not devoted to what the ethical considerations were when embarking on the dissertation or research projects.

According to Bryman and Bell (2007), among others, the following main principles are related to ethical considerations in dissertations:

1. There should be no risk to participants; and, even if minor ones are expected, this should be clearly stated and possible solutions offered to minimise such risks. The well-being of participants must thus be a priority during all stages of the survey/interview, and participants must not develop feelings of embarrassment or uneasiness. In such cases, they must be allowed to withdraw unconditionally.
2. Participants must be requested to fill in a consent form where the main objectives of the project (without exaggeration and potential deception) and its research methodology is adequately explained. They should be assured that it is purely voluntary and that anonymity and confidentiality will be preserved. It is also important to give contact details to address queries if any.
3. It is also very important to provide details of affiliations with the organisation in question: there should be no conflict of interest, such as a manager interviewing a subordinate, etc. The main sources of funding as well as sponsors must be clearly elicited.
4. Honesty and transparency must prevail throughout the research project, and any gifts associated with participation must be clearly stated and described, in particular the criteria for receiving such gifts.

Based on the above, to address ethical aspects of a dissertation or research project in an effective manner, the following points should be clearly explained to all stakeholders in the written work and presentation:

1. Participation is voluntary and respondents are free to withdraw.
2. Respondents are presented with a consent form that they duly sign before participation.
3. No discrimination of any kind to be practised.

4. Privacy and anonymity of respondents is prioritised. Data protection must be ensured.
5. To avoid plagiarism, all citations must be properly referenced in the recommended style.
6. Findings must be presented free from bias, and all analyses and discussions must be factual, without 'cooking' of results.

Most universities have their own code of ethical practice. It is critical that students thoroughly adhere to this code in every aspect of their research and declare their adherence in the ethical considerations part of the dissertation.

DISCUSSION

In this chapter we presented the main ethical factors to consider when undertaking marketing research. After defining what ethics is all about, we discussed some of the most important factors that ought to govern ethical practice in the research journey and project.

Some organisations have taken the lead in publishing codes of conduct in the ethical research behaviour domain to uphold integrity in marketing research projects. It is therefore no longer possible to claim ignorance to support bad or ethically wrong practice. We make the following recommendations after having thoroughly revised and differentiated the good from the bad, and we openly acknowledge the suggestions made so far to enable healthy marketing research practices.

Since there are various stakeholders concerned in marketing research, with the respondents probably being the most important, it is imperative to identify and address the ethical dilemmas that may occur throughout the research process as these may adversely impact management action.

Today we debate and have clearer ideas on such issues as consumer rights and protection through various channels, including consumer associations, government bodies, pressure groups that militate for the rights and privileges of customers, academia, business associations, etc. The focus of marketing research today is not about safeguarding the rights of the marketers per se, but protecting the rights and privacy of participants in marketing research projects.

With innovation and advances in technology, new methods of conducting marketing research will continue to emerge. It will become easier to access more respondents from diverse groups, for example minors. Researchers need to address ethical challenges such as informed consent, anonymity, confidentiality and causing embarrassment and distress to respondents, among others. In short, businesses need to adopt and communicate corporate ethics guidelines to all concerned with marketing research in the organisation.

For students undertaking research, it is vital to explain clearly how ethical issues are addressed in their work. This may take the form of what was done to protect the rights and identity of respondents, who should be able to participate voluntarily without being forced or coerced in any manner. This serves as a model for practitioners and novice or budding researchers, including students. For instance, it is most helpful to discuss at length any difficult ethical issues encountered and how these were dealt with to minimise negative consequences – this will add to checklists that might already be available and thus strengthen available guidelines.

All researchers should take responsibility for adopting ethical principles throughout the marketing research process to protect all stakeholders' interests, including their own. Ethical marketing conduct will contribute to achieving sustainable marketing goals.

REFERENCES

Akaah, I.P. (1997). Influence of deontological and teleological factors on research ethics evaluations. *Journal of Business Research*, 39(2), pp. 71–80.

Boyd, H.W., Walker, O.C. and Larréché, J.-C. (1998). *Marketing Management: A Strategic Approach with a Global Orientation* (3rd ed.). Boston: Irwin/McGraw-Hill.

Bryman, A. and Bell, E. (2007). *Business Research Methods* (2nd ed.). New York: Oxford University Press.

Chapman, R.G. (1989). Problem-definition in marketing research studies. *Journal of Consumer Marketing*, 6(2), pp. 51–59.

Dean, D.D., Payne, D.M. and Landry, B.J.L. (2016). Data mining: An ethical baseline for online privacy policies. *Journal of Enterprise Information Management*, 29(4), pp. 482–504.

Denzin, N.K. and Lincoln, Y.S. (2005), Strategies of qualitative inquiry. In Denzin, N.K. and Lincoln, Y.S. (Eds.), *Principles and Practice in Management and Business Research*. Aldershot: Dartmouth, pp. 35–62.

Drummond, H. (1992). Another fine mess: Time for quality in decision making. *Journal of General Management*, 18(1), pp. 1–14.

Hemsley, S. (2017). How brands are taking advantage of innovations in market research. *Marketing Week*, 26 October. https://www.marketingweek.com/2017/10/26/market-research-innovations/ (Accessed on 18 February 2019).

Kotler, P. and Armstrong, G. (2010). *Principles of Marketing* (13th ed.). Upper Saddle River, NJ: Pearson Pearson/Prentice Hall.

Krasonikolakis, I. and Pouloudi, N. (2015). 3D online environments: Ethical challenges for marketing research. *Journal of Information, Communication and Ethics in Society*, 13(3/4), pp. 218–234.

Kuyumdzhieva, A. (2018). Ethics challenges in the digital era: Focus on medical research. In Koporc, Z. (Ed.), *Ethics and Integrity in Health and Life Sciences Research*. Bingley: Emerald, pp. 45–62. Published online: 14 November 2018.

Laczniak, G.J. and Murphy, P.E. (1991). Fostering ethical marketing decisions. *Journal of Business Ethics*, 10(4), pp. 259–271.

Malhotra, N.K. and Miller, G.L. (1998). An integrated model for ethical decisions in marketing research. *Journal of Business Ethics*, 17, pp. 263–280.

Malhotra, N.K. and Peterson, M. (2001). Marketing research in the new millennium: Emerging issues and trends. *Marketing Intelligence and Planning*, 19(4), pp. 216–235.

Malhotra, N.K. and Peterson, M. (2006). *Basic Marketing Research: A Decision Making Approach* (2nd ed.). Upper Saddle River, NJ: Pearson/Prentice Hall.

Malhotra, N.K., Agarwal, J. and Peterson, M. (1996). Methodological issues in cross-cultural marketing research: A state-of-the-art review. *International Marketing Review*, 13(5), pp. 7–43.

Oliver, J. and Eales, K. (2008). Research ethics: Re-evaluating the consequentialist perspective of using covert participant observation in management research. *Qualitative Market Research*, 11(3), pp. 344–357.

Pearson, G. (2009). The researcher as hooligan. *International Journal of Social Research Methodology*, 12(3), pp. 244–255.

Proctor, T. and Jamieson, B. (2004). *Marketing Research*. Edinburgh Business School, Heriot-Watt University. Harlow: Pearson.

Sanjari, M., Bahramnezhad, F., Fomani, F.K., Shoghi, M. and Cheraghi, M.A. (2014). Ethical challenges of researchers in qualitative studies: The necessity to develop a specific guideline. *Journal of Medical Ethics and History of Medicine*, 7, 14. Published online 4 August.

Steiner, A.G. and Steiner, F.J. (1999). *Business, Government, and Society: A Managerial Perspective – Text and Cases* (6th ed.). New York: McGraw-Hill.

Twedt, D.W. (1963). Why a marketing research code of ethics? *Journal of Marketing*, 27(4), pp. 48–50.

Walton, C.C. (1977). *The Ethics of Corporate Conduct*. Englewood Cliffs, NJ: Prentice Hall.

Other Sources

Marketing Research Association. (2013). *MRA Members Will . . . MRA Code of Marketing Research Standards*. https://www.insightsassociation.org/sites/default/files/misc_files/mra_code.pdf (Accessed on 20 February 2019).

Scientific American. Use of cookies. https://www.scientificamerican.com/page/use-of-cookies/ (Accessed on 23 March 2019).

Index